Walls and Mirrors

Walls and Mirrors

Mexican Americans, Mexican Immigrants, and the Politics of Ethnicity

DAVID G. GUTIÉRREZ

University of California Press

BERKELEY   LOS ANGELES   LONDON

Chapter 6 is reprinted in revised form by permission of the *Journal of American Ethnic History*. The original article is *"Sin Fronteras? Chicanos, Mexican Americans, and the Emergence of the Contemporary Mexican Immigration Debate, 1968–1978," Journal of American Ethnic History* 10, no. 4 (Summer 1991): 5–37.

University of California Press
Berkeley and Los Angeles, California

University of California Press, Ltd.
London, England

Library of Congress Cataloging-in-Publication Data

Gutiérrez, David (David G.)
    Walls and mirrors : Mexican Americans, Mexican immigrants, and
the politics of ethnicity / David G. Gutiérrez.
        p.   cm.
    Includes bibliographical references (p.) and index.
    ISBN 0-520-08322-9 (alk. paper) ; ISBN 0-520-20219-8 (pbk. :
alk. paper)
    1. Mexican Americans—Politics and government.   2. Mexicans—
United States—Politics and government.   3. United States—
Emigration and immigration—History—20th century.   4. Mexico—
Emigration and immigration—History—20th century.   I. Title.
E184.M5G86   1995
323.1′168073—dc20   94-1892

Printed in the United States of America

08   07   06   05   04   03   02   01   00
9   8   7   6   5   4

The paper used in this publication meets the minimum requirements
of ANSI/ NISO Z39.48-1992 (R 1997) (*Permanence of Paper*). ∞

For Rose and Dad,
and for Mrs. R.

Dime con quien andes y te diré quien eres.
Tell me with whom you walk and I will tell you who you are.

—Mexican proverb

Contents

Acknowledgments

Completion of this book was greatly facilitated by the generous support I received from a number of institutions and individuals. I am particularly indebted to the Dorothy Danforth Compton Foundation, the Ford Foundation/National Research Council, the John Randolph Haynes and Dora Haynes Foundation, and the Chicano Fellows Program at Stanford University for providing financial assistance that allowed me time to complete the research for this project and to prepare the manuscript. I am also grateful for the generous faculty development assistance I received from the Dean of the College of Humanities at the University of Utah, the University of California's UC Mexus Program, and the Office of the Vice-Chancellor for Academic Affairs and the Office of the Dean of Arts and Humanities at the University of California, San Diego. Many thanks also to Alex Saragoza, Rosa Johnson, and the staff of the Chicano Studies Program at the University of California, Berkeley, for making my stay there so pleasant and fruitful, and to Tomás Almaguer and Howard Michaelson for so generously sharing their homes with me.

The professional staffs at all the libraries in which I conducted research for this project were invariably helpful and supportive. I would like to thank the staffs at the Bancroft Library, the Huntington Library, the Chicano Studies Library at the University of California, Berkeley, and the Departments of Special Collections at California State University, Los Angeles, Green Library at Stanford, University Research Library at the University of California, Los Angeles, and the Benson Latin American Library at the University of Texas, Austin. Special thanks go to Carol Rudisell and to my friend and colleague Roberto Trujillo at Green Library for their help and for their unflagging enthusiasm for this project. I am also deeply indebted to Martin Ridge, not only for his role in securing financial support for this work at the Huntington Library but also for his guidance and encouragement throughout my career.

I have been blessed with a great many colleagues and mentors who have also become dear friends over the years. At the University of California, Santa Barbara, Otis Graham, Isidro Ortiz, Christine Iriart, and Dick Oglesby all inspired my work through their examples as teachers and as human beings. During my years in Washington, Congressman Ed Roybal, Harry Pachón, Nelle Sandridge, Hy Frankel, and Raquel Márquez Frankel helped shape this study by giving generously of their time, experience, and acute insights into the workings of the political process. *Gracias* also to Rudy de la Garza for his gracious hospitality during my first memorable stay in Austin and to Al Camarillo, David Montejano, George Sánchez, and Emilio Zamora for unselfishly sharing with me key primary documents and their own unpublished work in progress. I am grateful to Laura Hyams for her support of my work at an early stage and for believing in this book at a time I didn't quite believe in it myself.

My greatest debt of gratitude is to my graduate advisor at Stanford, Albert Camarillo. As any of Al's students will attest, it is difficult to imagine working with an academic advisor more giving of himself as scholar, teacher, and friend. I feel privileged and honored to have worked with him. One of the other benefits of knowing Al has been the joy of becoming part of his extended family, and I thank Al, Susan, Greg, Lauren, and Slim for sharing their happiness with me.

Tomás Almaguer has played a similarly powerful role in my life. I am grateful to him not only for sharing his honest criticism and the insight developed in his long experience in Chicano Studies but also, and more important, for being an understanding and supportive friend even when he disagreed with me. Along with Al and Tomás, Ramón Gutiérrez has been a consistent source of inspiration and encouragement, and I thank him for helping make my transition back to California as stimulating and rewarding as it has been. Two other friends, Peggy Pascoe and Bill Deverell, have lived through this project from its inception, and I owe each of them more than they will ever know. It is impossible for me to adequately express my thanks to Peggy Pascoe for her continuing friendship, for many years of gentle but incisive criticism, and for helping me learn the ropes first as a graduate student and then as a green assistant professor. My debt to Bill over the years goes far beyond what I owe him as a colleague, critic, and confidant—I am honored that he considers me his friend.

Several other dear friends gave up valuable time to read and criticize previous drafts of this study. I am especially indebted to the finest wordsmith I know, Mrs. Elizabeth Rosenfield, for showing so much patience, good humor, and good will toward this manuscript and its author. I am grateful too, to Ramón Gutiérrez, Patricia Nelson Limerick, and Richard White, each of whom tried to hold me to the same high standards they have achieved in their work. I also deeply appreciate the incisive readings of the entire manuscript I received from my friends and colleagues Vicki Ruiz, George Sánchez, and Alex Saragoza and from Chuck Allen, Mary Lillis Allen, Camille Guerin-Gonzales, Gayle Gullet, Susan Johnson, Mark Kleinman, Jim Lehning, Ben Márquez, Valerie Matsumoto, Luis Murillo, Pamela Radcliff, Christine Sierra, and my brothers Ed Escobar and Rick Olguín, who lent their expertise to various sections of the book. I would be remiss if I did not also express my thanks and appreciation to the talented young scholars who served as research assistants. The research efforts and critical insights of Andrea Otañez and Leanne Armijo at the University of Utah, Ron López at Berkeley, Raúl Ramos at Yale and the University of California, Los Angeles, Steve Pitti at Stanford University, and Susie Porter at the University of California, San Diego, helped make this a much stronger study.

I owe a debt of personal gratitude to several other individuals. As part of my research I had the great privilege of interviewing some of the people who made the history discussed in the book. I respectfully thank Chole Alatorre, Albert Armendáriz, Sr., Bert Corona, Antonio Ríos, Antonio Rodríguez, Edward R. Roybal, Manuel Ruiz, Jr., and my favorite historians, my grandparents Sara and Ernesto Gutiérrez, for sharing their memories with me.

Finally, I'd like to thank several people who influenced this work in ways that transcend the academy. First, my love and thanks to my family, Rose, Ernie, Sara, Julie, and Cris Gutiérrez for showing me how rich and diverse Mexican American life and culture can be. I owe a debt to Joe and Bonita Trotter that I can never repay. For more than twenty-five years they have supported my education through good times and bad, and they have enriched my life through their example. Like Joe and Bonita, Ron Collins's enthusiasm for teaching showed me what is best about public education and, in the process, lit a fire in me that is still burning. I try to follow his example. I feel similarly privileged to call Mrs. Elizabeth Rosenfield a friend. The book's dedication is but a small reflection of my admiration, love, and respect for a woman who has lived through most of the history described in this book.

And last, to those who know me best, *los hijos del desierto*, Kevin Bender, Billy D., Pam Fink, Michael Koomey, Howard Michaelson, Stuart Swanson, and especially to my wife and partner Jane Sullivan, my deepest thanks and gratitude for teaching me the rules of the desert—and for forgiving me when I break them.

Introduction

In the three decades since 1960 the growth of the United States' Hispanic, or Latino,[1] population has become an increasingly controversial issue. Increasing at a rate that far exceeds that of any other minority group, the number of Americans of Latino descent rose from just under 7 million persons in 1960 to approximately 10.5 million in 1970, 14.6 million in 1980, and an estimated 20 million in 1990.[2] The number of ethnic Mexicans,[3] who historically have constituted the largest subpopulation of Latinos and who now represent approximately 60 percent of the total, has grown at a similar rate. In the same thirty years the number of Mexican Americans and Mexican immigrants residing in the United States grew from approximately 3.5 million in 1960 to 4.5 million in 1970, 8.7 million in 1980, and an estimated 13.4 million in 1990.[4]

Although much of the growth of both the ethnic Mexican and the larger Latino population has resulted from high rates of natural increase, immigration has been the major contributor to the recent surge in the number of Latinos in the United States. Such large-scale immigration—especially the undocumented flow that has occurred outside legally sanctioned channels—has deeply concerned and alarmed many Americans. Echoing the fears of previous generations who questioned the nation's capacity to absorb millions of non-English-speaking foreigners, many Americans now consider immigration to be one of the most pressing issues in national politics.[5] The public debate over these issues has been particularly intense since the early 1970s. With politicians, journalists, lobby groups, and labor unions all joining the fray, the debate over immigration has raged during the administrations of every president from Nixon to Clinton.

Partly as a reflection of the contentiousness of this debate, scholarly interest in immigration has grown exponentially since the 1970s. Attracting the attention of demographers, ethnographers, legal scholars, sociologists, anthropologists, political scientists, historians, and scholars from many other disciplines, the phenomenon of international migration has become one of the most dynamic areas of research in the humanities and social sciences. Despite this growing interest, however, several areas of research remain unexplored. Surprisingly, one of the least-understood dimensions of the debate over the immigration issue in the United States is the response the controversy has elicited among Mexican Americans and other long-term Latino residents. Although Mexican Americans and, more recently, other U.S. Latinos have been among those most directly affected by sustained immigration from Mexico and Latin America, relatively little is known about how they have reacted to the steady influx of immigrants into their communities over the course of this century.[6] There are probably many explanations for the relative dearth of knowledge about this question, but I would argue that one of the primary reasons researchers have not pursued the issue is that until fairly recently few Americans have recognized much of a distinction between long-term U.S. residents of Mexican and Latin descent and more recent immigrants from Mexico and other nations of Latin America. Latinos themselves, however, have always been aware of the subtle and not-so-subtle social, cultural, and political distinctions that divide them.

I first became aware of and interested in the significance of the differences Latinos perceive among themselves as a boy growing up in the Boyle Heights neighborhood of East Los Angeles, an area in which Mexican Americans and Mexican immigrants have lived together for more than a century. Even as a child I was struck by what often seemed to me to be almost comical love/hate relationships between U.S.-born Mexican Americans and more recent immigrants from Mexico. In my own family, for example, I often heard my relatives complain about lenient immigration policies even though virtually every one of them had parents or grandparents who had emigrated to the United States from Mexico. My family griped about many different aspects of immigration, but their most common complaints were that Mexican wetbacks or illegals, as they often called them, were displacing Mexican American workers, depressing wages, and undermining union-organizing efforts. More important, from their point of view, the mass immigration of so-called backward, un-Americanized illegal aliens reinforced the negative stereotypes Anglo Americans held about all Mexicans, regardless of citizenship status, including those, like my family, who had lived in the United States for many generations.

On the other hand, in our neighborhood I also saw numerous examples of cordial and mutually supportive relations between U.S. natives and immigrants of Mexican descent. For example, it was not at all unusual to hear my grandfather (whose father had immigrated to the United States from the Yucatán at the turn of the century) lambasting wetbacks, while my grandmother (whose parents had immigrated to the United States from Chihuahua in 1902) was in the process of sponsoring a Mexican neighbor for American citizenship, making a collection of money or preparing food for an immigrant family celebrating a birth or mourning a death, standing as *madrina* (godmother) for an immigrant's baby during baptism, or just congenially conversing—in Spanish, of course—with one of our many illegal alien friends. And, despite my grandfather's frequent harangues about wetbacks, on many occasions I witnessed him offering one of his illegal friends a small loan or a ride to the store or the bus stop, enjoying a drink or a smoke, watching the bullfights on television, or just shooting the breeze on the front porch. As a boy I cheerfully accepted this seemingly contradictory behavior as one of the mysterious quirks of the adult world.

I didn't think much about my grandparents' interactions with their immigrant neighbors again until years later, when I once again found myself pondering, albeit in a much different context, the peculiarities of Mexican American/Mexican immigrant relations. After I graduated from college I accepted a job as a staff member of the newly established Congressional Hispanic Caucus in Washington, D.C., during the last two years of the Carter administration. As a legislative assistant whose responsibilities included monitoring immigration-policy issues, I was particularly intrigued by the unanimous position the members of the Hispanic Caucus had adopted on the increasingly volatile Mexican immigration issue. Although I understood (and generally agreed with) the caucus members' stand on the immigration debate, I also knew from personal experience that many of their Mexican American and other Latino constituents were opposed to lenient immigration policies toward Mexico and Latin America. Indeed, a number of public opinion polls conducted in the late 1970s seemed to indicate that Mexican Americans and other Americans of Latin descent appeared to support immigration reform in percentages similar to those recorded in the general population. Despite this, members of the Hispanic Caucus strongly opposed efforts on Capitol Hill to restrict immigration from Mexico. From their point of view the restrictionist mood in Congress represented a serious threat both to the human rights of Latino immigrants and to the civil rights of American citizens of Latin descent. Members of the Hispanic Caucus argued that, if enacted, laws designed to control undocumented immigration by imposing legal penalties on habitual employers of undocumented workers, instituting counterfeit-proof worker-identification systems, and increasing enforcement personnel along the

U.S.–Mexico border would inevitably threaten anyone who even looked Hispanic in American society. Thus for the next seven years the Congressional Hispanic Caucus (along with virtually every other major national Latino civil rights and advocacy organization) led the fight against efforts in Congress to enact such immigration policies.

When I left Washington in 1980 to begin graduate study in American history I resolved to explore, in a more formal academic manner, the divisions over the immigration issue that I had observed in two very different contexts. By focusing on the historical origins and evolution of Mexican Americans' views about Mexican immigrants, I hoped eventually to shed light on what appeared to me to be an intriguing contradiction. My belief was that by exploring the differences that divided and the commonalities that bound the two groups—the walls and mirrors that so clearly characterized their relationship in the United States—I could illuminate some puzzling, unexplored dimensions of Mexican American political and social history, of the processes involved in immigrant settlement and adaptation, and of the larger national debate over immigration policy toward Mexico.

My initial research confirmed my sense that Mexican Americans had always been deeply divided over the immigration issue. And in many ways this made perfect sense. Although virtually all immigrant groups have faced similar challenges in their attempts to negotiate the distance between their old lives in their natal countries and their new lives in the United States, Mexican Americans and permanent settlers from Mexico have found their own adaptations significantly more complicated. Unlike most other immigrant/ethnic groups, whose ties to their former culture were gradually attenuated by the vast distances involved in their migration to the United States, the contiguity of Mexico along a two-thousand-mile-long border virtually guaranteed that Mexican Americans would remain in particularly close contact with both sojourners and settlers from Mexico.

Although Mexican Americans' attitudes about this situation have varied widely, the debate among Mexican Americans over their relationship to Mexicans and Mexican culture historically has fallen between two essentially polar positions. One end of the spectrum of opinion has been occupied by those Mexican Americans who tend to view Mexican immigrants as a threat. Individuals subscribing to this point of view generally acknowledge the deep historical, cultural, and kinship ties that bind Mexican Americans to Mexican immigrants, but, like some of my relatives, they believe that unrestricted immigration has undermined Mexican Americans' life chances by increasing economic competition and contributing to the reinforcement of negative racial and cultural stereotypes held by white Americans. More common among the small middle-class elements of the Mexican American population (but clearly present among many working-class Mexican Americans as well), the position advanced by these individuals consequently tended to emphasize the social, cultural, and political distinctions that separate Mexican immigrants from American citizens of Mexican descent. Logically, Mexican Americans who subscribe to this set of assumptions have also tended to argue that immigration from Mexico should be tightly controlled. As one historian of the Mexican American experience has explained it, although these Mexican Americans felt sympathy for Mexican immigrants, they "sincerely believed that the native Mexican American came first and priority lay with his [*sic*] welfare. If the [Mexican immigrant] had to suffer because of this belief, that was unfortunate, but so was the [Mexican American] who could not feed his family because of their presence."[7]

Other Mexican Americans have maintained very different opinions about the immigration controversy. Seeing themselves reflected in the people they call *los recién llegados* (recent arrivals), Mexican Americans occupying this end of the spectrum of opinion have tended to express more empathy for immigrants from Mexico. More common among (but again, not limited exclusively to) those Mexican Americans who, in terms of class position and cultural orientation, closely resemble recent immigrants, this sympathetic point of view stems from belief that the affinities between Mexican Americans and Mexican immigrants based on ties of culture, kinship, and friendship are much more important than any differences that divide them. Although working-class Mexican Americans are painfully aware that Mexican immigrants have competed with them for scarce jobs, housing, and social services and that the immigrants have contributed to the perpetuation of racial animosities between Anglos and Mexicans, they have drawn very different conclusions from these circumstances. Noting that Americans seem to discriminate against Mexicans whether they are U.S. citizens or not, Mexican Americans oriented in this way can see little difference between their position in American society and that of more recent immigrants. From their point of view, as one elderly Mexican American woman put it to the historian Albert Camarillo, "We were all poor. We were all in the same situation."[8]

Although this difference of opinion reflects what first appeared to me to be a fairly unambiguous disagreement about U.S. immigration policy, the more I delved into the archival sources on the issue, the more convinced I became that the disagreement actually represents much more than just this. I slowly began to realize that Mexican Americans' views about Mexican immigrants were part of a much broader and deeper debate about the historical evolution of Mexican Americans' own sense of cultural and political identity. Indeed, as I began to discern repeating patterns in the immigration debate I came to believe that Mexican Americans' views about Mexican immigrants and immigration policy often reveal more about their own sense of ethnic and political identity than about their feelings concerning the immigration debate. This was so, I concluded, because the virtually constant influx of Mexican immigrants into existing Mexican American communities in this century continually compelled Mexican Americans of all walks of life to consider, and to make choices about, questions of personal identity and the salience of their own ethnicity.

In short, for nearly a century the more-or-less constant presence of large numbers of Mexican immigrants in Mexican American communities has forced Mexican Americans to come to daily decisions about who they are—politically, socially, and culturally—in comparison to more recent immigrants from Mexico. This has been particularly true of those Mexican Americans active in political efforts to better conditions for the Mexican-descent population of the United States. To such individuals the immigration issue has always represented much more than merely establishing a border policy with Mexico. Forced virtually every day to deal with the both the positive and negative effects of Mexican immigration while struggling to win basic civil rights for their constituents, such activists have had to come to some fundamental decisions about just who their constituents are. Feeling the conflicting pressures exerted by their cultural affinities on the one hand and their desire to achieve at least functional political and social integration as American citizens on the other, Mexican American activists often found themselves in an ambiguous moral and existential borderland in which questions of political and cultural identity were muddled in ways most Americans have never had to consider. The fact that a great many Mexican Americans eventually married Mexican immigrants and raised children who were American citizens by birth confused the social landscape even more.

Consequently, in the process of coming to decisions about Mexican immigrants, Mexican American activists first had to make judgments about their own sense of culture, about their ethnic self-identification and national allegiances, and about the role they saw themselves playing in American society. Whether they chose to work only on behalf of American citizens or decided that their efforts should focus on what they considered to be a broader cultural community including immigrants, such decisions speak volumes about Mexican American activists' political and cultural orientations in a society that has continually been transformed by constant immigration.

Thus, although I started out with an examination of what I thought was a fairly narrow set of questions about immigration and U.S. immigration policy, I have discovered that the historical debate over immigration reflects even deeper, persistent differences among Mexican Americans and permanent Mexican immigrants over their political, social, and cultural future in the United States.

Given the controversy in the social sciences over several of the terms used thus far—particularly *ethnicity* and *ethnic identity*—some clarification of terminology is warranted here. Understanding and usage of these terms have undergone such dramatic and rapid transformations in the past twenty-five years that scholars disagree strongly as to what the concepts now represent. Perhaps the most fundamental controversy over the use of these categories involves the dispute over whether the phenomenon termed *ethnicity* represents primordial, immutable, preconscious aspects of a group's social identity (or sense of peoplehood) or merely strategies for pursuing group interests in society and comprises, therefore, situational, circumstantial, or optional components of individual and group identity.[9] Recognizing the broad range of the theoretical debate on ethnic phenomena, this study relies primarily on E. K. Francis's classic formulation and on Stuart Hall's more recent ruminations on ethnicity. Although they differ significantly in the emphases of their theoretical musings, both scholars argue the importance of recognizing ethnicity as a socially constructed category that involves both primordial elements, such as phenotype, culture, and language, and strategic, or ideological, elements that involve, in Francis's words, "mental processes [of resistance] based on abstraction and hypostatical transposition of characteristics from the primary to the secondary group."[10]

In the historical analysis of Mexican American/Mexican immigrant relations, the applicability of this synthetic conceptual framework is clear. At the moment of their original annexation into the United States in 1848, the first generation of Mexican Americans represented a primordial ethnic group by virtue of the fact that, at the stroke of a pen, they had instantaneously been rendered an ethnic minority of a much larger society. Over the course of a century, however, Mexican Americans increasingly became a situational or circumstantial ethnic group as a result of the persistent racism and discrimination they experienced in the United States. Generally defined by other Americans as Mexicans despite the fact that they were American citizens, Mexican Americans' own sense of distinctiveness was constantly reinforced by the discriminatory treatment afforded them. Thus external ascriptive factors were added to the already complex matrix contributing to the evolution of Mexican American ethnic identity. Finally, immigration from Mexico—sporadic in the nineteenth century but steadily growing throughout the twentieth century—complicated this situation immeasurably by constantly reinforcing Mexican cultural practices and use of the Spanish language in existing Mexican American communities, by intensifying American prejudices against Mexicans, and, most important, by contributing to the steady growth of the ethnic Mexican population of the United States. In addition to the struggle to carve out a niche for themselves in American society, Mexican Americans faced the dilemma of deciding how to respond to the growing numbers of Mexican nationals in their midst—a dilemma that persists to the present.

Although many of the conclusions presented in *Walls and Mirrors* are relevant to the American Southwest as a region, this study focuses on the two largest southwestern states—California and Texas. Analysis of these two states is especially pertinent to Mexican American history because a significant majority of both natives and immigrants of Mexican descent have lived there throughout this century and because the two states have served—and continue to serve—as the main entrepôts for the overwhelming majority of Mexican immigrants.[11] Both states, in addition, have had long traditions of organized Mexican American political activism. Dating from the late nineteenth century, virtually every major Mexican American advocacy, civil rights, labor, and political organization—including such well-known groups as the League of United Latin American Citizens (LULAC, formed in Texas in 1929), the American G.I. Forum (founded in Texas in 1947), the Community Service Organization (CSO, established in California in 1947), the Mexican American Political Association (MAPA, founded in California in 1959), and the United Farm Workers Union (formed in California in 1962) and many lesser-known mutual-aid and fraternal associations—traces its origins to one of the two states. In addition, innumerable Mexican American and Mexican immigrant political leaders and community, labor, and student activists prominent in the long debate over the significance and meanings of Mexican immigration have hailed from California or Texas.

It should be recognized that my focus on the changing positions, tactics, and rhetoric of politically involved Mexican American and Mexican immigrant activists and organizations does not necessarily represent a cross-section of the ethnic Mexican population over time. As is true in the general population, such groups and individuals are different from the majority by virtue of the degree of their political commitment and actions. Nevertheless, I hope to demonstrate that these activists not only played a crucial role in formulating, articulating, and acting on the pressing issues facing their communities but also successfully mobilized and empowered

Mexican Americans and Mexican immigrants to play more effective roles in shaping their own destinies in the United States. Thus, although historical interpretation of ethnic Mexicans' responses to immigration and other political issues does not represent a scientific gauge by which to measure precisely changes in public opinion, analysis of these evolving views over a long period of time does provide important insights into the intellectual and political development of several generations of politically active ethnic Mexicans in the American Southwest.

The book is generally organized chronologically, although there is significant thematic overlap between chapters. Chapter 1 provides an overview of the evolution of Mexican American society in the years following the Mexican Cession and delineates some of the major issues influencing the development of Mexican American political culture following the change to American sovereignty. In this chapter I argue that although most Mexican Americans retained their Mexican cultural orientations and maintained strong affinities for Mexico, significant social, cultural, and political cleavages divided Mexican Americans from Mexicans even before the United States annexed Mexico's northern provinces. Moreover, I argue that the mutually perceived differences between Mexicans and Mexican Americans, combined with the class, regional, and cultural diversity of the Mexican American population of the nineteenth-century Southwest, not only profoundly influenced the subsequent relations between citizens and aliens but also helped shape the main currents of Mexican American political and social thought in the twentieth century.

Chapter 2 carries the analysis into the first two decades of the twentieth century, focusing on the emergence of Mexican immigration as an important issue in American politics generally and, for Mexican Americans specifically, in the years when hundreds of thousands of Mexican immigrants poured into the United States seeking work. The chapter examines the evolution of mutually held perceptions and attitudes among Mexican Americans, Mexican immigrants, and the American public in the years immediately preceding the Great Depression, an era in which both Mexican Americans and Mexican immigrants experienced increasing discrimination and animosity in the United States. Chapter 3 explores the ways in which the pressures building in the 1920s finally exploded into active campaigns to rid the country of the so-called Mexican Problem in the 1930s. Although Mexican immigrants had been actively recruited by American employers during the previous quarter-century, by the late 1920s large numbers of Americans were calling for their expulsion from the country.

Caught in an atmosphere of rising anti-Mexican hysteria, Mexican Americans began to develop two very different strains of thought on the related issues of Mexican immigration and the social, economic, and political future of the Mexican American population of the United States. Though only vaguely defined at the time, these two often diametrically opposed perspectives helped shape both the contours of subsequent debate over the immigration issue and the development of Mexican Americans' political thought and civil rights efforts from the 1920s through the present period.

Chapter 4 presents an analysis of the reemergence of Mexican immigration as an issue of national political significance during World War II. The chapter demonstrates that in the fluid and volatile social context of the war the debate over Mexican immigration took on new, even more complex dimensions. The two strains of political thought that had crystallized among Mexican Americans during the 1920s and 1930s continued to shape their positions on the immigration debate. At the same time, shifts in the general pattern of civil rights rhetoric among American minorities, combined with the institutionalization of the so-called Bracero Program (a federal program that allowed the temporary employment of hundreds of thousands of Mexican laborers in American agriculture), set the stage for a broad and deep reevaluation among Mexican Americans of both the significance of ongoing immigration and the political and social salience of their own sense of ethnicity.

Chapter 5 explores the evolution of the these complex issues during yet another stressful period for racial and ethnic minorities in the United States: the Cold War decade of the 1950s. Assessing the role of the Bracero Program in stimulating both increased legal and illegal immigration from Mexico, the chapter delves into the often contradictory positions that Mexican American political and civil rights activists articulated between the late 1940s and the early 1960s. The chapter shows that although restrictionist sentiments seemed to dominate public discourse on the issue during this era, closer examination reveals that Mexican Americans were already beginning to express doubts about the constitutional and moral basis of the U.S. government's increasingly repressive policies toward Mexican immigrants. I argue that although they were still in a formative stage, the doubts that emerged in the 1950s in many ways laid the foundation for the emergence in the 1960s and 1970s of dramatic new positions on the now closely related issues of Mexican immigration and Mexican American ethnicity.

The final chapter of *Walls and Mirrors* examines the complex interplay between the florescence of Mexican American militant political activism in the Chicano movement of the 1960s and 1970s and the controversy surrounding the contemporary Mexican immigration issue. I argue that the emergence of an unprecedentedly strident assertion of Chicano ethnicity among young Mexican American activists was integrally related to the dramatic changes occurring in Mexican Americans' conceptualization of, and expressed opinions on, the debate over Mexican immigration to the United States.

The epilogue provides a brief discussion of the evolution of the deeply divisive debate over immigration since the 1980s. By analyzing the development of the current national debate over immigration, I hope to offer both an alternative interpretation of the contemporary controversy and a summary of the main arguments advanced in the body of the book.

1   Legacies of Conquest

On February 2, 1848, delegates representing the governments of the Republic of Mexico and the United States met in the dusty village of Guadalupe Hidalgo on the outskirts of Mexico City to sign the treaty ending the Mexican War. After more than two months of negotiations, and after nearly two years of bloody conflict that had left more than 63,000 dead on both sides, the Treaty of Guadalupe Hidalgo ended what was at that time the bloodiest and costliest war in American history. With most of the terms dictated by the victorious Americans, the treaty established a new border between the two nations, provided official recognition of the United States' previous annexation of Texas, and provided for the payment by the United States of 15 million dollars to Mexico in exchange for Mexico's former northern provinces. It ceded to the United States one-third of Mexico's territory—including Texas, more than half—which now comprises all or part of California, Arizona, Nevada, Utah, Wyoming, Colorado, Kansas, Oklahoma, and New Mexico.

The treaty also forever transformed the destiny of the estimated 75,000 to 100,000 Mexicans who remained in what had become the American Southwest. Although the Treaty of Guadalupe Hidalgo formally extended the full protection of the U.S. Constitution and "all the rights of citizens" to those individuals who chose to remain in the territory north of the new international border, Americans' past actions toward the ethnic and racial minorities that composed part of their society made it unlikely that the new Mexican American minority would be afforded anything near equal rights in American society. Indeed, in the half century following the annexation of Mexico's former northern provinces, the ethnic Mexican population of the region was slowly but surely relegated to an inferior, caste-like status in the region's evolving social system. Mexicans were quickly outnumbered by American immigrants; and, facing pervasive ethnocentrism and racial prejudice in their own homelands, they were gradually divested of both political and economic influence in all areas except northern New Mexico and south Texas (where they continued to hold large numerical majorities until the late nineteenth century). By the turn of the century most Mexican Americans found themselves in a position in society not much better than that occupied by Indians and African Americans elsewhere in the United States.

Over the course of the nineteenth century, however, these hardships played an important countervailing role by laying the foundation for the eventual emergence of a new sense of solidarity among Mexican Americans in the Southwest. Before annexation Mexicans on the northern frontier had been isolated from the centers of Mexican civilization and society and from one another by the region's vast expanses of mountains and deserts. However, the combination of military conquest and the subsequent racial prejudice and social subordination helped pull Mexican Americans together by providing the political and social context in which a new sense of community and common purpose would develop. Although the fruits of these first stirrings of ethnic consciousness would not be seen until late in the nineteenth century, this rising level of ethnic awareness provided the basis on which Mexican Americans would later contest their political and socioeconomic subordination in American society.

The Ambiguities of Mexican American Citizenship

Given American arrogance and disdain toward Mexicans and their culture before the Mexican War, it is almost surprising that the United States extended such lenient terms toward the defeated Mexicans. In the years immediately preceding the outbreak of hostilities and during the war itself, many Americans had argued quite seriously that the United States should annex the whole of Mexico. With jingoist newspapers such as the *New York Herald* and the *New York Sun* and ultranationalists such as John L. O'Sullivan and William Walker leading the way, the most strident advocates of American expansionism argued that it was "God's will" that the United States eventually absorb all of Mexico—and perhaps South America as well.[1]

Yet advocates of the "All Mexico" position faced some formidable challenges in selling their views to American political leaders and the American public. Clearly, the most troubling of these were the problems involved in incorporating into American society the peoples who already lived in the coveted territory. It was one thing to call for an aggressive American march to the west and to the south, but quite another to envision the potential incorporation of even larger numbers of non-white, non-English-speaking people into the United States. Given the antipathy many Americans felt toward Mexico and Mexicans, this was a particularly thorny issue.

At the height of the debate over American territorial aggrandizement in the 1840s, the issue of subject peoples would come to dominate discussion. Indeed, as historian Reginald Horsman argued in his study of racialism and Manifest Destiny, in the months preceding the outbreak of war, "the bitter dispute concerning the annexation of Mexican territory was primarily an argument not about territory but about Mexicans." "Though God might . . . guid[e] the Americans to the conquest of Mexico," Horsman observed, "He had not provided a detailed plan for American rule over Mexican people."[2]

Americans advanced a number of views as to what was to become of the people who might be acquired with any annexed territory. Some attempted to argue that such persons would simply melt into American society as they experienced the benefits of American civilization. For example, in presenting his rationale for America's Manifest Destiny, John L. O'Sullivan asserted that an American conquest of Mexico—particularly of Mexico's northern provinces—would be welcomed by Mexican citizens who had come to despise the arrogance and neglect they had traditionally received from their government in Mexico City. In O'Sullivan's view the Mexican residents of the northern provinces would welcome the advance of American civilization because "an irresistible army of Anglo-Saxon[s]" would bring with them "the plough and the rifle . . . schools and colleges, courts and representative halls, mills and meeting houses."[3] A journalist advanced a similar argument in a November 1847 article in the *New York Sun*, observing that "the [Mexican] race is perfectly accustomed to being conquered, and the only new lesson we shall teach is that our victories will give liberty, safety, and prosperity to the vanquished, if they know enough to profit by the appearance of our stars." "To *liberate* and *ennoble*," the *Sun* reporter editorialized, "not to *enslave* and *debase*—is our mission."[4]

Other Americans were not nearly so optimistic about the possibility of absorbing into the American orbit hundreds of thousands, if not more, racially mixed, Spanish-speaking people. Indeed, throughout the war many Americans argued that the annexation of densely populated Mexican territory would help create a new, potentially disastrous "race problem" in the United States. Responding to word of the fall of New Mexico to General Kearny's army in 1846, the opposition *Richmond Whig* argued this point forcefully, asserting, "We have far more to dread from the acquisition of a debased population who have been so summarily manufactured into American citizens than to hope from the extension of our territorial limits."[5] The *Illinois State Register* made a similar point, arguing against any American attempt to assimilate a mixed race "but little removed above the negro."[6] Not surprisingly, the firebrand racist senator from South Carolina, John C. Calhoun, added his objection to the possible incorporation into the Union of large numbers of Mexicans. Arguing that Mexicans represented a motley amalgamation of "impure races, not [even] as good as the Cherokees or Choctaws," Calhoun asked, "Can we incorporate a people so dissimilar to us in every respect—so little qualified for free and popular government—without certain destruction to our political institutions?"[7] As the war wound down in Mexico in late 1847, most members of Congress answered Calhoun's rhetorical question in the negative. Indeed, as the American army made its final advance on Mexico City, most American political leaders seemed to have agreed with Michigan Senator Lewis Cass, who asserted, "We do not want the people of Mexico, either as citizens or subjects. All we want is a portion of territory, which they nominally hold, generally uninhabited, or, where inhabited at all, sparsely so, and with a population, which would soon recede, or identify itself with ours."[8]

With such a broad range of people voicing opposition to plans to annex all of Mexico, American expansionists were forced to temper their desires for territory. Consequently, as American forces made their final push toward Mexico City, President James K. Polk and his cabinet scaled back their territorial aspirations to demand a Rio Grande border and the annexation of New Mexico and Alta California. Despite Senator Cass's predictions about the fate of the Mexican citizens who would come with any annexed territory, however, the issue of nationality and citizenship presented American negotiators with some nettlesome problems.

It is one of the ironies of Western history that the complex diplomatic and political issues raised by the impending American annexation of Mexican territory were ultimately resolved (to the extent they could be resolved) not in the Congress or in the court of American public opinion but by a State Department bureaucrat in Mexico City operating without the official sanction of his government. Nicholas P. Trist, the chief clerk of the U.S. Department of State, had been sent to Mexico by President Polk to negotiate a draft treaty after Gen. Winfield Scott had begun his march on the Mexican capital following the fall of Veracruz in March 1847. Polk, however, soon grew disenchanted with Trist's handling of the negotiations, thinking him too lenient with the Mexicans, and in October of that year ordered his representative to break off negotiations immediately and return to Washington. Trist decided that he was close to reaching an agreement with the Mexican government, so, largely on his own initiative, he ignored Polk's dispatches and continued to negotiate.[9]

With the American army already occupying the capital, Mexican negotiators realized that buying time was about the best they could expect to achieve in the treaty negotiations. Nevertheless, from the outset the Mexican delegation insisted that the United States provide guarantees with regard to the rights of the Mexican nationals who chose to remain in the annexed territories. Indeed, according to Trist's memoirs, despite the many other pressing issues facing the Mexican delegation, "the condition of the inhabitants of the ceded or transferred territory is the topic upon which most time [was] expended" during the treaty negotiations.[10] Although the Mexican government clearly was in no position to wrest significant concessions from the United States, the Mexican delegates were instructed to press the Americans on the question of the fate of Mexican citizens who remained in the conquered territories.[11]

Mexico did not achieve all it had hoped in negotiations with the Americans, but when the Treaty of Guadalupe Hidalgo was finally signed in February 1848 the Mexican delegation had achieved remarkable success in convincing the American government to accede to its essential wishes on the issue of its former citizens. Under the terms of the treaty initially agreed to by the negotiators in Mexico, Mexicans remaining in U.S. territory were to have three basic options. According to Section IX of the treaty, they could "remove" themselves south of the new international border, they could retain their Mexican citizenship in the United States with the status of permanent resident aliens by publicly announcing their intention, or, if they chose neither option within one year of the treaty's effective date, they would be considered to have "elected" to become citizens of the United States.[12]

Although Section IX subsequently was amended by the U.S. Senate, the terms of the bilateral protocol signed by representatives of both nations at Querétaro, Mexico, in May 1848 concerning Mexican nationals in the annexed territory remained essentially unchanged. Under the terms of the amended, final version of the treaty, those former citizens of Mexico who remained in American territory and chose not to retain Mexican citizenship were to be

> incorporated into the Union of the United States, and admitted as soon as possible, according to the principles of the Federal Constitution, to the enjoyment of all the rights of citizens of the United States. In the meantime, they shall be maintained and protected in

the enjoyment of their liberty, their property, and the civil rights now vested in them according to the Mexican laws. With respect to political rights, their condition shall be on an equality with that of the inhabitants of the other territories of the United States. . . .[13]

In theory the signing of the Treaty of Guadalupe Hidalgo and the subsequent Querétaro Protocol seemed to solve the problems associated with the incorporation into the American polity of a large foreign population by extending to them rights similar to those enjoyed by other citizens of the United States. In practice, however, the newly "created" Mexican American population faced two major obstacles to the free exercise of their civil rights in American society. The more fundamental of these concerned their legal status in the United States. As Richard Griswold del Castillo points out, although the treaty seemed to extend to Mexico's former nationals in the annexed territory "all the rights of citizens" of the United States, the wording of the treaty actually left the decision as to the timing and conditions conferring citizenship to the U.S. Congress.[14]

Over the long run the second set of obstacles confronting Mexican Americans proved to be even more important in shaping patterns of interethnic relations in the nineteenth-century Southwest. Although the treaty offered Mexican Americans at least nominal protection of their rights of person and property, it could do little to transform the biased views of Mexicans that Americans continued to entertain. Indeed, the bitterness and hatred toward Mexicans stimulated by the recent war in many ways intensified Anglo Americans' hostility toward "Mexicans"—including those who, at least in theory, had become members of American society. Horsman notes that, if anything, "The total Mexican defeat convinced the Americans that their original judgement of the Mexican race had been correct."[15] The impact of these persistently negative attitudes toward Mexicans was felt by Mexican Americans throughout the annexed territories in the months and years following the end of the war, but the most dramatic manifestations of Americans' racist tendencies emerged in California and Texas.

Of course, as numerous scholars of nineteenth-century California have noted, Americans had developed negative impressions of Mexican California well before the Mexican War. In his popular adventure travelogue *Two Years before the Mast*, for example, Richard Henry Dana had painted an unflattering portrait of the Californios that strongly influenced American popular perceptions of northern Mexican society. Although Dana expressed qualified admiration of some aspects of Californio society and lifestyle, in general he dismissed Californios as "thriftless, proud, and very much given to gaming." As for Mexican women, Dana admired their "dark beauty" but also noted that they were "but of little education . . . and none of the best morality." He was enthusiastic, however, about the territory the Mexicans inhabited. Musing over the Californios' lackadaisical development of "California's four or five hundred miles of sea-coast, . . . good harbors, . . . fine forests, . . . and herds of cattle," Dana was moved to wonder. "In the hands of an enterprising people, what a country this might be!"[16]

Following California's annexation and the discovery of gold soon thereafter, Americans' expressed attitudes about Mexicans and their lands quickly lost this tone of idle speculation. Drawn to California by the discovery of gold in the foothills of the Sierra Nevada in early 1848, nearly 200,000 immigrants poured into California over the next two years, reducing the Spanish-speaking population to a tiny ethnic minority virtually overnight. Among the initial immigrants to the goldfields were an estimated ten to twenty thousand Mexican prospectors from Sonora. Because they brought their expertise in precious-metal mining with them to California, they were at first welcomed by American prospectors eager to learn Mexican techniques. Once American prospectors learned these methods, however, and as pressure on the goldfields intensified, Mexican miners came to be seen as unwanted "foreign" competition. Thus, in 1849 and increasingly in the early 1850s, American prospectors forcefully expelled Mexican, Mexican American, and other Latin American "greasers" from the goldfields. In addition, responding to pressures exerted by American miners, in 1850 the California Legislature passed the so-called Foreign Miners Tax designed to discourage foreign prospectors—especially Mexicans—from gold mining. Those who persisted in the fields or refused to pay the tax were intimidated, beaten, or killed; throughout the 1850s violent crimes against Mexicans in California increased dramatically.[17]

In Texas, large-scale American immigration and the legacy of fierce racial animosity left by the Texas Revolution and the Mexican War stimulated a process of ethnic polarization even earlier than in California. Ironically, much of this ethnic polarization occurred as a result of the "success" of Mexico's colonization law of 1824. Originally passed in an effort to encourage immigration to the sparsely populated Texas frontier, the law soon attracted thousands of American immigrants (and their slaves). Although the new immigrants were required by law to renounce their former citizenship and become loyal citizens of the Republic of Mexico, by the early 1830s the colonization law had created an extremely unstable situation in which American immigrants probably outnumbered Mexicans in Texas by as much as ten to one. This imbalance continued after Texas was annexed by the United States. With a population estimated at somewhere between fourteen and twenty-three thousand (no more than 17 percent of Texas's total population), by the early 1850s Mexican Americans in Texas had become a small minority of a rapidly growing population of American and European immigrants. Just as important, Mexicans had become a spatially segregated minority as well. As a result of the racial hatred inflamed by such incidents as the massacres at the Alamo and Goliad in 1836, most Mexicans had been forced out of their former strongholds in the San Antonio area and became concentrated in the southern reaches of the state between the Nueces River and the Rio Grande.[18] As Texas historian Arnoldo de León noted in his work on the evolution of racial attitudes in nineteenth-century Texas, the mythology surrounding the Texas Revolution contributed to the emergence of lasting stereotypes of "Mexican depravity and violence, a theme which became pervasive once Anglos made closer contact with . . . the Hispanic population following the [Mexican] war. . . . Firebrands spoke alarmingly of savage, degenerate, half-civilized, and barbarous Mexicans committing massacres and atrocities."[19]

As thousands more American immigrants (a majority of whom originated in slave-holding southern states) poured into Texas after the Mexican War, such negative views of Mexicans spread throughout the state. To many of these new immigrants Mexicans represented a primitive "mongrel race," little better than the "wild" Indian tribes who still controlled the northern areas of Texas. Indeed, in the view of some American settlers in the state, Mexicans were inferior even, as Brownsville resident Oscar M. Addison put it in 1854, "to common nig[g]ers."[20]

The Socioeconomic Impact of Annexation in California

Combined with the pervasiveness of negative American attitudes toward Mexicans, the change in sovereignty over Mexico's former northern provinces deeply affected the lives of the nearly 100,000 ethnic Mexicans who had become American citizens under the terms of the Treaty of Guadalupe Hidalgo. Incorporated into the United States by conquest and soon overwhelmed in most areas of the Southwest by the rapid influx of Anglo American and European immigrants, most Mexican Americans found themselves occupying an extremely tenuous position in the rapidly changing Americanized Southwest. Generally perceived and defined by their American conquerors as an inferior, backward people, the vast majority of the Mexican American population faced serious obstacles to the free enjoyment of their new status as American citizens.

The most pressing issue facing Mexican Americans in the years following annexation was their weakened position in the changing regional economy. Despite having been guaranteed equal protection under the law by the Treaty of 1848, most Mexican Americans found that their opportunities for economic advancement in the new political economy were severely circumscribed. Indeed, within two decades of the American conquest it had become clear that, with few exceptions, Mexican Americans had been relegated to a stigmatized, subordinate position in the social and economic hierarchies.

In postwar California several developments contributed to the gradual erosion of Mexican Americans' socioeconomic position. The first of these stemmed from the massive influx of immigrants into the territory following the discovery of gold in early 1848. Most of the prospectors who entered California soon left the arduous work of the goldfields and began to settle in northern California, often on large tracts of land held by members of the Californio elite. The squatters placed intense pressure on Mexican landowners, who were attempting to hold on to their ranchos. As the mining boom subsided in the 1850s and 1860s and as Anglo American and European immigrants drifted away from the Sierra foothills, this process of displacement was replicated in the southern California "cow counties." Even a brief survey of demographic changes in California towns and cities underscores the magnitude and rapidity of these shifts. In Los Angeles, for example, the ethnic Mexican population dwindled from 82 percent of the city's population in 1850 to about 20 percent in 1880. In Santa Barbara the Mexican population dropped from 70 percent of the total in 1860 to less than 50 percent in 1870 and to 27 percent in 1880. In San Diego Mexican Americans' numbers dropped from 28 percent of the total in 1860 to only 8 percent in 1870.[21]

Mass immigration into California set in motion a series of related developments that undermined Mexican Americans' position in the state's evolving economy. As the large numbers of immigrants encroached on existing Mexican American communities, patterns of residential and social segregation began to emerge. It is important to note, as numerous scholars have, that the trend toward residential segregation in California represented a complex set of social forces. On one hand, the gradual concentration of Mexican Americans into smaller ethnic enclaves clearly reflected a combination of population pressures on Mexican neighborhoods and the desire of Anglo Americans to live apart from the lower-class "greasers" they encountered. On the other hand, however, the process of ethnic enclavement evolving in the region also involved a strong desire among Mexican Americans themselves to maintain boundaries between their communities and the Norteamericanos. Their decision to live in separate areas stemmed in part from their effort to maintain some semblance of their former community life. As Griswold del Castillo argues, in some respects "the creation of . . . barrio[s] was a positive accomplishment. The barrio gave a geographic identity, a feeling of being at home, to the dispossessed and the poor. It was a place, a traditional place, that offered some security in the midst of . . . social and economic turmoil."[22] And, as Albert Camarillo notes, withdrawal into segregated barrios allowed Mexican Americans to continue to function "within a closed Mexican social universe. Faced with their new-found status as a segregated minority and confronted by a hostile outside world, the Mexican community entered a phase of social change and adaptation . . . [that] ensured the continuity of Mexican society" in California.[23]

The mass migration of American settlers and the emerging patterns of ethnic segregation in California were accompanied and intensified by the transplantation of a new political and legal system to Mexico's former province. Bringing with them an American tradition of elections, criminal justice, and law enforcement, American immigrants quickly imposed their system of law and government on California. Of all the changes wrought by the shift in legal systems, perhaps the most important involved land law. This issue was crucial in California and other areas of the Southwest because so much of the regional economy under Mexican rule had been based on agriculture and the raising of livestock.

Most of the clashes between the American and Mexican legal traditions derived from the problems associated with confirming Mexican land titles. An early draft of Article X of the Treaty of Guadalupe Hidalgo had stipulated that "all grants of land made by the Mexican government or by the competent authorities, in territories previously appertaining to Mexico . . . shall be respected as valid, to the same extent that the same grants would be valid, if the said territories had remained within the limits of Mexico."[24] The U.S. Senate, however, refused to ratify this clause of the treaty. Fearing that Article X would throw the question of land titles in Texas (which, of course, had been annexed by the United States *before* the Mexican War) into a hopeless quagmire, the Senate simply deleted the offending article from the treaty. Secretary of State James Buchanan attempted to put the best face on the Senate's action by explaining to Mexico's Foreign Relations minister that Article X was "unnecessary" because, as he put it, "the present treaty provides amply and specifically in its 8th and 9th articles for the security of property of every kind belonging to Mexicans, whether acquired under Mexican grants or otherwise in the acquired territory." "The property of foreigners under our Constitution and laws," Buchanan concluded, "will be equally secure without any Treaty stipulation."[25]

Buchanan's assurances to the contrary notwithstanding, the change in sovereignty over Mexico's former territories raised complex questions about legal titles to land, some of which remain in dispute to the present day. It was not so much that Americans ran roughshod over the legal rights of Mexican landowners as that different legal traditions of property rights came into conflict. Under Mexican law (and Spanish law before that), procedures regulating property ownership, boundaries, and transfers were based as much on tradition and respect for authority as they were on codified, uniform statutes. For example, under Spanish and Mexican law, it was not at all uncommon to mark property boundaries with cow skulls, rocks, trees, and other such ephemeral landmarks.[26] Needless to say, such seemingly casual stewardship of private property was unfathomable to the notoriously litigious Americans. Nonetheless, the American Court of Land Claims set up in California in 1851 to adjudicate land-grant claims often ruled in favor of Mexican claimants.[27] Yet the combined pressure of the extremely high cost of legal representation, the imposition of property taxes (as opposed to the Mexican ad valorem system of taxing goods produced on the land), the rapid collapse of the livestock market after the Gold Rush, and the unrelenting pressure of squatters on Mexican Americans' lands ultimately spelled doom for almost all of the Californio propertied elite. By the mid-1850s in the north and the early 1870s in the south, the Californios' real estate holdings had dwindled to a tiny fraction of what they had been during the "Golden Age of the Ranchos."[28]

Combined with the rapid erosion of Mexican Americans' economic position in the 1860s and 1870s, existing patterns of American prejudice toward Mexicans created an environment in which the annexed ethnic Mexican population in the Southwest also lost political influence. It is important to recognize here that the rate at which Mexican Americans' influence in political affairs eroded in different areas varied substantially, depending on the presence or absence of such factors as the survival of local propertied elites, the ratio of Mexican Americans to Anglo Americans, and the specific legal structures that evolved in the various states and territories. Thus, whereas Spanish-speaking propertied elites in New Mexico were able to continue in positions of political influence until well into the twentieth century, it was generally true that Mexican Americans in other areas of the Southwest steadily lost political clout following annexation.

Historians of the Mexican American experience in California have demonstrated that Mexican Americans' political disfranchisement stemmed from the rapid demographic and economic transformation of their society after 1848. Between 1848 and the 1880s huge influxes of white immigrants, increasing Anglo domination over local economies, and a corresponding decrease in the wealth and property holdings of the former Mexican elite combined to erode Mexican Americans' influence in politics. California's constitution reiterated many of the civil guarantees extended to the Mexican population by the Treaty of Guadalupe Hidalgo, and Mexican Americans continued to influence local politics by electing some of their own in areas (such as Santa Barbara and Los Angeles) where they retained sizable minorities, but by the 1870s, and certainly by the 1880s, unfavorable population ratios, combined with Americans' use of gerrymandering and other forms of ethnic exclusion, gradually forced Mexican Americans out of the political arena. Consequently, by the turn of the century Mexican Americans had lost virtually all direct voice in local and state political affairs.[29]

The dramatic decline of the Californio elite was only one part of Mexican Americans' decline in economic, social, and political status in the society that evolved under American rule. On the broadest level, Mexican Americans experienced vast structural displacement as the local economy shifted rapidly from a pastoral one, based predominantly on ranching and subsistence farming, to a capitalist one, increasingly based on commercial agriculture, trade, and later, the large-scale infrastructural development of the region. Before 1848 the vast majority of Mexican American laborers had been employed by the Mexican landholding elite in skilled and semi-skilled jobs as blacksmiths, harness and saddle makers, leather workers, vaqueros, or *trasquiladores* (sheepshearers). When the ranch economy was rapidly supplanted by the more diversified market economy introduced by American immigrants after the Gold Rush, the traditional occupational structure of the region was transformed. In the two decades after California entered the Union in 1850, Mexican American workers found most of their traditional occupations rendered obsolete.[30]

Displaced from their former occupations, Mexican Americans were forced to seek work in a transformed labor market in which higher-paying occupations were dominated by Anglo American workers. Finding their access to skilled occupations, professions, and service jobs severely restricted, Mexican American workers were compelled either to accept semiskilled or unskilled occupations or to enter the growing stream of migrant agricultural workers. To make matters worse, the concentration of Mexican American workers in these low-status occupations in many ways helped to reinforce and perpetuate negative stereotypes about "Mexicans'" native abilities, for over time Americans in the Southwest came to associate

Mexican Americans with unskilled labor. Indeed, this status became institutionalized in some ways by the emergence of an ethnic division of labor characterized by a dual wage structure, in which Mexican workers were consistently paid less than "white" workers performing the same work. By the turn of the century the dual wage system was a characteristic feature of virtually all industries employing Mexican and other ethnic workers throughout the Southwest.[31]

Developments in Texas

As in California, the demographics of post-annexation Texas played a strong role in shaping the future status of Mexican Americans in the society that evolved in the state. Although a small number of the Texas landholding elite (particularly in the border region) were able to retain some control over their property—and thus a degree of political influence—for decades following the Mexican War, Tejanos in general experienced patterns of land loss similar to those occurring elsewhere in the Southwest. As in California, most of the Mexican land grants held by Mexican American landowners were eventually confirmed in Texas courts, but high legal fees, unscrupulous lawyers, and unpredictable markets combined to displace Mexican Americans from their former lands.[32] Summarizing the various factors affecting the Mexican American ranching elite in Texas, one historian notes that although "a segment of the landed Mexican elite . . . successfully commercialized, assimilated a mercantile outlook, and [thus] retained a patrimony of land and workers," the vast majority of Tejano landowners did not, "either because they failed to acquire an export-related source of capital or because they retained a complacent attitude toward merchandising." "Eventually," he continues, "taxes, drought, and disastrous fluctuations of the cattle market, the need to sink wells and improve cattle stock, and the expense of surveying and defending land titles combined to displace the 'unproductive' [Mexican American] landowner." The result was that "by 1900 the Mexican upper class would become nonexistent except in a few border enclaves."[33]

Mass immigration from other parts of the United States, together with the Mexican ranching elite's loss of land, deeply influenced the structural position of Mexican American workers in the evolving regional economy. As a number of Texas scholars recently demonstrated, working-class Tejanos steadily lost economic ground in the five decades following the Mexican War. Moreover, as control over the primary source of wealth became increasingly concentrated in the hands of the new immigrants, landholding Mexican Americans experienced a corresponding loss of property. And, again as in California, this shift in control of the local economy was accompanied by a clear trend in which Mexican Americans slipped into the lowest levels of the maturing capitalist labor market. Whereas in 1850 Mexican American workers in Texas had been fairly evenly distributed among the occupational classifications of independent ranch-farm owner-operator, skilled worker, and semiskilled and unskilled laborer, by the 1870s a disproportionate number of Mexican American workers were employed in the rapidly expanding "unspecialized labor" sector. By the turn of the century almost two-thirds of Texas-born Mexican American workers toiled in unspecialized, unskilled and semiskilled labor categories. As in other parts of the Southwest, by 1900 Mexican Americans in Texas made up part of an regional economy characterized by a clear ethnic division of labor in which they were trapped in the least-skilled and lowest-paid jobs.[34]

The process of the political disfranchisement of Mexican Americans that accompanied these economic changes was somewhat more complex in Texas than in California. On one hand, the climate of racial enmity against Mexican Americans in Texas was generally much worse than in California. Although violence and legislative repression against Mexican Americans were not uncommon in California, in Texas racial animosities arising from the Texas Revolution of the 1830s and Mexican-American War of the 1840s had been continually reinforced in subsequent years by intermittent violence between Anglos and Mexicans along the border. Interethnic tensions were exacerbated by the Texas Rangers, who often took it upon themselves to "keep the Mexicans in their place" through intimidation and violence. As one Texas scholar notes, by the 1860s and 1870s the Texas Rangers had become a paramilitary "corps that enjoyed the tacit sanction of the white community to do to Mexicans in the name of the law what others did extra-legally."[35]

Despite endemic racial conflict and the periodic repression of Mexicans by the Texas Rangers, however, a few "Texas Mexicans" were able to retain a degree of influence in local political affairs, particularly in areas where Mexican Americans continued to hold large numerical majorities. In towns with large Mexican populations, such as El Paso, Laredo, Brownsville, or Corpus Christi, Mexican Americans remained active in the new political order until the late nineteenth century. In other cases Mexican American political and social elites forged successful, if tenuous, coalitions with Anglo leaders that helped to perpetuate their influence until after the turn of the century.[36] When the railroads opened South Texas to settlement and development, however, large-scale migrations of Anglo American and European immigrants quickly changed the demographic structure—and thus the political structure—of the region. By the 1910s Anglos had achieved political domination even in those areas that remained largely ethnically Mexican.

Anglo Texans further consolidated their growing political power in the state through various legislative means. For example, in a series of moves initially designed to exclude East Texas blacks from the franchise, Anglos also effectively constrained or eliminated many Mexican Americans from political participation. One of the most effective methods of limiting the franchise was the utilization of the so-called White Man's Primaries. Implemented in the last quarter of the nineteenth century in several Texas counties (including Bexar County, which encompassed San Antonio), White Man's Primaries limited the franchise exclusively to "qualified, white" voters—a set of criteria which allowed local whites wide latitude in determining voter eligibility. In 1923 the Texas legislature established the white primary statewide.[37] Another measure designed primarily to obstruct black voters, the poll tax, was enacted by the legislature in 1902. The poll tax, required of all voters except those over sixty years of age or "otherwise qualified," ranged from $1.50 to $1.75 per voter. Roughly equivalent to a full day's pay for black and Mexican workers, the poll tax effectively constrained thousands from participation in elections.[38]

In those areas of Texas in which Mexican Americans constituted a vital swing vote, machine politics dominated the scene. Common in the border counties, the development of political machines reflected the need of Anglo immigrants to garner support of local Mexican elites in their attempts to gain control of local politics. As David Montejano explains in his study of South Texas society, "In the case of the Texas-Mexican border region and generally in the annexed Southwest, the ability to govern in the immediate postwar period was secured through an accommodation between the victorious Anglos and the defeated Mexican elite, with the latter [left] in command of the Mexican communities."[39] Building on existing patterns of paternalistic relations between the Tejano land-owning elite and the working-class Mexicans who worked for them during the Mexican era, Anglo political bosses attempted to adopt and refine traditional Mexican forms of deferential social relations in their efforts to extend control over the new political system. Allying themselves with Mexican American *patrones*, or local bosses, Anglo political bosses provided patronage and/or cash payments to these "sub-bosses" in exchange for the working-class Mexican American vote they delivered. At election time the patrones, after consultation with such Anglo bosses as James Wells, Archie Parr, or those associated with the infamous El Paso "Ring," would "instruct" the votes of their Mexican American constituents. In exchange for their votes, working-class Tejanos received considerations ranging from cash payments on election day to emergency loans or other assistance during the rest of the year. These inducements helped to perpetuate existing patterns of social relations in which working-class Tejanos were tied to Mexican and Anglo bosses by bonds of mutual dependence. Thus, for many Tejanos of the border region, voting and other forms of political activity were seen less as active participation in American politics than as an almost natural extension of the same mutually beneficial transactions that had characterized Tejano society prior to the Mexican American War. As one scholar of the Texas boss system notes,

> Lacking any tradition of participation in electoral politics, [Tejanos] did not view themselves as independent voters or as an aggrieved interest group with the potential power to organize and force their demands on public officials. Instead, the heritage of peonage conditioned the Hispanic workers and farmers to define their political roles in terms of political obligation. They voted for a particular candidate not because of his qualifications or campaign promises, but because they felt indebted to the candidate . . . or to their employers, who supported the machine ticket.[40]

Early Manifestations of Ethnic Awareness

The military conquest, annexation, and subsequent racial prejudice and economic displacement experienced by Mexican Americans placed intense strains on the culture and style of life they had developed over two centuries of continuous residence in the Southwest. As American and other immigrants poured into the region, bringing with them their systems of government, social norms, and institutions, the resident Mexican population faced an extremely difficult set of challenges. Most of this first generation of Mexican Americans had little choice but to try to adapt and accommodate themselves to the changes confronting their society. For the majority of Mexican Americans the general climate of anti-Mexican prejudice and their own withdrawal from extensive contacts with the Anglo American interlopers served as formidable barriers to achieving even the most basic forms of integration, much less full-blown assimilation into the society of which they had become a part.

On the other hand, the intense pressures that annexation exerted on the traditional northern Mexican social order had unforeseen effects on the Mexican American population. There is no question that Mexican Americans suffered from Anglo Americans' tendency to stigmatize them by generically defining and thus, to a large degree, dismissing them as inferior "Mexicans" in what had juridically become part of the United States. At the same time, however, Americans' prejudices and discriminatory practices helped lay the foundation for the gradual emergence and development of new forms of ethnic awareness among the Spanish-speaking population of the Southwest. Collective ethnic awareness developed slowly over a number of years and varied significantly in content and expression depending on local circumstances, including local economic conditions, the ratio of Anglo to Mexican residents in a given area, proximity to the border, the extent of interethnic contact, and other factors. But by the 1870s scattered evidence indicates that Mexican Americans in various locales had begun to forge an affirmative sense of themselves as an ethnic minority of a larger society. In some ways it was indeed the immense challenge of adapting to a new political and social order, combined with Mexican Americans' ongoing experience of prejudice and discrimination, that provided a basis for solidarity among a group of people who had previously had few bases of community or collective action. The experience of prejudice and discrimination helped Mexican Americans to create a self-conscious ethnic collectivity where one did not exist before.

Scholars have noted similar dynamics among a broad variety of peoples and cultures in many areas of the world. For example, in his broadly comparative work on the genesis and evolution of ethnic and/or national identities in minority populations in Europe, Africa, and the Middle East, the British scholar Anthony D. Smith details the complex nature of evolving interethnic or interracial relations in different societies. Smith notes that the common process of ascription—the act of a dominant or superordinate group assigning a priori characteristics and labels to another group—often serves unexpected or even contradictory functions, particularly in situations where the subordinate group has been involuntarily incorporated into a new society. Smith argues that it is common for such newly created minority populations to develop a new sense of identity as a natural defense mechanism or as part of a larger "oppositional strategy" against the prejudice and discrimination shown them by the majority or dominant group. As Smith points out, the process of forging a generally accepted collective self-identity in an ethnic minority population often "is simply the converse of [discrimination's] distancing role. Just as [discrimination based on] colour can point up dissimilarity and distance, so may it reveal similarity and proximity," among racial or cultural minorities. Similarly, discrimination by a dominant group over a subordinate group may serve as a catalyst, encouraging members of minority populations to overcome lines of internal stratification that divided them in the past. Seeking new areas of commonality, they often "invent" a new (or renewed) sense of community in an attempt to better conditions for their group as a whole (however that group or community is ultimately defined). As Smith notes,

"This is particularly apparent where group conflicts polarise members of different colour [or cultural] communities. The need for self-defence, for organisation and leadership, in the face of threat or attack inspires a desire for some rationale for the community, some set of justifications and explanations for their need to unite and mobilise."[41]

Although no one has yet produced a systematic study of the development of Mexican American ethnic identity after 1848, scholars of nineteenth-century Mexican American history have provided strong indications that a process similar to that which Smith describes was surfacing in different local contexts among the recently "created" Mexican American population in California, New Mexico, and Texas. By the 1850s Mexican Americans throughout the Southwest had begun to speak of themselves as members of a Mexican American community, or, more commonly, as members of a broader linguistic/cultural community that was distinct from the North Americans. More importantly, Mexican Americans in communities across the region had taken the first steps toward mobilizing and organizing themselves based on this nascent sense of collective identity.

This is not to assert, however, that Mexican Americans responded uniformly to the changes wrought by annexation. On the contrary, to achieve any level of collective ethnic awareness or solidarity, Mexican Americans first had to contend with the internal class, regional, and other differences that traditionally divided the Mexican population of the north. As David Weber, Ramón A. Gutiérrez, and other Southwest historians have argued, in the quarter century before annexation, many, if not most, Spanish-speaking residents of Mexico's northern provinces did not even identify themselves as Mexicans and instead probably thought of themselves first as Nuevomexicanos, Tejanos, or Californios. As Weber puts it, "Loyalty to one's locality, one's *patria chica* [little nation, or locale], frequently took precedence over loyalty to the patria, or nation as a whole."[42]

Given their long isolation on the fringes of the Mexican nation, these local attachments are hardly surprising. Considering themselves *hijos del país* (sons of the country), Mexicans in the various northern centers of settlement had driven deep roots into the regions where their families had lived for generations. Indeed, regional loyalties were so strong that many natives of the far-flung northern provinces—particularly members of the local elites—tended to view Mexican colonial administrators, soldiers, settlers, and sojourners as *extranjeros* (foreigners or outsiders)—despite the fact that both Norteños and Mexicans from Mexico were technically Mexicans. In fact, during the early Mexican Republic the Norteños' petulant attitude toward the patria was so strong that revolts periodically broke out against Mexican authority in Alta California, Nuevo Mexico, and Tejas.

Weber notes that in California "even casual visitors . . . noted the hostility and 'deep hatred' that the Californios held toward Mexicans from 'la otra banda,' or 'other shore' as Californios termed central Mexico."[43]

For their part, Mexicans who visited the northern provinces were also aware of the social distance that had grown between the Norteños and Mexicans from the fatherland. This was clear in the observations made by Lt. José María Sánchez, an artillery officer who traveled with Inspector General Manuel Mier y Terán on his tour of Texas in 1828. Commenting on the Mexican residents of Nacogdoches, Texas, Sánchez noted with regret that

> The Mexicans that live here are very humble people, and perhaps their intentions are good, but because of their education and environment they are ignorant not only of the customs of our great cities, but even of the occurrences of our Revolution, excepting a few persons who have heard about them. Accustomed to the continued trade with the North Americans, they have adopted their customs and habits, and one may say truly that they are not Mexicans except by birth, for they even speak Spanish with marked incorrectness.[44]

Society in nineteenth-century northwestern Mexico was stratified in ways that militated against the development of a strong sense of ethnic or cultural community. It was hierarchically organized into a social pyramid ordered by a combination of factors, including accumulated wealth and claimed lines of descent. By 1800 Hispanic society in the north was dominated by a small minority of wealthy landowners who claimed descent from the original Spanish settlers of New Spain. The exact shape of the social pyramid varied from region to region in the northern provinces, but in general Hispanic society in the early nineteenth century was divided into three fairly distinct strata. At the bottom were the Christianized or, more accurately, detribalized Indians (known as *genízaros* in New Mexico and neophytes in California) who worked for large landowners in a status resembling indentured servitude or for the many Catholic missions that dotted the northern frontier. Smallholder mestizos occupied the next tier. Although most people in this stratum, like the Christianized Indians, toiled at subsistence agriculture, ranch labor, artisanal crafts, and, toward the end of the Mexican period, as paid day laborers, the mestizos could—and did—claim at least some Spanish blood and thus were considered to be *gente de razón* (people of reason) as opposed to the savage Indians, who were deemed *gente sin razón* (people without reason). The final and smallest stratum of Hispanic frontier society consisted of the large landowners, government and military administrators, merchants, and in some cases, Catholic church officials who dominated the political economy. As Gutiérrez noted in his richly detailed work on the colonial and Mexican-era north, the landed aristocracy maintained and extended its dominance of northern society through a complex system of claimed European descent, the accumulation of wealth, and the strict supervision of marriage and women's sexuality.[45]

Many of the lines of internal differentiation that had evolved in northwestern Mexico persisted after the American conquest. As Gutiérrez and others have argued, although Anglo Americans may have seen the emerging patterns of ethnic relations in the Southwest as a question concerning simple categorical differences between Americans, Mexicans, and Indians, Mexican Americans continued to recognize important status distinctions among themselves, which they attempted to maintain even after the change in sovereignty. Indeed, Mexican Americans' attempts to grapple with the social status issues raised by their incorporation into American society closely mirrored the lines of internal stratification that traditionally had divided them.

Take, for example, the different ways the various strata of Mexican society reacted to the American takeover and to Americans' subsequent tendency to view Mexicans simply as "Mexicans." Upper-class Mexican Americans contested Anglo Americans' efforts to classify (and thus to denigrate) them as Mexicans by denying and/or reconstructing their ethnic heritage. Traditionally considering themselves to be of inherently higher status than the Mexican working masses by virtue of their class standing and their *calidad* and their sense of *limpieza de sangre* (that is, their social "quality" based on their supposed "pure" European blood), members of the Californio, Tejano, and Nuevomexicano elite tried to persuade incoming American immigrants to recognize and acknowledge these status distinctions. In the early part of the nineteenth century this strategy worked because many Americans found it in their interest to forge economic, political, and, in many cases, matrimonial alliances with members of the existing Spanish-speaking elite. Seeking to maximize their influence with the extant indigenous elite, the first American immigrants to the region tended to acknowledge the status distinctions the elite tried so hard to maintain between themselves and the Mexican working class.[46]

After annexation these status distinctions remained crucial to the Spanish-speaking elite's attempts to insulate themselves from the stigma associated with the Mexican label. By referring to themselves as Spanish in their dealings with Anglo Americans, members of the indigenous elite hoped to escape the prejudice exhibited toward Mexicans in the Southwest.

They accomplished this, in part, by meticulously laying the foundation for what Carey McWilliams wryly termed the "Spanish fantasy heritage" of the Southwest. Existing historical evidence demonstrates that only a tiny fraction of the original Hispanic colonists of the Southwest could legitimately claim pure Spanish descent, the overwhelming majority being descended from Mexico's vast mestizo population. Nevertheless, many of the elite families insisted on referring to themselves as *españoles*, or Spaniards, to distance themselves from what they defined as the *gente corriente*, the common or vulgar working-class people. As the position of the ethnic Mexican population eroded in subsequent years, the descendants of the former elite *gente de razón* families clung to such status distinctions even more tenaciously. By the last decades of the nineteenth century their efforts in this direction had become almost comical. As McWilliams noted of this trend in California, "By a definition provided by the *Californios* themselves, [a Mexican American] who achieves success in the borderlands is 'Spanish,' one who doesn't is 'Mexican'."[47]

This strategy of denying mestizo descent was not the only option available to Mexican Americans as they attempted to deal with the many contradictions inherent in being Mexican in what had become an American society. Members of the working-class majority also grappled with the ambiguities inherent in their new status as ethnic Americans. Consequently, some began to articulate a sense of identity that represented a conscious attempt to meld their Mexican/Spanish colonial cultural heritage with their new political status as American citizens. Although it is impossible to recreate a representative cross-section of Mexican American public opinion on the issue of ethnic or community identity in the decades following annexation, scattered evidence does indicate that soon after the Mexican cession Mexican Americans were actively engaged in a process of assessing their new position in American society. As Griswold del Castillo notes in his study of the Los Angeles Mexican community, local attachments and loyalties continued to exert a strong influence on the social identity of Mexican Americans in the Southwest, but the transfer of sovereignty over their homelands stimulated a strong tendency "to move from particular [local] allegiances toward a more general group solidarity."[48]

Much of the impetus for moving toward a more inclusive sense of community stemmed from Mexican Americans' need to assert a positive sense of "peoplehood" in the face of the Anglo Americans' attempts to denigrate them as racial and cultural inferiors. One strategy, as we have seen, involved withdrawal into the confines of the barrios. Painfully aware of how Americans felt about them, many working-class Mexican Americans simply attempted to avoid unnecessary contact with the American immigrants. More important, in a weak position to alter their ethnic heritage by constructing a myth of upper-class European descent, they took solace instead in observing their own variants of Mexican culture in the relative privacy of their neighborhoods or in the more isolated rural areas in Texas, northern New Mexico, and southern Colorado that the Americans had not yet overrun. By isolating themselves in segregated barrios, colonias, and rural *rancherías*, working-class Mexican Americans could, and largely did, continue to live their lives in a manner similar to that which existed prior to annexation. Although there is no question that life in their impoverished neighborhoods reflected Mexican Americans' eroding economic and social standing, segregation in some ways contributed to a process of community formation, or reformation, rather than the dissolution or fading away of Mexican American communities that many Americans had expected or hoped for.

To working-class Mexican Americans urban barrios and rural colonias functioned as sanctuaries from the bewildering changes occurring around them. Anglos may have gained control of the political and economic lifeblood of the Southwest, but within the boundaries of their own neighborhoods Mexican Americans protected many of their cultural practices and rituals. In their own enclaves Mexican Americans continued to converse in Spanish, observed Roman Catholic rituals and celebrations, and entertained themselves in the style to which they had grown accustomed, all largely without interference from the Norteamericanos. In addition, working-class Mexican Americans courted, raised families, and perpetuated their traditional practice of *compadrazgo*—the system of ritual godparent sponsorship which bound them to one another through complex fictive kinship networks—without interference from the American immigrants who were otherwise transforming their society.[49]

Some Mexican Americans developed other, more activist, methods of contesting their subordination in the new society of the Southwest. One way they contested their ascribed inferior ethnic status was to form their own voluntary organizations. One of the earliest and most ubiquitous forms of association among Mexican Americans and Mexican immigrants was the *mutualista*, or mutual-aid association. Like mutual-assistance and fraternal associations formed by other immigrant groups in the United States, Mexican mutualistas provided the working class and poor with a broad range of benefits and services they otherwise could not afford. By pooling their limited resources, members provided themselves with a number of benefits and services including funeral, disability, and other types of insurance, credit, and cultural events and entertainment.[50] Originating in Mexico during the early nineteenth century, by the 1870s similar organizations had been established throughout Mexico and the Hispanic Southwest.

Other Mexican Americans employed more extreme measures to contest challenges to their dignity and to the general process of social subordination they experienced. As several social historians have demonstrated, when local conditions became intolerable Mexican Americans across the Southwest resorted to violence and/or acts of social banditry in their efforts, as one scholar put it, to retain "some measure of self-determination in the face of an increasingly oppressive new regime."[51]

Over the long run, however, the development among Mexican Americans of a sense of themselves *as* Mexican Americans provided a far more important defense against discriminatory practices than did armed resistance or the formation of formal voluntary organizations. One of the clearest reflections of the evolution of this new sense of collective identity is seen in the gradual changes in the various terms Mexican Americans used to describe themselves. As we have seen, prior to extensive American penetration into northwestern Mexico in the early nineteenth century, residents of that area identified primarily with their localities rather than with the Republic of Mexico. After the Mexican War, however, the common experience of military defeat, widespread discrimination, and increasing poverty created conditions under which many Mexicans in the annexed territories began, in effect, to turn inward. Recognizing that they clearly were not accepted as Americans, many logically began to think of themselves as Mexicanos or as members of a larger, pan-Hispanic community of *La Raza* (the race or the people).

Although La Raza is a term that today has come to mean the entire mestizo population of greater Latin America, in the last third of the nineteenth century Mexican Americans often employed the term to describe the Mexican "race" on both sides of the new border. Use of group terms such as La Raza varied widely from region to region, but given the historical heterogeneity of the Spanish-speaking population the use of such terminology by Mexican Americans to describe campaigns of protest and resistance in Texas, New Mexico, and California is remarkable. In California, for example, Mexican Americans ranging from Francisco P. Ramírez, editor and publisher of the Los Angeles Spanish-language weekly *El Clamor Público*, to the social bandit Tiburcio Vásquez, advocated the creation of a new sense of ethnic solidarity among members of what the newspaper variously described as *la población Mexicana* (the Mexican population [of California]), *nuestros compatriotas* (our compatriots), *nuestra población California y*

Mexicana (our population of [Mexican] Californians and Mexicans [from Mexico]), *la raza española* (the Hispanic race or people), or *nuestra raza* (our people).[52]

These terms were popularized by the rapid proliferation of Spanish-language newspapers and the fraternal, mutual-aid, and Mexican patriotic associations that sprang up in the Southwest after annexation. Their use marked the birth of an oppositional strategy that acknowledged the common oppression Mexican Americans suffered in American society while offering an alternative, positive label that countered the stigmatized status many Americans sought to impose on Mexicans. As Griswold del Castillo describes the emergence of the term in California,

> The increasing use of "La Raza" as a generic term in the Spanish-language press was evidence of a new kind of ethnic consciousness. . . . La Raza connoted racial, spiritual, and blood ties with the Latin American people, particularly with Mexico. And La Raza emerged as the single most important symbol of ethnic pride and identification. There were many ways of using this term, depending on the context. "La Raza Mexicana," "La Raza Hispano-Americana," "La Raza Española," and "La Raza Latina" were all used to convey a sense of the racial, class, and national variety within the Spanish-speaking community. But in general the use of "La Raza" implied membership in a cultural tradition that was separate from the . . . "norteamericanos."[53]

According to de León and other historians of nineteenth-century Texas, an even more intense process of ethnic redefinition and boundary marking occurred among Tejanos after 1848. With the vast majority of the surviving Mexican American population pushed into ethnic enclaves hugging the new border after the Mexican War, the demarcation between Anglo and Mexican was more clearly marked in Texas than anywhere else in the Southwest. Consequently, in the Nueces Strip—the territory between the Nueces River and the Rio Grande—and in other communities along the Rio Grande where Mexicans Americans and Mexican sojourners predominated, Mexican Americans doggedly retained a strong sense of Mexican identity for decades following their political incorporation into the United States. Although Tejanos suffered from the effects of discrimination and economic subordination as much, if not more, than did Mexican Americans in other parts of the Southwest, the Tejanos, as de León notes, "continued their own cultural patterns, making bearable their life as poor and marginal people." Despite their incorporation into American society and in many ways because of their annexation into a foreign nation, most Mexican

Americans in nineteenth-century Texas continued, as de León notes, to emphasize what they called *lo mexicano* (a sense of Mexicanness) as the cornerstone of their collective identity. Indeed, as de León and other Texas historians have argued, "'*lo mexicano*' prevailed over '*lo americano*' [a sense of Americanness], manifested in the population predominance of Mexicans, in the use of the Spanish language and Mexican work patterns, in the persistence of Mexican social traditions, and in the influence, however subtle, that the northern states of Mexico had on the area." In short, although Mexican Americans in the border region of Texas were no longer citizens of Mexico, Texas largely remained "a place where Tejanos could move about as Mexicans instead of Americans, if they had to."[54]

The success of Mexican Americans in maintaining a distinctive culture in the Southwest did not lie in the fact that they violently or even overtly resisted Anglo Americans' steady encroachments on their way of life. Rather, the ultimate political and social significance of the perpetuation of distinct Mexican American communities throughout the Southwest lay in the fact that Mexican Americans were able to survive and persist as an ethnically distinct people despite the change in political sovereignty over their homeland. In technical, political terms, although Mexican Americans, by virtue of their new status as American citizens, were no longer Mexicans, American racism and Mexican Americans' de facto subordinate status in the new social order encouraged them to consider themselves Mexicans in a way they never had before.

The irony in this situation was that Mexican Americans confounded Anglo Americans' expectations in at least two ways. In developing a new sense of community based both on a common Mexican cultural heritage and the common experience of racial prejudice in the United States, Mexican Americans were able to transform Anglo Americans' efforts to stigmatize them as racial inferiors into a positive strategy of self-affirmation as Mexicans in American society. At the same time, Mexican Americans' success in generating such new bases for solidarity went a long way toward guaranteeing the survival and growth of a distinct, if syncretic, variant of Mexican culture in what had become part of the United States. This was the last thing the proponents of Manifest Destiny had in mind when they had predicted the eventual fading away of the region's ethnic Mexican population.

The evolution of a society bifurcated in this manner spoke to a fundamental contradiction with which most Americans had yet to come to grips—a contradiction that would ultimately raise serious questions about the nature of the society the Americans had transplanted in the Southwest.

For in formally granting the ethnic Mexican population in the Southwest all the rights of American citizens in 1848, and yet denying them the possibility of exercising those rights, Americans planted the seeds of continuing ethnic discord in the region. As the ethnic Mexican population suddenly exploded in the last decades of the century due to the large numbers of immigrants that began to pour into the region from Mexico, the contradiction between the promise of the Treaty of Guadalupe Hidalgo and the American Constitution and the reality of American interracial and interethnic relations in the Southwest would take on even greater significance.

2   Economic Development and Immigration, 1890–1920

When Frederick Jackson Turner published his famous essay on the closing of the American frontier in 1893, ethnic Mexicans had become a tiny fraction of the total population of the region that had once been their domain. Indeed, for most Americans living in the Southwest in the last decades of the nineteenth century, the Mexican presence in the region seemed a distant memory. Continuing immigration from other parts of the United States resulted in the rapid growth of the non-Mexican population of the region, to the extent that, with the exception of northern New Mexico and isolated pockets of south Texas, Mexican Americans had seemingly disappeared from the landscape. Geographically isolated and mired in the lowest levels of the region's economy, by the 1890s the United States' Mexican American population had become, in one scholar's apt phrase, "the forgotten people."[1]

Americans would soon recognize, however, that the disappearance of the Mexican American population was illusory. In fact, although their numbers expanded at a much lower rate than those of the non-Mexican population, the Mexican American population had also continued to grow throughout the nineteenth century. Moreover, as the century drew to a close, the resident ethnic Mexican population began to grow at a significantly higher rate.

Some of this growth was attributable to natural increase, but most of it was the result of the steady increase in the rate of immigration from Mexico. Displaced from the land by the draconian land policies instituted by Mexican dictator Porfirio Díaz and drawn to the United States by the rapidly diversifying and expanding southwestern economy, the number of Mexican immigrants entering the United States climbed steadily after

1890. When the Mexican people revolted against Díaz's regime in 1910, the stream of Mexicans into the United States increased even more. By the 1920s their rate of entry for a short time rivaled the great European migrations of the late nineteenth century. Although immigration and demographic statistics for this era are notoriously inaccurate, most scholars concur that at least one million, and possibly as many as a million and a half Mexican immigrants entered the United States between 1890 and 1929.

Very few Americans recognized it at the time, but immigration of this magnitude added a new dimension to the already complex patterns of social relationships that had evolved in the Southwest since the Mexican Cession. Accustomed as they had become to seeing Mexicans as an inherently inferior and internally undifferentiated racial minority, most Americans failed to recognize the significance of large-scale Mexican immigration for the simple reason that they recognized no distinctions between Americans of Mexican descent and more recent immigrants from Mexico. This was true largely because the vast majority of Americans never came into direct contact with the resident Mexican population. Because most Mexican workers took jobs and found housing in or adjacent to extant urban barrios and isolated rural communities inhabited by Mexican Americans, few Anglo Americans realized that Mexican immigrants had both contributed to a dramatic expansion of the resident ethnic population and created many new tensions in existing Mexican American enclaves.

The effects of large-scale immigration were readily apparent, however, to Americans of Mexican descent. Although the increasing flow of immigrants into the Southwest was welcomed by some Mexican Americans because the immigrants helped to rejuvenate Mexican culture, customs, and use of Spanish in their communities, immigration of this magnitude also tended to exacerbate the many social, economic, and political problems Mexican Americans faced in American society. Already struggling to maintain some kind of niche in a society that seemed to have little use for them, many Mexican Americans viewed the rising rate of immigration from Mexico with concern and uneasiness. Although many Mexican Americans could not help but identify and empathize with the Mexican people they called *los recién llegados*—the recent arrivals—others were concerned about the potential negative influence the new immigrants might have on the Mexican people already living in the United States.

Regional Economic Development

The rapid expansion of the Southwest's ethnic Mexican population was the result of a number of interrelated economic and political developments that unfolded in both the United States and Mexico during the last quarter of the nineteenth century. Up to then the American Southwest's economy had grown only slowly, subject to the vagaries of mining booms and busts, real estate speculation, and forays into the large-scale capitalist "bonanza farming" of the 1870s and 1880s. In the last decades of the century, however, important infrastructural and technological advances in the region— particularly the extension of vast railway networks, the introduction of the refrigerated boxcar, and the construction of an intricate network of privately and publicly financed irrigation projects—laid the foundations for one of the most explosive periods of economic growth in American history.

The construction and expansion of the great western railroads—the Union Pacific, the Atchison, Topeka & Santa Fe, the Southern Pacific, and others—tied the region both to the national economy of the United States and to the newly constructed Mexican rail system, thus enabling western entrepreneurs to transport and market their goods in unprecedented quantities. In 1880 the Southwest had only 7,436 miles of track; by 1920 it was criss-crossed by more than 36,000 miles of track.[2] The expansion of irrigated agriculture in the arid Southwest was even more impressive. In 1890 the combined total of irrigated land in California, Nevada, Utah, and Arizona amounted to a mere 1,575,000 acres. By 1902 California alone had nearly two million acres under irrigation, and the other states followed close behind. After the Newlands Federal Reclamation Act was passed in 1902, millions more acres of former desert land were reclaimed, allowing production of an unheard of cornucopia of hundreds of different varieties of crops. By 1909 nearly 14 million acres were under irrigation in the Southwest.[3]

In California the combined effects of these developments—particularly the expansion of the railroads and the rapid growth of highly specialized irrigated agriculture—were dramatic. The extension of the Southern Pacific into Los Angeles (and the heart of the state's citrus growing region) in 1876 and the link with the Santa Fe in 1887 allowed southern California growers to increase production and reach distant markets. As irrigation systems slowly snaked into new areas throughout the state, millions of additional acres of rich agricultural land were brought into intensive production. By 1910 California claimed 2.6 million acres; by 1920 irrigated acreage in the state had increased to more than four million.[4] As a result the value of California's crops—particularly fruits, nuts, citrus, and vegetables—rose spectacularly in the first third of the twentieth century. Between 1900 and 1920, for example, orange production quadrupled, and lemon production quintupled. Overall the value of the state's fresh fruit and nut crops jumped from $29 million in 1900 to almost $49 million in 1910. By 1930 California alone accounted for one-third of the United

States' fresh fruit, one-fourth of its vegetables, eight-tenths of its wine, and nearly the entire American output of almonds, artichokes, figs, nectarines, olives, dates, and lemons.[5]

To accomplish this massive increase in agricultural production, California growers expanded the scale of their enterprises and in the process laid the foundations for the development of American corporate agriculture, or agribusiness. Employing economies of scale by expanding the acreage under cultivation, by the turn of the century California growers had already established a pattern of encompassing prime agricultural land into huge corporate farms. By the late 1920s California alone contained nearly 40 percent of all large-scale farms. (A large-scale farm was defined by the U.S. Department of Agriculture as a one with an annual crop worth at least $30,000.) Although these large-scale corporate farms, which social critic Carey McWilliams termed "factories in the fields," represented only 2.1 percent of all farms in the state, the agribusiness giants accounted for almost 29 percent of the overall value of crops produced in California.[6]

Texas's economic growth during the same period, though not quite as spectacular, was impressive nonetheless. With the extension of the railroads into southern and western Texas during the first two decades of the century, vast new areas were opened to mining, livestock raising, and agriculture—especially the cultivation of citrus fruits, vegetables, and cotton, perennially Texas's top cash crop. As a result of the development of a reliable method of transportation, cotton cultivation, long restricted to the eastern portion of the immense state, rapidly expanded into central, west, and south Texas. When cotton production in the state peaked in the mid-1920s, almost seventeen million acres were under cultivation. Texas accounted for between 35 and 42 percent of the total United States' cotton crop and an amazing 20 to 30 percent of the world crop.[7]

The concomitant growth of Texas's rail network and irrigation systems spurred growth in other areas of agriculture. The extension of the Gulf Coast Line into the Rio Grande Valley in 1904, with connections into what soon became known as the Winter Garden region (Zavala, Dimmitt, and La Salle counties) in 1911 and the completion of the Southern Pacific line into south Texas in 1925 made possible the integration of the Texas economy into national markets and provided an unprecedented boom to the local economy as well.

Labor and the Southwestern Economy

The rapid expansion and growing scale of the agricultural, mining, transportation, and construction sectors of the southwestern economy would not have been possible without a massive infusion of labor. Indeed, the lack of a reliable source of affordable labor, combined with the extreme environmental conditions of the Southwest, had always presented would-be capitalists with a vexing obstacle to large-scale development of the region. Consequently, as American entrepreneurs experimented with various technologies to overcome the physical obstacles to development, they also undertook a long series of experiments designed to fill their growing need for cheap labor.

American employers first looked to the Far East as the solution to their labor problems. After the Gold Rush peaked in California, railroad companies and some agricultural employers began to import large numbers of Chinese laborers. By the late 1850s and early 1860s thousands of Chinese railroad workers were employed in the West. Soon other employers were also utilizing Chinese labor. By 1880 more than 100,000 Chinese were employed in a wide array of occupations, ranging from work on the railroads, in agriculture, and in mining, to work as domestics, in restaurants, and in laundries. The use of Chinese laborers stimulated fierce opposition among American workers and some small businesses, however, and as early as the 1860s opposition began to coalesce into what became a virulent anti-Chinese movement. As the Chinese were subjected to nativist violence and intimidation in many locations in the West throughout this period, political pressure steadily increased to restrict further Chinese immigration into the United States. As a result Chinese workers were ultimately barred from entry into the country by the passage of the federal Chinese Exclusion Act of 1882.[8]

As anti-Chinese hysteria played itself out in California and other locales in the West, American employers turned to Japan as a potential labor panacea. Beginning in the late 1880s Japanese workers began to enter the United States in numbers similar to those that had been recorded for Chinese workers earlier in the century. Although American corporate farmers initially believed that Japanese labor represented the ideal answer to their labor woes, it soon became clear that Japanese immigrants were not behaving according to plan. American growers became alarmed, in particular, at the Japanese tendency to form cooperatives, pool resources, buy or lease land, and ultimately compete against their former employers. This entrepreneurial talent was clearly not what American employers had in mind when they began to recruit Japanese workers, so by the early years of the twentieth century small farmers and some corporate agricultural concerns started to lobby the California legislature to enact measures designed to limit Japanese investments in land and small businesses. Such pressures increased until 1908, when the governments of the United States and Japan quietly struck a so-called Gentlemen's Agreement that, in effect, severely restricted subsequent immigration from Japan. The ethnic Japanese population of the West continued to grow through both natural increase and limited immigration, but the experiment in the large-scale use of Japanese workers had come to an end before World War I.[9]

The Early Use of Mexican Labor

Frustrated by these early attempts to stabilize the regional labor supply in the rail, mining, construction, and agricultural industries, American employers began to look to Mexico as a source of cheap labor. Although Mexican Americans and some Mexican immigrant workers had been utilized in the lower-skilled segments of the regional labor market since the mid-nineteenth century, by the 1880s the demand for labor began to outstrip local supply. When the Chinese Exclusion Act and the Gentlemen's Agreement significantly reduced the available labor supply, employers began to hire Mexican immigrants to fill the steadily increasing demand for low-skilled, low-wage jobs in the southwestern economy.

Fortunately for American entrepreneurs, their increasing demand for labor coincided with the serious deterioration of the position of workers in Mexico during the Porfiriato. Forced off the land and into a growing migratory labor stream by the movement toward export-crop farming under Díaz's regime, thousands of Mexican workers had begun to wander within Mexico well before they thought of making the journey north to the United States. But facing the painful realities of declining wages combined with rapidly rising food prices, growing numbers of landless Mexican workers began to look to the United States for work. As one historian of the period noted, "The men, women, and children of rural Mexico paid a horribly disproportionate price to pull their country into the twentieth century. It was natural that they sought better conditions for themselves elsewhere."[10]

As real wages in Mexico dropped and the price of food continued its precipitous climb in the late 1880s and early 1890s, increasing numbers of Mexican peasant workers began to move north. This movement was aided and abetted by American labor agents, who traveled into the interior of Mexico seeking agricultural and railroad construction and maintenance workers. Accruing lucrative profits by charging the immigrants for supplies and transportation and the American employers for utilizing their services, these employment agencies did a booming business in the Southwest up through the 1920s.[11]

Statistics on Mexican migration during this period, as already noted, are notoriously inaccurate, but extrapolation from Mexican and United States census sources reveals the increasing magnitude of the immigrant flow. In 1880 the number of U.S. residents born in Mexico was probably no more than 68,000. By 1890 the Mexican-born population had increased moderately, to approximately 78,000.[12] In the 1890s the rate of immigration increased appreciably, when approximately 50,000 new immigrants entered the United States. After the turn of the century, however, the rate of Mexican immigration rose dramatically. Between 1900 and 1910 the Mexican-born population grew from approximately 103,000 to almost 222,000, statistics that almost surely significantly underestimated the number of Mexican immigrants who had entered the country undetected. By 1920 the Mexican-born population residing in the United States had more than doubled, to at least 478,000 individuals.[13]

Mexican immigrants filled a wide variety of occupations, ranging from agricultural labor, mine work, and railroad construction and maintenance, to common day labor on innumerable construction sites throughout the Southwest. By 1910 Mexican immigrant workers had become the backbone of the work force in many industries and could be found in smaller numbers working as auto and steel workers in the Great Lakes region and as fishermen and cannery workers in Alaska. By the 1920s Mexican immigrant and Mexican American workers dominated the unskilled and semiskilled sectors of the regional labor market. In California, for example, ethnic Mexican workers made up nearly 17 percent of the unskilled construction labor force and as much as three-quarters of the state's farm labor force. In Texas Mexican workers proved even more crucial to economic development. With no other source of labor available, Texas entrepreneurs had first turned to Mexican immigrant laborers in the 1890s to perform back-breaking "grubbing" work clearing brush from fields. After the turn of the century growing numbers of Mexicans entered the work force in cotton cultivation. By 1940 Mexican immigrants and Mexican Americans constituted an estimated three-quarters of the migratory laborers working in the state's cotton fields. Ethnic Mexican workers were not restricted to agricultural labor: by the late 1920s Mexicans also constituted an estimated 75 percent of all unskilled construction workers in Texas. By then Mexican labor dominated most sectors of low-wage work in the Southwest, accounting for an estimated 65 to 85 percent of the work force in vegetables, fruit, and truck crops, more than half of the workers in the sugar-beet industry, 60 percent of the common labor in the mining industry, and 60 to 90 percent of the track crews on the regional railroads.[14]

Early Rationales for the Use of Mexican Labor

Given the long history of racial antipathy toward Mexicans in the Southwest, it may seem surprising that Mexican immigrants were allowed to become such a vital component of the region's economy during the first thirty years of this century. Indeed, in the era of Manifest Destiny most expansionists had argued that Mexicans and other inferior races would gradually disappear after Americans established hegemony over the Southwest. The need for cheap labor, however, provided a powerful inducement to southwestern capitalists to change their thinking about Mexicans. Faced with the persistence of anti-Mexican sentiment among the American public, employers had to devise ways to justify the recruitment and employment of large numbers of Mexican workers.

Most employers invoked many of the same negative racial and cultural stereotypes Americans had developed over the years about Mexicans to explain their use of them as low-paid labor. Thus in the years after 1910 southwestern economic interests exploited Americans' traditional perceptions of Mexicans as an inherently backward, slow, docile, indolent, and tractable people. By the mid-1910s southwestern employers argued that these characteristics constituted the very virtues that made Mexicans an ideal (and cheap) labor force.

The basic tenets of the elaborate rationale American employers first developed about the use of Mexican labor would be heard again and again over the course of the next sixty years. Spokesmen for the Southwest's commercial farmers, mine operators, railroad corporations, and large construction firms reiterated their old complaints about the region's chronic labor shortage. Second, they argued with no small justification that the kind of work required by these industries was not work that white Americans would tolerate. The hours were too long, wages too low, and working conditions too harsh to attract white American workers in sufficient numbers to fill the ever-growing demands for labor in the Southwest. And last, American advocates of the use of Mexican labor blandly asserted that Mexicans were a race that was both culturally and physiologically suited to perform the arduous manual labor required in these industries.

The articulation of these beliefs can be found in a broad range of sources in the first two decades of the century. As early as 1908 the U.S. government economist Victor S. Clark argued that despite their racial and cultural shortcomings Mexican workers were "docile, patient, usually orderly in camp, fairly intelligent under competent supervision, obedient and cheap."[15] In 1911, a special congressional panel (subsequently known as the Dillingham Commission) convened to review U.S. immigration policy made similar observations about Mexican labor in its report to Congress. Although the commission expressed some reservations about the racial characteristics of Mexican workers, it nevertheless concluded that

> Mexican immigrants are providing a fairly acceptable supply of labor in a limited territory in which it is difficult to secure others, and their competitive ability is limited because of their more or less temporary residence and their personal qualities, so that their incoming does not involve the same detriment to labor conditions as is involved in the immigration of other races who also work at comparatively low wages. While the Mexicans are not easily assimilated, this is not of very great importance as long as most of them return to their native land after a short time.[16]

As increasing numbers of Mexican immigrants entered the labor market after World War I, however, southwestern industrial and agricultural spokesmen recognized the need to allay other Americans' fears about what many perceived as an invasion of foreign workers. In an era in which American nativists clamored for ever more stringent restrictions on the immigration of non-Nordic peoples to the United States, advocates of the use of Mexican labor had to tread a very fine line in developing and advancing their arguments. Consequently, in a pattern that characterized the region's debate over Mexican immigration for the next six decades, employers and their allies tried to dampen criticisms of the use of Mexican labor. To this end they developed a public relations strategy that painstakingly explained the reasons why Mexican immigrant workers did not represent a threat to American workers or to the cultural (and racial) homogeneity of American society.

Regional employers and their supporters in the federal government hammered away at points they believed would positively influence American public opinion. In testimony before the House Immigration and Naturalization Committee in 1930, Harry Chandler, publisher and chief stockholder of the *Los Angeles Times*, attempted to do just this. "Mexicans never have created problems in Los Angeles," he argued. On the contrary,

> the peon who comes here is an innocent, friendly, kindly individual. He has to be industrious, for he has to work in order to live. He has in him 85 percent Indian blood on the average and every American who knows anything about Indian characteristics can measure from that the Mexican peon who comes to work in the United States. They are not enterprising, of course, like other races, but they are more desirable from our standpoint than any other class of labor that comes, and they create fewer problems.[17]

Another theme southwestern corporate and business interests (and their congressional allies) emphasized was that Mexicans were doing work that was beneath American workers. As Colorado Congressman Edward Taylor put it in 1926,

> The American laboring people will not get down on their hands and knees in the dirt and pull weeds and thin these beets, and break their backs doing that kind of work. In fact there are very few people who can stand that kind of work. No matter how much they are paid, they can not and will not do it. That kind of labor is hard tedious work.[18]

Ralph Taylor of the California Agricultural Legislative Committee made a similar point in a prepared statement he read during hearings held in 1930. "American whites," he insisted, "have been educated away from hard, physical labor, particularly common labor, and more particularly itinerant labor, and even the proponents of exclusion grant that the education of the American for higher pursuits is entirely legitimate and proper." "They fail, however, to recognize," he continued, "that the menial tasks must be performed by someone, and have thus far utterly failed to tell us where the people to do these tasks are to come from."[19]

Other spokesmen for southwestern capitalist interests explained their use of Mexican workers in more graphic racial terms. For example, George P. Clements of the Los Angeles Chamber of Commerce spent much of his career extolling the racial virtues of Mexican immigrant labor; in the process, he revised and expanded the employers' case for the use of such labor in the American economy. Elaborating on arguments others had made before him, Clements held not only that Mexicans would accept jobs which white American workers would not take but also that Mexicans were genetically suited to the harsh working conditions of the desert Southwest. Arguing this point to a group of southern California lemon growers in the fall of 1929, Clements stated, "Much of California's agricultural labor requirements consists of those tasks to which the Oriental and Mexican, due to their crouching and bending habits, are fully adapted, while the white is physically unable to adapt himself to them."[20] Clements also added other none-too-subtle racial arguments about the possible alternatives to Mexican labor. "If we cannot get the Mexican to supply . . . casual labor," he asserted in a letter to the U.S. Chamber of Commerce, "we have but one place to turn—the Porto Rican [sic] negro or as he is commonly known, 'the Portuguese nigger.'" "I do not think," he continued, "I need to stress the biological problem, particularly in California and the border states where so many of our people are dark skinned. [The Puerto Rican] is an American citizen, and once coming to us becomes a real social problem as well as adding to our American negro problem which is all ready [sic] sufficiently serious to have become a national question." Concluding with a warning, Clements intoned, "Picture to yourself the 136,000 California farmers, the highest type of agricultural people in the world living ideal rural lives to the greater part isolated, with 150,000 hybrid negroes tramping over the state. Is there any wonder we want to keep our Mexican labor?"[21] Congressman Taylor of Colorado concurred with this assessment, having noted in 1926 that Americans had already become used to working with Mexicans after one hundred years of close contact with Mexican Americans in the United States. As he put it, "It is not at all like we were importing inhabitants of a foreign country. We understood each other. They have no influence whatever upon our habits of life or form of civilization. They simply want work. . . . Generally speaking they are not immigrants at all. They do not try to buy or colonize our land, and they hope some day to be able to own a piece of land in their own country."[22]

Taylor's comments pointed to what was perhaps the most important part of the southwestern employers' argument, namely that Mexicans were a temporary foreign work force and therefore represented no lasting social or economic threat to American citizens. Arguing in all seriousness that Mexicans had an ingrained homing instinct like that of migratory birds, western lobbyists repeatedly assured congressional committees that Mexican workers came to the United States seeking only to earn a stake before they ultimately returned to Mexico. As S. Parker Frisselle, a spokesman for the California Farm Bureau Federation, put it during congressional hearings on the use of Mexican immigrant labor in 1926, "My experience of the Mexican is that he is a 'homer.' Like a pigeon, he goes back to roost. He is not a man that comes into this country for anything except our dollars and our work; and the railroads, and all of us, have been unsuccessful in keeping him here because he is a 'homer.' Those who know the Mexican know that that is a fact." Indeed, when asked by House Immigration Committee Chairman Albert Johnson whether he had any "idea of the established Mexican population" of California, Frisselle replied flatly, "There is no such thing, in my opinion, as an established Mexican population."[23] Texas Congressman Olger B. Burtness made much the same argument in particularly frank and revealing testimony before a House immigration committee in 1928. Trying to convince the committee that Texas needed Mexican immigrant labor, Burtness insisted that Mexicans had no impact on local society. As he put it,

> I am not going to stand here and tell you that [Mexicans] are the
> best people on the face of the earth, or that they will have made
> wonderful citizens or that in a few years their sons and daughters
> will be graduating from our high schools and soon acting as our
> preachers and lawyers and doctors and as our professors in colleges
> or anything . . . of that sort. If they were going to do that I don't
> know that we would want them.[24]

Over time, southwestern extractive, agricultural, and transportation
corporations, such as the American Smelting and Refining Corporation of
El Paso, the Phelps-Dodge Corporation, the Amalgamated Sugar Company, and the Southern Pacific Railroad, and lobby groups, such as the U.S.
Chamber of Commerce, the U.S. Sugar Manufacturers' Association, the
Farm Bureau Federations of California and Texas, the Arizona Wool Growers Association, and many others, honed their arguments for the use of
Mexican immigrant labor to an even finer edge. By the mid-1920s the litany espoused by southwestern economic concerns about the benefits of
temporary Mexican labor was presented to the American public as a set of
scientific facts. For example, in hearings before a congressional immigration committee in 1928, a representative of a lobby organization known as
the Agricultural Labor Committee of California laid out a detailed racial,
cultural, and economic justification for the widespread use of Mexican labor in the West and Southwest which combined most of the arguments that
other lobbyists had slowly developed since the turn of the century. The
lobbyist blithely noted that

> The Mexican immigrant fills the requirements of farm labor in Cal-
> ifornia and the Southwest as no other laborer could. He [sic] with-
> stands the high temperature and is adapted to field conditions. He
> goes from one locality to the other as the season's activities require
> his services. He takes care of highly perishable products as they de-
> mand picking. He does heavy field work, which other laborers do
> not desire and are unsuited to perform. His migratory character
> makes him fit into the need of each locality for transient and mo-
> bile labor.[25]

Other advocates articulated similar views. The region's corporate lobbyists, though they admitted that their industries might have become ov-
erreliant on temporary foreign labor, insisted that Mexican immigrants
had become indispensable to the economic well-being of the Southwest.
During hearings over proposed restrictions on Mexican immigration in the
late 1920s, Alfred P. Thom, a representative of the American Railroad Association, sounded an almost plaintive note on this point. "The labor sit-

uation in the territory referred to may have been due to a lack of foresight," he asserted,

> but it is a fact, and it is a fact that statesmen must deal with. The question arises as to what is going to be the economic effect upon that vast territory and its vast agricultural industry, if the supply of common labor is made inadequate. What could be more destructive of the prosperity of a people; of their contentment; of their general welfare; than to have their entire labor situation disrupted?[26]

Stating the position of the Southwest's capitalist interests about as forthrightly as one could, Thom concluded, "We are not employing men on account of their dispositions. We are employing them to have them exercise their strong backs at hard work. We are not employing them because they are of a high type of intellectuality [for] if we employed men because of their mental attainments, we could not employ either Mexicans or these colored people. We employ these men because we have the world's work to do and we must do it well."[27]

Evolution of the Restrictionist Debate

At the same time that such southwestern industrial and agricultural lobbyists as Ralph Taylor, George Clements, and Alfred Thom were advancing their case for the suitability of Mexican immigrant labor, forces were building within the regional society that would severely undermine their efforts. The most serious of these was the resurgence of anti-Mexican sentiment that was prevalent during and after World War I. Although some Americans had expressed vocal opposition to Mexican immigration even before the war, in the late 1910s and early 1920s the immigration debate assumed new levels of vituperation.

Much of the increase in anti-Mexican sentiment stemmed from the generally high levels of xenophobia and nativism that had increasingly characterized American society since the last years of the nineteenth century. Alarmed at the rapid increase in immigration from southern and eastern Europe and convinced that the so-called new immigrants were racially and culturally inferior to white Americans of Anglo-Saxon heritage, American protectionists had begun to agitate for restrictive federal immigration legislation as early as the mid-1880s. Led by such nativist spokesmen as Madison Grant, Henry Cabot Lodge, and Prescott W. Hall and by an array of restrictionist organizations as diverse as the American Protective Association, the Immigration Restriction League, the Daughters of the American Revolution, the American Federation of Labor, and the Ku Klux Klan, anti-immigration activists increased pressure on Congress to adopt stringent requirements for entry into the United States. Congress responded to these pressures by slowly revising U.S. immigration law in an effort to stem the flow of undesirable immigrants. Although the immigration reforms enacted by Congress in this period did not go nearly far enough toward meeting the demands of the restrictionists, by the 1880s and into the first two decades of this century several measures were passed that tightened control of the nation's borders. For example, between 1882 and 1917 Congress passed legislation establishing head taxes, preventing anarchists from entering the country, and barring entry to "persons suffering from . . . loathsome or dangerous contagious disease[s]." In addition, restrictionists in Congress mounted a major effort to impose literacy requirements on prospective immigrants. Arguing that such limitations represented a radical departure from the American tradition of encouraging new immigrants, several administrations opposed literacy legislation, with Presidents Grover Cleveland, William Howard Taft, and Woodrow Wilson vetoing such bills in 1896, 1898, 1902, 1906, 1913, and 1915. Beginning in 1917, however, Congress passed the first of what would become a long series of increasingly exclusionary immigration statutes. Laws passed in 1917 and 1921 and the omnibus Johnson-Reid Immigration Act of 1924 not only imposed strict literacy requirements but also established a stringent national-origins quota system, which placed severe limitations on immigration from southern and eastern Europe, the Far East, Africa, and most countries of the Middle East.[28]

Mexican immigrants initially were not subject to most of these restrictions. Bowing to the intense pressure exerted by southwestern agriculture, transportation, and construction lobbyists, Congress either exempted Mexican immigrants from the restrictive provisions of the new laws or relaxed them through various administrative procedures. As a partial consequence of these practices, Mexican immigration continued to increase steadily in the years after World War I.[29]

To advocates of immigration restriction, loopholes that allowed Mexicans to enter the United States in such numbers were unconscionable. Although Mexican immigrants were not yet considered quite the menace that immigrants from southern and eastern Europe represented, as early as 1910 some influential Americans had already voiced concern about their poor health and hygiene, "cultural backwardness," and general "unassimilability."[30] Over time, however, restrictionist sentiment against Mexicans became more pronounced. For example, during House debate on Mexican immigration quotas in April 1924 Congressman Albert H. Vestal of Indiana asked, "What is the use of closing the front door to keep out undesirables from Europe when you permit Mexicans to come in here by the back

door by the thousands and thousands?"[31] From the point of view of a growing number of Americans, the rapid growth of the Mexican population represented just as serious a threat to the racial, cultural, and social integrity
of the United States as did the entry of any of the other undesirable peoples. Indeed, by the mid-1920s many Americans were beginning to conclude that Mexicans were inferior even to the lowliest European immigrants. As one scholar of Mexican immigration in this period observed, "In
[the nativists'] eyes, Mexicans were racially inferior [even] to southern and
eastern Europeans since they were of predominantly Indian stock. . . . The
addition of hundreds of thousands of 'low-grade' Indian-Spanish hybrids
to the United States could result only in disaster for the nation's future racial integrity."[32] According to the restrictionists Mexican immigration, if
allowed to continue unabated, would surely "change the complexion of
[the Southwest] . . . and bring about a hyphenized, politically unstabilized,
Latinized majority throughout the [region]."[33] In the opinion of the vocal
East Texas Congressman John C. Box, Mexican immigration was bound to
create in the Southwest a race problem which would exceed that of the
South. "We are treading in the steps that men have been walking for over
a hundred years," Box argued in 1928.

> When the Constitutional Convention met in Annapolis in 1787 this
> question came up when they were determining whether or not
> they would import Africans in the South, and it was generally in-
> sisted that they ought to be brought in, because the South could
> not clear its lands and do its work without them. I live in the
> South. I am very much devoted to my whole country and my local
> country. I know Mr. Madison told them that if they carried this on
> the injury would be incurable. All the strife that we had for 50
> years before the Civil War, in which most of us in that country lost
> everything that our fathers would have left to us, we have reaped
> as the consequences of a great race question. . . . The country has
> adopted [a] restrictive [immigration] policy. If it had adopted it in
> the constitutional convention, if it had been possible to do so, the
> country would have been a hundred percent better off right now.[34]

Acting on this basic assumption, immigration restrictionists like Box
mounted a concerted campaign designed to counter the arguments earlier
advanced by the proponents of Mexican labor. Although the restrictionists
shared many of the ethnocentric or racist assumptions held by their opponents, spokesmen for this position turned these assumptions on their
heads, arguing that the characteristics southwestern employers had long
touted as reasons for the use of Mexican labor were precisely why Mexican
immigrants should be *barred* from the United States. The restrictionists'

fundamental premise was that Mexicans constituted an inherently "un-assimilable" group. In many ways building on the same racial stereotypes that had shaped Americans' views of Mexicans during the debate over the acquisition of Mexican territory in the 1840s, anti-Mexican activists re-stated the old assertion that the process of racial amalgamation between Spaniards and Indians in Mexico and Latin America had created a race of people that combined the worst characteristics of each group. Articulating one of the most extreme positions on this issue in early 1928, Box char-acterized the "Mexican peon" as "a mixture of Mediterranean-blooded Spanish peasants with low-grade Indians who did not fight to extinction but submitted and multiplied as serfs. . . . This blend of low-grade Span-iard, peonized Indian, and negro slave mixe[d] with negroes, mulattoes, and other mongrels, and some sorry whites already here." In Box's view, the only way to protect "American racial stock from further degradation or change through mongrelization" was to bar all future immigration from Mexico.[35] Other restrictionists were even more rabid in their assessment of Mexicans, as an editorial in a local Los Angeles magazine made clear in January 1928. In the view of its author, Mexicans were "diseased of body, subnormal intellectually, and moral morons of the most hopeless type." "It is true," the author editorialized, "that our civilization has swallowed and digested a good many nasty doses, but the gagging point has about been reached."[36] Collecting data for his study of the Mexican immigration issue, Vanderbilt University economist Roy L. Garis presented a similar view of Mexicans in his report to the House Committee on Immigration. Quoting what he claimed was a letter sent to him by a "concerned American living in a border city," Garis inserted into the committee's record a virulent racist representation of Mexicans which characterized them as having

> minds [that] run to nothing higher than the animal functions—eat,
> sleep, and sexual debauchery. In every huddle of Mexicans one
> meets the same idleness, hordes of hungry dogs and filthy children
> with faces plastered with flies, disease, lice, human filth, stench,
> promiscuous fornication, bastardy, lounging, apathetic peons and
> lazy squaws, beans and dried chili, liquor, general squalor, and envy
> and hatred of the Gringo. These people sleep by day and prowl by
> night like coyotes, stealing anything they can get their hands on,
> no matter how useless to them it may be. Nothing left outside is
> safe unless padlocked or chained down.[37]

American immigration restrictionists hoped to bolster this line of ar-gument by asserting that lenient U.S. immigration policies would inevi-tably result in the creation of a serious new race problem in the United

States. Undoubtedly influenced by the racial strife that had erupted in Texas, Chicago, East St. Louis, and other areas at the end of World War I, restrictionists argued that similar outbreaks might occur if Mexican immigration continued unabated. This fear was explicitly expressed in a 1928 report of the American Eugenics Society, which warned that

> Our great Southwest is rapidly creating for itself a new racial problem, as our old South did when it imported slave labor from Africa. The Mexican birth rate is high, and every Mexican child born on American soil is an American citizen, who, on attaining his or her majority, will have a vote. This is not a question of pocketbook or of the "need of labor" or of economics. It is a question of the character of future races. It is eugenics, not economics.[38]

Thus for restrictionists the question, as Garis put it, was "whether we shall preserve the Southwest as a future home for millions of the white race or permit [it] . . . to be used . . . as a dumping ground for the human hordes of poverty stricken peon Indians of Mexico." "We must decide now before it is too late," he argued, "whether we wish the complete Mexicanization of this section of our country with all which it implies—enormous decreases in the value of all property; the economic organization based upon peon labor, exploitation, and oppression; the complete nullification of the benefits derived from the restriction of European and the exclusion of Oriental immigration; a lowering of our standards of morals and of our political and social ideals; the creation of a race problem that will dwarf the negro problem of the South; and the practical destruction, at least for centuries, of all that is worthwhile in our white civilization."[39]

Restrictionists augmented such flagrantly racist arguments by insisting that Mexicans were depriving American citizens of jobs. As important sectors of the American economy slipped into recession in the mid-1920s, immigration restrictionists intensified their accusations against the Mexican peons they saw competing with American citizens. As a member of the Texas State Chamber of Commerce put it, Mexican workers "living constantly on the ragged edge of starvation" were driving hard-working Americans out of jobs. "The competition of Mexican labor in every walk of life," he argued, "is so intense that no room or opportunity exists for the American who wants to work for sufficient wages to support himself and his family. This is resulting in this country's being almost taken over by the Mexican citizens because the American cannot compete with the low wages of the Mexican."[40] The *Saturday Evening Post,* long an advocate of immigration restriction, advanced similar arguments throughout this period, and by the end of the 1920s the magazine had come to a conclusion that summed up the restrictionists' position on the Mexican question. "Mexican exclusion," the *Post* editorialized, "is [the American worker's] only salvation."[41]

The Dilemma of Mexican Immigration

Although the debate that raged among Americans over the so-called Mexican Problem reflected many of the demographic, economic, and social changes that had altered the face of southwestern society in the 1910s and early 1920s, the rhetoric employed by both sides of the immigration debate made it abundantly clear that many Americans continued to view Mexicans as faceless abstractions rather than as a group of human beings. For the proponents of the use of foreign labor, Mexicans represented little more than a huge, tractable labor pool to be exploited at the whim of American industry. To immigration restrictionists Mexicans constituted a foreign menace both to the cultural and racial homogeneity of American society and to the institutional foundations on which the nation had been built. Thus, whether one argued that Mexicans should be allowed to work in the United States or not, Americans continued to subscribe to stereotypical images of Mexicans as members of an inferior, debased race. Moreover, habituated after nearly a century of Mexicans being viewed as filling no other niche than that of cheap labor, few Americans could recognize meaningful individual distinctions among them. As one historian notes of the first quarter of the twentieth century, "The pervasive employment of Mexicans in agriculture, construction, and track maintenance in the United States helped to implant the peon image of the Mexican firmly in the American mind, and the terms 'Mexican' and 'peon' became inextricably fused. To Americans, who defined Mexicans by and identified them with the work they did, the servile peon was antithetical to the rugged, self-reliant yeoman who had made their nation prosperous and progressive."[42]

Americans' myopia about Mexicans blinded them to the fact that immigration from Mexico had also created a deeply complex and troubling set of issues for the Southwest's growing ethnic Mexican population. The arrival of so many Mexican immigrant workers in a political environment that was already hostile toward Mexicans stimulated deeply ambivalent responses in the Mexican American communities of the Southwest. Of course, in many ways Mexican immigrants rejuvenated and enriched the social and cultural life of those communities. Pouring into the region and settling in, or next to, existing Mexican American barrios and colonias in Texas, Arizona, and California (and to a lesser degree, New Mexico, Colorado, and some areas of the industrial Midwest), Mexican men, women, and children dramatically expanded the Mexican cultural community of the United States. By bringing the Spanish language, Mexican customs and folkways, or merely the latest news from the hinterlands of Mexico, Mexican immigrants helped to reinforce the distinctive Mexican atmosphere of existing Mexican American enclaves. Indeed, by the mid-1920s the influx of new immigrants was so large that the immigrant population soon vastly outnumbered the native-born population in many areas and thus changed the character of Mexican American neighborhoods that had stood for more than a century.

This was particularly true in California and Texas, the ultimate destinations for the majority of recent immigrants from Mexico. In California, for example, the ethnic Mexican population of Los Angeles County mushroomed after the turn of the century, growing from less than 5,000 in 1900 to numbers estimated to be as high as 29,000 in 1910, 50,000 in 1920, and perhaps 190,000 in 1930.[43] Similar rates of population growth occurred in Texas. According to U.S. census data (which most historians believe may have underestimated the resident ethnic Mexican population by as much as 30 percent), the Mexican American–Mexican immigrant enclaves of San Antonio and El Paso grew from 41,469 and 39,571, respectively, in 1920, to 82,373 and 58,291 respectively, in 1930. Enclaves in other, smaller Texas towns and rural areas grew at similar rates.[44] Statewide statistics on the growth of the Mexican immigrant population were similar, with that of Texas growing from 71,062 in 1900 to 262,672 in 1930 and that of California from 8,086 to 191,346 in the same period.[45]

Not all Mexican Americans regarded this process of Mexicanization as a positive development. Although Mexican immigration helped to reinforce culturally and to expand existing Mexican American enclaves, large-scale immigration also created tensions and social friction between Mexican Americans and the recent arrivals from Mexico. Although all of the recent immigrants shared a common language and cultural heritage with their Mexican American neighbors (and many shared even more intimate friendship and kinship ties), contact and interaction between natives and immigrants of Mexican descent in the United States were also marked by conflict and mutual distrust.

The uneasiness Mexican immigrants and Mexican Americans felt toward one another came from several sources. Some of the friction apparent between U.S.-born Mexican Americans and Mexican immigrants in the twentieth century could be traced to a tradition of misunderstanding and suspicion that had divided the residents of Mexico's northern frontier provinces from the Mexicanos *del otro lado* (Mexicans "from the other side" of the border) since early in the nineteenth century. As noted previously, at that time the independent Norteños often chafed at the arrogance and cultural chauvinism displayed by Mexican government and military officials. In the view of many nineteenth-century Californios, Nuevomexicanos, and Tejanos, working-class Mexicans "from the other side" were even worse. From their point of view, common Mexicanos from Mexico were little more than uncultured, vulgar peasants.

During the Gold Rush in California these sentiments often devolved into displays of open derision as the Californios reacted to the influx of Sonoran *cholos* (Spanish slang for lower-class Mexicans) who entered the goldfields in the 1840s and 1850s. Though the Californios shared the Sonorans' language, culture, and, until 1848, nationality, Mexican Californians tended to look upon their former countrymen as social inferiors. As one historian of the period noted, to the Californios "the Mexican [immigrant generally] was of a lower social order, a peon or cholo, on whom many Californians looked with contempt. The Sonoran, moreover, was easily identified by his dress, especially by his white trousers; he was consequently nicknamed *calzonero blanco*, and considered fair game [for exploitation] by the Californian."[46]

Although intraethnic conflict of this magnitude was rare between Tejanos and Mexican immigrants in Texas, several scholars have noted that nativity sometimes played a role in dividing Mexicans from south of the Río Bravo from those who lived in Texas. The imposition of new political boundaries, first by the Texas Revolution of 1836 and later by the Mexican War, inevitably contributed to the development of social and cultural ambiguities between ethnic Mexicans who lived on either side of the new international border. Tensions between Tejanos and Mexicanos were most apparent during the unsettled period following the Texas Revolution and the Mexican War. Tejanos were caught in an intense struggle for their political and cultural loyalties to Anglo Texans on one side and to Mexicans from Mexico on the other; and in the 1830s and 1840s they found themselves increasingly alienated from both groups. This was particularly true for those Tejanos who fought on the side of the Americans in the revolt against Santa Anna in 1835 and 1836. Trapped between their Mexican cultural and national heritage and the exigencies of the Texas insurgency, these Tejanos found themselves in a political and social no-man's land after San Jacinto.[47]

After the Mexican American War, however, contiguity to northern Mexico along the long border, a highly concentrated population of Mexicans in the territory between the Nueces River and the Rio Grande, and frequent travel in both directions across the frontier ensured that intraethnic relationships would not deteriorate to the level to which they had in California. Even so, relationships between Tejanos and Mexicans in Texas were often strained.[48]

The migration of hundreds of thousands of Mexican immigrants into the Southwest after the turn of the century created an even more complex and volatile set of issues for the growing ethnic Mexican population of the border region. Thrown together in a sociopolitical context in which Mexican Americans occupied an inferior social status and Mexican immigrants were, by definition, aliens, both groups found themselves viewed as outsiders in American society. Consequently, as immigration rates increased Mexican Americans and Mexican immigrants confronted each other in an ambiguous and often contradictory social milieu where potentially crucial distinctions between native and foreigner, citizen and alien, and American and Mexican, were called into question.

These confusing issues played themselves out in countless ways in the everyday interactions between U.S.-born Mexican Americans and recent Mexican immigrants. But as Albert Camarillo notes in his perceptive study of the growth of the ethnic Mexican population in southern California, three sets of factors contributed in general to what he calls the growing "schism within the Chicano community" in the late nineteenth and early twentieth centuries. The most obvious of these was the growing sense among many U.S.-born Mexican Americans that the recent arrivals represented an economic threat. Despite the cultural affinities Mexican Americans may have felt toward immigrants from Mexico, as their numbers grew, many Mexican Americans began to worry that the recent arrivals were depressing wages, competing with them for scarce jobs and housing, and undercutting their efforts to achieve better working conditions.

The second set of factors was more subtle and complex and can be traced to the internal heterogeneity of Mexican society. As we have seen, most Americans did not recognize any meaningful distinctions between a Mexican born in Mexico and a Mexican born and raised in the United States. Mexicans and Mexican Americans, however, were well aware of the many regional differences that had long characterized Mexican society, both within the Mexican Republic and in the extended Hispanic-Mexican Southwest. Although Mexican Americans often resembled recent immigrants physically, spoke the same language, and shared many customs, subtle, mutually recognized distinctions in language usage and vernacular, folkways, and social mores often served as internal boundaries demarcating various subgroupings of Mexicans from one another. Just as local attachments and customs in present-day Mexico continue to distinguish a

Mexican from Jalisco or Yucatán, say, from a Mexican from Mexico City or Chihuahua, similar distinctions often separated Mexican immigrants from Mexican Americans in the early years of this century.[49]

The third—and perhaps most important—set of factors that contributed to the schism involved Americans' attitudes toward Mexicans, or what Camarillo calls "the external prejudices of Anglo society." Already subject to the stigma of being Mexican in American society, many Mexican Americans feared that the mass immigration of impoverished, uneducated Mexican peasants would reinforce and inflame the negative stereotypes Americans already held about Mexicans. Consequently, as Camarillo notes, many U.S.-born Mexican Americans "kept their distance from the foreign-born . . . to try to avoid this negative association."[50]

The same kinds of cleavages that divided Mexican Americans from Mexican immigrants in the late nineteenth century persisted into the twentieth. Although most contemporary observers in the United States were unaware of the extent to which Mexican immigration had contributed to social tensions within expanding Mexican American–Mexican immigrant communities, some of the more sensitive observers began to notice a certain ambivalence in the relationships between U.S.-born Mexican Americans and recent immigrants from Mexico soon after the turn of the century. For example, commenting on the relationship between the two groups in 1908, U.S. government economist Victor S. Clark observed that

> The attitude of Americans of Mexican descent towards immigrants from Mexico seems to be friendly, except where there is direct competition between the two. In Colorado the former regard the latter as interlopers though they are not actively hostile to them. . . . In Texas, where there are no labor organizations among resident Mexicans, the latter oppose an influx of immigrants likely to lower wages; and in some cases they have lodged complaints of alleged violations of the contract labor laws.[51]

Americans who had extensive contacts with the ethnic Mexican population made similar kinds of observations. In Los Angeles, for example, Emory Bogardus, a prominent sociologist at the University of Southern California, noticed the same ambivalence. Although Bogardus himself perceived very few meaningful social or cultural distinctions between working-class Mexican Americans and recent Mexican immigrants in southern California, he noted that Mexican Americans in the Los Angeles area often voiced concern about immigrants competing with them for jobs and housing, and he reported that Mexican Americans worried about the use of Mexican immigrants as strikebreakers.[52]

Other early studies revealed many of the same tendencies. In one of the most detailed analyses of evolving Mexican American–Mexican immigrant relationships during this period, a research team led by the distinguished Mexican sociologist Manuel Gamio illuminated some of the most important sources of the ambivalence in relationships between the two groups. In the first important book-length study of the social impacts of Mexican immigration, *Mexican Immigration to the United States* (first published in 1930) and in a subsequent companion volume of interviews with Mexican Americans and Mexican immigrants entitled *The Mexican Immigrant: His Life Story* (first published in 1931 as *The Life Story of the Mexican Immigrant*), Gamio and his research team explored the complex and multifaceted migration and settlement patterns, social and cultural adaptation strategies, and main contours of inter- and intraethnic interactions that had evolved since the turn of the century.[53]

Reading these volumes today, one is immediately struck by the deep ambivalence Mexican Americans and Mexican immigrants apparently felt toward one another. Indeed, Gamio himself regarded this as one of the fundamental defining characteristics of the Mexican immigration phenomenon. Summarizing his findings, he observed, "The attitude of the Mexicans who are American citizens toward the immigrant is a curious one. Sometimes they speak slighteningly of the immigrants (possibly because the immigrants are their competitors in wages and jobs), and say that the immigrants should stay in Mexico. . . . Furthermore, they are displeased, possibly because of racial pride, at the miserable condition in which most Mexicans arrive." On the other hand, Gamio noted that the Mexican immigrant "considers the American of Mexican origin as a man without a country. He reminds him frequently of the inferior position to which he is relegated by the white American."[54]

Yet Gamio also noted the strong ties that bound Mexican Americans to Mexican immigrants and thus complicated the range of their interactions even further. He observed,

> Notwithstanding these differences in point of view between the Mexican immigrants and the Mexican-Americans—differences which in reality are of purely superficial and formal nature—both groups consider themselves as together composing that body called by them "The Race"; both are called Mexicans by white Americans; they live together in the same districts; they belong to the same social stratum; they talk the same language; they wear the same clothes and possess the same needs and ideals; and most significant of all, they frequently intermarry.[55]

Drawn from extensive interviews conducted by bilingual research teams in 1926 and 1927, Gamio's publications paint a poignant portrait of the attempts that ethnic Mexicans from both sides of the border made to define themselves and their sense of community (of course, each with reference to the other) in the bewildering and constantly changing social landscape of the Southwest. Both volumes are rife with examples of the ambivalence expressed by each group as Mexican Americans and Mexican immigrants grappled with the complex issues of national and cultural identity brought to the surface by the rapid growth of the ethnic Mexican population in the United States.

For example, in the space of a few sentences one of Gamio's Mexican American respondents expressed sentiments about Mexican Americans' relationship to Mexican immigrants and, by extension, about his sense of Mexican nationality that appear to be directly contradictory. Speculating about the possibility of war breaking out between the United States and Mexico, Gamio's respondent, "Elías Sepúlveda" of Nogales, Arizona, said, "One can't deny one's race. If there was a war between Mexico and the United States I wouldn't go shoot my own brothers. . . . I would rather be a prisoner than go fight against the country from which my fathers came. We are all Mexicans anyway because the *güeros* [Anglos] always treat us all alike." Yet almost in the same breath Sepúlveda went on to comment:

> They say that we are all Mexicans and we are that by blood but those of us who have been born in this country and speak English and know our rights don't let ourselves be maltreated like the poor fellows who come fresh from the other side. I believe that it would be a good thing to put a quota on the Mexican immigrants for it would be a good thing for them and for those who are already living here [because] the Mexicans who are already here wouldn't have so much competition from those who keep coming and they could earn better wages and the Americans wouldn't humiliate us so much because they believe that we are like those who come from Mexico.[56]

Another Mexican American, "Luis Albornoz," who had lived his entire life in Tito, New Mexico, expressed a similar level of mixed feelings about his ethnic identity, his national loyalties, and his relationships with recent immigrants from south of the border. Gamio wrote that "Sr. Albornoz says that he would have never married an American because his blood is Mexican and he doesn't care about the geographical-political division. He looks at the two countries with love."[57] Yet in the same conversation Gamio noted that Albornoz had "never been in Mexico and has never felt desires to go." Moreover, Gamio noticed "a certain tendency of Sr. Albornoz to look down on the humble Mexican workers; he believes that their faults cannot be corrected. When he deals with them he does so with a certain air of superiority. . . . Sr. Albornoz feels proud of being American and deplores the fact that Mexicans who come to the United States are uncultured immigrants, so they are despised; this makes him feel ashamed of being of Mexican descent."[58]

Many Mexican immigrants expressed their own ambivalence, if not outright resentment, about their experiences with Mexican Americans in the United States. Of course, much of this sentiment during this period derived from Mexican immigrants' belief that they would someday return permanently to Mexico, although by the mid-1920s a significant number of immigrants had already lived in the United States for more than twenty years. Considering themselves part of what they called *Mexico de afuera*—Mexico outside Mexico—they believed themselves the only true Mexicans and often dismissed the Mexican Americans, whom they called *pochos* (faded or bleached ones), as a mongrel people without a country or a true culture. For example, one of Gamio's respondents, who had resided in the United States for more than a quarter-century, asserted in no uncertain terms that he continued to consider himself a Mexican. "I would rather cut my throat," he said, "before changing my Mexican nationality. I prefer to lose with Mexico than to win with the United States. My country is before everything else and although it has been many years since I have been back I am only waiting until conditions get better, until there is absolute peace before I go back." Concluding on a poignant note, he mused, "I haven't lost hope of spending my last days in my own country."[59]

With regard to Mexican Americans, many of the immigrants interviewed by Gamio's research team made little attempt to disguise their disdain for what they perceived as Mexican American arrogance. One Mexican immigrant expressed this sense by stating,

> The so-called Pochos here don't like us. They think that because one comes from Mexico one is going to take the country away from them. But our worse enemies are the Mexicans who have lived here a great many years and have gotton [*sic*] settled and have become American citizens. They don't like us and they try to do us all the harm possible.[60]

Voicing a criticism of Mexican Americans that many Mexicans continue to make to the present day, another immigrant charged that Mexican Americans had "lost their culture." As he put it, "Mexicans who are born and educated here are people without a country."[61] Another young man interviewed by Gamio's survey team was more temperate in his criticism yet communicated essentially the same message. "I don't have anything against the Pochos," he said, "but the truth of the matter is that although they are Mexicans, for they are of our own blood because their parents were Mexicans, they pretend that they are Americans. They only want to talk in English and they speak Spanish very poorly. That is why I don't like them."[62]

These themes were corroborated and elaborated by the University of California's Paul Taylor. In a series of what probably are the most sensitive and penetrating studies of evolving Mexican American–Mexican immigrant relationships during in the 1920s and early 1930s, Taylor provided a richly detailed portrait of the intricacies and implications of the rapid growth of the United States' ethnic Mexican population in the first decades of the twentieth century. Conducting extensive research and interviews in Mexican American and Mexican enclaves throughout the United States, Taylor published his findings in the multivolume *Mexican Labor in the United States* and in *An American-Mexican Frontier: Nueces County, Texas.*

Unlike most Americans of his generation, Taylor recognized that the addition of hundreds of thousands of new immigrants into the existing population of Mexican Americans had created a potentially volatile social situation in Mexican American communities. Moreover, although he observed that most Mexicans in the United States—regardless of their nativity—considered themselves to be "essentially Mexicans," he also realized that mutually perceived differences within the resident ethnic Mexican population often served to reinforce important social cleavages within the group. And although many of his observations about native-immigrant interactions were similar to those made by other contemporary observers, he often drew conclusions about the political implications of divisions between the groups that others missed.

For example, Taylor, like Gamio, noted instances in which Mexican immigrants and Mexican Americans expressed empathy toward one another, as when one Mexican immigrant told Taylor about a time when he and his companions arrived in Ratón, New Mexico. "When we got there," the immigrant explained, "we were broke. A Spanish-American [that is, an American of Mexican descent] helped us. He was working at the Gardner Mine. He gave us meals for five days. There were nine in our own family. I will always give a Mexican a meal and I can always get one. We do not pay and it is not expected. The Spanish American customs are the same as ours."[63] Still, many of Taylor's Mexican American and immigrant respondents commented on the significant differences each perceived about the other. As one of Taylor's Mexican American respondents in the South Platte Valley of Colorado expressed it,

The Mexican [immigrants] are patriotic, but they are patriotic for
Mexico. This is even true even of children born here. They don't
know why they hate the United States, perhaps because they are
Indian. The Mexicans think the Spanish Americans should be pa-
triotic for Mexico because of blood and history. They say that the
Spanish Americans were sold in 1848, but the Spanish Americans
feel themselves to be American and 100 years ahead of the Old
Mexico Mexicans. [64]

Another of Taylor's Mexican American interviewees, a high school student, found similar areas of friction. "The Mexicans call us 'manitos,'" she
complained, "and say that we are neither Spanish, Mexican, nor American.
They say we have no country. The Mexicans say that we were sold to the
United States. In reply we call the Mexicans 'su[ru]matos' [a derogatory
term for immigrants from the south]." [65]

For their part, Mexican immigrants often expressed similarly negative
sentiments toward their Mexican American neighbors. One Mexican immigrant student went so far as to tell Taylor that "Mexicans hate the Spanish Americans more than [even] the Americans because the Spanish Americans feel superior." "When I came here," the student continued, "I found
that my Mexican friends did not like the Spanish Americans. The Mexicans say, 'Santa Anna sold the Spanish Americans for some chewing to-
bacco.'" [66] That some Mexican Americans recognized the animosity immigrants felt toward them was clear in the statement of a Mexican American
member of the American Legion in Texas who told Taylor, "The Mexicans
on the other side of the river hate the Texas-Mexicans and call us
[a]gringados [that is, Americanized or "whitened" Mexicans]. When we
meet in uniform at the Legion picnic at Piedras Negras, some of them called
us [a]gringados, and they sometimes do it when they are mad." [67]

Conclusion

Although records on the social implications of the evolving relationships
between Mexican Americans and Mexican immigrants in the first decades
of the twentieth century are frustratingly fragmentary, the evidence gathered by scholars such as Taylor, Bogardus, and Gamio provides important
early insights into the dynamics of an interaction destined to transform
southwestern ethnic politics over the next half century. On the most basic
level, the evidence gathered by these researchers indicates that sustained
large-scale immigration from Mexico helped to rejuvenate a strong Mexican cultural presence in the United States. With hundreds of thousands of
immigrants settling in or near existing Mexican American communities

after the turn of the century, the culture, language, and customs most Americans believed had disappeared in the United States experienced a new flowering in Mexico's former northern territories.

Although these developments were welcomed by Mexican Americans who continued to feel strong cultural attachments to the Mexican people and to Mexico, the rapid growth of the United States' ethnic Mexican population raised some troubling issues for both Mexican Americans and Mexican immigrants. As the testimonies gathered by Taylor and Gamio so clearly point out, the most pressing of these concerned basic issues of survival. For these Mexican Americans the cultural and other affinities they felt toward Mexico and Mexicans would simply have to take a back seat to their own perceived self-interest. Forced to compete against the recent arrivals for scarce jobs, housing, and access to social services in a social and political context in which Mexicans were already stigmatized, many Mexican Americans argued that large-scale immigration represented a clear danger to ethnic Mexicans already living in the United States.

At another level, potential ethnic solidarity between U.S.-born Mexican Americans and recent immigrants was undermined by the subtle internal differences that had always characterized Mexican society and culture. Sensitive to regional variations in customs, language usage, and social mores, Mexican Americans and Mexican immigrants often found as many reasons to distrust and dislike one another as they found reasons for amity. In the increasingly pressurized social context of the Southwest, these mutually recognized distinctions would often be much more significant than they would have been in a less politically charged atmosphere.

The various cleavages that divided Mexican immigrants from Americans of Mexican descent were reflections of much deeper social changes occurring in the Southwest. Although few observers were aware of it at the time, the primary reason sustained Mexican immigration created tensions in Mexican American communities was that immigration had strongly altered the context of social relationships in the region. Before 1900 Mexican Americans had effectively utilized their sense of Mexicanness as a boundary-marking mechanism that in many ways protected them from, or at least buffered, the prejudice and discrimination they experienced in American society. By maintaining elements of Hispanic-Mexican culture and identifying themselves as Mexicanos, as Hispanoamericanos, or as members of the more metaphysical La Raza, Mexican Americans had asserted an oppositional set of defining characteristics that helped demarcate their community from the Norteamericanos. Thus, although the bifurcation between "us" and "them" that was largely accepted by both Mexican Americans and Anglo Americans on one level reflected the racially stratified character of southwestern society, by providing Mexican Americans with a basis of solidarity and action these ethnic boundaries served as an effective defense mechanism against discrimination.

The influx of large numbers of immigrants from Mexico after the turn of the century upset this bifurcated social ordering by introducing a huge new set of actors. Prior to 1910 it had been fairly easy for Mexican Americans to define themselves vis-à-vis Anglo Americans by adhering to a formula that simply distinguished "us" from "them," but the presence of a large population of Mexicans "from the other side" greatly complicated the boundary-marking process. Although many Mexican Americans may have continued to consider themselves culturally Mexican when comparing themselves to Anglo Americans, the unprecedented influx of Mexicans from Mexico raised some confusing questions about what now defined a Mexican in the United States. As increasing numbers of Mexican immigrants entered their communities, Mexican Americans were compelled to reconsider the criteria by which they defined themselves.

A Mexican ballad popular in the border region around the turn of the century reveals that these questions were not far from the minds of immigrants and natives when they pondered the implications of the growth of their numbers in the Southwest. Facing each other in a society in which both groups were deemed inferior, Mexican Americans and Mexican immigrants were confronted with excruciating choices about their ultimate cultural and national identities and loyalties. In a commentary that undoubtedly struck a chord with ethnic Mexicans from both sides of the border, "El Corrido del Norte" proclaimed:

Nací en la frontera	I was born on the border
de acá de este lado	though here on this side
de acá de este lado	though here on this side
puro mexicano	I'm a pure Mexican
por más que la gente	even though people
me juzque tejano	may think I'm Texan
yo les aseguro	I now assure you
que soy mexicano	that I'm all Mexican
de acá de este lado	from here on this side
Porque uso de lado	Just because I wear
el sombrero vaquero	a large cowboy hat
y cargo pistola	and carry a pistol
y chamarra de cuero,	and a leather jacket,
y porque acostumbro	and because I'm used to
el cigarro de hoja	rolling my own
y en el cuello llevo	and wearing around my neck

mi mascada roja,	a red silk handkerchief
se creen otra cosa	people believe otherwise
. . . .	. . . .
Nací en la frontera	I was born on the border
de acá de este lado	though here on this side
de acá de este lado	though here on this side
puro mexicano,	I'm a pure Mexican
por más que la gente	even though people
me juzque tejano	may think I'm a Texan
yo les aseguro	I now assure you
que soy mexicano	that I'm all Mexican
de acá de este lado	from here on this side.[68]

When considered along with the ambivalence and uncertainty expressed by so many of Taylor's and Gamio's respondents, "El Corrido del Norte" suggests that Mexican Americans and Mexican immigrants themselves had not yet made difficult decisions about the complex cultural and national questions raised by the growth of the ethnic Mexican population of the United States. However, as the rate of immigration reached a peak in the 1920s, Mexican Americans and Mexican immigrants would discover that political developments in the United States would soon compel them to make such choices. As more Americans became aware and alarmed over the rapid growth of the resident ethnic Mexican population and as the American economy rapidly slid toward a deep depression at the end of the decade, Mexican Americans and Mexican residents of the United States would be forced to consider, and to make initial decisions about, those issues of ethnic and national identity that Mexican immigration brought to the surface of regional politics.

3   The Shifting Politics of Ethnicity
     in the Interwar Period

The competition and social tensions that so deeply affected relationships between Mexican Americans and Mexican immigrants after the turn of the century became even more acute in the 1920s. Because an average of more than 25,000 Mexican immigrants entered the United States each year between 1920 and 1929, many Mexican Americans believed that their initial concerns about *los recién llegados* had been justified. As the first era of mass Mexican immigration reached a peak in the late 1920s, the problems of economic competition, overcrowding, eroding wage rates, and employers' use of immigrant workers as strikebreakers exacerbated the resentments and misunderstandings that had surfaced earlier between Mexican Americans and Mexican immigrants.

More important, immigration of this magnitude clearly had contributed to a resurgence of anti-Mexican sentiment in the United States. Having long believed (or at least having convinced themselves) that the Mexican population of the region had receded before the advance of American civilization in the last years of the previous century, many Americans were surprised by the rapid expansion of the Southwest's ethnic Mexican population between 1910 and 1929. Some westerners, as we have seen, had grudgingly come to accept the use of Mexican workers as a necessary or even vital component of their region's economic growth, but as the American economy weakened and slipped into periodic recessions after World War I, many Americans who had taken a complacent view of Mexican immigration began to reconsider their position. Believing that Mexican immigrants were responsible for the displacement of American citizen workers, by the early 1920s a growing chorus of critics called for the imposition of strict controls on immigration from Mexico.

The intensification of anti-Mexican sentiment, combined with the increasing public clamor to restrict immigration from Mexico and to deport or repatriate Mexican nationals who resided in the United States, placed immense political and social pressures on Americans of Mexican descent. They were torn between the strong cultural affinities they felt toward Mexico and Mexicans on one hand and their desire to be accepted—or, at the very least, to be allowed to function—as equal members of American society on the other. By the late 1920s and early 1930s many Mexican Americans were forced to choose between their cultural loyalties and their determination to defend their political-legal status as citizens of the United States. In short, with hundreds of thousands of new immigrants swelling the ranks of the Mexican community in the Southwest, Mexican Americans and Mexicans from Mexico had constantly to consider how they felt about each other. Should they cooperate with one another in the United States by drawing on their common cultural heritage to build ethnic solidarity, or had a half-century of political separation created unbridgeable social, cultural, and political cleavages between them?

Although it was impossible for Mexican Americans to come to definitive conclusions about any of these painful issues, by the mid-1920s two fairly polarized points of view had surfaced. One pole of the continuum of public opinion on these complex questions was occupied by those individuals who viewed recent Mexican immigrants with empathy. This perspective, more common among (but not limited to) working-class Mexican Americans and those long-term Mexican residents of the United States who felt strong cultural ties to Mexico, was also informed by a sense of solidarity born of a common experience of discrimination in American society. Mexican Americans and resident Mexican nationals who held this view were painfully aware that the structure of the regional labor market forced them to compete with one another for jobs, housing, and public services, but they demonstrated a strong inclination to work together to address the common problems facing their extended communities. Observing that Mexican Americans and recent immigrants seemed to experience similar levels of economic, political, and social discrimination regardless of their citizenship status, many Mexican Americans and resident Mexican immigrants could see little reason either to abandon their cultural heritage by attempting to assimilate into American society or their cultural ties to one another. From their point of view the similarities between them far outweighed whatever invidious distinctions others might see. Some doggedly maintained a sense of themselves as *mexicanos de afuera* (Mexicans living outside Mexico); others tried to redefine what it meant to be American by carving out an intermediate niche in which they combined their Mexican cultural heritage with the idea that they were, in fact, members of American society.

The other pole of the continuum was occupied for the most part by the various segments of Mexican American society who had come to accept, however reluctantly, the reality of their permanent incorporation into American society. The basic tenet of this perspective was that Mexican Americans were in fact Americans and therefore should make every effort to assimilate into the American social and cultural mainstream. Mexican Americans who held this view were also deeply torn by ambivalent attitudes about their ethnic heritage and, in many cases, by the fact that they had friends and relatives who were immigrants, but they came to the painful conclusion that the needs and interests of American citizens simply had to take precedence over the problems faced by the growing Mexican immigrant population.

These positions were far from completely gelled in the early 1920s and 1930s. Indeed, the issues involved in the immigration question—issues of national loyalty, of cultural identification, and of competing visions for the future of the ethnic Mexican population of the Southwest—were so complex and pervasive that it was impossible for Mexican Americans and Mexican immigrants to reach any broad consensus on them. Yet, under the intense pressure of the Great Depression, the various constituent cohorts of this population were eventually compelled—whether directly or indirectly—to decide where they stood on these sensitive questions. Although very few realized it at the time, the tentative, initial decisions they came to on these issues in the 1920s and 1930s were to define the shape and direction of both Mexican Americans' and Mexican immigrants' involvement in the American political arena for the next half century.

Recession, Restrictionism, and the Politicization of Ethnicity

In the first years of the century many Americans had come to acknowledge the contributions Mexican labor had made to the economic growth of the Southwest and to certain industries in other parts of the country. As the American economy began to falter in the 1920s, however, increasing numbers of Americans came to see Mexican immigrants as a menace to American workers. In this context the charges first raised by immigration restrictionists in the late 1910s and early 1920s acquired a new resonance among Americans. The suddenness of the change in attitude about Mexican labor was dramatic. For example, as late as September 1929 the *Imperial Valley Farmer*, the local newspaper of southern California's rich, irrigated Imperial Valley, was still estimating that "twenty thousand Mexican workers [will be] . . . the . . . necessary quota for ranch work, lettuce harvesting and all other branches of agricultural activity during the winter season. The general view is that there are slightly over half that to-day."[1] But after five years of depression the tone of local newspapers changed drastically. As the *Brawley News* editorialized in the spring of 1935, "There seems plenty of relief work for the aliens—but for the American pioneer, who battled scorpions, sidewinders, rattlesnakes, the ever-boiling sun of the desert . . . there seems to be nothing but the scrap heap. The sooner the slogan 'America for Americans' is adopted, the sooner will Americans be given the preference in all kinds of work—instead of aliens."[2]

As nationwide unemployment reached six million by the end of 1930 and eleven million by the end of 1932, Mexican workers were singled out as scapegoats in virtually every locale in which they lived in substantial numbers. In this atmosphere the nativist litany that had been employed against Mexicans in the 1920s—charges that they were disease ridden, that they committed crimes, that they displaced American workers, and that they were, in short, singularly un-American—was raised with new vehemence. Moreover, as the number of unemployed Mexican and Mexican American workers seeking relief from local welfare agencies began to rise, American communities across the country took steps to pressure Mexicans to return to Mexico. Consequently, by early 1930 many American cities, including Gary, Chicago, and Detroit in the Midwest and Denver, San Antonio, and numerous other cities in the Southwest had organized campaigns designed to oust Mexican workers from their communities.[3]

The largest and most publicized of the repatriation campaigns occurred in Los Angeles, which of course had one of the largest concentrations of Mexican immigrants. With the U.S. Department of Labor and Los Angeles city and county officials mounting a concerted campaign in 1930 and 1931, tens of thousands of Mexican nationals—and an unknown number of their American-born children—were pressured into returning to Mexico.[4] Nationwide, an average of almost 80,000 individuals was repatriated to Mexico each year between 1929 and 1937, with a reported 138,519 in 1931 alone. Although repatriation statistics, like most data concerning the ethnic Mexican population for this period, are highly unreliable, scholars estimate that at least 350,000, and perhaps as many as 600,000, persons of Mexican descent returned to Mexico during the depression decade.[5]

It should be emphasized that most Mexicans who returned to Mexico during this period were not formally deported. Because deportation proceedings involved—and still involve—cumbersome and time-consuming administrative procedures, most officials of the U.S. Department of Labor and the Border Patrol, local welfare agencies, and other government bodies encouraged Mexican aliens to depart voluntarily. For its part the Mexican government, through its consulates in the United States, also encouraged many of its nationals to return to Mexico, periodically offering to subsidize transportation costs and, in some cases, to resettle repatriates on government-sponsored agricultural tracts.[6] Consequently, during the depression most repatriations fell into what one scholar has aptly termed a "huge twilight zone between voluntary and forced migration."[7]

Despite the fact that few Mexicans were formally deported, repatriation for most individuals and families was a traumatic, disorienting, and sorrowful course undertaken under extreme duress. Many of the repatriates believed that Mexicans had been unfairly blamed for events over which they had no control. Despised and vilified after spending ten, fifteen, or even twenty or more productive years as hard-working, though isolated, members of the American working class, Mexican immigrant workers seemed to bear the brunt of Americans' resentment about the economic catastrophe. A famous *corrido* of the period underscores the sense of injustice and ingratitude many Mexicans clearly felt. "Los deportados" lamented,

Los güeros son muy malores[sic] se valen de la ocasión Y a todos los mexicanos nos tratan sin compasión	The Anglos are very bad fellows They take advantage And to all the Mexicans They treat us without pity
Hoy traen la gran polvareda y sin consideración Mujeres, niños, y ancianos nos llevan a la frontera, nos echan de esta nación	Today they bring great disturbance And without consideration Women, children, and old ones They take us to the border, They eject us from this country
Adiós paisanos queridos Ya nos van a deportar Pero no somos bandidos Venimos a camellar.	Goodbye dear countrymen They are going to deport us But we are not bandits We came to toil.[8]

As "Los Deportados" expressed so poignantly, the political climate symbolized by the repatriation campaigns placed intense political and social pressures on the ethnic Mexican population of the United States, which continued even after hundreds of thousands of Mexican nationals and their children had returned to Mexico. The scapegoating that occurred at this time rekindled Americans' disdain for working-class Mexicans, and as always, their disdain was directed at Mexican Americans as well as the newer immigrants. For Americans of Mexican descent this situation was like the rubbing of salt in old wounds. Torn between their cultural ties, their nationality, and their awareness that American citizenship did not necessarily protect them from such excesses, Mexican Americans faced some tough decisions as to what their attitudes toward the repatriation campaigns ought to be. As in previous periods of increasing social stress, in the late 1920s and 1930s opinion among Mexican Americans (and the Mexican nationals who remained in the United States) on the complex issues intertwined with the repatriation crisis remained deeply ambivalent. Between the late 1920s and the mid-1930s, however, opinion and debate on these questions began to harden and polarize.

LULAC and the Assimilationist Perspective

In the winter of 1921 an article by former Texas Congressman James L. Slayden appeared in an issue of the *Annals of the American Academy of Political and Social Science* that was devoted to Mexican immigration. A long-time observer of Mexican immigration trends in his state, Slayden proved to be one of the few Americans active in public life who was perceptive enough to recognize the deep impact mass Mexican immigration was having on the existing Mexican American population. From Slayden's point of view Mexican immigrants represented a threat to the existing Texas Mexican population not so much because immigrants competed with Mexican Americans for jobs and housing as because Anglo Texans generally refused to acknowledge any meaningful distinctions between Mexican Americans and Mexican immigrants. Whether one was a citizen of the United States made no difference: to white Texans a Mexican was a Mexican, and that was the end of it. As Slayden put it, "In Texas, the word 'Mexican' is used to indicate the race, not a citizen or subject of the country. There are probably 250,000 Mexicans in Texas who were born in the state but they are [defined as] 'Mexicans' just as all blacks are negroes though they may have five generations of American ancestors."[9]

While Slayden was making his observations about the peculiarities of racial classification in Texas, some Mexican Americans in that state were themselves pondering the implications of their ambiguous status in American society. As migration from Mexico continued into the 1920s they began to chafe at the thought that Americans were equating them with immigrants who, in many cases, had just recently entered the United States from the interior of Mexico. Although most of these native-born Texas Mexicans harbored no ill will toward their immigrant neighbors, worsening economic conditions and the intensification of anti-Mexican sentiment among Anglo Americans caused many of them to wonder whether the new immigrants were undermining their already tenuous position in Texas society. Having lived in the United States their entire lives, and in many cases having served the United States as members of the armed forces in World War I, increasing numbers of Texas Mexicans began to take exception to Anglo Americans' nonchalant dismissal of them as mere Mexicans. They gradually concluded that the only way to stop this indiscriminate lumping of American citizens with newly arrived Mexican immigrants was to take a stand against continuing large-scale immigration from Mexico. This was a painful decision, but from their point of view prudence dictated that Americans of Mexican descent had to be concerned with the immediate well-being and future health of Mexicans already in the United States. Mexico would simply have to take care of its own.

Although similar sentiments had been heard in Mexican American communities since the 1850s, these attitudes took on new salience with the establishment of a different type of Mexican American organization in Texas in the years immediately after World War I. Having returned from service in the armed forces, many Mexican Americans were no longer content to accept treatment as second-class citizens. Consequently, in the early 1920s Mexican American community leaders in several Texas cities established a number of new civic organizations designed to protect and advance the interests of their people. The three largest of these new groups were El Orden Hijos de América (The Order of the Sons of America), El Orden Caballeros de América (The Order of the Knights of America), and the League of Latin American Citizens. Such groups were formed by lower-middle-class members of the Texas Mexican community, and their leaders were typically attorneys, restaurateurs, teachers, printers, and small entrepreneurs serving the Spanish-speaking community. By 1927 these groups had established an extensive network of chapters throughout the state of Texas. The Sons of America, for example, had councils in Somerset, San Antonio, Pearsall, and Corpus Christi. The Knights of America were active primarily in the San Antonio area, and the League of Latin American Citizens had established chapters in the south Texas towns of Harlingen, Brownsville, Laredo, Gulf, Penitas, McAllen, La Grulla, and Encino.[10]

As their names indicated, these new organizations espoused a political perspective that departed significantly from the philosophies of older Mexican American voluntary associations, such as the mutualistas and honorific societies. Unlike earlier groups, which had based their organizations on the principle of mutual cooperation between Mexican immigrants and Americans of Mexican descent, from their inception the new organizations pointedly excluded non-American citizens from membership.

To these organizations, Mexican Americans were American citizens and thus should make every effort to assimilate into the American social and cultural mainstream. Although most were generally proud of their ethnic heritage, they believed that Mexican Americans had focused too much on maintaining their ethnicity and culture in the United States and, in the process, had hindered their progress as participating members of American society. Thus, while members of these new organizations continued to profess respect for Mexico and for their Mexican cultural heritage, they insisted that the best way to advance in American society was to convince other Americans that they too were loyal, upstanding American citizens. In keeping with these beliefs the new Mexican American organizations carefully cultivated what they considered to be an appropriate American public image by conducting their proceedings in English, by prominently displaying the American flag in their ceremonies, stationery, and official iconography, by singing such songs as "America" at their gatherings, and by opening their meetings with a recitation of the "George Washington Prayer."[11]

The political agendas of the Sons of America, the Knights of America, and the League of Latin American Citizens all reflected these basic premises. For example, the by-laws of the Sons of America articulated the political assumptions and general plan of action by asserting, "As workers in support of the ideal that citizens of the United States of America of Mexican or Spanish extraction, whether native or naturalized, [we] have a broad field of opportunity to protect and promote their interests as such; [and are committed] to elevate their moral, social and intellectual conditions; [and] to educate them . . . in the proper extension of their political rights."[12] Members hoped to implement these principles by organizing voter registration and poll-tax campaigns, by mounting battles against the segregation of Mexican Americans in public facilities, and by insisting on more adequate representation of Mexican Americans on Texas juries.[13]

Such ideas quickly gained currency after some of the Texas-based groups were consolidated into a new, larger organization just before the Great Depression. After a preliminary series of meetings in 1927 and 1928 in which the terms of consolidation of the various organizations were negotiated, the League of United Latin American Citizens (LULAC) was officially founded at a meeting in Corpus Christi on February 17, 1929. The original delegates met again at Corpus Christi in May of that year to codify the objectives agreed to in principle at the founding convention. Drafting a constitution and a formal statement of principles they called "The LULAC Code," Texans Manuel C. Gonzales, Alonso S. Perales, Benjamin Garza, J. T. Canales, Luis Wilmot, and others agreed to a series of objectives that came to define the organization's basic philosophy and political program for the next sixty years. Foremost among these objectives was a pledge to promote and develop among LULAC members what they called the "best and purest" form of Americanism. They also resolved to teach their children English and to inculcate in them a sense of their rights and responsibilities as American citizens, and they promised to fight discrimination against Mexican Americans wherever they encountered it.[14]

In many ways the new organization exemplified the integrationist strains of thought that had slowly evolved among some Mexican Americans over the previous years. LULAC's founders believed that Mexican Americans had for too long been denied the full enjoyment of their rights as American citizens and that it was now time to change the situation. Both LULAC's constitution and the LULAC Code emphasized that the best way to rectify the appalling conditions facing Mexican Americans was to organize as American citizens; thus LULAC's founders rejected outright the notion that they were merely Mexicans who happened to reside in the United States. Although LULAC members insisted that their organization did not represent a political club, most of the group's goals were clearly political in nature. Thus even though LULAC's by-laws specifically prohibited direct involvement in partisan elections, the group's leaders encouraged members to participate in politics and use their "vote and influence" to support "men who show by their deeds, respect and consideration for our people."[15] They remained extremely sensitive to the anti-Mexican sentiment that was building up in Texas and other parts of the Southwest during the first years of the depression, however, and so, from the outset, they were very careful to disavow the use of political tactics that might be interpreted as radical. Despite such caution, they asserted their strong commitment to "destroy any attempt to create racial prejudices against [Mexican Americans], and any infamous stigma which may be cast upon them [by] demand[ing] for them the respect and prerogatives which the Constitution grants us all."[16]

LULAC leaders consciously chose to emphasize the American side of their social identity as the primary basis for organization. Consequently, in pursuit of much-needed reforms they developed a political program designed to activate a sense of Americanism among their constituents. Considering themselves part of a progressive and enlightened leadership elite, LULAC's leaders set out to implement general goals and a political strategy that were similar in form and content to those advocated early in the century by W. E. B. DuBois and the National Association for the Advancement of Colored People: for "an educated elite" "to provide the masses with appropriate goals and lift them to civilization."[17] LULAC's political activities varied from chapter to chapter according to local political circumstances, but in general the organization adopted a three-pronged plan of attack in the 1930s and 1940s that strongly emphasized desegregated public education for Mexican American children; encouraged Mexican American citizens to register, pay their poll taxes, and vote; and supported aggressive local legal campaigns to combat discrimination against Mexican Americans in public facilities and on juries.

Although the depression constrained LULAC's organizing and prose-lytizing efforts, the organization proved remarkably successful in expanding its membership base after 1929. Utilizing "Flying Squadrons" of organizers who traveled to distant communities in cars or chartered buses, LULAC grew throughout the 1930s in Texas, and by the outbreak of World War II the organization had established viable chapters in New Mexico, Arizona, California, and Kansas. By the early 1940s LULAC claimed at least eighty dues-paying chapters nationwide, making it the largest and best-established Mexican American civil rights organization in the United States.[18]

LULAC also proved remarkably successful in achieving many of its stated political goals. Indeed, despite the generally hostile political environment facing Mexican Americans during this era, LULAC scored a number of significant legal victories in Texas, and the organization assisted Mexican Americans in other states in mounting effective challenges against local discriminatory practices. From 1929 through World War II LULAC organized successful voter registration and poll-tax drives, actively supported political candidates sympathetic to Mexican Americans, and aggressively attacked discriminatory laws and practices in communities throughout Texas and the Southwest. More important over the long run, LULAC also achieved a number of notable legal victories in the area of public education. Following a strategy in which it focused its energies on legal challenges to discriminatory practices in one community at a time, LULAC began to chip away at the structure of the de jure segregation of Mexican American students. For example, in the organization's first legal challenge in 1930, LULAC lawyers brought suit against the Del Rio, Texas, School District for discriminating against Mexican American students. LULAC ultimately lost most of the major points contested in *Independent School District v. Salvatierra*, but the case was only the opening salvo in what proved to be a long legal struggle in which LULAC and other groups successfully argued that discrimination violated the equal-protection and due-process clauses of the Fourteenth Amendment to the U.S. Constitution. Similar LULAC efforts in the 1940s and 1950s built on this important precedent and helped Mexican Americans and other minority groups attack the separate-but-equal doctrine that was ultimately overturned in the famous *Brown v. Board of Education* case in 1954.[19]

LULAC and the Paradox of
Ethnic Politics in the 1930s

Without a doubt, LULAC made important strides toward achieving its vision of the future of the Mexican American minority of the Southwest. At the same time, however, the organization's staunch integrationist political stance helped to expose, and ultimately to deepen, many of the most important social and cultural fissures that had developed in ethnic Mexican communities with the large influxes of immigrants during the previous two decades. Few could deny LULAC's success in building a viable advocacy organization, but by deciding to focus its efforts exclusively on behalf of the American-citizen population, LULAC in effect chose to abandon hundreds of thousands of other ethnic Mexicans who had also come to consider the United States their permanent home. Thus even though most of LULAC's leaders clearly believed that their exclusionary membership policies and political efforts on behalf of American citizens of Mexican descent represented a rational attempt to achieve the greatest good for the greatest number of Mexican Americans, their decision to exclude non-naturalized residents raised some troubling long-term questions as to how they proposed to define their constituency. The LULAC constitution seemed to imply that the organization would act on behalf of all Mexican Americans and thus, presumably, the American-born, American-citizen children of immigrants, but the group's decision to exclude the parents of these children raised some complex moral, cultural, and political questions.

LULAC activists did not miss the significance of the rapidly changing demographic structure of the Mexican American–Mexican immigrant population of the region. Indeed, they could hardly ignore these trends, given the fact that many of the organization's leaders and rank-and-file members had spouses, parents, and other close relatives and friends who had emigrated to the United States. Similarly, LULAC members were also clearly aware that decades of sustained immigration from Mexico had created what amounted to a broad, amorphous, social borderland in which the distinctions between what was Mexican and what was American had become confused and blurred. With the influx of so many immigrants changing the social landscape of the five border states, it was impossible not to recognize that, for better or worse, the Southwest had to a large degree become re-Mexicanized.

The organization as much as acknowledged this fact by publishing in the *LULAC News* a bit of doggerel that made light of the cultural and political ambiguities that so colored life in Texas and the border states. Though whimsical, "The Mexico-Texan" provides some telling insights into the uneasiness LULAC members must have felt, both about the changes that had unfolded since the turn of the century and about their reactions to those changes.

> The Mexico-Texan, a durn funny man,
> Who lives in the region that's north of the Gran.
> Of Mexican father, he born in thees part,
> And sometimes he rues it way down in hees heart.
> For the Mexico-Texan, he gotta no lan'
> He stomped on the neck on both sides of the Gran.
> The damn gringo lingo he no cannot spik,
> It twista da tong and it maka heem sik.
> A cit'zen of Texas they say that he ees. . . .
> But then—why call heem da Mexican grease?
> Soft talk and hard actions he can't understand,
> The Mexico-Texan, he gotta no lan'.
> Elections come 'round and the gringos are loud,
> They pat on hees back and maka heem proud.
> They give heem mezcal and they heem meet,
> They tell heem, "Amigo, we can't be defeat."
> But after election, he no gotta no fran
> The Mexico-Texan, he no gotta no lan'.
> Except for a few that in cunning are deft,
> He counta so much as an "o" to the left.
> He gotta no voice, all he gotta is da hand,
> To work like da burro—he gotta no lan'
> Only one way hees sorrows all drown,
> He'll get drunk as hell when next payday comes 'roun.
> For he has one advantage of all other men,
> Though the Mexico-Texan he gotta no lan'
> He can getta so drunk that he thinks he can fly,
> Both September da Sixteen and the Fourth of July.[20]

Even though "The Mexico-Texan" continues to elicit a smile a half-century after it first appeared, the poem's tone reflects the deep ambivalence both Mexican Americans and Mexican immigrants must have felt about living side by side in the United States. Like the Spanish-singing composer of "El Corrido del Norte," the author of "The Mexico-Texan" used a significant degree of irony and black humor that simultaneously celebrated and lamented the cultural ambiguities which large-scale immigration had reinforced in the Southwest.[21]

For LULAC's founders, however, the situation had become much less funny as the depression continued to take a heavy toll on Mexican Americans. In a social environment in which a sense of "us versus them" must have increased every time a Mexican American worker was slandered as a "greaser" or a "dirty Mexican" and thrown out of work, LULAC's organizers felt forced to conclude that a hard line had to be drawn between themselves and those they arbitrarily defined as alien. In 1929, and increasingly during the depression, LULAC insisted that it made little sense for Mexican Americans to organize politically if the border with Mexico remained open to the extent it had been earlier in the twentieth century.

Still, such a momentous decision inevitably raised important issues for an organization that had committed itself to fostering "the best and purest form of Americanism" among its members while admonishing them to "love the men of your race, take pride in your origins," and "learn to handle with purity the two most essential languages, English and Spanish."[22] By simultaneously adhering to these two sets of principles they were forced to walk a very fine line in their attempts to strike a balance between what must often have seemed to be contradictory objectives.

Nowhere were the inherent contradictions of this position more apparent than in LULAC's stance on Mexican immigration. Indeed, that the Mexican Americans who founded LULAC were aware of the sensitivity (and potential explosiveness) of their position was clear even before the organization was officially established in 1929. For example, when delegates of the Sons of America, the Knights of America, and the League of Latin American Citizens met to discuss possible unification, a motion that membership in the new organization be restricted exclusively to American citizens was presented to the assembly. According to one observer the motion created an immediate uproar in an audience that was composed largely of resident Mexican nationals. The witness reported that "a demonstration of dissatisfaction was made when the assembly was told by Judge [J. T.] Canales that the organization was to be composed only of American citizens, as it would be detrimental to aliens." According to this account, "More than ninety percent of the assembly left the hall in protest—leaving only a few delegates and visitors from Corpus Christi, San Antonio, and Brownsville."[23] That LULAC's organizers adopted this rather harsh position despite the fact that more than 90 percent of the organization's potential constituents walked out of the founding meeting is an indication of the extent to which these Mexican Americans were committed to drawing clear distinctions between themselves and more recent arrivals from Mexico.

Some scholars have interpreted LULAC's decision to exclude Mexican nationals from membership as an early indication of the middle-class composition and outlook of the group's members. In essence arguing that LULAC's founders were concerned primarily with asserting and consolidating their own class and political position in Texas and only secondarily with improving the social, economic, and political condition of Mexican Americans generally, such scholars have roundly criticized the organization's activities and motivations.[24] That interpretation is, I think, overly simplistic. Although LULAC probably did claim a higher proportion of middle-class members than did previous Mexican American organizations, a strict class analysis of the organization obscures and diminishes the group's motivations. Moreover, although much of LULAC's leadership cadre did come from professional and small-business backgrounds, the scant evidence that scholars have been able to turn up about the organization's early membership suggests that many of LULAC's rank-and-file members were either small farmers or ranchers or wage-laborers of various kinds.[25] Similarly, although some LULAC members did use language in their organizational campaigns and literature that made distinctions between "Americans of Latin extraction" and the "peon class" of common Mexican immigrant (and Mexican American?) workers, to interpret the organization's position simply or even primarily as a reflection of its members' class standing or aspirations does not do justice to the logic of their political views.

The ideological positions and views on immigration held by most of LULAC's leaders were pragmatic, political responses that reflected their honest perception of the social and political realities of Texas and the greater Southwest. From their point of view the basic issues facing LULAC—and Mexican Americans generally—were not merely questions of status preservation, self-aggrandizement, or the consolidation and expansion of the political influence of a few individuals. On the contrary, LULAC leaders seemed to believe that the essential challenge facing the Mexican American people was to develop and employ a political strategy that would enable them to organize most effectively for the achievement of meaningful social change. In their opinion this required that Mexican Americans first come to some difficult decisions regarding the boundaries of the community they hoped to organize. If that meant excluding those who had not been born (or naturalized) as citizens of the United States, so be it.

LULAC's spokespersons were firm and quite consistent in advancing this point of view in the coming years, but judging from the amount of time and ink they expended explaining and refining their position, their decisions regarding the boundaries of the community they claimed to represent continued to trouble them for years after that first momentous meeting in Corpus Christi. The problem was set out in 1928 in an exchange of correspondence between Alonso S. Perales and Ben Garza, prominent San Antonio community leaders and future LULAC presidents. While serving in the Department of State on a diplomatic posting to Nicaragua, Perales wrote that Mexican Americans could never expect to advance themselves unless individuals "of the better sort" seized the initiative. "Were I to criticize Nicaraguans for their filthy and backward towns and cities," he argued, "they would in all probability retort: 'How about your Mexican villages . . . in San Antonio, Houston, Dallas and other Texas cities and towns?' I believe I would have to agree with them that our Mexican districts in the United States are just as filthy and backward as Managua." For Perales the fundamental issue involved was Mexican Americans' own responses to those conditions. "What are we Mexican Americans going to do about the matter?" he asked. "Are we going to continue in our backward state of the past, or are we going to get out of the rut, forge ahead and keep abreast of the hard-driving Anglo-Saxon? There is the big problem before us, my friend, and one that we Mexican Americans must solve if we have any sense of pride at all. Hence the need for a strong, powerful organization composed of and led by intelligent, energetic, progressive, honest and unselfish Mexican Americans."[26]

For Perales and other LULAC leaders the key to answering these questions lay in the melting pot. Thus, even though most of the organization's spokesmen continued to pontificate about veneration of their Mexican ethnic heritage and culture, as anti-Mexican sentiment intensified during the first years of the depression LULAC's rhetoric clearly tilted toward espousal of some type of melding of Mexican Americans into the American mainstream. As one scholar of the organization recently put it, LULAC's leaders were convinced that "it was not enough to cry out against discrimination. Mexican Americans also had to learn the culture, language, and political system of the United States in order to effectively wage their political struggle and integrate into the system. There was no other way to overcome discrimination and underdevelopment."[27] Consequently, in the 1930s LULAC's leaders consistently argued that Mexican Americans should appropriate and emulate what they considered to be the most salutary aspects of American culture. For example, in an editorial published in a 1932 issue of the *LULAC News*, LULAC's President-General Manuel C. Gonzales advocated that Mexican Americans "fuse" with Americans "known to be members of a vigorous and masterful race," because such "commingling . . . in the end tends to bring out the force and character and the fertility of intellect that create and perpetuate a leading nation."[28] Although Gonzales tempered these rather startling remarks by insisting that Mexican Americans should adopt American customs only "in so far as they may be good customs," he argued that LULAC's primary mission should be to "shed the light of knowledge of [American] patriotism [and] civic consciousness into the dark recesses of a willing but as yet partially dormant [Mexican American] people . . . that they may awaken to the beauty and glory of a new day—filled with opportunities that [are] today challenging us to an awakened reality."[29] From Gonzales's point of view Mexican Americans could not hope to "awaken to this new day" unless they first "accept[ed] the challenge" of becoming full-fledged Americans by "bow[ing] to . . . American citizenship," albeit, as he put it, "with dignity and pride [in] our racial origin." "God grant," he intoned, "that . . . respect and admiration for the land of my forefathers may grow from day to day— and our love, devotion, and loyalty to America, the land of our birth, may never be surpassed by anyone."[30]

Although Manuel Gonzales apparently sincerely believed that the strategy expressed in his editorial represented an altruistic agenda which would, in time, benefit the greatest number of Mexican Americans in the United States, at another level his views clearly reflected some of the difficult conclusions that LULAC's founders had reached when they decided to exclude unnaturalized Mexican nationals from their organization. Try as they might to convince others (and perhaps themselves) that they retained the same respect and admiration for Mexico and its people that they did for the United States, LULAC members consistently went to great lengths to explain to anyone who would listen that Americans of Mexican descent were different from (and by implication, somehow better than) Mexicans from the other side.

LULAC's leaders advanced this view with varying degrees of subtlety during the organization's first decade. Perales was probably most sympathetic to recent immigrants, but even he ultimately concluded that Mexican Americans had to turn their backs on their immigrant neighbors. As Perales saw it, the fundamental challenges facing his organization (and Mexican Americans generally) were "how to teach the average Anglo Americans to recognize the American Mexican as an 'American'; and at the same time, how to teach the American Mexican to realize and recognize the fact that he [is] an American, without arousing the national resentment, hatred, and animosity created in him by his daily treatment by other Americans."[31] The best way to achieve this, he insisted, was for "enlightened" Mexican Americans to assume leadership, organize, educate, and otherwise work within the existing American political system to achieve gradual, incremental reform and thus ultimate acceptance of Mexican Americans as full-fledged American citizens. This required that "intelligent and progressive" Mexican Americans focus their energies exclusively on American citizens of Mexican descent. According to Perales the unrestricted immigration of hundreds of thousands of Mexican workers had reinforced negative stereotypes to the point that "being considered a Mexican [in Texas] signifies contempt, abuses, and injustices." Perales concluded, therefore, that the first step toward the effective political organization of the Mexican American people had to be "to draw [a] line between the American citizen of Mexican descent, and the alien of the same extraction, residing in the United States in such close proximity to his mother country."[32] The drawing of such lines was deplorable but necessary, he believed, because of the bad image of Mexican Americans created by such great numbers of impoverished Mexican immigrant workers. Moreover, citizens and aliens could not possibly work together in the United States because "being consolidated in a single organization and their [national and cultural] tendencies being entirely opposed, conflict [between Mexican Americans and Mexican immigrants] would be inevitable. . . . Thus, unity of action would be lost and the organization disrupted." Speaking for LULAC's leadership cadre, Perales concluded, "The truth is that the Mexican American has before him a very serious problem and he has chosen the most practical road to solve it."[33]

Perales and other LULAC leaders insisted that they meant no disrespect toward Mexico or Mexicans. The members had no intention, Perales argued, of "segregat[ing] [them]selves maliciously . . . [or despising] their own brothers of race, the Mexican citizens for whom they always have had the most sincere affection." "No," he insisted, "it is one thing to deny one's racial origin and a very distinct thing to try and be a loyal and conscientious [American] citizen to struggle, on a basis of an indisputable patriotism, for one's rights and prerogatives. This last is what the American citizen of Latin origin [is] trying to do."[34] Only when Mexican Americans had secured their own rights would they be able to assist Mexican immigrants. As Perales put it, "The day that the Mexican American betters his condition and finds himself in a position of being able to make useful his rights of citizenship, that day he will be in a position to aid the Mexican citizen to [gain] his rights, and to collaborate with him in all that goes to assure his welfare and happiness."[35] Perales concluded with a plea to Mexicans both in Mexico and in the United States that "our dear brothers of race, the purely Mexican citizen, may not criticize the attitude of the Mexican American nor view his labor in a bad light." "Do not criticize," he urged, "but before all lend your determined moral support and wish us the best success in our undertakings."[36]

The lofty rhetoric began to break down as antipathy toward Mexicans deepened along with the depression. Thus, even as Perales was pleading with Mexican nationals to understand LULAC's motivations, in January 1930 he and Ben Garza offered their organization's qualified support of restrictive immigration legislation pending before a House subcommittee in Washington. They were careful to insist that LULAC would support the immigration bill if its sponsors could prove "that Mexicans—that is Mexicans from Mexico—are a menace to the American working man because

. . . they . . . lower wages," rather than basing the legislation strictly on racial criteria. It is significant, however, that LULAC had gone on public record in opposition to further immigration from Mexico a mere eleven months after its establishment.[37]

LULAC's position on the immigrant question would harden even more in the coming months, although this position often involved the performance of some logical and rhetorical gymnastics. Forced as they were to follow a logic grounded in what they considered to be the loftiest ideals of the American liberal democratic tradition, LULAC members had to employ some rather tortured reasoning when its members attempted to interpret the repressive anti-Mexican atmosphere surrounding the repatriation campaigns. Thus, rather than viewing the expulsion of Mexican immigrants as a logical outgrowth of racist attitudes that Americans had exhibited toward Mexicans ever since the nineteenth century, some of LULAC's spokesmen tried to reconstruct Mexican American history in a manner consistent with their great faith in the American democratic tradition. In their zeal to press their case they sometimes bent Texas history to the extent that Anglo Texans and Mexican Texans were portrayed as having always lived in racial harmony. Indeed, they baldly argued that Anglo Americans had never recognized prejudicial "differences or distinctions between old Texans of Anglo-Saxon descent and old Texans of Latin American descent" until large numbers of impoverished Mexican immigrants began to enter the United States, at which point "a different attitude developed from newcomers to Texas toward the laboring class of Mexican who came to work." The tragedy for Mexican Americans, as one LULAC member saw it, was that "this attitude has not been limited to alien laborers but has extended to United States Citizens." "In those communities which have been settled and developed since the year 1900," he continued, "there have been raised veritable barriers against Latin Americans indiscriminately and regardless of whether they are American citizens or not. They are discriminated against in the public schools, hotels, restaurants, barber shops, theaters, swimming pools and other places of amusements, because they belong to another race. Is it any wonder that their living conditions are a disgrace to the State of Texas?"[38]

Thus, according to an opinion published in LULAC's official newsletter, discrimination against Mexican Americans in the United States did not stem from the legacy of racism and economic exploitation dating from the Mexican Revolution and the Mexican War but derived almost exclusively from Anglo Americans' adverse reactions to Mexican immigrants who had recently entered the United States. This line of argument was made abundantly clear in a 1932 *LULAC News* editorial. Seeking to answer the rhe-

torical question, "Are Texas-Mexicans 'Americans'?" the unsigned article
asserted that "the Constitution of the United States provides that all persons born or naturalized in the United States are citizens of this country,
so it can be easily seen that the Latin-Americans born in Texas have a dou-
ble reason to say that they are Americans, first by force of treaty between
two great nations, and also by virtue of the provisions of the Federal Constitution." "Texas-Mexicans have never been considered as foreigners," the
author continued, "and so far as the great State of Texas is concerned, the
real, true-blue 'Americans' are native citizens of this State of Latin extraction." From LULAC's point of view it was crucial, therefore, that "the
greatest care . . . be exercised to distinguish between th[e Latin American]
citizen and the alien of Latin extraction."[39]

Competing Political Visions

LULAC's views on the intertwined issues of immigration, Mexican American ethnic identity, and political organization and activism were to prove
deeply influential in the interwar period. Indeed, many historians have argued that the establishment and growth of organizations like LULAC
marked a major turning point in Mexican American political and social history. According to this line of reasoning, LULAC's establishment marked
a political coming of age of a new generation of Mexican Americans. Such
scholars are convinced that this new generation's American nativity, up-
bringing, and political socialization strongly predisposed them to focus on
the American side of their social identity to a far greater degree than was
possible for their parents' generation. From this premise they argue that
the late 1930s and early 1940s marked a psychological watershed in which
huge numbers of Mexican Americans entered American social and cultural
life for the first time. As one historian put it, "Growing up in this country,
Mexican Americans were increasingly more acculturated, bilingual, and as
a result, more politically functional. Formally educated to a greater extent
than ever before, they became better socialized to their rights as U.S. citizens. . . . For Mexican Americans, there was no going back to Mexico. The
United States was their home."[40] Another historian has taken this argument even further, asserting that the rise of middle-class-oriented groups
such as LULAC represented "the emergence of a [new] collective Mexican
American mentality."[41] From this point of view LULAC's activities not only
represented a new form of political and social activism but also symbolized
a much larger social process in which "the majority of Mexicans [in the
United States] had moved . . . from a consciousness of [being] *'mexicanos
de afuera'* to [a sense of being] *'mexicanos de adentro'* [Mexican Ameri-

cans within or part of the United States]."[42] According to this interpretation, so sweeping was the change in consciousness that by the end of the Great Depression large numbers of Mexican Americans had come to adopt LULAC's "emphasis on Americanism . . . because it coincided with their rising expectations. They began to accept the themes of citizenship, Americanization, and integration."[43]

The kind of political philosophy and strategies advocated by organizations like LULAC represented a rising force in Mexican American ethnic politics in this era. In many ways, however, the emphasis scholars have placed on this strain of political thought has tended to obscure other important trends in Mexican American political and social history of the interwar period. That the Mexican American activists associated with LULAC and similar organizations deeply influenced popular political discourse on immigration and ethnic consciousness is indisputable. What is often lost in analysis of this period is the fact that, even at the height of their influence, groups such as LULAC directly represented only a small percentage of the total ethnic Mexican population.

Why, then, have so many scholars of the Mexican American experience implied or flatly asserted that the ideology and activities of such individuals as Alonso S. Perales, M. C. Gonzales, J. T. Canales, or Ben Garza and such groups as the Sons of America or LULAC defined the Mexican American mentality of the period? Clearly, part of the explanation lies in the success of these individuals and groups in articulating their political positions and winning concessions for their constituencies during a particularly difficult time. Given the attention LULAC attracted in the Southwest in the 1930s and 1940s, it is not at all surprising that scholars subsequently have focused on the legacies left by groups adhering to this particular political perspective. Moreover, scholars have probably paid more attention to these kinds of organizations because they generated a significant body of documentary records, newspaper articles, and correspondence that historians have been able to tap in their research.

It can be argued, however, that the very visibility and successes of these groups and individuals—and the survival of their documentary records—has helped to obscure the historical activities and significance of the hundreds of thousands of Mexican Americans and Mexican immigrants who did not participate in this particular brand of political activity. Many scholars have made the error of assuming that the historical silence of the working-class majority of ethnic Mexicans somehow indicated either that they tacitly accepted the assimilationists' vision of the future or, at the other extreme, that they were apolitical. Scattered historical evidence strongly suggests, however, that the political perspectives of Mexican

Americans and Mexican nationals residing in the United States had a much broader range than such an argument would indicate. Indeed, throughout this period Mexican Americans and Mexican immigrants articulated political views that were radically different from those advocated by the integrationists. Although many ordinary Mexican American and resident Mexican immigrant workers, if asked, may well have agreed and applauded LULAC's efforts on their behalf, other Mexican Americans and Mexican nationals responded differently.

When a team of researchers interviewed long-time Mexican residents of the colonia of Hick's Camp, California, outside the San Gabriel Valley community of El Monte, late in the depression decade, their views reflected a very different perspective on the social and political realities facing ethnic Mexicans from that offered by groups such as LULAC. Questioning a random sample of 67 of the 137 Hick's Camp families, in case after case the California Commission on Immigration and Housing survey team discovered the depth of the frustration and despair that Mexican and Mexican American residents felt about their experience in the United States. One immigrant, responding to a question as to why he had not become an American citizen after years of living in the United States, flatly stated, "I don't want to be a citizen. My wife doesn't want to be." "I'll tell you why," he continued. "[Mexicans] feel that Americans don't trust them and treat them equal. At the show they seat them separately. . . . If six Americans and six Mexicans go for a job and there are six job openings, they don't take three Americans and three Mexicans. No—they take the six they can tell are Americans by their color. When I go to a show they don't ask if I'm a citizen or not, but if I'm dark they put me on one side. The same with work. . . . That's why we don't want to be citizens."[44]

Another interviewee responded in similar fashion: "I'm not interested in being a citizen because first of all it would mean nothing to anyone—I would be a citizen in name only—with no privileges or considerations. I would still be [considered] a 'dirty Mexican.'" "Even if I had papers," he continued, "I would not have entry to the park, nor would they keep me from being segregated at the show." This individual went on to recount an incident of discrimination against a Mexican American veteran. The veteran, the immigrant recalled, "was proudly taking two American girls to a dance one evening and at the door of the dance he was turned away and told Mexicans were not admitted. The veteran produced his citizenship papers and then was told that he wasn't an American just because he had American citizenship papers—he was still a Mexican."[45] A female resident of the camp told the interviewers much the same thing: "I don't think I care to become a citizen. My husband was born here and is a citizen [and yet] he is still called a Mexican. To me that is not an insult—but it is meant as such. I like being a Mexican."[46]

Such comments pointed to a sentiment that stemmed from the experiences of a stratum of American society that had virtually no status before the law. Since the first large migrations of Mexicans at the turn of the century most Americans, giving no thought to the possibility that these workers might expect to build a future for themselves and their families, had simply expected Mexicans to perform their tasks and then depart, grateful for the opportunity to have worked in the United States. What so many Americans failed to understand was that thousands of Mexican immigrants—like so many previous immigrants to America—were human beings who had not come north merely to work but to find a better future. After twenty-five, thirty, or even forty years, however, it seemed to many that their hopes for equal status in American society would forever be denied.

One of the Mexicans interviewed by the California survey team expressed just this combination of bitterness and frustration in his comments. "I am clean," he said, "I bathe—I shave—I dress decently. My wife and I are decent people. [Yet] if we go to the theatre in El Monte we can't choose our own seats—we have to sit off to the side where we cannot see." In giving vent to his anger at having worked so hard and received so little recognition in return, this resident of Hick's Camp expressed a resentment and sense of injustice that more and more immigrants had come to feel throughout the previous decade. "I don't know why it is," he declared. "Mexicans were here before the Americans. We are more American than they. Whatever there is here, besides, we built. We built the roads. We built the railroads. We built the new hospital. We built the new City Hall in Los Angeles. They are lazy. When there is work to do the Americans won't do it. They sit on the side, and the Mexicans do the work! But they won't let us sit by them in the theatre!"[47]

When the social conditions and life circumstances of the vast majority of ethnic Mexicans are taken into account, it is not at all surprising that at least some Mexican Americans and resident immigrants would come to such conclusions. Already struggling economically before the depression, by the mid-1930s the great majority of Mexican American and Mexican immigrant families were living in some of the worst conditions to be found in America. Indeed, when measured by virtually any standard of public welfare, the ethnic Mexican population—regardless of formal citizenship status—lived in shocking conditions across the Southwest.

In 1937, for example, the so-called Mexican population of San Antonio, Texas (no distinction was made between Mexican American citizens and more recent Mexican immigrants) suffered a mortality rate from tuberculosis of 310 per 100,000, compared with a rate of 138 for blacks and 56 for Anglos. Infant mortality—the rate of deaths per thousand live births, exclusive of stillbirths—among ethnic Mexicans was a staggering 144 per 1,000 live births, compared with 105 for blacks and 51 for Anglos.[48] Conditions were little better in the more rural south Texas. Living at an income level far below the already abysmal poverty line of the period, Mexican and Mexican American families endured extremely primitive conditions. In 1938 a Works Projects Administration researcher described Mexicans' homes as "little more than shacks with dirt floors, tin roofs, flour sacks over the windows, [and] open toilets." "Few had electricity," he reported. "Fewer still had indoor plumbing." With people crowded almost three to a room, tuberculosis, enteritis, and infectious diarrhea were endemic, and although mortality rates of ethnic Mexicans were not quite as high in south Texas as in San Antonio, they remained three to four times greater than those of the general population.[49]

Working-class ethnic Mexican communities in California were no better off. In 1928 the Los Angeles County Health Department developed a numerical rating system for the county's housing stock that showed dwellings occupied by Mexicans to be the worst in the area. Including such components as window screens, toilets, food storage, and refrigeration, Mexican homes received an average rating of only 8.3, compared with a countywide average of 25.[50] In a similar survey of 357 ethnic Mexican families (totaling 1,668 individuals), 65 percent reported having very little meat in their normal diet (9 percent had none at all), 40 percent reported seldom having fresh vegetables, and only 45 percent said their children had milk on a daily basis.[51] As might be expected in such circumstances, even before the depths of the Great Depression Mexican Americans and Mexican immigrants in Los Angeles County suffered infant mortality rates that ranged from twice as high as to five times higher than those of the general population. In 1928 the infant mortality rate for the ethnic Mexican population was 116.8, compared with a rate of 51.7 for the so-called white population. The next year the infant mortality rate had dropped significantly to 39.6 for the white population but remained at 104.5 for Mexicans.[52] In another area, just outside the Los Angeles city limits, an inspector of the California Commission on Immigration and Housing reported that the Mexican labor camp he surveyed had the highest infant mortality rate in the entire country.[53]

Reported rates of infection by communicable disease—particularly tuberculosis—were similar to the infant-mortality statistics. The California State Mexican Fact-Finding Committee appointed by Governor C. C.

Young noted that of the cases of communicable disease reported in the ethnic Mexican population, nearly 25 percent "terminated fatally," a mortality rate twice that of the general population. Although by 1927 the death rate from communicable disease among Mexicans had dropped significantly, the rate remained nearly one-third higher than that afflicting the white population.[54] Observing the state of California's ethnic Mexican population in 1936, after nearly six years of depression, a California public-health official was moved to comment,

> It does not seem possible that conditions can be as deplorable as they are, and yet I have a schedule on each person interviewed, and the investigator returned so discouraged over conditions that she found that I do feel it is the duty of every person in California that has any interest in public welfare [to] make an effort [to establish] a state registration bureau so that there can be a distribution of labor and some minimum standards set up for at least shower baths, toilets, and some shelter for these people.[55]

Political Implications

Like the lower-middle-class members of LULAC, working-class Mexican Americans and Mexican immigrants were well aware of the political implications of the inferior socioeconomic position they occupied during the Great Depression. The repatriation campaigns, continuing discrimination, poor health and housing conditions, and their own steadily worsening economic situation confirmed their status as a subordinate caste. They saw a future for themselves in the United States, however, that was very different from the picture painted by LULAC.

To them, coping successfully with the deepening crisis of the barrios and colonias did not necessitate their becoming integrated or assimilated into American society—at least in the manner LULAC and similar groups proposed. Indeed, many ethnic Mexicans could see very little reason why they couldn't continue living culturally as Mexicans, even while living within the political boundaries of the United States. Separated in what one scholar calls "insular cultural communities,"[56] in which Mexican practices were observed as part of everyday life, they often responded to those who advocated assimilation and Americanization by insisting there was nothing inherently wrong about the way they lived their lives. In some ways such a perspective would seem to be a natural outgrowth of the experience of those who lived among people similar to themselves, but in other ways this point of view contained the seeds of what slowly developed into more coherent oppositional cultural strategies.

Individuals associated with groups such as LULAC based both their political strategies and their programs on the fundamental assumption that Mexican Americans and Mexican immigrants should attempt to adjust and adapt to American society by emulating, and ultimately conforming to, American social, cultural, and political mores. In the 1920s and 1930s, however, opposing views were increasingly adopted by other ethnic Mexicans residing in the United States. That many Mexican immigrants and at least some Mexican Americans would resist campaigns designed to dilute their cultural heritage is not at all surprising, especially in light of the demographic revolution that had transformed the Southwest since the turn of the century. The resident ethnic Mexican population was increasingly skewed toward U.S. citizens by the late 1930s, but American citizens still made up only one segment of the population. Indeed, detailed analysis of demographic data clarifies several points. The first is that although the American-citizen cohort of the resident ethnic Mexican population grew throughout this era, when the number of first-generation Mexican Americans is considered along with the resident immigrant population it is clear that a very large percentage of the total Mexican-descent population was of recent origin in the United States. In other words, when the number of resident Mexican nationals is combined with the number of American-born children of at least one Mexican-born parent, we discover that these recent Americans represented a very large fraction of the total resident ethnic Mexican population throughout the period—ranging from a high of at least 66 percent in 1930 to more than 45 percent in 1960.[57]

Data on language usage among ethnic Mexicans further undercuts the position of those who posit a rapid transformation of the Mexican American mentality. Again, although U.S. census data on language preferences and usage in ethnic Mexican population must be evaluated with caution because of the carelessness in which so-called Mexicans were enumerated, even a cursory review of aggregate language-usage trends among U.S.-born Mexican Americans and Mexican immigrants indicates that theories presupposing a linear, progressive acculturation of the Mexican American–Mexican immigrant population in this period should be reassessed. What the census data do suggest is that the number of persons who claimed Spanish as their mother tongue, whether foreign-born, U.S.-born of mixed parentage (that is, persons with one Mexican-born parent), or U.S.-born of American-born parents, grew rapidly between 1910 and 1940.[58] In the foreign-born cohort these numbers grew from 258,131 in 1910, to 556,111 in 1920, to 743,286 in 1930, then dropped to 428,360 in 1940, presumably as a result of the repatriations of the previous decade. Significantly, however, the mixed-parentage population claiming Spanish as its mother tongue grew at an even steeper rate, increasing from 190,067 in 1910, to 294,737 in 1920, and jumping to 714,060 in 1940. In addition, the 1940 census enumerated another 718,980 U.S.-born Mexican Americans of U.S. native parentage who continued to claim Spanish as their mother tongue.[59] Thus although Mexican Americans, Mexican immigrants, and the children of both these groups were experiencing powerful forces of interculturation resulting from their residence in the United States, it is also apparent that thousands continued to speak the language of their parents.[60]

Taken together, the data on nativity rates, language usage, socioeconomic conditions, and awareness of discrimination among citizen and noncitizen Americans of Mexican descent begin to suggest some of the complex—and potentially contradictory—trends that had been unfolding in the Southwest since the turn of the century. At the most fundamental level the demographic statistics demolished the old argument that Mexican immigrants had come to the United States only to earn a stake before returning to Mexico. Although hundreds of thousands of Mexicans did, in fact, return to Mexico during the 1930s, huge numbers settled in the United States. In the process they had created permanent ethnic enclaves in a broad band of territory extending from Brownsville in the southeast to Denver in the north and to San Diego, Los Angeles, and Santa Barbara in the west. Permanent settlement did not mean, however, that these immigrants and their American-born children had automatically become Americans, at least insofar as most other Americans would have defined the process. On the contrary, by settling in or near existing Mexican American barrios or colonias that were already largely spatially and culturally segregated, Mexican immigrants helped build communities that functioned very much like the ones they had left in Mexico. Living in a fairly familiar environment, surrounded by people who spoke their language, ate many of the same foods, enjoyed many of the same forms of entertainment, celebrated the same holidays, and shared many of the same religious practices and folkways, immigrants often did not have to venture outside the boundaries of the many "Mexican towns" that dotted the Southwest except to go to work.

Given these circumstances, it is not surprising that many of these individuals were reluctant to accept the blandishments of those Anglo Americans and Mexican Americans who argued for the rapid assimilation of the ethnic Mexican minority. Indeed, extant sources strongly suggest that, dating from the late nineteenth century and running throughout this period, working-class Mexican Americans and Mexican immigrants often developed oppositional political and cultural strategies that, like those voiced indirectly at Hick's Camp, flatly rejected the most cherished assumptions of those Americans who advocated assimilation and/or Americanization.[61]

These political and cultural perspectives had deep roots in the Mexican American past, but in the late 1920s and 1930s ethnic Mexicans gave voice to them with increasing frequency and intensity. Responding to what they viewed as unwarranted anti-Mexican repression of the era, Mexican American and Mexican immigrant activists—particularly those associated with the numerous strikes and other job actions that erupted in the 1920s and 1930s—increasingly ascribed their grievances to racial and class exploitation. Observing that their oppression seemed to occur without regard to their formal citizenship status, these activists tended to discount the importance of citizenship as an organizing tool. Instead, they began to forge political strategies that strongly emphasized the ethnocultural and class ties that bound Mexican workers to Mexican Americans. Historical evidence of the evolution among ethnic Mexican workers of the disparate movements that scholars in different contexts have called "strategies of cultural resistance" or "class-based oppositional subcultures" remains scattered and fragmentary.[62] Even so, evidence of this type of political and social thinking is sufficient to warrant serious reconsideration of the prevailing historical interpretation of the interwar period.

The Mutualista Tradition

One of the earliest manifestations of this kind of political activity was seen in the mutualista movement. As pointed out in Chapter 1, mutualistas had emerged in the mid-nineteenth century in Mexico, and by the 1870s mutual-aid organizations had been established in many ethnic Mexican enclaves throughout the Southwest.[63] Although most mutualistas functioned primarily as social-welfare associations and explicitly banned discussion of religious and political issues in their meetings, the prohibitions against substantive political discussion generally meant discussion of Mexican politics. Considering the intrigues and growing factional ferocity that characterized the last twenty years of the Porfiriato, it is not at all surprising that Mexicans remained sensitive to these issues even after they entered the United States. The proscriptions usually did not apply to discussing the common problems faced by ethnic Mexicans in American society. Recognizing that the issues facing Mexican Americans and immigrants in the United States were distinct from the political controversies raging in Mexico, members of the mutualistas often used their organizations as forums for discussing the issues of the day. As one scholar noted in a study of the emergence of Mexican mutual-aid societies in Texas, "Civil Rights issues [in the United States] were not considered politics, but rather vital, local 'problems' to be addressed by the community."[64]

One of the largest Mexican American mutual-aid alliances in the United States, the Alianza Hispano-Americana, founded in 1894 in Tucson, Arizona, involved itself in local and territorial politics soon after its establishment. Formed in response to Anglo attempts to exclude Tucson's Mexican Americans from participation in local politics, according to one scholar, the alliance "cross cut the social classes of the [Mexican] colony and made it possible for Mexicans to respond collectively to threats of Anglo discriminations." "Although its founders did not consider it to be a political association," this scholar notes, "it quickly became involved in city and territorial politics, the membership standing firmly against candidates with known records of discrimination."[65] After the turn of the century the alliance expanded its activities to include civil rights litigation on behalf of Mexican Americans and immigrants from Mexico and provided its members with legal assistance, both from its Tucson headquarters and from newly established chapters in Los Angeles, San Diego, and San Bernadino, California.[66]

Another prominent early example of political activity stemming from the mutualista movement was El Primer Congreso Mexicanista (the First Mexican Congress), held in Laredo, Texas, in September 1911. Called by Nicasio Idár, the influential south Texas publisher of the Spanish-language newspaper, *La Crónica,* the congress was designed to bring together the state's many mutual-aid and fraternal organizations to discuss ways to combat discrimination and increasing racial violence against Mexicans in the border region. Although no lasting unified Mexican American organization emerged from the congress, it was significant in that for a time it united the numerous Texas organizations serving Mexican Americans and Mexican immigrants and provided an important precedent for cooperative effort in the future.[67]

The activities of both the alliance and the congress revealed another important feature of the southwestern mutualistas: they were organizations formed in the United States that served both American citizens and immigrants of Mexican descent. Although there are examples of mutualistas that restricted membership to either Mexican Americans or Mexican immigrants, most of these organizations appear to have opened their membership to both American citizens and resident Mexican nationals. As a result, in many mutualistas membership was rather evenly divided between American-born and Mexican-born individuals. For example, in one of the few detailed studies of the internal workings of mutualistas, Julie Pycior pointed out that 38 percent of the largest mutualista in San Antonio were native-born American citizens, whereas 58 percent were Mexican citizens residing in the United States.[68] Other researchers reported similar membership compositions.[69]

Another important characteristic of mutual-aid associations in the Southwest was their predominantly working-class character. To be sure, middle-class Mexican Americans and Mexican immigrants (primarily entrepreneurs serving ethnic Mexican clientele) often played prominent leadership roles in mutual-aid and fraternal organizations, but in most cases the majority of the rank-and-file members were workers. Pycior noted that fully 81 percent of the membership of San Antonio's largest mutualista were either *jornaleros* (common day laborers) or skilled or semi-skilled workers.[70] Similarly, after conducting extensive field research in California, Colorado, Texas, and the Great Lakes industrial belt in the 1920s, Paul Taylor noted that "hardly without exception" mutualista membership was drawn from "laboring class Mexicans." Other scholars made similar observations.[71]

The mixed membership of these organizations served several important functions in the evolution of relationships between Mexican immigrants and Mexican Americans in the first third of the twentieth century. In many communities the mutualista acted as a crucial institutional buffer that eased new immigrants' adjustment to the United States. By providing a place where immigrants and citizens of Mexican descent could speak the same language, discuss common problems, and cooperatively provide themselves with needed services, mutualistas allowed immigrants to learn the ropes of living in the United States in a nonthreatening, supportive environment. In addition, the intimate contact that occurred between Mexican Americans and Mexican immigrants in the culturally familiar mutualistas helped to break down barriers between the two groups, improved communication, and promoted a spirit of cooperation among them. As Pycior noted in her study of San Antonio's mutualistas, "Many of the leaders came from Mexico and brought with them the mutualist tradition. They teamed with native-born Tejanos who knew the *colonia* and could organize membership drives." "Thus," she concluded, "from the beginning mutualistas fostered cooperation between members of La Raza from Mexico and those born in the United States. While native born and immigrant Mexicanos might be pitted against each other for jobs or housing, they often cooperated in the mutualist sphere."[72] Manuel Gamio made similar observations, noting that the mutualistas in the United States seemed to "awaken the desire for social cooperation [and] discipline the character and the labor of the working man." In his view the mutualistas enabled Mexican and Mexican American workers to become "better disciplined [and to] develop . . . initiative, greater competence, and better moral character."[73]

Some scholars have argued that cooperation between Mexican immigrants and Mexican Americans in the early part of the century in the mutualistas and in Mexican patriotic organizations such as the *comisiones honoríficos* (local committees set up to observe Mexican national holidays) represented little more than manifestations of a nostalgic and conservative (if not reactionary) orientation toward Mexico among working-class Mexican Americans and migrants to the United States. According to this line of argument, working-class Mexican Americans used these organizations primarily as an escape from the reality of their subordinate position in American society. By sustaining a nostalgic orientation toward Mexico, they could look forward to a time when they would return to their homeland, freed at last from the prejudices of American society. Thus mutualistas and similar groups served as little more than way stations for immigrants hoping to avoid confronting their oppression both in the United States and in Mexico. Viewed from this perspective the early Mexican American–Mexican immigrant organizations were sentimental anachronisms "without redeeming political virtue,"[74] concerned more with "maintaining the physical and cultural integrity of . . . Mexican communities" than with "overcoming discrimination and fighting for equality within [American] society."[75]

Such interpretations are partly accurate in that most mutualist organizations did emphasize Mexican Americans' and Mexican immigrants' common cultural heritage, used Spanish almost exclusively in official proceedings, and spent much time planning the celebrations of such Mexican patriotic events as the Cinco de Mayo (commemorating the Mexican victory over Emperor Maximilian's forces at Puebla in 1862) and the Dieciséis de Septiembre (Mexico's Independence Day). The varied activities of many mutual-aid organizations in Texas, Arizona, and California, however, provide evidence that the members of such organizations often had much more complex motivations and political agendas than this interpretation takes into account. Although the mutualistas and comisiones often did exhibit nostalgic forms of Mexican nationalism and strongly encouraged the maintenance of Mexican culture in the United States, the scope and thrust of their activities indicated a growing awareness of the importance of local American political issues—and a growing willingness to confront them. As Grebler, Moore, and Guzmán astutely observed, "the visible symbols of loyalty to Mexico [among Mexican Americans and Mexican immigrants residing in the United States] must be interpreted with reference to their functioning for Mexican Americans in *this* country, as well as their functioning for Mexicans vis-à-vis their motherland."[76]

This nascent cooperative spirit had far-reaching implications for the relationships evolving between Mexican Americans and Mexican immigrants after 1900. Although the cultural and patriotic emphasis of these organizations clearly was Mexican, it must be recognized that, in the end, the mutualistas' ceremonies, celebrations, and community activities served to foster solidarity among ethnic Mexicans who were, for better or worse, permanent residents of the United States. Rather than representing the reactionary tendencies of resident ethnic Mexicans, the activities of mutualistas should be viewed as manifestations of the first efforts at concerted collective action. The increasing political activities of these organizations after World War I provided strong evidence that they had built a strong foundation for future joint political activism among immigrants and natives based largely on mutually acknowledged ties of class and culture.

Labor Activism and Ethnic Political Mobilization

No arena better exemplified the cooperative efforts of Mexican Americans and Mexican immigrants to combat the crises facing their communities than the strikes and walkouts that occurred during the 1920s and 1930s. Throughout these decades ethnic Mexican workers engaged in spontaneous job actions, which in turn stimulated the development of new modes of political analysis among them. Because their employers generally recognized no difference between Mexicans from Mexico and Mexicans from the United States, Mexican American and Mexican immigrant workers often found themselves side by side in their labor struggles. Although much work remains to be done in documenting the evolution of joint Mexican immigrant–Mexican American labor activism in the early part of the century, recent scholarship has provided intriguing and suggestive glimpses into some of the ethnic and class dynamics of Mexican labor-organizing efforts in the Southwest.

In one of the first studies to explore early Mexican–Mexican American labor activism, historian Juan Gómez-Quiñones pointed out that although the incidence of militant labor activism among these workers did not reach a peak until the mid-1930s, ethnic Mexican workers had already established a significant pattern of labor activism between 1900 and 1920. Citing a long list of strikes involving Mexican American and Mexican immigrant workers in agriculture and in the mining, transportation, and construction industries, Gómez-Quiñones (and his students) argued that the strikers drew on a wide variety of ideological perspectives as they organized and struck against their employers. Mexican American and Mexican immigrant workers were influenced by their own strong traditions of mutualism and cooperation (indeed, many of the earliest strikes were coordinated by local mutualistas), but in many areas they were also influenced by, and worked closely with, labor organizers from unions such as the Industrial Workers of the World, the Western Federation of Miners, and various Socialist labor unions in both the United States and Mexico.[77]

Most of the early organizational and strike-directed efforts among ethnic Mexican workers in the United States began as protests over labor's traditional bread-and-butter issues: wages, hours, and working conditions. These were crucial issues since from the onset of industrialization in the Southwest ethnic Mexican workers from both sides of the border had been subject to occupational discrimination and arbitrary wage differentials. As early as the late nineteenth century Mexican American and Mexican immigrant workers had resorted to strikes to protest their abuse under the contract labor system, the company store, and Mexican wages.

The demands of Mexican workers soon encompassed much more than just bread-and-butter issues. Recognizing that their relegation to the bottom of the occupational and wage hierarchy followed from their exploited position as a despised racial minority, Mexican Americans and Mexican immigrants soon began to make demands that reflected this awareness. By the early twentieth century the rhetoric of striking ethnic Mexican workers throughout the Southwest made it clear that they were also concerned about their basic human and civil rights as full-time workers and residents of the United States. Indeed, as one labor historian noted in 1946, Mexican–Mexican American labor strife during the 1930s often "took the form of organized race conflict."[78]

For example, during the violent and protracted mine strikes that ravaged the Arizona copper industry between 1903 and 1917, Mexican American and Mexican immigrant workers quickly expanded their initial demands for higher wages and better working conditions to a larger discussion of the basic human worth of Mexican workers and their families. Led by local chapters of mutualistas such as the Alianza Hispano-Americana and La Liga Protectora Latina, ethnic Mexican laborers from both sides of the border worked together to press their demands for social justice.[79] Labor historians have shown that similar sentiments began to emerge among ethnic Mexican workers in Texas soon after the turn of the century. One, who explored the expansion of militant labor activity among Mexicano workers in south Texas, claims that Tejano and immigrant workers began to make demands combining class and ethnic concerns as early as 1902. According to this study Mexican workers, influenced by the liberal and Socialist ideologies surfacing in Mexico in opposition to Díaz's dictatorship and by the rise of the Socialist party in the United States, attempted to forge lasting unions that combined these strains of political thought with their own tradition of cooperation and ethnic solidarity that had first found voice in the mutualistas. In Texas, the author concludes, "while a strict interpretation of socialist trade union principles did not meet [all] the needs of Chicano workers," union leaders were able to organize Mexican and Mexican American workers by "appeal[ing] . . . to the workers' ethnic and class consciousness."[80]

In California, also, Mexican workers began to demonstrate a growing awareness of the connection between Anglo discrimination against Mexicans and their exploitation as workers. Despite a growing inclination to strike, however, most Mexican American and Mexican immigrant workers continued to make rather moderate demands of their employers. During a short-lived and ultimately unsuccessful strike by Mexican Americans and Mexican immigrant workers in the Imperial Valley in 1928, a representative of the workers' union noted plaintively that "During the year we scarcely work 185 days, of which we acquire the sum of $555 in which we couldn't meet our expenses of alimentation, clothing, house rent, medicine, automobile, and other small exigents." "As you understand," the strikers' spokesman continued (with no small understatement), "we live in the most unhonorable and miserable way."[81] Despite the seriousness of their predicament, however, the striking workers emphasized that they were only making what they considered to be fair demands. "The tendencies of this union," they asserted, "preclude any communistic idea. With due respect for the laws of the country, it will work within its limited sphere of action." Thus, although the union announced its intentions to "extend the bases of the Union . . . for the general benefit of the Mexican element," the strike leaders pledged to work "within . . . legal means . . . and respect the laws of the country so as to deserve in every case all due consideration."[82]

Such moderate rhetoric was to change very quickly during the depression, when a growing number of strikes erupted among ethnic Mexican workers in California, Texas, and other parts of the Southwest. In California, well over 160 major strikes occurred between 1933 and 1937 alone. In Texas, although labor actions erupted much less frequently, Mexican workers also struck in significant numbers.[83] Labor historians familiar with the oppressive conditions faced by ethnic Mexican workers have maintained that increasing militancy among them was inevitable. As one scholar argued in his study of depression-era California agricultural labor, "Since low wages, irregular employment, harsh and abusive working conditions, and an utterly degraded standard of living had been the prevailing facts of the California farmworkers' life for decades, the rise of an agricultural labor movement in the state at the beginning of the 1930s was due to more than a simple desire among workers to alleviate particularly oppressive features of their generally desperate economic situation." In this scholar's view it was, rather, "the product of a gradual realization among Mexican workers, who comprised a majority of the farm-labor force, that only through organization were they likely to mitigate their endemic powerlessness."[84]

The rapid proliferation of multiethnic labor organizations and the emergence across the Southwest of ad hoc coalitions of groups that espoused militant anticapitalist rhetoric speak to the fact that common economic deprivation and social discrimination had stimulated an unprecedented degree of labor militancy among ethnic Mexican workers. As before, most of the hundreds of labor conflicts involving the Spanish-speaking during the depression were initiated and organized along ethnic or nationalistic (Mexican) lines, often under the leadership of local mutualistas. One labor historian observed that "the discrimination which Mexicans . . . periodically encountered as distinct alien minorities . . . had the effect of stimulating them to organize in self-protection. Members of each race tended to withdraw within their own group, in associations whose ties were stronger than those of occupational interests alone." Such associations, he noted, laid the "preliminary groundwork for the development of a 'job-conscious' labor union movement" among Mexican and Mexican American workers.[85]

During the depression the tendency of ethnic Mexican workers to move back and forth frequently from their homes in towns and cities to their work in rural areas helped establish strong lines of communication between urban and rural dwellers. Just as Mexican American and Mexican immigrant workers had long used these informal lines of communication to locate work and exchange news, during this era of intense labor strife they also utilized word-of-mouth networks to keep themselves apprised of the issues and disputes that involved Spanish-speaking workers over huge areas of the Southwest.[86]

One of the earliest manifestations of these trends was in the activities of a group of Mexican and Mexican American agricultural workers in southern California during the autumn of 1927. An opening salvo in what would become a much larger series of labor-related protests that wracked California, Texas, and other southwestern states in the 1930s, these initial efforts of ethnic Mexican workers in the Los Angeles area established an important precedent that would deeply influence Mexican American political and social thought and activism even after the depression ended.

In November 1927 a committee of the Federación de Sociedades Mexicanas, an umbrella organization of Mexican and Mexican American mutual-aid, fraternal, and beneficent societies in Los Angeles and adjacent counties, passed a resolution calling for the immediate formation of Mexican trade unions as a way to combat inferior wages and working conditions in southern California. By early 1928 more than two thousand Mexican American and Mexican immigrant workers had joined together to form the Confederación de Uniones Obreras Mexicanas (CUOM), which was modeled closely after Mexico's largest labor organization, the Confederación Regional Obrera Mexicana (CROM).[87]

At first glance CUOM appeared to be very similar to other labor-oriented organizations that had been established by Spanish-speaking workers in the first decades of the century. Among the main principles CUOM adopted were the basic bread-and-butter demands of all labor unions, but it soon became clear that the union's leaders were thinking about much more than just these issues. Departing from the moderate positions advocated by the Imperial Valley strikers, CUOM's initial rhetoric often bordered on advocacy of class struggle, although its spokespersons were always careful to couch their demands in terms they believed conformed to American law. Thus, while CUOM proclaimed its belief that the "exploited class [in the United States], the greater part of which is made up of manual labor, is right in establishing a class struggle in order to effect an economic and moral betterment of its conditions, and at last its complete freedom from capitalist tyranny," its leaders carefully added that they did not intend to "agitate, nor to spread insolvent ideas." "All that is desired," they asserted, "is to equalize Mexican Labor to American Labor, and to obtain for them what the law justly allows."[88]

Nevertheless, CUOM advanced what was, for the time, a radical set of proposals concerning the social and cultural issues raised by the growth of a large population of ethnic Mexican workers in the Southwest. Significantly, the first of these proposals was that both the American and Mexican governments be encouraged to put a halt to further immigration from Mexico. In essence agreeing with the position LULAC advocated over the next few years, CUOM's leadership believed that they could not hope to improve conditions for Mexicans in the United States unless further immigration from Mexico were severely restricted. Acknowledging the region's deteriorating economic conditions, in May 1928 CUOM's first general convention in Los Angeles adopted a series of resolutions supporting a restrictive immigration policy toward Mexico. "In view of the fact that thousands of Mexican laborers in the United States [are] already suffering want and deprivations because of lack of work," one resolution read, "the Mexican government and the CROM [should] be urged to obstruct and discourage all further immigration to the United States." In addition, citing "the desperate position in which Mexicans in the United States find themselves" (sentiments that the local Spanish-language press had also begun to express), CUOM urged each of its members to write to relatives and friends in Mexico urging them not to come to the United States. Contending that further immigration was "harmful to the working men of both countries," CUOM went so far as to encourage all Mexican nationals who could repatriate themselves to Mexico voluntarily to do so. The labor organization then sent a series of petitions to Mexican President Plutarco Elías Calles, urging him to "limit and regulate Mexican immigration to this country."[89]

Thus to a large degree CUOM concurred with the position on immigration that LULAC eventually adopted in Texas. However, the labor organization differed radically from the Texas group when it came to the question of the maintenance of Mexican culture in the American Southwest. Although CUOM could see the wisdom of limiting further immigration into the region, it had a very different vision of the future of ethnic Mexicans who already resided in the United States. Far from advocating assimilation or even significant Americanization of its constituency, CUOM envisioned a separate, almost autonomous ethnic Mexican community in the states bordering Mexico. Whereas LULAC and other Mexican Americans responded to the oppressive conditions facing their communities by calling for their rapid assimilation into the American political and cultural mainstream, CUOM's leaders seemed to view these same conditions as solid reasons to encourage and foster Mexican ethnic solidarity within the United States. Their position seemed to imply at least a tacit recognition that most Americans wanted little to do with Mexicans under any circumstances, and they therefore turned to a policy that encouraged a form of self-segregation among ethnic Mexicans living in American territory—regardless of their formal citizenship status. Thus, where LULAC and similar groups called for a program of Americanization, naturalization, political education, and the acquisition of English as a strategy designed to facilitate Mexican Americans' eventual amalgamation into American society, CUOM sought to conserve among its members a virtually autonomous variant of Mexican culture in the United States. This commitment was made clear in CUOM's constitution, wherein the workers' confederation pledged

1) To animate by all possible [means] the conservation of our racial pride and patriotic principles; 2) To promote a strong cultural campaign giving preference to the education of our children, for which we shall build schools and libraries as possible; 3) To raise a beneficence fund toward helping our indigent countrymen and to build up or help other Mexican Societies for the establishment of exclusive Mexican hospitals, orphan asylums, alm houses, etc.; and 4) To constitute committees of defense which will have competent lawyers, paid by the Mexican colonies themselves so that these with the help of the [Mexican] consulate can effectively defend Mexican[s] who are put in jail, in many cases by mere ignorance of [American] law.[90]

Such culturally specific demands, made in the midst of a deepening recession and in an increasingly volatile atmosphere of antiforeign sentiment, provided a small indication of the extent to which some Mexican Americans and Mexican immigrant workers had begun to question prevailing notions about their economic role and their political and cultural status in American society. As the Great Depression deepened and anti-Mexican hysteria intensified in the 1930s, other ethnic Mexican activists would extend and refine similar arguments that stood as sharp alternatives to the ideology of the melting pot.

Ethnic Mexican workers also seemed to be strongly encouraged to press their job-related grievances by the inclusionary rhetoric of the new Roosevelt administration, particularly after the National Industrial Recovery Act was passed in 1933. As will be discussed later in this chapter and the next, although Mexican workers clearly placed too much faith in the New Deal's commitment to the principles of labor organization and collective bargaining, throughout the 1930s and increasingly during the 1940s Mexican American and Mexican immigrant labor activists repeatedly used President Roosevelt's rhetoric of fair play to press their demands for better wages and working conditions and for expanded cultural rights.

Historians still dispute the extent of Communist, Socialist, or anarcho-syndicalist influence among Mexican workers in the United States, but it is clear that Communist-affiliated labor organizers did play important roles in contributing to the continued development of a sense of ethnic and class solidarity and in providing support and/or coordination for the strike efforts of predominantly ethnic Mexican work forces in the 1930s. Beginning with the January 1930 walkout of Mexican workers in California's Imperial Valley and continuing through the major strikes that crippled California agriculture in 1933 and 1934, Communist organizers associated with the Trade Union Unity League and, later, with the Cannery and Agricultural Workers Industrial Union supported Mexican workers.[91] In Texas, although Communist influence in Mexican labor organization and action was less pronounced, Mexican American Communist labor organizers, including Emma Tenayuca and ethnic Mexican workers associated with various local chapters of the Workers Alliance, provided strong leadership and organizing skills under particularly explosive circumstances.[92]

Communist labor organizers may have played important support roles, but it was the workers themselves who supplied the drive and commitment to pursue their goals in an extremely hostile and at times violent atmosphere.[93] Throughout the 1930s ethnic Mexican workers' rhetoric in strike actions provided an intriguing mix of Mexican nationalism with the workers' interpretation of idealistic American democratic principles. In a case one labor historian has examined, when cotton workers went out in a strike that eventually involved 50,000 workers in California in 1933, they named their strike headquarters and the streets in their temporary tent city after Mexican revolutionary figures or Mexican cities[94]—yet they made appeals to Americans' democratic traditions and what they hoped was their sense of fair play. They issued circulars in Spanish in which they not only demanded better wages, abolition of child labor, sick pay, and Social Security but also insisted that they were committed to fighting for these reforms without regard to workers' race, color, religion, or citizenship status.[95]

What is so remarkable about the outbreak of such job actions was the similarity of the rhetoric employed by Mexican and Mexican American activists in widely scattered incidents across the Southwest. In California, beginning with the Imperial Valley strike of 1930 and continuing with the strikes that erupted up and down the state until 1934, citizen and Mexican national workers combined their demands for better wages and conditions with an increasing insistence that they should have the same rights as any other American worker, despite the fact that they often organized along stridently Mexican nationalistic lines. The specific causes and intensity of the many strikes that ravaged California agriculture between 1930 and 1934 varied from region to region, but Mexican American and Mexican organizers consistently used appeals to ethnonational and class solidarity to encourage workers.[96] Moreover, drawing on the social networks they had developed over a quarter-century of laboring in the United States, citizen and alien workers often pooled their resources and relied upon one another as they struggled against their Anglo employers. As one author points out in her study of the 1933 cotton strike, ethnic Mexican enclaves served as bastions of "Mexican culture in predominantly Anglo towns which became central meeting places where workers met, talked, sang songs, swapped stories, exchanged information . . . and relaxed." Although Mexican and

Mexican American workers continued to face harassment, intimidation, and violence throughout the depression, "racial discrimination, poor conditions, segregation, and alienation from Anglo American culture heightened their sense as Mexicans" and "served as a unifying force" in their labor activities in California.[97]

In Texas a tradition of paternalistic labor relations, a comparatively repressive political atmosphere, and the huge distances ethnic Mexicans traveled in the migratory agricultural labor stream combined to militate against the level of labor unionism that evolved in California. Nonetheless, ethnic Mexicans there also developed political strategies that flatly rejected much of what LULAC advocated. Thus, even though Stuart Jamieson noted that, in comparison with California and some other areas of the Southwest, strikes in Texas tended to be "few, sporadic, and local," he documented a long series of job actions collectively undertaken by Mexican Americans and Mexican immigrants after 1910. Moreover, with the formation of various Workers' Alliances during the depression, ethnic Mexican workers in Texas demonstrated an increasing tendency to strike and take other labor-related actions.[98]

Ideological Legacies of the Great Depression

The widely scattered labor-organizing efforts and strikes by Mexican American and Mexican immigrant workers laid the groundwork for the gradual emergence of new forms of political analysis and organization in the years before World War II. Building on more than thirty years' experience working in the regional economy and drawing on the organizational skills and political insights developed in local organizations such as the mutualistas and the first ad hoc labor unions, by the mid-1930s Mexican American and Mexican labor and community activists had developed a set of alternative political positions that stood in stark contrast to those offered by the advocates of assimilation. These alternative modes of political analysis among Mexican Americans and resident Mexican nationals were given voice in many ways. In Texas one of the most fully developed refinements of an antiassimilationist perspective during this period was articulated by the Mexican American Communist labor leader Emma Tenayuca and her husband, Homer Brooks. As an early leader of the famous San Antonio pecan-shellers' strike of 1938, Tenayuca attempted to apply the experiences she gained as a militant organizer in developing a theoretical explication of what she and Brooks called "the Mexican question in the Southwest."[99] First published in 1939 in *The Communist* (the Communist party's theoretical journal), "The Mexican Question in the United States" represented an attempt to apply a Communist analysis to the historical experience of Mexican Americans and Mexican immigrants in the United States, but the article was also a synthesis of some of the views that had evolved among Mexican American and Mexican labor leaders after years of organizing efforts in the Southwest. Applying Lenin's and Stalin's concept of a nation as a "stable community of language, territory, economic life, and psychological make-up manifested in a community of culture" to the situation of ethnic Mexicans in the United States, Tenayuca and Brooks concluded that although the ethnic Mexican people north of the border represented an "oppressed national group," they still should be considered an organic part of American society, rather than as a separate nation.[100] Thus although the two activists acknowledged that Mexican Americans and Mexican immigrants had experienced social ostracism and de facto segregation for more than a century, they maintained that "their economic life inextricably connect[s] them, not only with each other, but with the Anglo-American population in each of these separated Mexican communities." "Therefore," they concluded, "their economic, and hence, their political interests are welded to those of the Anglo-American people of the Southwest."[101]

Tenayuca and Brooks's initial propositions led them to elaborate on a fact that had become readily apparent to large numbers of native-born and Mexican-born workers as they worked side by side in the fields and the factories and engaged in the innumerable walkouts and strikes of the 1930s. In their view there simply existed "no sharp distinction between the two groups, either in their social conditions or in their treatment at the hands of the Anglo-American bourgeoisie." The American conquest of 1848, the long subsequent history of racial discrimination and oppression, and the continued economic exploitation and political subjugation of the Mexican people, whether citizen or alien, had effectively rendered the ethnic Mexican population of the Southwest "one people."

Based on this important assumption, Tenayuca and Brooks articulated a position that had been implicit in the rhetoric and actions of many Mexican American and Mexican immigrant mutual-aid and labor organizations since before World War I. They argued that Mexican nationals, because of their "historical rights in th[e] territory" and the fact that United States capitalists had actively recruited them in more prosperous times, had earned the right to work and live in the United States "regardless of their citizenship." Indeed, the two went so far as to demand a virtually open border with Mexico, calling for "the abolition of all restrictions—economic, political, and cultural—and for the due recognition of the historic rights of the Mexican people in this territory."[102]

Tenayuca and Brooks's position on the rights of Mexican nationals in the United States marked an important ideological departure, and in some ways it had even more far-reaching implications for American citizens of Mexican descent. For although ethnic Mexicans' future might be welded to that of other Americans, this did not imply that Mexican Americans should attempt to assimilate into American culture by conforming to Anglo norms. On the contrary, Tenayuca and Brooks explicitly rejected LULAC's melting-pot strategy, dismissing it as a "sterile path." They insisted that Anglo Americans themselves should shoulder the responsibility for correcting the inferior position Mexican Americans and Mexican immigrants occupied in American society. Thus, in effect, the Texas Communists stood the traditional ideology of assimilation on its head, demanding that Americans recognize the contributions of the Mexican people and the value of their culture rather than expect them to assimilate into the mainstream. Moreover, they considered it imperative that Americans be forced to recognize and acknowledge the fact that, for better or worse, their own formal and informal immigration, labor, and business policies and practices had fundamentally transformed the ethnic and class composition of society in the Southwest.

Clearly, that position marked a radical departure from the views most Americans held about what ought to happen to immigrants. The argument served as a clear example of the kind of oppositional political perspective that would be heard with increasing frequency among working-class ethnic Mexican activists in the coming years. Tenayuca and Brooks insisted that Americans recognize that their expectations that Mexican residents abandon their culture when offered so little in return was both repressive and unrealistic. Instead, they argued that Americans recognize and accept the importance of Mexican workers to the development of the region. Indeed, in developing this position, they went so far as to argue that Americans should learn to tolerate the biculturalism that already existed in the Southwest. In pursuit of this goal they called for federally supported programs of "educational and cultural equality" that included "equal educational facilities for the Mexican population; no discrimination against children of Mexican parentage; [and] a special system of schooling to meet the needs of migratory families." More than that, they demanded equal status for "the study of the Spanish language and *the use of Spanish as well as English in the public schools and universities* in communities where Mexicans are a majority; [and] the granting of equal status to the Spanish language . . . in those counties and states where the Mexican people form a large part of the total population."[103]

Although the Communist position on the Mexican question, as explicated by Tenayuca and Brooks, was one of the most extreme options articulated by ethnic Mexican activists during this period, basic elements of their point of view characterized the positions put forth by other important Mexican American and Mexican immigrant activists. Neither communism nor socialism was accepted by the majority of the native and immigrant population even in the darkest days of the depression, but the rhetoric and logic of the militant labor movement contributed to the emergence of important new political alternatives among members of the ethnic Mexican working class.

One of the most important manifestations of the continuing evolution of such alternatives was the founding of the United Cannery, Agricultural, Packing, and Allied Workers of America (UCAPAWA) in July 1937. An affiliate of the upstart Congress of Industrial Organizations, UCAPAWA in many ways continued the struggle to better conditions and wages that these workers had begun in the late 1920s. Breaking new ground in its attempts to form a nationwide union of agricultural workers, UCAPAWA also established important precedents in its efforts to recruit and organize Mexican American and women workers into the ranks of an American labor organization.[104]

Significant in Mexican American labor history for these reasons alone, UCAPAWA was also important in the way it addressed the Mexican immigrant question. In a sharp departure from virtually every previous major American labor union, UCAPAWA from its inception argued that resident immigrant workers had a right to work in the United States and to participate in the American labor movement. Recognizing that Mexican immigrant workers had become a vital part of many American industries, UCAPAWA resolved to attempt to organize the thousands of immigrants who worked in American agriculture, including those who had entered the United States illegally.[105] Although it would be years before other major American labor organizations considered the tactic of attempting to organize undocumented or illegal immigrant workers, UCAPAWA set an important precedent that would be followed decades later by such groups as the International Ladies' Garment Workers' Union and the United Farm Workers Union.

UCAPAWA's immediate influence in the agricultural labor force was short-lived, however, due to the union's decision in 1938 to focus its energies on organizing packing-shed and cannery workers rather than workers in the fields. Nevertheless, the union's philosophy strongly influenced working-class Mexican American labor and community organizations founded in the next several months. Undoubtedly, the most important of these new organizations was El Congreso de Pueblos de Habla Española (the Congress of Spanish-Speaking Peoples). Organized in 1938 by a coalition of labor and local Mexican American and Mexican community activists, the congress represented one of the most dramatic examples of an expanding range of attitudes among ethnic Mexicans on the broad issue of immigration, civil and political rights, and the general status of the Mexican-descent minority of the United States. Moreover, it proved to be a crucial training ground for a generation of Mexican American and immigrant political and social activists. George Sánchez, Eduardo Quevedo, Luisa Moreno, Josefina Fierro de Bright, Bert Corona, and others were all original congress members, and all remained active in Mexican American–Mexican immigrant politics into the 1940s, the 1950s, and, in the case of Quevedo and Corona, into the 1960s and beyond. Moreover, unlike most previous Mexican American organizations, the congress was able to attract the support of a broad range of non–Mexican Americans in their civil rights and advocacy efforts. Largely via contacts made through Josefina Fierro de Bright's husband, screenwriter John Bright, congress leaders gained the endorsement of several Hollywood personalities, including Anthony Quinn, Orson Welles, Joseph Cotton, and Rita Hayworth, and attracted the support of such liberal California politicians as Governor Culbert Olson, state Attorney General Robert Kenney, Los Angeles Mayor Fletcher Bowron, and the Los Angeles County Board of Supervisor's John Anson Ford, all of whom sent representatives to the convocation. Thus although the congress, like UCAPAWA, had a short tenure as an active organization, it in many ways marked a watershed in Mexican American political history.[106]

The Congress of Spanish-Speaking Peoples was originally organized largely through the efforts of Luisa Moreno. A Guatemalan expatriate and veteran labor organizer, Moreno gained early organizing experience working with Latino garment workers in New York City, cigar makers in Florida, and pecan shellers in San Antonio and, eventually, as a UCAPAWA organizer in the Southwest. She and other congress organizers drew on an extensive network of activists among labor, mutual-aid, and fraternal organizations. In 1938 and early 1939 they issued calls to action through UCAPAWA, local chapters of the Workers Alliance in New Mexico, Colorado, Texas, Arizona, and California, and other contacts in the United States and Mexico.[107]

Attracting nearly 1,000 delegates representing 128 Latino-oriented organizations from across the United States and Mexico, the First National Congress of Spanish-Speaking Peoples met in Los Angeles April 28–30, 1939. In many respects the agenda set by the congress was built on platforms that had been hammered out by previous labor-oriented Mexican American and Mexican immigrant organizations since the 1920s. According to the agenda printed by the congress organizers, the most pressing issues facing the conference were education, housing and health, discrimination and segregation, and the complex issues involved in citizenship and naturalization.[108] The platform broke new ground in a number of areas, but the group's most important contribution was its insistence that all Spanish-speaking people—citizens and aliens alike—work together to better their conditions as residents of the United States.

Congress members believed that equality and integration were worthy goals, but for this organization, integration had little to do with the assimilationist program proposed by groups such as LULAC. Rejecting those Mexican Americans' attempts to dissociate themselves from recent immigrants (and by extension, from the working-class Mexican American majority) congress leaders stated flatly that "in all their fundamental characteristics the situations of all three groups are identical. All face essentially the same discrimination—the same restriction of opportunity, the same conditions of employment and living." From the coalition's point of view, although "the problems of the Mexican Americans may differ somewhat from those of the Spanish-Americans [that is, New Mexican Hispanos] and the problems of the non-citizens may differ from those of other groups, . . . these are differences of degree rather than kind." The organization concluded, therefore, that "only the unity of all three groups and the cooperation of other progressive Americans and in constructive thought and actions will bring about positive advances."[109]

From this seemingly simple assertion the congress advanced a political point of view that marked a significant departure from the views espoused by both the Anglo American and Mexican American advocates of Americanization. It colored the congress's positions on all of the issues on the agenda, but it was particularly striking in the Congreso's stance on civil liberties, immigration, and naturalization and citizenship, for, as the "Call to Action" put it, "Here is where our people are most affected." Delegates issued a resolution calling for a congressional investigation into the deplorable conditions facing the nation's Spanish-speaking residents. What made the demands so notable was not that congress leaders raised these questions but that they challenged the very assumptions on which Americans had for so many years based their attitudes toward Mexicans. The congress began by asserting that "the conditions under which the Spanish-speaking people live in the Southwest[:] discrimination in the right of employment, differentials in wage payments, discrimination in relief, lack of cultural opportunities, lack of civil and political rights in many sections, in brief a condition under which . . . the Spanish-speaking people are denied the rights of 'liberty and the pursuit of happiness' . . . are completely at variance with American standards."[110]

But rather than arguing, as LULAC's leaders did, that unrestricted Mexican immigration was primarily responsible for creating and perpetuating these conditions, congress leaders were straightforward, arguing that Americans themselves must accept responsibility for the ethnically bifurcated and increasingly polarized society that had evolved in the American Southwest. It is here that the congress parted ways most dramatically with the advocates of assimilation and Americanization. Indeed, like Tenayuca and Brooks, it argued for what was, in effect, the opposite position. Instead of demanding that Mexicans prove their loyalty to American values, ideals, and institutions, congress members argued that Americans themselves should begin to live up to the high democratic standards and principles they claimed to venerate. Indeed, as they saw it, hard-working Mexican American and Mexican immigrant laborers had already earned the right to an equal place in American society; they insisted that it was "the American people, all of them, [who] owe an enormous cultural and physical debt to the Spanish-speaking people."[111]

In the context of the xenophobia and general assumptions of Mexican cultural inferiority so often expressed by Americans during the 1930s, the congress's direct challenge to the dominant political and social canon of the period was a bold act. Departing from the positions advanced by the most visible Mexican American political activists and hewing closer to the position advocated by the most politically radical sectors of the Spanish-speaking population, the congress proclaimed that Mexican aliens living in the United States had already, in the most profound sense, become American by virtue of their hard work, their sacrifices, and their many contributions to the building of American society. Members readily acknowledged the importance of encouraging Mexican nationals to become naturalized American citizens because of the greater legal protection citizenship afforded foreign nationals. At the same time, however, they insisted that "in every way except the possession of citizenship papers," these individuals were already "as thoroughly a part of American society as the citizen population," and thus were entitled to the same rights and privileges accorded citizens.[112] As Moreno later put it in a speech she would repeat many times in the coming years, "These people are not aliens—they have contributed their endurance, sacrifices, youth and labor to the Southwest. Indirectly, they have paid more taxes than all the stockholders of California's industrialized agriculture, the sugar beet companies and the large cotton interests that operate or have operated with the labor of Mexican workers." She argued passionately that people who had sacrificed, worked in good faith, invested in property and homes, and raised their American children in hopes of bettering their position—in effect, people who had pursued the American Dream—had earned the right to live in their adopted country. As she put it, "a people who have lived twenty and thirty years in this country, tied by family relations with early settlers, with American-born children, cannot be uprooted without the complete destruction of the faintest semblance of democracy and human liberties for the whole population."[113]

Congress members built on these beliefs in hammering out a platform that not only flatly rejected the notion of assimilation but actually called for the protection and expansion of the cultural rights of Spanish-speaking people. Departing from the comparatively conservative views of LULAC as well as from the cultural prescriptions of even the most liberal American proponents of Americanization, the congress went so far as to demand de jure recognition of a bilingual-bicultural society that already existed in fact. Moreover, the congress added what many Americans surely would have considered insult to injury when it justified its position by asserting that the "cultural heritage of the Spanish-speaking people is part of the common heritage of the American people as a whole and should be *preserved and extended* for the common benefit of all the American people."[114] Far from encouraging the Southwest's Spanish-speaking residents to assimilate by conforming to the American cultural mainstream, the Congreso encouraged "Spanish-speaking parents in the home to inculcate in their children a *fuller* appreciation of their cultural background."[115] Indeed, in a resolution that surely would have shocked and outraged the most strident advocates of Americanization ideology, delegates took their cultural demands one step further, calling for "the preservation of the language and cultural heritage of the Spanish-speaking people by obtaining for Spanish recognition and official status alongside . . . English in locations where the Spanish-speaking people constitute an important group, and educational facilities in both languages [as part of] an immediate campaign to wipe out illiteracy."[116]

Conclusion

Although the manpower demands of World War II soon decimated the ranks of the Congress of Spanish-Speaking Peoples, it made contributions to the struggle for the civil and human rights of Mexican Americans and Mexican immigrants that far outlasted its short tenure as an active organization. Because many of its members went on to work in other Mexican American and immigrant advocacy organizations after the war, its legacy would be felt in grass-roots political organizations for the next forty years.

The congress made a number of important ideological contributions to Mexican Americans' and Mexican immigrants' ongoing struggle to achieve social justice in the United States. Clearly the most important of these contributions was the fostering and encouragement of ethnocultural and class solidarity among people who, in the previous quarter-century, had found many reasons to distrust each other. Rejecting the views of those Mexican Americans who advocated the erection of strict boundaries between Mexican immigrants and Americans of Mexican descent, congress organizers chose instead to emphasize the cultural and class similarities of the two groups as the primary basis for organization. Implicitly arguing that barriers between U.S. citizens of Mexican descent and resident Mexican nationals did nothing but ratify the same kinds of invidious distinctions that Americans for so long had imposed on Mexican Americans, the congress seized the initiative and boldly transformed the terms of debate on both the immigrant question and on the broader issues associated with Mexican Americans' own civil rights campaign. By explicitly linking the plight of Mexican immigrant (and other Spanish-speaking) workers to Mexican Americans' own ongoing struggle to gain equal rights as American citizens, it broke important new ground in public discourse on the status and potential modes of incorporation of the nation's immigrant and ethnic minorities.

Congress activists such as Luisa Moreno, Bert Corona, and Josefina Fierro argued aggressively that noncitizen Mexican immigrants had earned an equal, or even superior, claim to the full benefits and responsibilities of American citizenship. In so doing they advanced a position that had powerful implications not only for the struggle for Mexicans' and Mexican Americans' civil rights but for the entire constellation of issues concerning the future of a multiethnic society in the American Southwest. By rejecting the assumptions held by most integrationist organizations that immigrant and ethnic groups should spare no effort in adopting American social and cultural norms and mores once they entered the United States, the congress's platform opened up a whole new set of possibilities for ethnic Mexican political activism, even if discussion of those possibilities occurred largely among the members of the group itself. Although congress activists might agree with LULAC and similar organizations that naturalization and participation in American-style politics were tools that immigrants and ethnics could employ, they stridently insisted that Americans could no longer demand one-way assimilation—Americans would have to start living up to the democratic principles they claimed to represent.

In articulating this view, the congress and similar groups also challenged many prevailing notions about what it meant to be American on the eve of World War II. By skillfully manipulating the rhetoric of American democracy and equality during a period of increasing international tension, the activists associated with such organizations sought to transform mainstream American perceptions about what constituted a proper American. Tapping into a growing public awareness and concern about the implications of fascist expansion in Europe and elsewhere in the world, they asserted that democracy started at home, an argument that would be employed with greater force and frequency once the United States entered the war. With specific reference to Mexican immigrant families, activists associated with organizations like the congress argued that it was time to extend the blessings of American democracy to the ethnic Mexican residents who had in effect already become model Americans through their hard work and sacrifice. Drawing on positions that had first been articulated by many of the first joint Mexican American–Mexican immigrant labor organizations after the turn of the century, activists who shared the congress's vision demanded that Americans recognize that the United States' immigration, business, and labor policies and practices had fundamentally transformed the social and cultural makeup of the Southwest. Such activists insisted that Americans in good conscience could not have it both ways—they could not simultaneously exploit the labor and the goodwill of ethnic Mexican people, deny them any real possibility of assimilating into the social or cultural mainstream, and then expect them not to continue to cherish and defend their own cultural traditions and practices. By persisting in the practice of discrimination and segregation and blocking any real possibilities that would allow Mexicans entrance into the mainstream of American life, Americans helped to perpetuate conditions which virtually guaranteed that the majority of working-class Mexican Americans and resident immigrants would continue to follow lifeways that were considered foreign by other Americans. For Mexican American and Mexican labor and local community activists ranging from those associated with CUOM in southern California to Emma Tenayuca and UCAPAWA organizers in Texas, the so-called Mexican problem was only a problem insofar as Americans refused to take responsibility for their actions. Moreover, they then compounded the issue by blaming ethnic Mexicans for creating an increasingly socially and culturally stratified society. What was radical about this position was not merely that these activists and organizers demanded full civil rights for Mexican American and Mexican immigrant workers but also that they insisted on the recognition and extension of full cultural rights for ethnic Mexican residents as well. Thus, far from contributing to the emergence of an ethnic consensus among the Southwest's Mexican American and Mexican immigrant residents, the depression era helped to sharpen and accelerate the processes of internal political and cultural differentiation and stratification that had emerged during the great Mexican diaspora of the first years of the century.

4   The Contradictions of Ethnic Politics, 1940–1950

It has become commonplace in historical literature to note that World War II marked a turning point in Mexican American history. Most ethnic Mexicans in the Southwest remained well outside the mainstream of American social, cultural, and political life for years after the United States officially entered the war, but the demand for manpower in the armed forces and in war-production industries allowed hundreds of thousands of ethnic Mexicans to enter new, higher-paying occupations and therefore helped open the way for Mexican Americans (and some Mexican immigrants) to improve their position in American society. In addition, many scholars have pointed out that World War II marked a political coming of age of the Mexican American population. Because a majority of the resident ethnic Mexican population were native-born U.S. citizens and thus were strongly predisposed to focus on the American side of their social identity rather than on the Mexican, some historians have argued that a new mentality emerged among them during this period. According to this interpretation the new mentality was reinforced by the United States' entry into the war. As one historian recently asserted,

> The convulsions of the Great Depression combined with new economic and political opportunities during World War II and with the historic discrimination in the Southwest against Mexicans and rising expectations among Mexican Americans to give birth to a new leadership, cognizant of its rights as U.S. citizens and determined to achieve them. . . . Together this generation forged a spirited and persistent struggle for civil rights, for first-class citizenship, and for a secure identity for Americans of Mexican descent. Mexican Americans identified with the World War II slogan: 'Americans All.'[1]

Such statements accurately portray the experiences of a large proportion of the United States' ethnic Mexican population during this crucial period, but they have also distorted our understanding of the war era by implying that Mexican Americans and resident Mexican nationals uniformly developed a new collective mentality and that the political and cultural conflicts which had divided them as recently as 1939 had somehow been resolved. Although thousands of Mexican Americans did begin to think of themselves more as Americans than as Mexicans during the 1940s, thousands more remained deeply ambivalent about their cultural and national identities even at the height of the war.

In some ways this was to be expected. A majority of the resident ethnic Mexican population in 1940 were U.S. citizens, but at least 60 percent of this population were either unnaturalized Mexican nationals or were the first U.S.-born generation of Mexican immigrant parents. These demographic characteristics continued to have profound political, social, and cultural implications throughout the 1940s. Moreover, in the highly charged atmosphere of ultrapatriotism, xenophobia, and jingoism that accompanied American preparations for war, Mexican Americans and other minority groups were subjected to even greater pressures to conform to American norms. As they had during the depression, the most visible Mexican American community leaders and organizations responded by redoubling their efforts to convince other Americans that Mexican Americans were loyal, patriotic citizens. But these activists also recognized that many thousands of their constituents remained profoundly alienated from this kind of rhetoric, and they realized that in some ways they faced an even more daunting challenge in attempting to convince ordinary Mexican Americans and resident Mexican nationals that the high-minded, inclusionary rhetoric of the war was more than just one more empty promise.

This situation was destined to become even more complicated once Mexican immigrants again began to trickle into the Southwest. For more than a decade very few Mexicans had been allowed to enter the United States, but in 1942 the federal government announced the creation of the Emergency Farm Labor Program, which in effect reopened the border to Mexican workers. Although very few recognized the significance of this development at the time, the first modest importations of Mexican laborers that summer signified the beginning of a new era of large-scale legal as well as officially unsanctioned Mexican immigration to the United States. The program also helped reopen the old debates among ethnic Mexicans of both nationalities over immigration policy, their ethnic identity, and their children's future in American society. Preoccupation with other issues kept most Mexican American political activists from recognizing the full implications of the resumption of labor migration from Mexico during the war, but when peace returned it soon became clear that the renewal of both legal and unsanctioned labor migration from Mexico had reopened debates over questions they thought had long since been put to rest.

The Problem of the Second Generation

When the United States entered the war in December 1941, few Americans still considered immigration to be a pressing political question. Restrictive federal policies passed in the 1920s, combined with the dampening effect of the depression, helped quell debate on this traditionally divisive issue.[2] Mexican Americans, however, still considered immigration—or, more specifically, the effects of previous periods of immigration—a vital concern. Among the most obvious of these effects were the various conflicts that erupted between U.S.-born Mexican American children and their Mexican immigrant parents. Commonly referred to collectively as the problem of the second generation (even though they occurred primarily between immigrant parents and what was actually the first U.S.-born generation), intergenerational tensions stemmed from a range of sources, including language differences, disputes over diet in the home, outright rejection of parental authority, and, at the extreme, juvenile delinquency and crime among U.S.-born Mexican American youth.

Although such problems seemed to have emerged suddenly in the early 1940s, observers of the ethnic Mexican population actually had noted similar cultural and generational fissures soon after the first immigrants settled in the United States earlier in the century. For example, in the 1920s Manuel Gamio cited a corrido that provided an clear indication of the conflicts many Mexican families experienced as they watched their countrymen and their children adopt American ways:

Andas por [ahí] luciendo	You go [around] showing off
gran automóvil	In a big automobile
me llamas desgraciado	And you call me a pauper
y muerto de hambre	And dead with hunger,
y es que ya no te acuerdas	And what you don't remember is
cuando en mi rancho	That on my farm
andabas casi en cueros	You went around almost naked
y sin huaraches.	And without sandals.
Así pasa a muchos	This happens to many
que aquí conozco	That I know here
Cuando aprenden un poco	When they learn a little
de americano	American
y se visten catrines	And dress up like dudes,

y van al baile.	And go to the dance.
Y el que niega su raza	But he who denies his race
ni madre tiene	Is the most miserable creature.
pues no hay nada en el mundo	There is nothing in the world
tan asqueroso.	So vile as he.[3]

"El Enganchado" ("The Hooked One"), another popular corrido of the Mexican diaspora, was even more straightforward in its portrayal of the disruptions caused by the clash of cultures in the Southwest. Voicing protest against the erosion of Mexican culture among his countrymen in the United States, "El Enganchado" laments,

> Many Mexicans don't care to speak
> The language their mothers taught them
> And go about saying they are "Spanish"
> And deny their country's flag.
> Some are darker than *chapote* [tar]
> But they pretend to be Saxon;
> They go about powdered to the back of the neck
> And wear skirts for trousers.
>
> The girls go about almost naked
> And call *la tienda* "estor"
> They go around with dirt-streaked legs
> But with those stockings of chiffon.
>
> Even my old woman has changed on me—
> She wears a bob-tailed dress of silk,
> Goes about painted like a *piñata*
> And goes at night to the dancing hall.
> My kids speak perfect English
> And have no use for our Spanish
> They call me "fader" and don't work
> And are crazy about the "Charleston."
> I'm tired of all this nonsense
> I'm going back to Michoacán;
> As a parting memory I leave the old woman
> To see if someone else wants to burden himself.[4]

In the 1920s and 1930s all of the early scholars of Mexican immigration, including Paul Taylor, Emory Bogardus, and Ernesto Galarza, made observations that seem to confirm the main theme of "El Enganchado." For example, Bogardus, in his work on immigrants in southern California, noted deepening rifts between Mexican American youth and their Mexican parents. "Their fathers and mothers are not only not becoming American citizens," he wrote, "but are protesting against becoming such, although they, the children, as native-born individuals are being trained in public schools and in American environments."[5] "Loyalty to Mexico supersedes loyalty to the United States," Bogardus observed in another article. "They hear their elders laugh at a Mexican who becomes an American citizen because American citizenship does not mean anything to a Mexican—even after [becoming an American citizen] he is still treated as a Mexican by Anglo Americans." Mexican American youth, Bogardus concluded, were "stimulated to contradict themselves—at home to act as loyal Mexicans, and away at school, as loyal Americans."[6]

In 1929 Galarza, himself an immigrant who would spend the next half-century as a labor activist and scholar observing and commenting on the evolution of Mexican–Mexican American culture and society in the United States, also noted the tensions emerging among the American-born children of Mexican immigrants, particularly when they entered American schools. "The public schools," he observed, "have a distinct effect on the second generation of the immigrant group."

> The children begin to feel contempt for field labor and disdain for the sweat and grime which permeate the life of their parents. . . . Pride of birth is forgotten and in its place creeps a desire to imitate their playfellows in what appeals to them as distinctly American . . . and while this is going on, they fail to find a secure place in the social scheme of their adopted country.[7]

Zoot-Suiters and Pachucos

Bogardus and Galarza pointed to what by 1940 had become widely regarded by Mexican Americans as perhaps the most pressing social problem facing their communities. They recognized that even though Mexican immigration had virtually ceased during the Great Depression Mexican American and resident Mexican nationals faced the delayed effects of more than a quarter-century of large-scale migrations from Mexico. Nothing provides a clearer picture of how profoundly years of Mexican immigration transformed Mexican American society than the generational profile of the resident ethnic Mexican population in 1940.

Although the Census Bureau's efforts to gain a more accurate count of the United States' ethnic Mexican population in the 1940 census once again fell short, its data do provide a rough outline of the region's demographic structure.[8] The Census Bureau departed from its most recent enumerating criteria by attempting to count American ethnic groups according to their mother tongue, "the principle language spoken in the home in [the immigrant's] earliest childhood." Census data indicate that the Mexican-stock population (that is, the Mexican-descent population excluding natives of native parents) comprised approximately 377,000 resident Mexican aliens and approximately 700,000 Mexican Americans with at least one parent who had been born in Mexico.[9] Population data for California and Texas reveal similar demographic profiles. The Census Bureau's published data indicate that in 1940 U.S.-born Mexican Americans of U.S.-born parents numbered approximately 64,000 in California and 272,000 in Texas.[10] In addition, although the presence of an unknown number of undocumented aliens skew the findings, in California the census indicates a population of at least 134,000 foreign-born Mexicans and approximately 220,000 U.S.-born Mexican Americans of foreign or mixed parentage.[11] In Texas the corresponding figures are 160,000 resident Mexican aliens and 325,000 U.S.-born Mexican Americans of foreign or mixed parentage, respectively.[12] Taken together, and allowing for an undercount of both natives of native parents and undocumented Mexican nationals, these statistics indicate that by 1940 resident Mexican immigrants and their offspring significantly outnumbered the native-of-native-parents cohort of the Mexican-descent population.

In addition to this high ratio of immigrants and first-generation offspring to the native-of-native-parents cohort, the census revealed that Mexican nationals remained reluctant to became naturalized American citizens. Despite recent memories of the repatriation of hundreds of thousands of legally unprotected noncitizens during the depression, Mexican residents of the United States continued to refuse to take even the first steps toward acquiring American citizenship. The 1940 census indicates that more than 86 percent of the 377,000 Mexican nationals enumerated—many of whom had lived in the United States for decades—had made no attempt to become naturalized American citizens.[13] In southern California numerous observers added anecdotal evidence that helped explain these trends. For example, Ruth Tuck, in her 1946 study of the Mexican neighborhoods of Pomona, California, commented that of the unnaturalized Mexican residents she interviewed, "every one" indicated an intention "to stay in the United States permanently and considered it his [sic] country. No one had the slightest desire or intention of returning to Mexico." "Still," she observed, "few in this group had any definite plans for becoming naturalized citizens of the United States." "One gathered," she concluded, "that naturalization would be deferred and postponed until death overtook the immigrant group, still aliens in a country which they had lived most of their lives."[14]

The distinctive characteristics of the resident ethnic Mexican population proved to have important social and political implications during the war years. Although the majority of the so-called second generation of Mexican American youth had been born and raised in the United States, it was clear that thousands remained "caught between two cultures," to use a phrase popular among sociologists of the day. The problem might have been ignored had it remained confined within the boundaries of the barrios, but by the early 1940s public officials and law-enforcement agencies began to view the so-called crisis of Latin American youth as a potentially dangerous social issue affecting the broader community. Indeed, as tensions and uncertainty built up both before and immediately after the attack on Pearl Harbor, the problem of the second generation contributed to a rapid erosion of interethnic relationships that soon reached crisis proportions in southern California.

Among the most important causes of the deteriorating interethnic relationships in the region was Anglo reaction to the emergence of a "pachuco gang" subculture among "second generation" youth. Although the origins of such groups are obscure, several contemporary accounts indicate that some young Mexican Americans and Mexican nationals had coalesced into neighborhood clubs, or gangs, by the late 1920s and early 1930s. These groups of pachucos (sometimes called *cholos*) were characterized by their use of a hybrid English-Spanish slang dialect known as *caló*, the adornment of their bodies with tattoos, and, most conspicuously, by a distinctive style of dress, the zoot suit. Zoot suits were part of a fashion ensemble that included long jackets with exaggerated shoulders, pegged pant legs, thick-soled shoes, long watch chains, and wide-brimmed pancake hats worn over duck-tail haircuts that were then in style not only among many young Mexican Americans but among some urban African American and Filipino youths as well.

Pachucos apparently first appeared in the environs of El Paso, Texas, in the late 1920s and early 1930s. Commonly viewed as the natural outcome of large numbers of ethnic youth coming of age under impoverished conditions, contemporary observers noted that pachucos seemed intent on rebelling against both the world of their parents and that of the American mainstream. The pachuco phenomenon initially attracted little public attention, however, because it seemed to be confined to the barrios. Isolated within ethnic Mexican enclaves, such as Maravilla, Dogtown, El Hoyo, The Flats, Alpine, Happy Valley, Simon's, or Palo Verde in Los Angeles, or in the Mexican barrios of Chihuahuita or El Segundo in El Paso or on the west side of San Antonio, pachucos at first must have seemed to be little more than exaggerated examples of the common stereotype so many Americans had already developed about their Mexican neighbors.[15]

By the time the United States entered World War II, however, official concern about the apparent spread of such subcultural groups had grown substantially. Two events that took place soon after the Japanese attack on Pearl Harbor, the so-called Sleepy Lagoon incident of 1942 and the Zoot-Suit Riots of 1943, dramatically increased the public's awareness and concern over pachucos and over the problem of Latin American youth in general.

The basic outlines of these two events are well known and need only a brief review here.[16] In August 1942 a young Mexican American youth, José Díaz, was found dead near Sleepy Lagoon, a water-filled gravel pit in south-central Los Angeles traditionally used by local Mexican American children as a swimming hole. According to police reports Díaz was killed after an altercation between two Mexican gangs at a party near the pond. On the basis of highly circumstantial evidence the Los Angeles police charged that Díaz, who may have been associated with a group known as the Downey Boys, had been murdered by members of a gang known as the 38th Street Club, and they summarily arrested twenty-two club members on charges of murder and conspiracy. In January 1943, after a sensational and highly irregular trial, an all-white jury convicted seventeen of the defendants of charges ranging from assault and battery to first-degree murder.

In the summer of 1943 another outbreak of violence, the Zoot-Suit Riots, underscored the increasing volatility of ethnic and race relations in wartime Los Angeles. Misleadingly labeled, the Zoot-Suit Riots referred to a period of violence between American servicemen and Mexican American youths that took place between June 3 and June 13 in downtown and east Los Angeles. Although the so-called riots actually were a series of physical assaults by American servicemen—and some civilians—on young Mexican Americans, the events were widely publicized in the local and national press as yet another example of Mexicans' inherent barbarity, hooliganism, and questionable loyalty. Reacting particularly to young Mexican Americans' zoot suits—and apparently to their demeanor or attitude as well—roving crowds of servicemen and civilians sought out young Mexican Americans in theaters, on streetcars, and on the streets of the downtown area and in outlying neighborhoods. No one was killed during the violence, but scores of Mexican Americans were stripped, had their hair shorn, and were beaten by the mobs, only to be arrested later by Los Angeles police officers for disturbing the peace.

Much as the repatriation campaigns of the previous decade contributed to the inflammation of anti-Mexican attitudes among white Americans, the Sleepy Lagoon case and the Zoot-Suit Riots dramatically intensified racial tensions between the Mexican and Anglo communities in southern

California during the war. With local Los Angeles newspapers such as the *Times* and *Herald-Express* and national publications such as *Time* and *Life* all blaring lurid headlines about "marauding Latin gangs" and "roving wolf-packs" of Mexican American youths, it is not at all surprising that existing racial stereotypes were reinforced by the reportage.[17] In addition to the sensational press coverage, official reports as to what had occurred between servicemen and Mexican zoot-suiters almost uniformly assigned responsibility for the riots to young Mexican Americans. Seemingly caught by surprise at the reemergence of the "Mexican problem" in the new guise of the "pachuco menace," Los Angeles law-enforcement officials responded in the local press by painting zoot-suiters, pachucos, and Latin gangs as the predictable results of the primitive and backward culture of the "Mexican colony." Much as the press and local officials had inflamed public opinion in the early 1930s by charging Mexican residents with everything from innate immorality to genetically determined mental retardation, similar charges were raised in the explosive atmosphere of a nation at war.

Perhaps the most egregious example of the new xenophobia directed toward Mexicans in southern California was the infamous report issued in 1943 by the so-called Foreign Relations Bureau of the Los Angeles County Sheriff's Department. Written by Lt. Ed Duran Ayres, the "Report on Mexicans" built and elaborated on stereotypes of Mexicans that were by then well over a century old. In the report Ayres developed an elaborate sociobiological description of Mexicans' innate proclivities. Contending, among other things, that Mexicans were naturally disposed to violence, with biological urges "to kill, or at least to let blood," he traced this supposedly instinctive tendency to their alleged descent from "Asiatic nomads" and to the predominance of "Indian blood" in their racial composition. In Ayres's view, "utter disregard for the value of life" had been universal throughout the Americas among the Indian population, which, he concluded, "of course is well known to everyone."[18]

Although such charges against Mexican Americans were not at all new or unusual, in the tense atmosphere of the months after Pearl Harbor any discussion of a group's un-Americanness could quickly acquire more threatening connotations. Already jittery from the colossal surprise of the Japanese attack on the American fleet, many Americans were quick to imagine internal enemies bent on sabotaging the Allied war effort. Consequently, Mexican American youngsters had been subject to harassment and illegal searches by Los Angeles law-enforcement officials for months before the outbreak of the "riots."[19] After the dramatic Sleepy Lagoon trials and later, during the Zoot-Suit Riots, many journalists and public officials began to use even harsher rhetoric in criticizing Mexican youngsters. Indeed, some zealots went so far as to portray the Sleepy Lagoon and Zoot-Suit incidents as examples of Communist "agitation, conspiratorial intrigue, and adroit manipulation of human relationships," designed to subvert the Allied war effort.[20]

By late summer rhetoric had become so heated that police officials and journalists were no longer content with merely lambasting the zoot-suiters and pachucos themselves. They now directed their attention to those Mexican Americans who attempted to come to the defense of the Sleepy Lagoon defendants and zoot-suiters who had been caught in police dragnets. Charging that Mexican American civil rights activists were fostering "disrespect for law and order, and the economic system it [sic] protects," officials such as Los Angeles Chief of Police C. B. Horrall denounced the Sleepy Lagoon Defense Committee as a "Communist front organization" directed by "trained rabble rousers" who had "contributed to the [zoot-suit] conflagration by constantly stirring and fomenting antagonisms through hysterical activities."[21] Similarly, when the California Joint Un-American Activities Committee convened to investigate conditions in Mexican barrios, it was careful to assert that "the Mexican people and Americans of Mexican origin are not under investigation by the committee," but the committee's subsequent actions and rhetoric revealed that Mexican Americans' motives in fact were in question. Indeed, the Tenney Committee on Un-American Activities tended to see virtually all of the events in Los Angeles as part of a vast Communist-directed conspiracy. According to the committee's report,

> the Communist Party press, pursuing the party line on racial agitation, continually fed the fires of racial antagonism by charging that Mexican youth in the United States was being subjected to police brutality, race discrimination, segregation, and humiliation. Communist inspired and dominated organizations were created for the alleged defense of the Mexican minority. Meetings were organized in Mexican districts in Los Angeles, where trained rabble-rousers orated of [sic] police brutality against minority groups, of the unfair treatment of the Mexican and the Negro population, and of racial discrimination and segregation.[22]

Mexican American Organizational Responses

The renewed and widespread ethnic hostility directed toward ethnic Mexicans during the early months of the war initially forced many Mexican American community leaders into defensive positions. Compelled to scramble during a period of intensifying xenophobia, Mexican American civil rights leaders had to be extremely careful about the way they couched their responses to charges of disloyalty. This did not mean, however, that Mexican Americans ceased to press their case for civil rights. On the contrary, Mexican American community advocates soon discovered that in some ways the heightened tensions of wartime could work to their advantage. Keenly aware that the federal government needed to mobilize full support for the war effort, many Mexican American groups quickly employed political rhetoric and tactics that echoed wartime concerns by emphasizing their community's fundamental Americanness, loyalty, and patriotism. If Americans like Franklin Roosevelt and Nelson Rockefeller could utilize wartime rhetoric and appeals to patriotism to argue for racial and ethnic harmony in the national interest, Mexican American representatives could, and increasingly did, utilize the same rationale to further their own political goals.

In California Mexican American responses to the public furor over the Sleepy Lagoon and Zoot-Suit incidents provide clear examples of ways in which Mexican American activists began to manipulate wartime rhetoric in their civil rights efforts. From the time the first organizations and committees were formed in response to the perceived crisis of Mexican American youth, political activists consistently attempted to seize the high ground of patriotism and American unity in attempts to advance their arguments for social justice. For example, Mexican Americans in prominent coalition organizations founded during this period, such as the Sleepy Lagoon Defense Committee and the Los Angeles Citizens' Committee for the Defense of Latin American Youth, aggressively employed rhetoric that emphasized the American nationality of the vast majority of California's Mexican-descent population.

The Sleepy Lagoon Defense Committee was perhaps the best known and most influential Mexican American–oriented advocacy organization to emerge in California during this period. Organized shortly before the 38th Street Club defendants went on trial in Los Angeles, the committee eventually succeeded in getting the Sleepy Lagoon convictions overturned on appeal. The committee proved to be particularly effective because it represented an unprecedented coalition of articulate, forceful Mexican American advocates and liberal Anglo community activists. Among the well-known Mexican American members were Josefina Fierro de Bright, executive secretary of the Congress of Spanish-Speaking Peoples; Bert Corona, another congress member who was also affiliated with Local 26 of the International Longshoremen and Warehousemen's Union; Jess Armenta, a southern California organizer with the CIO-affiliated Laundry Workers Union; and screen stars Rita Hayworth and Anthony Quinn. Among the committee's Anglo representatives and financial contributors were actors Henry Fonda and Joseph Cotton; screenwriter John Bright, Josefina Fierro's husband; actor/director Orson Welles; state CIO President Philip M. Connelly; veteran Communist organizer LaRue McCormick; Jerome Posner of the Amalgamated Clothing Workers Union; activist/author Carey McWilliams, who also had been director of California's Department of Immigration and Housing under liberal Democratic Governor Culbert Olson; Al Waxman, editor of Los Angeles' *Eastside Journal*; and Guy T. Nunn, representative for minority groups on the newly established Federal War Manpower Commission.[23]

Drawing on the kind of anti-Fascist rhetoric that groups such as the Congress of Spanish-Speaking Peoples had begun to develop in the late 1930s, the Sleepy Lagoon Defense Committee set an example that would be followed by other Mexican American advocates during the war years. The committee employed what appeared to be explicitly assimilationist rhetoric that emphasized American patriotism as well as the critical need for Pan-American unity in wartime. The basic premise of the committee's defense of the Sleepy Lagoon defendants was that the boys in question were Americans who, solely because of their ethnic background, had been deprived of their rights and freedom in a manner that was antithetical to American democratic ideals. But the committee also added a new twist to the old integrationist argument by arguing that the fight for the "Sleepy Lagoon boys"—and the wartime quest for Mexican American civil rights generally—represented "an integral part of the welding of Allied unity for the winning of the war," strongly implying that Roosevelt's pledge to uphold the principle of the self-determination of oppressed peoples was meaningless unless it was first extended to America's own minority groups.[24] As one committee publication put it,

> It wasn't only seventeen boys who were on trial. It was the whole of the Mexican people, and their children and grandchildren. It was the whole of Latin America with its 130,000,000 people. It was the Good Neighbor Policy. It was the United Nations and all for which they fight.[25]

The committee also aggressively confronted those who questioned the political loyalties of southern California's Mexican colony. Indeed, committee members often tried to invert the kinds of charges that were being hurled against Mexican Americans. For example, committee publications and press releases insisted that much of the anti-Mexican hysteria surrounding the Sleepy Lagoon case had nothing to do with the Mexicans' disloyalty but was itself the pernicious result of Fascist fifth-column activity in the barrios.[26] In the committee's own highly charged rhetoric, the issue was not merely that of the railroading of several Mexican American boys due to racial prejudice but also, and more important, involved the broader issue of what the committee called the "Nazi logic . . . which guided the judge and jury and dictated the verdict and the sentence."[27] "We are at war!" the committee thundered. "We are at war not only with the armies of the Axis powers, but with the poison gas of their doctrine, with the 'biological basis' of Hitler and with his theories of race supremacy."[28]

Another influential organization that pursued this general rhetorical tack was the Los Angeles Citizens' Committee for Latin American Youth, established by the Los Angeles County Board of Supervisors in 1941 to address the many problems facing the second generation of Latin American youth, particularly juvenile delinquency. Chaired by local Mexican American attorney Manuel Ruiz, Jr., the committee included among its members influential Mexican Americans such as Bert Corona, Dr. Reynaldo Carreón of the Mexican Welfare Committee, Peter Salas of the Mexican Chamber of Commerce, Dr. José Díaz of the Mexican Relief Committee, Luis Díaz Flores of *La Opinión*, and long-time Mexican American activist Eduardo Quevedo, national president of the Congress of Spanish-Speaking Peoples. Prominent Anglo members (mainly in ex officio capacities) included the Los Angeles County Sheriff Eugene Biscailuz, Los Angeles Chief of Police C. B. Horrall, and Monsignor Thomas J. O'Dwyer of the Los Angeles Catholic Archdiocese.[29]

The committee's membership, program, and rhetoric generally reflected both the popular conceptions of the nature of the Mexican problem and the reformist strategy deemed best to address it. Indeed, the committee's political perspective, as expressed in its public statements and positions, was derived from the same integrationist, liberal position that characterized most prominent Mexican American organizations in California and elsewhere during the war. Mexican American members of the committee, however, tended to take the assimilationist rhetoric employed by other wartime groups one step farther. For example, while arguing, like the Sleepy Lagoon Defense Committee, that "raising . . . social and economic levels and promoting the full community integration of this minority is no longer a reformist or humanitarian movement, but a war-imposed necessity,"[30] the Los Angeles Citizens' Committee for Latin American Youth insisted that the general public be made aware that the vast majority of the so-called Mexican youth disparaged in the press were in fact American citizens. But Ruiz, in particular, was not content to let the matter lie there: he went so far as to deny that Mexican Americans even constituted an ethnic minority. During the public turmoil surrounding the Sleepy Lagoon case, for example, he took exception to a series of derogatory articles published in the *Los Angeles Times* and the *Los Angeles Examiner*, which consistently described Eastside gang members as "Mexican youths." "Such a blunder is incomprehensible," Ruiz argued. "The word Mexican denotes a nationality not a race," he insisted, adding that if the press investigated further, it would "undoubtedly ascertain that the alleged 'Mexican youths' involved in the gang fights are American youths born and raised in this vicinity."[31]

Pursuing this logic throughout the growing controversy over Latin American youth gangs between 1941 and 1943, the committee forcefully responded to police and media insinuations that Mexicans were somehow culturally predisposed to antisocial behavior. For example, in a petition to the City and County of Los Angeles the committee voiced its strong objection to the perpetuation of such misconceptions, arguing that "[we] cannot support the hypothesis that the American way of living is the solution to the juvenile delinquency problem any more than [we] could submit that the Mexican way of living would constitute such a solution."[32] From the committee's perspective the key to the problem encountered by the second generation of Mexican American youth lay not in their alleged propensity to violence or their clannishness but in the generally oppressive conditions in which they lived. While acknowledging the tremendous difficulties young Mexican Americans faced in their efforts to reconcile the world of their parents and that of American society, the committee advanced an argument that remains influential to the present day. Articulating an early version of the liberal Mexican American response to charges that Mexican American poverty and "backwardness" derived from the "social pathologies" inherent in "Mexican culture," Ruiz and other committee members pointed to socioeconomic factors, such as underemployment, lack of education, poor housing and health care, widespread prejudice and discrimination, and "the lack of sufficient Spanish-speaking officials in the community" as the underlying causes of alienation and anomie in the barrios.[33] Carey McWilliams stated the essential elements of this perspective most succinctly when he asserted in 1942 that "the root of the problem is not traceable to the mere fact that a child happens to have parents who were born outside of this country" but rather originated in the "social conditions and attitudes which make the child constantly aware of a sense of difference."[34]

The Civil Rights Struggle in Texas

In the early months of the war the civil rights rhetoric used by Mexican Americans in Texas was remarkably similar to that used by their counterparts in California. Although Mexican Americans in Texas did not experience the kind of dramatic ethnic flare-up represented in the Sleepy Lagoon or Zoot-Suit incidents, activists there continued to struggle with a long list of grievances, including deeply rooted prejudice and discrimination against Mexican Americans in schools and other public facilities, exclusion from juries, discriminatory real estate and insurance policies, voting abuses, and, after 1941, disparities in Selective Service practices.[35]

Like their counterparts in California, however, Texas Mexican American activists were quick to recognize the political possibilities the war unexpectedly offered them. For example, as early as December 1941 LULAC's president-general, George Sánchez, began exploring various ways to pressure the federal government to take immediate action to guarantee Mexican Americans' full civil rights, pressure that he would continue to exert for the next twenty years. In a letter to wartime Coordinator of Inter-American Affairs Nelson Rockefeller, Sánchez argued that Mexican Americans were "an orphan people" insofar as the federal government was concerned. Mexican Americans, he argued,

> are without benefit of lobby because of the very nature of their social and economic status. . . . They are . . . segregated and demeaned. Even the descendants of the Spanish colonials, who have belonged here for three centuries and more, are "forgotten people on the other side of the railroad tracks." "Mexican" has become a term of opprobrium, applied indiscriminately to citizen and alien alike, and associated with discriminatory practices in wage scales and employment procedures, in education, in the exercise of civil rights and the like. In effect, many of these people live in a veritable concentration camp.[36]

Sánchez proposed that Rockefeller use his authority to encourage the federal government to create a national Latin American Research and Policies Commission to study these issues and then to develop policy recommendations designed to alleviate such conditions in Mexican American communities.

When Sánchez received no action on this proposal he attempted to increase pressure on Rockefeller by pointing out just how critical these issues were to the Allied war effort. Citing in particular the persistence of discrimination against Americans of Mexican descent in public facilities such as movie theaters, swimming pools, and restaurants (which still commonly exhibited signs stating "No Dogs or Mexicans Allowed"), Sánchez was not shy about issuing veiled threats as to potential outcomes of such practices. "I want to underline the critical nature of the . . . situation facing these people and the urgent character of their problems as they affect national defense and international goodwill," he wrote in a follow-up letter to

Rockefeller in early 1942. "I can't emphasize this too much," Sánchez continued.

> Every day I am under pressure to bring the matter into the open
> for a public airing—a procedure fraught with danger to all con-
> cerned. . . . Personally, I view these tendencies with both fear and
> deep sorrow. These people are fundamentally loyal and well-
> meaning, but after all, they are becoming desperate at a seemingly
> impossible and unjust situation. They are citizens and they resent
> both the conditions with which the environment confronts them
> and, above all, the seeming lack of governmental interest in the
> matter. You are no doubt aware of the fact that this affects not only
> our internal situation but that it is highly significant in our rela-
> tions with the Mexican Republic.[37]

Later that year, in an attempt to drum up support for his proposal, Sánchez expanded his critique in a series of letters to the president of the
American Civil Liberties Union. Pressing home his point about the dele-
terious effect continuing discrimination would exert on the Allied war effort, Sánchez wrote, "These conditions constitute a tremendous drag upon
the morale of some two and a half million people in this area. This is a dangerous situation in its effects upon productive manpower and whole-
hearted cooperation in the defense effort as well as in the possibilities it
presents to subversive elements." "In addition," Sánchez concluded, "the
biggest single drawback to good relations with Latin America, particularly
Mexico, is to be found in the mistreatment of our Spanish-speaking citizens and of the nationals of those countries."[38]

Other Mexican Americans in Texas used similar tactics during the war
to press for equal rights. Indeed, by the mid-1940s it had become quite
common for Mexican Americans in Texas to voice their grievances over
discriminatory treatment in terms of the harm discrimination against
Mexicans did to the war effort. A telegram sent by a group of Mexican
American residents of Weslaco, Texas, to a member of the state legislature
in May 1943 was typical of the skillful use of Good Neighbor rhetoric Mexican Americans employed during the war. Complaining that they, along
with a group of uniformed Mexican American servicemen, had been denied
entrance to amusement parks in both McAllen and Mission in the spring
of 1943, Hector Valdez, Hector Benítez, José Garza, and their friends im-
plored State Representative J. T. Canales to "give us your liberal attention
. . . on behalf of these proud young fighters of Democracy and Liberty
. . . so that we may have conquered those saboteurs who do more damage
at home than abroad."[39] Canales responded in kind, noting in a letter to

Sánchez that "I am almost sure that this is the under-hand work of some persons, who are masquera[d]ing under the cloaks of loyal American citizens, but who in fact are either spies or traitors to our country." "If something is not done to stop this," Canales concluded, "the friendly relations that have heretofore existed between the citizens of our Country and the citizens of Mexico will take a serious turn for the worse and it will certainly endanger our war efforts."[40]

The Bracero Program

Renewing their arguments that they were just as American as any Anglo, Mexican American activists hoped finally to convince both the government and, eventually, the public at large that they had earned a place as fully vested citizens of the United States. Given the enthusiasm with which they enlisted in the American armed forces and the distinction with which they subsequently served in the war, Mexican Americans may well have taken major steps toward overcoming what had become deeply entrenched patterns of discrimination. But as Mexican American political leaders were to discover, the renewal of immigration from Mexico in the early 1940s was destined once again to upset the best-laid plans and strategies of individuals and organizations active in the Mexican American civil rights campaign.

When it became clear that the United States needed to dramatically increase production of food and fiber as the Allies fought to stop Hitler's advances, southwestern employers once again raised a hue and cry about severe labor shortages. Their complaints intensified after President Roosevelt signed the Selective Service Act in September 1940. Soon thereafter, southwestern corporate agricultural and other interests moved to renew the joint lobbying effort that had worked so effectively before the depression. Within weeks such industry groups as the American Farm Bureau Federation, the Vegetable Growers Association of America, the Amalgamated Sugar Company, the National Cotton Council, and others descended on Washington in a concerted effort to convince Congress that the country's war-mobilization efforts would be seriously undermined unless growers were once again allowed to recruit and employ workers from Mexico.[41] Members of the legislative and executive branches of the government resisted these pressures for some months, arguing that an adequate domestic supply of labor was already in place, but once the armed forces began to draft American men in earnest after Pearl Harbor, official resistance to reinstituting some type of emergency foreign labor program began to break down.

Consequently, in late 1941 and early 1942 the U.S. government made its first overtures to Mexico concerning a bilateral labor agreement. Although the Mexican government understandably was reluctant to enter into any kind of labor agreement with the United States without first gaining ironclad assurances that Mexican workers' interests would be protected, in August 1942 the two nations came to terms on the essential elements of what was announced as an emergency—and temporary—foreign farm labor program. Under the terms of the initial agreements, the Emergency Farm Labor Program (soon dubbed the Bracero Program after a Spanish term for farm laborer) was to guarantee the rights of both American citizens and Mexican workers. The exact terms of the program would change during subsequent negotiations, but in general braceros could be certified for employment in the United States only if the secretary of labor officially verified that local shortages of domestic (that is, American-citizen) labor existed and made sure that the employment of braceros would not adversely affect prevailing local wages and working conditions. As for the braceros themselves, the agreements guaranteed that Mexican contract workers would be exempt from service in the U.S. military, that they would not be subject to racial discrimination while in the United States, and that they would be provided certain wage levels, working conditions, food, housing, basic living expenses, and travel back to Mexico upon the expiration of their contracts.[42]

In September 1942 the program began quietly with the transportation of 500 Mexican contract workers from the interior of Mexico to the sugar-beet fields outside Stockton, California. The number of Mexican workers contracted grew steadily throughout the war years, from 4,189 in 1942 to a peak of 62,091 in 1944. By 1947 nearly 220,000 braceros had worked under contract in the United States, almost 57 percent of them on large-scale corporate farms in California.[43]

Announcement of the Emergency Farm Labor Program initially stimulated very little public discussion, even among Mexican American organizations with long records of opposition to immigration from Mexico. This apparently was true both because war mobilization tended to divert attention from the farm-labor negotiations and because the federal government tried to avoid the publicity and the potential for controversy inherent in the recruitment of foreign laborers.[44] Despite the chilling effect war mobilization had on minority dissent, however, it was not long before Mexican Americans began to express their opinions on the reopening of the border to Mexican nationals. Although their criticism was muted somewhat by the exigencies of the war, at least some Mexican American leaders recognized that reopening the border would undermine their renewed campaign to emphasize the fundamental Americanness of their constituents. U.S. government officials did their best to reassure Mexican Americans that the braceros would be in the United States only temporarily, but Mexican American advocates publicly and privately expressed doubts about this as the negotiations progressed. For example, when early word of the bilateral farm-labor negotiations leaked in California in the spring and summer of 1942, representatives of several Mexican American–oriented organizations registered their concern about the labor importation scheme. Among these organizations were the Cannery and Agricultural Workers Union (the organizational successor of UCAPAWA), the newly established Federation of Spanish-American Voters of California, and even the Congress of Spanish-Speaking Peoples. Although most of these groups remained sympathetic to the position of Mexican immigrant workers in the United States, they worried that a renewal of large-scale farm-labor recruitment inevitably would undermine the economic and social position of both Mexican American U.S. citizens and the Mexican laborers themselves. They also were concerned that the renewal of immigration, even under such emergency conditions, would inevitably contribute to the hardening of negative stereotypes about Mexicans held by white Americans.[45]

Such concerns were raised soon after the bracero negotiations were made public. After a series of meetings with Mexican American community representatives in Los Angeles in the spring of 1942, U.S. Department of Agriculture representative Davis McIntire reported to Washington that although Mexican American leaders were strongly behind the war effort,

> at the same time they are keenly sensitive to the low-caste position of the Mexican in American society, resentful of the discrimination against the Mexican, and rather bitter over the long record of exploitation and injustice to which the Mexicans have been subjected in this country. All with whom we have talked were very skeptical of the proposals to import Mexican labor; they seemed to feel that such importation would be the beginning of another period of exploitation of the "greenhorns." If our contacts in the Mexican Colony of Los Angeles are at all representative of opinion in Mexico (and the California Mexican leaders are in close touch with affairs in Mexico and make frequent trips there), then importation of Mexican laborers is a very delicate issue from the standpoint of relations with the Mexican people.[46]

If anything, McIntire underestimated just how delicate the bracero issue would soon become. Over the coming months other Mexican American organizations were even more suspicious of the government's intentions. An exchange of letters between LULAC representatives in California and Texas in the summer of 1941 made it clear that members of that organization were deeply concerned about the implications of renewed immigration from Mexico even before the Bracero Program was officially announced. "Again history begins to repeat itself in the American Southwest," wrote Theodore Chacón, president of LULAC's San Gabriel, California, Council to George Sánchez. "Agricultural interests . . . have [requested] the Immigration bureau to lower immigration restrictions to allow cotton pickers and other farm laborers to cross the border from Mexico." From Chacón's perspective, reopening the border with Mexico could mean only disaster for Mexican Americans who already lived in the United States. "During the last World War there was a similar shortage of labor in the United States," Chacón pointed out, "[and] to remedy this condition over a million Mexicans were brought from the Republic of Mexico." "These same Mexicans and their children have lived to constitute the 'Mexican problem' in the economic, political, and social structure of the Southwest states." In Chacón's mind the only way this could be rectified was to maintain a hard line against a renewal of Mexican immigration. As he put it, "If . . . segregation in the public schools, where begins the education of the American and foreign-born Mexican, an education predetermined to make of him a moral, economic, and social delinquent, is the way the American people have solved the 'Mexican problem,' the more reason, then, why the Bureau of Immigration in Washington should refuse to allow Mexicans now living in Mexico from becoming social pariahs in the United States. Definitively, the immigration quotas and standards should not be lowered to further perpetuate injustices upon a humble, defenseless, and disunited people."[47]

Mexican Americans associated with newer organizations took an even dimmer view of the possible renewal of any type of immigration from Mexico. An organization known as the Mexican American Movement (MAM, originally established in 1938 as the Mexican Youth Conference) vehemently opposed any resumption of immigration from Mexico. Made up of young, upwardly mobile, relatively well-educated Mexican Americans in the Los Angeles area, MAM, like other contemporary Mexican American civil rights and service organizations, adhered to a stridently assimilationist political philosophy, pledging to work "to improve conditions among our Mexican American and Mexican people living in the United States" and to promote "citizenship, higher education . . . and a more active participation in civic and cultural activities by those of our national descent."[48]

Following their commitment to such goals, MAM members apparently believed that immigration from Mexico lay at the very heart of most of the social problems facing Mexican Americans in the Southwest. During the Zoot-Suit Riots, for example, MAM's Paul Coronel rejected the notion that Anglo society was somehow responsible for creating and perpetuating the conditions that led to the problems of the second generation, including juvenile delinquency. Coronel insisted that Mexican Americans had no one but themselves to blame. "We need to recognize our own faults," he argued. "Our parents [have] not encouraged education among our youth. We Mexicans have found it difficult to dismiss our cultural heritage, our Spanish language, our food habits, and the like." As a result, Coronel argued, "The Mexican American population has failed to intermingle with the rest of the American population in social and civic activities. There has been a failure to adopt American citizenship." "Due mainly to the above reasons," he concluded, "the Mexican American has failed to improve his economic and social status."[49]

From MAM members' perspective, the answer to the chronic social problems facing the Mexican American population was clear: Mexican Americans needed to accept what the organization called "the impervious [*sic*] necessity of producing good American citizens of Mexican descent," and they needed to adopt a strict position both against renewed immigration from Mexico and, just as important, against the maintenance of Mexican culture among Mexican Americans.[50] A series of editorials published in *The Mexican Voice* in the fall of 1938 made this clear. "We discriminate and segregate ourselves in many ways," read one. "We shouldn't. We may be darker (yet many of us are very fair), and we may have a different background, but we are Americans! This is our country. Very few of us pin our future [on] Mexico. Our future is here." "Isn't it logical then," the author asked, "that we *should stand for Americanism?*"[51]

Although MAM, like LULAC, tried to temper its assimilationist rhetoric by asserting that "being an American citizen is not denouncing that you are a Mexican," more often than not the organization exhorted Mexican Americans to become Americans politically and culturally. From MAM's point of view, Mexican aliens who refused to take out citizenship papers, particularly those who had lived in the United States for many years, did themselves and their communities a great disservice, a position that was clearly implied in an article MAM published without comment in *The Mexican Voice* in 1940. "Apparently one is better off to be an alien in this country," the author argued, "for aliens are not allowed to work on government projects and, instead, county charities provide aliens and their families food, clothing, shelter, and medical care without work." "All we are doing," the writer continued, "is paying [t]his kind of alien to have more and more children, which he refuses to raise according to our standard of living by not making them attend school."[52] "If you choose to remain [in the United States]," read another editorial, "stay and become a decent American citizen. Raise up our name so that your children will feel as citizens, of this, their country, and not suffer that bad reputation a few have given us." "If you desire to remain here, if your future is here," the *Voice* editor concluded, "you must become a citizen, an American; you can't be a 'man without a country.'"[53]

Braceros and Texas Politics

Although, in broad outline, the debate over the related issues of the Bracero Program and the political and cultural future of the ethnic Mexican population in Texas was similar to that heard in California, the debate in Texas over the use of braceros tended to be much more intense. To a large degree the difference in intensity of feeling about these questions among Tejano civil rights activists stemmed from their long experience in fighting for more restrictive immigration policies toward Mexico. Recognizing that a renewal in the use of foreign labor represented a threat to the chronically underemployed, predominantly rural Mexican American work force, Mexican American activists in Texas voiced some of the strongest protests against the program. At the same time, however, many of these activists were also keenly aware that the wartime demand for labor had provided them with an important negotiating tool—and they used this effectively throughout the war. Mexican Americans in Texas also found themselves in a unique position because of the interest the Mexican government took in the persistence of civil rights abuses against Mexican nationals. From the very beginning of the binational negotiations the Mexican government used the Emergency Farm Labor Program as a bargaining chip in its efforts to better conditions in Texas for both Mexican nationals and Mexican Americans. Knowing that the U.S. government was interested in guaranteeing a reliable source of labor, in controlling incipient Fascist groups in Latin America, and in implementing the so-called Good Neighbor Policy toward Latin America, Mexican government officials pressed for Mexico's interests. Although the ongoing negotiations over the terms and implementation of the Bracero Program primarily focused on conditions for the braceros themselves, in Texas the public debate over the issue touched on a much broader group of domestic and foreign policy issues, including Mexican American civil rights.

The growing interplay between the Good Neighbor Policy, the Bracero Program, and the civil rights of Spanish-speaking Texans was just the latest phase of the Mexican government's attempted intercessions on behalf of Mexicans in the United States. Since the turn of the century Mexican consulates in the United States had often served as intermediaries between Mexican nationals—and American citizens of Mexican descent—and various American government agencies in discrimination and civil rights disputes.[54] Furthermore, as already noted, Mexico's thousand-mile-long border with Texas, the large concentrations of Mexican nationals and Mexican Americans in the Rio Grande valley and south Texas, and a long history of easy movement in either direction across the border ensured close interaction between the consulates and ethnic Mexican residents of both nationalities.

That interaction was destined to increase significantly during World War II. As the Texas economy began to recover and then expand after 1940—especially in agriculture, oil production, and the military and defense industries—manpower needs rose apace. In the agricultural sector these trends contributed to an estimated decrease in the local farm-labor supply of 260,000–300,000 workers between 1940 and 1944 as workers streamed into higher-paying jobs in the cities, were drafted, or moved out of state. Of the estimated 100,000 workers remaining in the migrant pool, some 85 percent were Mexican Americans and resident Mexican nationals.[55]

In California the Emergency Farm Labor Program was implemented with sufficient dispatch that braceros were working in local fields in time for the fall 1942 harvest. In Texas, however, bracero negotiations were rocky. As in California, Texas growers, long committed to maintaining a farm-labor surplus to insure a flexible labor supply at low wages, began to lobby for relaxation of strict immigration policies toward Mexico even before the United States entered the war.[56] But many Texas growers found the proposed guarantees of braceros' rights to be onerous intrusions into the so-called free market. From their point of view the law of supply and demand should be allowed to operate in Texas the way it always had. Consequently, growers' spokesmen lobbied intensively for what basically amounted to an open border with Mexico. In testimony before a Senate Appropriations subcommittee in the spring of 1943 Edward O'Neal, president of the American Farm Bureau Federation, unabashedly argued that from the growers' perspective the "old system" had "worked just fine until the Administration got to fooling with it." According to O'Neal, the Bracero Program "just played havoc with it and messed it all up . . . with a lot of rules and regulations; [guaranteed] wages and hours . . . [and] working conditions and that sort of thing. Where in former years all you had to do was go to Mexico and look at the men who came in and worked under the old conditions . . . they got Mexicans in large numbers to come over and do this work." O'Neal concluded his testimony by arguing that "Mexicans [used to come] to this country without the wages-and-hours agreement . . . by the thousands, were well paid and went back home, their economic status . . . so much better than the average Mexican."[57]

The Mexican government, to say the least, was not impressed with such arguments, asserting that these moves represented a fundamental violation of the bilateral agreement struck between the federal governments of Mexico and the United States. Moreover, the Mexican government was acutely sensitive to a growing public outcry in Mexico about continuing civil rights abuses of Mexican nationals and Mexican Americans in Texas. As negotiations between Mexican and Texas state government officials dragged into weeks, and then months, one popular Mexico City periodical went so far as to charge that the United States, "while opposing the racial theories of Germany, feeds, sustains, and cultivates this racism in its own territories against Mexicans."[58] Facing this kind of criticism and citing Texan recalcitrance in the area of civil rights, in June 1943 the Mexican government took the unprecedented step of officially banning the importation of braceros to Texas, an act that represented, in the words of Foreign Minister Ezequiel Padilla, "a just resentment against the discriminatory treatment of our nationals."[59]

These developments had dramatic—and largely unexpected—consequences for the Mexican American population of Texas, especially when the state government took immediate steps to respond to Mexico's announcement of a bracero moratorium. Forced for perhaps the first time in its history to address the issue of the now explicitly linked issues of the status of Mexican Americans and Mexican immigrants within its borders, the state government took the first halting steps toward guaranteeing at least a modicum of rights to Texas's ethnic Mexican residents. Consequently, after a series of somewhat frantic negotiations with Mexican representatives, Governor Coke R. Stevenson proclaimed in August 1943 that Texas would henceforth adhere to the spirit of the Good Neighbor Policy. The governor also urged all citizens of Texas to uphold a related antidiscrimination resolution that the Texas legislature had passed earlier in the year. On September 4, 1943, the governor also announced that he had agreed to create the Texas Good Neighbor Commission, an agency designed to hear discrimination complaints and to publicize the state's new policy with regard to Latin Americans.[60]

The Good Neighbor Commission's broad objectives, as stated at its establishment, were "to promote the principles of Christ in human relations throughout the state of Texas," "to preserve the honor and prestige of Texas before the nation, before our allies, and before the world," and "to educate

[the] present adult Anglo population on the history and culture of Mexico, on inter-American relations, and on the problems faced by Latin Americans in Texas."[61] With specific regard to the issues raised with Mexico over the bracero agreement, the commission also pledged "to promote friendship, understanding, and respect between Anglo American and Latin American citizens of the community." This, in the commission's view at least, would "insur[e] the continuance of cordial relations between Texas and Mexico." The commission also promised "to investigate fully, in case problems in human relations arise between Anglo Americans and Latin American citizens of the community."[62]

"Wetbacks" and Braceros

In most concrete respects these commitments did little during the war era to alleviate the pervasive discrimination that had been practiced against Mexicans for more than a century. They did, however, have important symbolic value that Mexican American activists used to advance their civil rights concerns in the 1940s and beyond. Taking advantage of the liberal, pluralistic rhetoric inherent in the Good Neighbor Policy and in broader wartime statements of national principles, Mexican American activists in Texas, like their counterparts in California and elsewhere in the Southwest, achieved some gains in the fight against segregation in schools and other public facilities, in the struggle to gain access to higher paying jobs, and, perhaps most important, in their efforts merely to gain recognition as fully vested citizens of the United States.[63]

When the war ended Mexican Americans had good reason to expect that the progress they had made would continue as the United States entered what promised to be a new era of liberalized race relations. The booming wartime economy had opened up to allow Mexican Americans and other minority groups unprecedented access, and although the federal government had consistently dragged its feet in implementing antidiscrimination policies, discrimination in many sectors of American life including the military, defense industries, and some branches of government seemed to decrease during the 1940s. Moreover, with thousands of Mexican American combat veterans returning to the United States after having served their country with honor and distinction, their political spokespersons looked forward to a period in which Americans of Mexican descent might at long last be accepted as first-class citizens.

Unexpectedly, the reinstitutionalization of officially sanctioned foreign labor programs during the 1940s, however, presented Mexican Americans with a new set of obstacles to achieving their dream of full integration. In the spirit of wartime unity most Mexican American community activists had reluctantly acquiesced to the Bracero Program, but they clearly expected it to die after the war. But when corporate agricultural lobbyists successfully convinced Congress to extend the so-called Emergency Farm Labor Program after the war, Mexican American civil rights activists suddenly realized that labor migration from Mexico had once again become a vital concern. To make matters worse, these activists soon realized that the use of bracero labor had stimulated a huge increase in the number of undocumented migrants who poured into the United States seeking work.[64] Indeed, evidence indicated that the flow of undocumented immigration from Mexico into the United States in the late 1940s exceeded that of the 1920s, when the border had seemed open virtually to all comers. As early as 1945 some observers were estimating that the flow of undocumented entries in the United States from Mexico already surpassed the numbers of workers who had entered under the Bracero Program. As in previous periods of large-scale immigration from Mexico, undocumented Mexican workers were induced to come to the United States through a combination of factors, including the lure of higher wages, the blandishments of labor recruiters, and, perhaps most important, the encouragement they received from friends and relatives who had already made the journey north.

Whatever the reason, the Bracero Program clearly contributed to unprecedented population movements from the interior of Mexico northward toward the U.S.–Mexico border and from there into the United States. The U.S. Immigration and Naturalization Service (INS) reported apprehending an annual average of only 7,023 undocumented migrants between 1940 and 1943, but the number rose from 29,176 in 1944 to 69,111 in 1945, to 101,478 in 1946, and to nearly 200,000 in 1947. Between 1947 and 1954 (when the INS claimed to have apprehended nearly 1.1 million nonsanctioned immigrants under its infamous Operation Wetback) an average of more than 500,000 undocumented migrants were apprehended each year.[65]

Most Mexican American political and civil rights activists were appalled that the wetback issue had once again been thrust into regional politics. Having believed that the depression had finally created a situation in which the resident ethnic Mexican population stabilized, they had looked forward to a time after the war when they could begin to implement programs that would facilitate the integration of Mexican Americans and permanent resident aliens into the American mainstream. The apparent institutionalization of the Bracero Program and the attendant massive increase in undocumented immigration presented major obstacles to achieving Mexican Americans' civil rights and economic objectives. Consequently, beginning almost immediately after the war, Mexican American activists across the Southwest began what was to be a long and hard campaign intended both to abolish the Bracero Program and to impose strict new controls on future immigration from Mexico.

As before, LULAC was among the foremost opponents of the Bracero Program and the use of wetback labor. If anything, LULAC's long-standing positions stressing the need for Mexican Americans to assimilate on one hand and to support restrictive immigration policies toward Mexico on the other intensified during the 1940s and early 1950s. The rhetoric of the war fit nicely with what LULAC members had been advocating since the 1920s, so the organization stepped up its use of the rhetoric of assimilation and American patriotism during the war years. An incident that began in 1943 provides a good example of the extremes to which some LULAC members were willing to take this position. Taking exception to the continued use of the term Latin American in the organization's official name, these members argued that LULAC's name should be changed so that its acronym would henceforth stand for the League of United *Loyal* American Citizens. Arguing that it was "ironic" that a "people who have worked incessantly to attain the rights and privileges of . . . American[s], who have labored so diligently to make themselves unadulterated Americans, and who desire so deeply to be accepted as and called Americans without any distinction still find themselves classified as a peculiar type of American." "If the League persists in segregating itself because of its name," the dissidents asked, "how can it expect the general public to feel otherwise?"[66] From their point of view continuing to identify themselves as a minority group could only reinforce the kind of discriminatory behavior by Anglos against Mexicans that LULAC had fought to defeat. As one LULAC member in Austin, Texas, put it in 1946,

> The American citizen of Mexican ancestry is weak because he is a minority citizen. Discrimination will pursue him until he blends with the majority group of this country enough to lose his present identity. This is a discouragingly slow process . . . [but] if we fail to do it, we shall continue to be discriminated against, insulted and abused; and complaining of injustice in the name of democracy will not help us. We shall simply be begging for things that must be paid for. Democracy does not provide for mendicants of this type.[67]

LULAC's position on braceros and wetbacks predictably followed similar lines. Like other major Mexican American organizations active during the war and the early 1950s, LULAC continued to promote fundamental patriotism and Americanism among Mexican Americans even while it advocated Americanization and naturalization for the resident alien population. Given the organization's continuing emphasis on what it termed assimilation, it is not surprising that much of LULAC's official position on the Bracero Program and illegal immigration in the 1940s rested on its long-stated policy stressing the fundamental distinctions between citizens and aliens. Arguing that the "avalanche of illegal Mexican labor signifies the lowering of wage standards almost to a peonage level and will force thousands of native born and naturalized Americans to uproot their families, suspend the education of their children and migrate to other states in search of a living wage," LULAC went on record as opposed to the Mexican farm-labor programs, passing resolutions to that effect in 1942, 1944, and 1953.[68] With regard to the large and growing resident alien population, LULAC continued to advocate Americanization—primarily through education (emphasizing the acquisition of English) and citizenship training— as the only proper long-term strategy. To this end, by 1946 LULAC had initiated a small number of citizenship and English-language classes for Mexican aliens in Texas.[69]

Although LULAC was the most visible Mexican American organization involved in the battle against the use of undocumented migrant labor and the continuation of the Bracero Program, George Sánchez of the University of Texas probably formulated and advanced the most sophisticated arguments concerning these issues. Already a veteran of more than twenty years of activism on behalf of the ethnic Mexican minority of the United States, by the mid-1940s Sánchez had come to believe that the use of bracero and wetback labor represented the most serious economic, political, and cultural threat Mexican Americans faced. From Sánchez's point of view Mexican immigrants exacerbated virtually any problem Mexican Americans confronted in their everyday lives. For example, in 1948 Sánchez wrote to his friend Ernesto Galarza about the negative economic impact Mexican nationals were exerting on the Mexican American population. "As you know," Sánchez wrote, "the root of much of the evil as regards 'Mexicans' in the United States stems from the fact that, just across the border, there is a reservoir of cheap labor that growers in the United States can tap at will." "The alien worker," he continued, "becomes, in effect, a strike-breaker or 'scab' who is used as a potent club to prevent the 'Mexican' already here from improving his lot."[70] "I am firmly convinced," he added a few months later, "that unless we stop the wetback, we might just as well throw in the sponge on practically everything else except political action."[71]

In 1949 Sánchez expanded his argument by pointing out to an American Federation of Labor official that undocumented workers were not just displacing Mexican Americans in agriculture, but were also taking jobs "in the railroads, smelters, urban jobs [and] factories. Most of them work under conditions that border on peonage at dismally low wage rates." "More often than not," he asserted, "each wetback displaces an entire resident family and causes those displaced persons to become migrants [and] inhabitants of the slums."[72] Sánchez was even more concerned about the long-term cultural impact that unrestricted Mexican immigration would have on the United States' ethnic Mexican population. Quoted in a 1951 *New York Times* article provocatively entitled "Peons in West Lowering Culture," Sánchez averred that, "from a cultural standpoint, the influx of a million or more wetbacks a year transforms the Spanish-speaking people of the Southwest from an ethnic group which might be assimilated with reasonable facility into what I call a culturally indigestible peninsula of Mexico. The 'wet' migration tends to nullify processes of social integration going back 300 or 350 years, and I would say at the present time has set the whole assimilation process back at least twenty years."[73]

Sánchez hoped to force action on these questions by exposing the abuses inherent in the use of bracero and illegal alien labor. Consequently, in 1947 he began to plan a series of studies he believed would ultimately swing public opinion on these issues. His efforts eventually resulted in the publication or public delivery of a series of long articles co-authored by Lyle Saunders, Olen Leonard and himself between 1949 and 1951.[74] Marshaling a team that conducted extensive field research in the lower Rio Grande Valley in 1948 and 1949, Sánchez and his colleagues developed what they believed to be an ironclad case against the use of imported Mexican labor in the region—and by extension, in the Southwest as a whole.

Each of the reports produced during this period had a slightly different focus and emphasis, but collectively Sánchez, Saunders, and Leonard argued that illegal alien labor and, to a lesser extent, bracero labor harmed Mexican American workers in three major areas. The first, of course, concerned the negative economic effects of these labor practices. Employing a series of arguments that had first been heard among Mexican Americans during World War I, the researchers argued that the use of Mexican labor virtually guaranteed that the majority of working-class Mexican Americans would continue to live in poverty, because foreign laborers tended to depress wages, undercut unionization efforts, and posed serious health risks to the communities in which they settled. As serious as these threats were, the research team argued that the fact that Mexican immigrant labor retarded assimilation and helped perpetuate ethnic antagonisms toward ethnic Mexicans represented far more menacing long-term problems. As Saunders put it in a draft of the "Lower Rio Grande Report,"

> It is something of an understatement to point out that the wetback hardly represents the best in Mexican culture. Being poor, unedu-cated, unskilled, and underfed, and frequently, unclean, he has little to endear him to a people who highly value material success, knowledge, skills, good health and cleanliness. And since he speaks Spanish, looks like the native Spanish-speaking population, and ob-viously has many things in common with them, it is quite natural for the Anglo to lump them all together in his thinking and to as-cribe to all the characteristics of some.[75]

Although Sánchez, Saunders, and Leonard were roundly criticized by both Anglos and some Mexican Americans in Texas for the thrust and wording of their reports, their work reflected the tenor of mainstream Mexican American criticism of the use of bracero and undocumented Mex-ican labor in the late 1940s and early 1950s.

Alternative Positions

Although most mainstream Mexican American civil rights activists turned a jaundiced eye toward the renewal of the Mexican immigration contro-versy during the 1940s, closer analysis of the period suggests that a much broader range of political opinion on the question persisted in ethnic Mex-ican communities of the Southwest throughout this period. An energetic and expansive patriotic rhetoric emphasizing Americanism dominated po-litical discourse of the period, but Mexican Americans nevertheless contin-ued to maintain strongly divergent views about the significance of renewed immigration from Mexico. Even though the atmosphere of war muted eth-nic dissent, no amount of ideological pressure could eradicate the sense among many ethnic Mexicans that they were not yet accepted as Ameri-cans.

It is also important to remember that Mexican residents were not mo-tivated only by the negative experiences of their lives—many chose to maintain certain cultural and social boundaries that by their very nature served as barriers to the kind of assimilation Americans traditionally pre-scribed for immigrant groups. With their perceptions distorted by deeply ingrained ethnocentrism and national chauvinism, many Americans in the Southwest simply found it impossible to recognize that a large and growing segment of their society apparently had no intention of abandoning its own distinct cultural practices in favor of those which Anglo Americans considered to be so much more superior.[76]

Moreover, blinded by an uncritical acceptance of the ideology of assimilation, many Americans failed to recognize the extent to which U.S. immigration and labor policies had contributed to the development of a parallel society in the Southwest. Complete with a complex and growing infrastructure of diverse small businesses, owner-occupied homes, restaurants, bars, bordellos, newspapers, radio stations, record shops and recording studios, and various organizations and associations, this parallel society seemingly had emerged out of nowhere. Replenished by influxes of new immigrants, the hybrid society reflected the persistence and growth of a distinct Mexican–Mexican American culture within the political boundaries of the United States. Of course, continuous exposure to elements of American popular culture powerfully influenced the evolution of this syncretic culture, but the fact remained that significant numbers of ethnic Mexicans in the 1940s and 1950s showed no signs of abandoning the folkways, customs, and religious and linguistic practices that made their neighborhoods and communities distinct from the typically American communities which surrounded them. With all the elements of these insular communities in place, it is not at all surprising that so many ethnic Mexicans apparently felt so little need to abandon their cultural practices in the United States. To them, compulsory Americanization, particularly in the ways it traditionally had been prescribed, was largely irrelevant to their daily lives.

The activities of some oppositional Mexican American groups during the early years of World War II provide good examples of how these alternative cultural sensibilities played themselves out in the political arena. Although the political atmosphere of the period made it difficult, if not impossible, for Mexican American community activists to advocate immigrants' rights to the extent, for instance, that the Congress of Spanish-Speaking Peoples had in previous years, at least some Mexican Americans made gestures in that direction during the war. Not surprisingly, Mexican Americans associated with CIO-affiliated unions were particularly active in this regard. As mentioned previously, in both California and Texas in the late 1930s the most active and militant Mexican American and Mexican immigrant political advocates often came from the ranks of CIO unions. Though military conscription cut into the ranks of these unions during the war, it was at this time that Mexican Americans gradually began to gain lower-level leadership positions in them. In California, in addition to such long-time labor leaders as Bert Corona and Luisa Moreno, many other Mexican American activists were influential in other local labor organizations. These included Balt Yanez, Gilbert Anaya, and Antonio Ríos of the Steelworkers; Jess Armenta of the Transportation Workers; Armando Dávila of the Furniture Workers; Frank López of UCAPAWA; and Rosendo Rivera of the Electrical Workers, who also became president of the Congress of Spanish-Speaking Peoples during the war.[77]

The emergence of such individuals in the trade union movement during the war significantly influenced the positions on the immigration question subsequently adopted by working-class Mexican American activists. As in the 1930s, union organizing experience helped to train a different cohort of local activists concerned with Mexican American and Mexican immigrant issues. Just as important, the mutual cooperation between citizens and nationals in such organizations helped to promote discussion of alternative positions on ethnic political action and the status of immigrants in American society. The alternatives discussed were similar to those first advanced by groups such as CUOM, UCAPAWA, and the Congress of Spanish-Speaking Peoples.

Signs that Mexican American and Mexican immigrant activists were continuing to explore such alternatives could be seen in the earliest stages of war mobilization. In 1941, for example, the CIO in Los Angeles created a Committee to Aid Mexican Workers, largely as a result of the initiative taken by local Mexican American trade unionists. Although the committee was short-lived, its creation marked a continuation of the kinds of concerns that UCAPAWA and the Congress of Spanish-Speaking Peoples had tried to advance in the 1930s. In addition to its basic representation of Spanish-speaking workers, the committee also played an important role in advocating the rights of ethnic Mexican workers (regardless of citizenship) and in providing war-industry job training, English-language classes, and citizenship and naturalization counseling. Committee members also played strong supporting roles in a number of civil rights campaigns during the war, ranging from the defense of the Sleepy Lagoon defendants and victims of the Zoot-Suit Riots to struggles against housing discrimination and police brutality.[78]

One of the strongest examples of Mexican American support for noncitizen workers, however, immediately followed the United States' entry into the war. The federal Office of Production Management acknowledged a severe labor shortage and thus announced in January 1942 the abolition of legal barriers "to the employment of aliens in any factories having war contracts." Nevertheless, many employers in defense industries continued to refuse to hire resident Mexican aliens, no matter how long they had lived in the United States.[79] Consequently, the agenda of a meeting called by Mexican American union activists later that winter to discuss continuing discrimination against Mexican American workers was quickly expanded to include discussion of the employment of Mexican nationals in war-related industries. During the meeting Bert Corona, an activist associated with the Longshoremen's Union, a founding member of the Congress of Spanish-Speaking Peoples, and a member of the Los Angeles Citizens' Committee for Latin American Youth, argued that the committee should support the proposition that Mexican aliens be allowed to work in the U.S. defense industry. Protesting that long-term resident Mexican aliens were being illegally denied jobs in war-related industries, Corona suggested that industries "with the largest number of openings" be strongly encouraged to "launch [job recruitment] campaigns in . . . Mexican communities through the Spanish-language press, Spanish radio programs and billboards in the Spanish language to . . . fill openings in our production effort."[80]

Corona's actions provide an important indication that at least some Mexican American activists continued to work on behalf of Mexican immigrant workers even during the pressure-packed first months of the war. Obviously influenced by his work with the Congress of Spanish-Speaking Peoples, Corona based his advocacy of immigrants' rights on his belief that long-term resident aliens had earned the right to work in the United States. Moreover, Corona argued forcefully that the issue of the welfare of the resident alien population was integrally tied to the civil rights and welfare of Mexican Americans. From his point of view, Mexican Americans should consider discriminatory practices against Mexican nationals as a direct threat to American citizens of Mexican descent as well.

Other Mexican American activists seemed to be influenced by the logic of this position. For example, even Los Angeles attorney Manuel Ruiz, who generally espoused strongly assimilationist positions in his capacity as chairman of the Los Angeles Committee for Latin American Youth, added his protests against hiring practices that discriminated against Mexican nationals. Consequently, in April 1942 Ruiz sent a letter to the California state commissioner of labor in which he decried the "deplorable" lack of local compliance with President Roosevelt's recently announced Executive Order 8802, which prohibited discrimination in war industries based on "race, creed, color, or national origin." Demanding an immediate forceful response from the labor commissioner, Ruiz argued that job discrimination against "aliens of Mexican extraction" was "contrary to the spirit of the proclamation of the president of the United States."[81] In November of that year, the committee pressed its protest farther, requesting that the mayor of Los Angeles make every effort to enforce existing policy on nondiscrimination against citizens and aliens of Mexican extraction.[82]

Significantly, within a very short time Mexican American activists began to extend the same kind of support voiced for resident Mexican nationals to braceros who had begun to enter the local work force in agriculture and, to a lesser extent, in the railroad industry. Although most Mexican American advocacy organizations were at best lukewarm in their support of the Bracero Program, on several occasions Mexican American representatives on the newly renamed Los Angeles Coordinating Council on Latin American Youth took action in support of braceros whose rights or contracts had been violated while they were working in the United States. In one case, veteran Mexican American activist Eduardo Quevedo, president of the Congress of Spanish-Speaking Peoples, personally intervened on behalf of 110 Mexican contract railroad workers who quit their jobs in a dispute over violations of their contracts.[83] In terms very similar to those used by the congress in its activities on behalf of Mexican aliens, Quevedo proved to be an eloquent spokesman for a position that in many ways ran counter to the prevailing ideological currents of World War II. While testifying before a U.S. Senate subcommittee, he argued that Mexican Americans and Mexican immigrants together had earned the right to work and live in the United States and that they deserved respect, consideration, and equal treatment for their efforts. Speaking on behalf of both citizens and aliens of Mexican descent, he told the subcommittee, "We want to assume all our responsibilities and obligations to our government; we want to do our duty. . . . We do not want any special privileges whatsoever. We do not even want a job, or feel we are entitled to a job, just because we happen to be of a certain racial extraction." Quevedo concluded, however, by asserting that "inasmuch as we accept our duties and responsibilities as Americans, we do not want to be deprived of a job on account of our ancestry or national origin or race."[84]

Conclusion

Although these disparate responses represented the opinions of only a small number of Mexican Americans in California during the war, the positions they adopted on the related issues of the resident alien population and, after 1942, on the status of braceros in the United States indicated that much of the spirit of cooperation between Mexican Americans and Mexican immigrants evident during the depression continued into the 1940s. Despite the intense pressure to disavow conflicting ethnic or national loyalties during the war, some intrepid Mexican American activists apparently believed that the issue had become far too complex for such simple and unambiguous ideological positions.

Nevertheless, the view that unnaturalized Mexican nationals represented a threat to the social and political position of Mexican American citizens was increasingly influential among most Mexican American groups during the war. Reflecting the ideological atmosphere of wartime America, as well as the effects of the higher levels of education, gradual upward mobility, and the unmistakable cultural assimilation of some members of Mexican American society, the view was widely publicized by groups such as the Sleepy Lagoon Defense Committee and MAM and by quasi-official agencies such as the Los Angeles Committee for Latin American Youth.

Ironically, it would take the reopening of the border to Mexican immigrant labor in 1942 to jar Mexican American activists on both sides of the issue into renewed awareness that previous periods of immigration had created a large subpopulation of Mexican Americans for whom Americanism and assimilation had little appeal. Although working-class and ethnically oriented organizations such as the Congress of Spanish-Speaking Peoples and UCAPAWA had recognized this development during the depression, by the mid-1940s even assimilationist groups were compelled to rethink their positions on the problems facing the U.S.-born children of earlier immigrants. With the establishment of the Emergency Farm Labor Program, these issues came into even sharper relief as political activists once again faced coming to some hard decisions about the significance of the distinctions that existed between themselves, the long-term resident alien population, and newcomers from Mexico.

Most Mexican Americans clearly opposed the renewal of mass labor migrations from Mexico, but many expressed their ambivalence on this complex question by attempting to defend the rights of Mexican nationals already in the country and, in some cases, by coming to aid of newly arrived braceros. In the midst of the war, such paradoxical views necessarily remained the position of only a courageous minority, but as Mexican Americans and Mexican immigrants once again became the target of political repression in the early 1950s, Mexican American public opinion on these issues would undergo a remarkable transformation.

5   Ethnic Politics, Immigration Policy, and the Cold War

World War II appeared to mark a significant victory for Mexican American activists and organizations that had pursued an integrationist civil rights strategy. Shrewdly manipulating wartime rhetoric during a period in which discussions of human rights and the self-determination of peoples dominated both domestic and international political discourse, Mexican American civil rights activists had achieved unprecedented political leverage. With tens of thousands of Mexican American combat veterans returning to their homes, Mexican American community leaders in the Southwest had every reason to expect to push their civil rights demands farther in the 1950s.

However, the continuation of the Bracero Program and the reemergence of the so-called wetback problem seemed to threaten virtually all of the gains Mexican American leaders had fought so hard to attain in the 1940s. With Mexican immigrant workers pouring into the Southwest, Mexican American political advocates and organizations worried that, like previous periods of large-scale migration from Mexico, this one would undermine the limited economic, social, and political opportunities Mexican Americans had available to them. Consequently, soon after the war ended most major Mexican American organizations redoubled their efforts to win repeal of the bracero agreements and to convince Congress to impose strict new limits on future immigration from south of the border. Although they may well have sympathized with unfortunate immigrants who entered the country seeking only to make a living, most of the Mexican Americans who were active in public life insisted that the rights of American citizens had to come first.

Not all Mexican Americans viewed the renewed controversy over Mexican immigration exactly in this light, however. A small but growing number of Mexican Americans had begun to argue that Mexican immigrants' plight in the United States was closely linked to Mexican Americans' own political struggles. From their perspective the growing controversy over legal and illegal Mexican immigrants was diverting attention from the true source of Mexican Americans' depressed position—the persistence of discriminatory policies and practices that allowed the exploitation of Mexican Americans and other ethnic minorities in American society to continue.

Although this point of view remained well outside the mainstream of Mexican American public opinion in the 1940s, arguments supporting it resonated with more people in the 1950s, particularly after new federal immigration and naturalization laws were passed in 1950 and 1952. The laws were not drafted specifically to deal with the new Mexican problem of the 1950s, but Mexican Americans could not help noticing that ethnic Mexican residents of both nationalities once again seemed to be bearing the brunt of the government's new restrictive immigration and antisubversive policies.

This new awareness contributed to a gradual yet unmistakable shift in the political perspectives of many Mexican Americans. As the repressive and discriminatory aspects of such laws as the Internal Security Act of 1950 and the McCarran-Walter Act of 1952 became clear and as Mexican Americans watched federal agents engage in massive sweeps of their neighborhoods during the so-called Operation Wetback in 1954, more and more of them began to realize how closely their own civil liberties were tied to the legal and political status of Mexican immigrants. Consequently, much as they had reacted to what they considered the scapegoating of Mexicans during the Great Depression, many veteran and new community activists came to see the mass deportations, coerced repatriations, and breakup of Mexican American families as symptoms of a much larger system of race and class exploitation. In the face of a growing impression that the government's actions were also designed to rid the nation of vocal Mexican American and Mexican immigrant labor leaders, Mexican American and Mexican immigrant advocates began to fight back.

The Bracero Program and the Wetback Issue

As the apprehensions of undocumented Mexican workers continued to rise dramatically in the early 1950s, Mexican American community leaders and civil rights organizations intensified their protests against illegal immigration and the continued use of bracero labor. LULAC remained the most visible of the Mexican American organizations to press this case after the war, but by the late 1940s other groups had begun to enter the fray.

The most aggressive of these new organizations was the American G.I. Forum of Texas. It was founded by a group of Mexican American veterans in 1949 in response to an unusual case of discrimination in the small town of Three Rivers, Texas. When a funeral parlor refused to bury the remains of Mexican American veteran Félix Longoria in the local community cemetery because the dead soldier was a "Mexican," a group of veterans, led by Corpus Christi physician Hector P. García, organized the G.I. Forum in protest. Enlisting the aid of then-Senator Lyndon B. Johnson, García and the G.I. Forum ultimately arranged to have Longoria's remains interred with full military honors in Arlington National Cemetery.[1]

After the infamous Three Rivers Incident the G.I. Forum expanded quickly throughout Texas and other states in the Southwest, drawing its membership primarily from Mexican American veterans of World War II. By the early 1950s it had established a reputation as one of the most effective Mexican American advocacy organizations in the nation. Although the forum, like LULAC, maintained that it was a nonpolitical association, it was active in political issues from the outset.

Like the older Texas group, the G.I. Forum considered the Mexican immigration question to be the most important political and social issue facing Mexican Americans. Thus soon after its establishment the forum undertook a broad-based campaign to convince Congress to end the Bracero Program and to impose strict new regulations on future immigration from south of the border. Arguing along lines similar to those previously advanced by other anti-bracero groups, members of the forum conducted policy research, testified before congressional committees, and otherwise actively campaigned against the Bracero Program and illegal immigration. For example, in 1951 the forum adopted resolutions that urged more stringent regulation of the "wetback tide" and commended the Immigration and Naturalization Service (INS) for its efforts in deporting illegal aliens.

The forum received far greater publicity on the immigration issue in 1953, however, after it published (along with the Texas State Council of the American Federation of Labor) a broadside against undocumented workers entitled *What Price Wetbacks?*[2] Arguing that illegal immigration represented "the fundamental problem facing the Spanish-speaking population of the Southwest," it issued a blistering critique of government and business policies and practices that encouraged clandestine labor migration into the United States. Moreover, breaking new ground among Mexican American civil rights groups, the forum advocated the passage of specific legislative measures rather than just voicing abstract opposition to undocumented migration from Mexico. In 1953 the organization advocated many of the same immigration reform proposals that Congress ended up debating and passing more than three decades later, including: "enforceable pen-

alt[ies] for harboring or aiding an alien, . . . confiscation of vehicles used
to transport aliens, and . . . enforceable penalt[ies] for the employment of
illegal aliens."[3] With regard to the Bracero Program itself, the forum, while
acknowledging that "genuine labor shortage[s] may exist and that it may
be necessary to continue to contract alien labor in limited numbers," voiced
its unwavering opposition to the use of braceros whenever they displaced
American citizens.[4]

The American G. I. Forum, like LULAC, argued strongly that civil rights
efforts must be focused on U.S. citizens of Mexican descent. Much like
LULAC during the 1930s, forum members argued that unless Mexican
American organizations concentrated their efforts on improving conditions for the existing resident population it would remain difficult, if not
impossible, to achieve their stated goals. As a historian of the organization argued, "The Forum sincerely believed that the native Mexican American came first and priority lay with his welfare. If the bracero or *mojado*
("wet one" or wetback) had to suffer because of this belief, that was unfortunate, but so was the Mexicano who could not feed his family because
of their presence."[5]

Forum members insisted that much of the poverty, ill health, underemployment, and low educational attainment of the Mexican American
population was tied at least indirectly to the adverse impact of Mexican immigration. In testimony before the President's Commission on Migratory
Labor in 1950, García summarized his organization's concerns by asking,
"Would thirty thousand Americans migrate . . . if they did not have to?
Would they expose their children to sickness and death if they did not have
to? Would they leave their homes and schools to migrate to uncertainty if
they could make a living at home?"[6] Forum members had already come to
their own conclusions on these questions. As far as they were concerned,
whatever good the Bracero Program had contributed to the nation during
the war had been "subverted to the crass desires of American ranchers and
farmers at the expense of American citizen labor which is being displaced
in increasing numbers and whose wages are being depressed more and
more."[7] Maintaining this basic position throughout the 1950s, the organization expanded its demands in 1957 by insisting that action also be
taken "against Mexican residents who commute across the border bridges
to work in the states, [and] to bar Oriental labor from the country."[8]

Ernesto Galarza and the Bracero Issue

Of all the individuals who had reason to contemplate the ramifications of
the issue of Mexican immigration, Ernesto Galarza probably wrestled with
the question the longest. Born in the village of Jalcocotán, Nayarit, he had

a long and distinguished career as a scholar, community activist, union organizer, and spokesman of the Mexican American community. An immigrant himself, Galarza spent the greater part of six decades criticizing what he considered to be the fundamentally exploitative character of American immigration and labor policies concerning Mexicans. Beginning in the late 1920s he expressed a point of view on immigration, labor, and the nature of Mexican culture in the United States that strongly influenced both his contemporaries and a subsequent generation of Mexican American activists and community leaders.[9] He died in San Jose, California, in 1983.

During his long career of activism Galarza proved himself an articulate and often controversial spokesman for farmworkers, many thousands of whom were, of course, Mexican Americans and Mexican nationals. During the 1940s and 1950s his primary forum for voicing his views on farm-labor issues was the National Agricultural Workers' Union (NAWU, first known as the National Farm Workers Union). Formed in the mid-1940s as an offshoot of H. L. Mitchell's Southern Tenant Farmers Union, the NAWU had, of necessity, to confront the bracero issue throughout its tumultuous history. As the union's director of research and education, Galarza actively campaigned against the Bracero Program from 1948 through 1960, concentrating most of his efforts in California.

Although Galarza's views on the bracero issue clearly reflected his trade-unionist orientation, the NAWU's arguments encapsulated many of the more general objections Mexican American organizations had previously advanced during the bracero debate. To Galarza and the NAWU, the bracero system represented on the most basic level the most recent attempts by American agribusinesses to rationalize and consolidate their control over the farm-labor market, something the growers themselves readily admitted. The *Associated Farmer*, the official publication of the Associated Farmers of California, put it frankly in 1943. The magazine's editor graciously allowed that California growers "certainly appreciated having obtained Mexican nationals to help them in their desperate farm labor situation," but he went on to warn readers "not [to] depend too much on any labor supply that must be received through any government agency." "Our labor supply," he concluded, "is our problem and we must attempt to solve it to the best of our ability through those channels which do not depend on any activities beyond those which we can institute and administer."[10]

On the surface, the NAWU's objections to what Galarza termed administered labor migration were simple and straightforward. The issues boiled down to the fundamental bread-and-butter questions raised by organized labor throughout the century. From the union's point of view, of course, the Emergency Farm Labor Program and its successors were implemented not to fill any real gaps on the farm-labor supply but rather because growers found it in their interest to maintain a large, flexible, and, above all, tractable labor supply. Thus it followed from the union's perspective that Mexican workers displaced domestic workers (although, interestingly, domestic workers were sometimes defined to include both citizens and resident aliens). The NAWU also argued that braceros exerted extreme downward pressure on wages, that their employment helped perpetuate dismal working conditions, and that their presence undermined labor-organizing efforts. As union representatives put it in 1948, although "the labor movement has recognized the important contribution to war production that the Mexican Nationals made . . . organized labor has not lost sight of the fact that this type of agreement, and the manner in which it has been negotiated and administered [that is, without union input], holds serious threats against the living standards of the workers of both Mexico and the United States."[11] In articulating these objections the union's spokespersons argued that, rather than import foreign workers, Congress should pass legislation guaranteeing American farmworkers the same rights as those afforded braceros: a set minimum wage, job-placement assistance, low-cost transportation, adequate housing and health care, and the right to collective bargaining. NAWU organizers also advocated the strict enforcement of child-labor laws, provision of child care for field workers, and the licensing and strict regulation of farm-labor contractors. From the union's point of view, with such guarantees in place domestic workers would eagerly seek farm labor, and the so-called labor shortage would disappear.[12]

Soon after the war, however, it became increasingly apparent to the union that the so-called wetback issue represented even more of a threat to citizen workers than did the formal Bracero Program. By 1948 national press coverage and numerous incidents along the border, such as the near-riot of Mexicans attempting to cross the border at El Paso, Texas, had catapulted the issue of illegal Mexican immigration back into national prominence. For Galarza and the NAWU, undocumented immigration severely compounded the problems the Bracero Program had already presented Mexican American labor. George Sánchez argued just this point in a letter to Galarza in 1948, insisting that the presence of thousands of wetbacks, combined with the availability of large numbers of legally contracted braceros, provided a ready and growing "reservoir of strike breakers."[13] From Galarza's point of view the advantage to corporate growers, and the threat to domestic farmworkers, was obvious: "The Mexicans are in no position to bargain for wages with corporations. They do not speak English. They are completely ignorant of any legal obligations that employers may have.

They cannot file claims. . . . They cannot invoke the protection of the Mexican consuls. They are, in short, perfect strike breakers."[14]

Galarza, however, was one of the first to recognize that the continuation of the Bracero Program and the related increases in undocumented immigration had implications for the existing Mexican American community that went beyond strictly economic or labor concerns. Although much of his rhetoric and tactics still clearly reflected his trade-unionist orientation, by the early 1950s his public statements and published tracts indicated that he had significantly reconsidered the broad social and cultural dimensions of the immigration question.

Above and beyond his concern with the economic impact of the large-scale surreptitious entry of Mexican immigrants into the United States, Galarza, like Sánchez, saw the wetback issue as perpetuating and intensifying anti-Mexican bigotry in the Southwest. Illegal aliens had contributed to what he saw as the dangerous and accelerating degradation of Mexican American workers "as a class" in American society. Reminiscing about his experiences in California, Galarza described a situation that existed in virtually every barrio and colonia in the Southwest when he wrote, "There were always the single men who as seasonal migrants drifted through the skid rows of Sacramento, Fresno, Los Angeles, and Marysville. . . . The domestic workers as a whole were portrayed as bums, drunks, thieves, post office robbers, telephone booth pilferers, and malingerers."[15] Contrary to such popular stereotypes, Galarza insisted that labor migrations were not matters of choice. As he argued in 1954, the migrant stream was a stark reminder of "the flight of people who can find no work in their community or who are offered work on such low terms that they cannot rear a family or maintain an approximately American standard of living." "They are not bums and drifters," he continued, but "Americans who feel the common American urge to settle down, establish a home, rear a family, and take a responsible part in community life."[16] He argued that Mexican Americans' growing frustration over their inability to achieve any of these simple goals would eventually create a "brew of . . . racial strife," between Mexican American workers and both braceros and wetbacks.[17]

But Galarza was also keenly aware that Mexican Americans continued to have strong emotional attachments to Mexicans from the other side, something other researchers of the period noted as well. Margaret Clark, in her work in the barrios of San Jose, California, in the mid-1950s, commented on the deep ambivalence Mexican Americans and Mexican immigrants seemed to feel toward one another as they lived their lives in close proximity. "The general feeling among resident Mexican Americans," she wrote, "is that the importation of braceros . . . increases job competition and keeps farm wages pitifully low." But as one barrio resident told her,

I've been following the crops in California for about twelve years, and I still don't know if I'm for or against the braceros. I guess that's because I first came to this country as a bracero myself in 1944, and know something about their problems. But I also know that when the braceros come in, the wages stay very low; that's pretty bad for people who have to earn their whole year's income just during the harvest season.[18]

Lyle Saunders and Olen Leonard drew similar conclusions in their study of relationships between Mexican American and Mexican immigrants in South Texas. Although many Mexican Americans there obviously resented the presence of large numbers of recent immigrants, the researchers noted,

There is [also] a certain affinity [between them] which comes about partly because of the fact that they share a common language and have many other cultural traits in common and partly through the fact that they tend to be thought of as one group by the English speaking people of the Valley. . . . In a strange land whose customs and language are much different from those of his own country, the wetback naturally establishes contacts with those most like himself. He does his shopping in the "Mexican" section of town; . . . he rents a shack on the back of one of the lots owned and inhabited by a Spanish-speaking family; he turns to Spanish-speaking truckers for employment; when he has money he patronizes cantinas and pool halls in the "Mexican" area; he attends social affairs and *bailes* [dances] with the Spanish-speaking people; he may go out with or even marry the daughter of Spanish-speaking citizens.[19]

For his part Galarza, perhaps more than any of his Mexican American contemporaries, seemed to recognize that the immigration debate affected the lives of Mexican Americans and Mexican immigrants on many levels other than merely the economic. Consequently, throughout the 1950s he advanced arguments that increasingly diverted blame from individual braceros and wetbacks while pointing the finger at government and business. For example, although much of the NAWU's criticism of the Bracero Program through the years was directed at American corporations, by the early 1950s the union had begun to expand its analysis and critique to hold both the U.S. and Mexican governments accountable for allowing illegal immigration to continue. Thus the union at one point argued that the U.S. government (and the American taxpayer) had provided Mexico with a safety valve for its own misguided economic and social policies. Later he added another innovative tactic to his strategy for effecting the demise of the Bracero Program: he pointed out that the foreign labor program should be outlawed because it violated the Mexican Constitution.[20] As he argued before a House committee in 1955, "The Mexican government has hit upon a very interesting fiscal device for subsidizing its misery. It is taking out of the wage tax on the lowest paid American worker . . . thereby obtaining a slightly higher standard of living to which our underpaid workers are already forced."[21]

Galarza eventually insisted that his union's primary concern was not with individual legal or illegal immigrants, whom he generally viewed as merely trying to make a living. In an interview late in his life, Galarza noted that the NAWU gradually shifted its strategy on the immigration question away from discussion of impoverished Mexican workers themselves and tried to publicize the inherently exploitative and systemic nature of the issue. As he put it,

> Our view was that the so-called wetback is a product of the political and social conditions of Mexico; and consequently we favored a campaign of publicity, confrontation, documentation, [and] protest . . . that zero[ed] in not on the wetback as a person, but on the Mexican government and its policy.[22]

The other major plank in the union's platform, of course, was to continue to hammer home the point that braceros were injuring American citizens. Using rhetoric that became increasingly strident as the excesses of the Bracero Program reached their peak in the mid-1950s, Galarza repeatedly admonished congressional committees to recognize that the real issue facing them was the widespread and continuing discrimination against American citizens. While pointedly reminding committee members that under the terms of the program braceros enjoyed "protections and guarantees . . . not . . . available to American citizens," Galarza contended that as a result, "discrimination against citizens of the United States has now become fundamental public policy in the United States."[23] Continuing along such policy lines was folly not only for Mexican Americans but for the nation as a whole. Stating what he considered to be the ultimate issues involved, he argued, "If you are ready to commit your government to a permanent policy of taking in this tremendous torrent of thousands and thousands of people who are driven from pillar to post, who have nothing to eat, who are on the verge of starvation, I say let us do it honestly, openly, and frankly." But in the context of the displacement and abuse of American farmworkers he continued, "Let us not cover it up with a myth which has been proved to be such over and over on the record, that we are doing it because there is a need for such labor in this country."[24]

Immigration and Anti-Communism

Galarza's contentions spoke to a subtle yet important broadening of the immigration debate that was developing among Mexican American activists in the early 1950s. As evident in his arguments, much of the NAWU's opposition to Mexican immigrants rested on the same economic competition arguments that had been heard since the 1920s. And yet in much the same manner that organizations such as UCAPAWA and the Congress of Spanish-Speaking Peoples had developed their views on the issue, as already noted by the 1950s Galarza and the NAWU had begun to think of the problem as encompassing much more than its strictly economic aspects. Although many of their arguments were clearly rhetorical and instrumental, by the late 1940s at least some Mexican American activists seemed to be reconsidering their views on the relationship of Mexican Americans to Mexican immigrants residing in the United States. This process of reassessment would receive a powerful additional boost after Congress passed the landmark acts of 1950 and 1952.

Reflecting the nation's growing preoccupation with the threat of communism both within and from outside its borders, Congress passed these two laws in an effort to shield the United States from the perceived peril. The Internal Security Act of 1950 was passed as a means for prosecuting anyone who had ever been even nominally affiliated with a Communist, Socialist, or other organization deemed subversive. Of even greater impact was the passage (over President Harry Truman's veto) of the Immigration and Nationality Act of 1952. This omnibus legislation, known popularly as the McCarran-Walter Act after its chief congressional sponsors, Senator Pat McCarran of Nevada and Congressman Francis Walter of Pennsylvania, liberalized some parts of the nation's general immigration statutes. At the same time it instituted strict new guidelines regarding qualifications for entry into the country, for the naturalization of aliens, and for the denaturalization of American citizens. Of particular concern to Mexican residents was a provision of the McCarran-Walter Act that greatly expanded the grounds on which unnaturalized aliens could be expelled from the country. In essence this provision decreed that any alien who had entered the United States since 1924 was subject to summary deportation from the United States—regardless of his or her character, length of stay in the United States, employment record, or familial relationship to bona fide American citizens.[25]

Enforcement of such legislation had potentially disastrous ramifications for the resident ethnic Mexican population for the simple reason that large numbers of resident Mexican nationals had not become naturalized American citizens. According to the 1950 census, of the 2,281,710 Spanish-speaking individuals enumerated in the five southwestern states (California, Arizona, New Mexico, Colorado, and Texas), approximately 83 percent were native-born or naturalized U.S. citizens, whereas approximately 16 percent reported Mexican nativity. As always, the data demonstrating overwhelming American nativity of the population helped to obscure the fact that a large proportion of Mexican American families had at least some members who were Mexican nationals. Indeed, when viewed in this way the 1950 census indicates that the combined population of resident Mexican aliens and Mexican Americans with at least one parent who had been born in Mexico amounted to 55 percent of the total ethnic Mexican population of the United States.[26]

Few Mexican Americans seemed to recognize the significance of such demographics however, for reaction in the Mexican American community to changes in immigration policy was fairly muted. Indeed, when the McCarran-Walter Act was passed, most Mexican American activists seemed to support its major provisions, especially those that mandated strict control of the border. In addition, many Mexican American organizational spokesmen seemed to have succumbed to the increasingly common cold war notion that Communists were somehow slipping into the country along with illegal aliens from Mexico and other Latin American nations. Echoing the growing number of reports in the press about such Communist infiltration, organizations ranging from LULAC and the American G.I. Forum to the NAWU all raised the specter of communism as part of their general arguments for immigration reform during the early 1950s. During congressional hearings on extension of the Bracero Program in 1951, for example, union president H. L. Mitchell expressed concern "that there is no provision [in the extension bill] for the proper screening of foreign workers to keep out foreign agents." In 1953 Mitchell elaborated on his fears in testimony before the House Committee on Agriculture:

> Not only are the illegal aliens a menace to the American citizens with whom they compete for jobs in large scale agriculture, but it is also well known that the Communist Party is most active in all countries south of us, and that Mexico City is a center of their operation. U.S. Immigration authorities have reported that Communist agents come across the border both in the guise of wetbacks and as legally contracted workers.

Other spokespersons for Mexican American interests voiced similar concerns.[27]

Another subtle indication of the political tenor of the times was a change made in the "LULAC Code" in the early 1950s. From the time of the group's founding until about 1950 the code, while obviously emphasizing the organization's Americanism and patriotism, also included admonitions to the membership to: "Love the men of your race, be proud of your origin and maintain it immaculate, respect your glorious past and help defend the rights of your own people"; and to "Study the past of your own, and of the country to which you owe your allegiance, [and] learn how to master with purity the most essential languages—English and Spanish." Some time in the late 1940s or early 1950s, however, these provisions had been stricken from the Code, leaving a document that emphasized the organization's American side while almost totally dismissing its former nod to the Mexican cultural heritage.[28] LULAC publications underscored the shift in the organization's ideological position. For example, in a version of the organization's "Aims and Purposes" published in the twenty-fifth anniversary edition of the *LULAC News* all reference to the value of Spanish-language maintenance was deleted in favor of a clause which pledged "to foster the acquisition and facile use of the official language of our country that we may thereby equip ourselves and our families for the fullest enjoyment of our rights and privileges and the efficient discharge of our duties to this, our country."[29]

It was not long, however, before politically active Mexican Americans began to realize that many of the reforms that they had initially welcomed in legislation such as the Internal Security and McCarran-Walter acts were now being used against both Mexican immigrants and their American-born children. Having lobbied against the Bracero Program for so long, most Mexican American advocates had welcomed such legislation as a long-needed step in the right direction, but as enforcement of the McCarran-Walter Act once again seemed to fall disproportionately on the ethnic Mexican populace, Mexican Americans began to protest.

This process of reassessment was greatly accelerated when the INS initiated its so-called Operation Wetback in the spring of 1954. Apparently designed both to stem the influx of undocumented workers into the United States and to pressure the Mexican government to agree to renew the bracero agreement, Operation Wetback instituted widely publicized sweeps of suspected illegal aliens, especially in the Southwest. By September of that year the INS claimed to have expelled more than one million illegal aliens from the United States.[30]

Mexican American activists reacted to many aspects of Operation Wetback, but the issue that clearly created the greatest resentment was the breakup of Mexican American families stemming from the INS's deportation of long-term Mexican residents. Belatedly recognizing that the deportation provisions of the laws could affect tens of thousands of Mexican American families, Mexican American advocates from across the political spectrum began to rethink their position on immigration. Not even the most politically conservative Mexican American organizations could ignore the fact that INS dragnets not only were affecting putative illegal aliens but also were devastating Mexican American families, disrupting businesses in Mexican neighborhoods, and fanning interethnic animosities throughout the border region.

Consequently, the positions of even hard-line restrictionist organizations, such as LULAC, the American G.I. Forum, and Galarza's NAWU, began to change on various levels. One early protest took place during LULAC's twenty-fourth annual convention in Albuquerque in June 1953. Arguing that "there are thousands [of Mexican nationals] who have intermarried with American citizens [and] are now parents of members of the United States Armed Forces," delegates handily passed a resolution "condemning the McCarran Act [that is, the Internal Security Act] as an oppressive and unjust law towards minorities," and requested that U.S. Attorney General Herbert Brownell take steps to ensure that "deportable aliens who are parents of members of the . . . Armed Forces be allowed to remain in the United States and legalize their status without returning to Mexico."[31]

LULAC's rhetoric on the issue of mass deportations continued to soften over the next twelve months, even though many LULAC members still expressed concern over the adverse effects of undocumented immigrants on Mexican American citizens. The best example of this softening position could be seen in the pages of the *LULAC News*. For the first time articles began to appear that expressed concern over the exploitation of wetbacks as well as the impact immigrants were having on U.S. citizens. Thus although an article published in the May 1954 *LULAC News* continued to advocate positions on the immigrant question that LULAC had supported for years, the author also expressed concern over the treatment of Mexican aliens, pointing out that most returned to Mexico "broken men, with strength spent and exhausted by the senseless struggles of a life revolving around slavish, ill-paid labor, and the degradation of jail and prison cells." In a notable break from the rhetoric of the past, the author went on to express admiration for "the courageous spirit of men who leave their own country to tackle hardships and uncertainties in the hope that they may improve the material lot of their families."[32] LULAC subsequently reinforced this position by officially endorsing the views of the Reverend Matthew Kelly of the Catholic Bishops' Committee for the Spanish-Speaking in the Southwest, who argued that "wetback traffic benefits no one except the employer who pays the unfortunate aliens as little as seventeen cents an hour. There is no good reason to tolerate such a situation."[33]

Broadened understanding of the many dimensions of the immigration question also became more evident in LULAC's internal discussions and debates—though the group's continuing ambivalence on the issue remained clear. When the INS began to apprehend undocumented aliens in Texas during Operation Wetback in the spring of 1954, LULAC, which among Mexican American groups remained the most supportive of the government's anti-Communist and anti-immigrant campaigns, heartily endorsed the agency's efforts. In a series of articles in the *LULAC News*, the organization called on the Mexican American community to cooperate with immigration officials and castigated those who opposed the sweeps as "men who have developed a belated and spurious solicitude in the wetbacks' welfare."[34]

In the spring of 1954, however, LULAC's national president, Albert Armendáriz, became embroiled in these issues after a LULAC member protested the organization's apparent drift in position on the immigration debate. Responding to the member's resignation in an open letter to the organization's general membership, Armendáriz addressed both what he considered to be LULAC's mission and the larger question of what it meant to be a Mexican American in postwar society. Although he agreed that one of the organization's basic principles had always been "that we must integrate with our fellow Americans," he raised the question of the costs of such integration. "Are we committed," he asked, "to the idea that we must also lose all vestige of a culture and heritage we possess, and which is undoubtedly part of our very being? Does integration . . . mean the breaking of all ties with our ancestors?" To him the answers to these questions clearly were negative. Departing from LULAC's previous official position on the issue, Armendáriz argued that, from his point of view at least, assimilation at the expense of tradition and culture was unacceptable. LULAC, and Mexican Americans generally, needed to act

> with the absolute knowledge that our culture and background are equally virtuous than [sic] the culture and background of our European or any other neighbors, that we can't and mustn't feel ashamed of it, but should endeavor to make the better aspects of it a part of the American way of life; realizing that in this, we have made a great contribution to the joys of life in these United States.[35]

The significance of Armendáriz's position lay in its rationale. Although LULAC had been founded on the assumption that Mexican Americans needed to maintain strict boundaries between themselves and Mexican immigrants, in 1954 the organization's national president was arguing that sustained immigration from Mexico dictated that LULAC change its perspective. In Armendáriz's view, at least, not only was "the ideal of integration as the sole purpose of LULAC unwise, but [it] is doomed to failure." Armendáriz tempered his comments by expressing his belief that a "sudden stoppage of immigration would find us completely integrated within a single generation," but he argued nevertheless that Mexican Americans had to face the reality of continuing immigration from Mexico. LULAC members had to acknowledge that they faced a unique situation: not only was their community being constantly replenished culturally by Mexican immigrants, but the "constant influx of immigrants (braceros and wetbacks too) . . . make the process of integration a perpetual one."[36]

This discussion proved to be just one round of a sustained debate within the organization. At LULAC's next national convention the members carried the debate onto the floor. The delegates reaffirmed their long-held belief that "wholesale importation of wetback laborers" represented "a menace to the social, economic, and educational well being of American born citizens of Mexican descent." Nevertheless, after what was reported as "spirited debate," LULAC members went on record in opposition to the McCarran-Walter Act because, as they put it, the law was "oppressive and unjust and creating great hardships to thousands of families in the deportation of aliens who entered the country illegally but have established residence." LULAC's El Paso council (Armendáriz's local council) went farther, offering a resolution which proposed that Mexican aliens who had married an American wife, had American-born children, were law-abiding, and had maintained steady employment "should be permitted and allowed to legalize their residence in the United States without . . . having to return to Mexico."[37]

Although the El Paso council's resolution ultimately was tabled for further discussion, the very fact that LULAC's national membership was discussing the immigration issue in these terms represented a significant shift of opinion within the group. The ostensible issue at hand was the status of Mexican immigrants in American society, but by the summer of 1954 some LULAC members were explicitly linking the issue of immigrants' rights to their own campaign to achieve civil rights for American citizens of Mexican descent. More important, a few were linking the immigration issue to reconsideration of the boundaries of the community LULAC had long claimed to represent.

In many ways, the organization's consideration of the wetback question and of a response to the McCarran-Walter Act had forced LULAC members to contemplate the criteria on which to base the eligibility of Mexican aliens for membership in their community. Finally recognizing that the Mexican American population had always included significant numbers of unnaturalized Mexican residents, their spouses, and their American-born children, some LULAC members were coming to realize that they needed to reconsider some of their most cherished political assumptions. The realization caused some LULAC members—including its national president—to adopt positions that in many ways were remarkably similar to the positions that leftist groups such as the Congress of Spanish-Speaking Peoples had advocated some years before. Although LULAC as a whole ultimately backed off from full endorsement of the notion that unnaturalized long-term Mexican residents should be considered as fully vested equal members in either the Mexican American community or American society, the organization from that time forward advocated clemency for long-term resident aliens.[38]

Other influential Mexican American leaders and organizations also reappraised the significance of immigration. As we have seen, even Ernesto Galarza and the NAWU eventually had to acknowledge the larger implications for the Mexican American population of the bracero-wetback debate.[39] Although Galarza continued to criticize American immigration and business policies and practices throughout his long career, he realized over the years that the immigration issue had become inextricably enmeshed with Mexican Americans' future in the United States. Indeed, he sometimes argued that the essential conflict was not immigration per se, but what he saw as the excruciating confusion in cultural and political identities that mass immigration had created in the Southwest's ethnic Mexican population.

From Galarza's point of view the key to the problem of self-identification for all ethnic Mexicans in the United States derived from "the slow erosion of the inward process of [Mexican] culture," caused by the inexorable interculturation that all Mexican immigrants and Mexican Americans experienced in the United States. Galarza argued that as Mexican immigrants slowly lost what he called their "collectivist and communitarian traditions" as they settled in American towns and cities, ethnic Mexicans and their children ultimately had "no alternatives to acculturation and assimilation by the Anglo."[40] The constant stream of immigrants from Mexico ultimately disrupted the process of acculturation, however, because for all intents and purposes the new immigrants remained outside the political community of the United States. By being part of what Galarza called "a culture in process," both Mexican Americans and Mexican immigrants were thus caught in a twilight world in which it was virtually impossible for them collectively to engage in effective political or social action in American society. The situation was further complicated by the government's active collusion in perpetuating the political powerlessness of ethnic Mexicans by condoning the use of Mexican labor while simultaneously whipping up anti-immigrant hysteria against wetbacks. As Galarza wryly noted in 1955, after Operation Wetback had ended, "while one agency of the United States government rounded up the illegal aliens and deported them to Mexico . . . [an]other government agency was busily engaged in recruiting workers in Mexico to return them to U.S. farms."[41]

Ethnic Political Mobilization in California

By the early 1950s in California, Mexican American activists were engaged in an even more sweeping reassessment of the significance of the immigrant question. Indeed, as noted earlier, a tradition of mutual aid and cooperation between citizen and alien Mexicanos historically had been fostered there even at times of extreme pressure, such as the depression and World War II. Despite the enormous pressure on minority groups to stifle their demands during such periods of crisis, scattered evidence suggests that, regardless of the prevailing political atmosphere, some Mexican American activists continued to act on their belief in the fundamental link between Mexican Americans' struggle for civil rights and the status of resident Mexican aliens.

During the 1950s instances of cooperation between Mexican Americans and Mexican immigrants increased dramatically, particularly among new organizations that had appeared in southern California after the war. One of the most important of the organizations to emerge during this period of intensified Mexican American political activity was the Community Service Organization (CSO). Founded in September 1947, the CSO was an outgrowth of Edward Roybal's unsuccessful bid for the Los Angeles ninth district council seat that year. Roybal, a Mexican American born in New Mexico, had been educated in California and for some time had been a social worker with the California Tuberculosis and Health Association. Much of the impetus behind the establishment of the CSO, which was composed largely of Roybal campaign workers, was the simple desire to retire Roybal's campaign debts. However, the fledgling organization soon attracted the attention of Fred Ross, an organizer affiliated with the Industrial Areas Foundation (IAF) and the American Council on Race Relations. The IAF, funded largely by Chicago philanthropist Marshall Field and run by veteran community activist Saul Alinsky, supported local community organization efforts and had achieved notable successes in Chicago's Back-of-the-Yards Movement in the 1930s and 1940s.[42] By early 1948 the IAF provided the main source of funding for the new Los Angeles barrio organization.[43]

Although the IAF grant to the CSO prohibited direct participation in partisan politics, the CSO—like so many other Mexican American–oriented organizations—was inherently political from the outset. Indeed, several of the CSO's founders, including Antonio Ríos and Gilbert Anaya (both activists with the Steelworkers' Union and future presidents of the organization), initially wanted to name the group the Community Political Organization.[44] From Ross's and the IAF's point of view the CSO experiment was an important first step toward the effective organization of what was still commonly seen as a politically disorganized, and therefore politically ineffective, minority group.[45] From the local Mexican American activists' perspective, the CSO, with IAF monetary and professional support, presented entirely new avenues for community political organization and activism. After its establishment, the CSO concentrated its community service efforts on nonpartisan voter registration and education drives, neighborhood improvement, legal advice, youth activities, health screening and referral, and legislative advocacy at the local and state levels.[46]

Although the new organization could not actually campaign for candidates because of the IAF restrictions, the CSO immediately distinguished itself by mounting a huge, nonpartisan voter-registration campaign in East Los Angeles before the 1949 municipal elections. The campaign met with unprecedented success. The CSO registered more than 15,000 new voters—mostly Mexican Americans—in Los Angeles' ninth councilmanic district.[47] The registration drive proved decisive, for Edward Roybal won the City Council seat and thus became the first Spanish-surnamed person elected to that body since 1888. Whereas former Congreso president Eduardo Quevedo had received only 2,227 of the 17,683 votes cast when he ran for the same seat in the 1945 primary, in 1949 Roybal defeated the incumbent councilman by a vote of 20,472 to 11,956.[48] In 1945 fewer than 39 percent of the district's eligible voters had voted; in 1949, largely through the CSO's registration and get-out-the-vote efforts, more than 82 percent of the eligible voters went to the polls.[49]

From its inception the CSO, like LULAC, concerned itself with the distinctions that traditionally had divided citizens from noncitizens in the ethnic Mexican community. For example, the tone of a CSO pamphlet published in the mid-1950s was very similar to that of some of LULAC's publications. "What makes a nation indivisible?" it asked. "What generates this goal of unity, of oneness, of 'togetherness' that holds the people of a country steadfast? Citizenship, with its assurance of protection of home and family when it assures justice and a voice in the government."[50] Similarly, in response to the heightened concern in the Spanish-speaking community about immigration matters that followed the passage of the Internal Security and the McCarran-Walter acts, the CSO, like so many previous Mexican American groups, emphasized the importance of citizenship training and naturalization to its noncitizen members and to the resident alien community at large. By 1955 the CSO was conducting 450 citizenship classes throughout California. Within a year and a half of the program's initiation the CSO had "graduated" more than 5,000 new American citizens.[51] By 1960 the organization claimed to have assisted more than 40,000 Mexican nationals in obtaining American citizenship.[52]

The CSO differed from most previous Mexican American advocacy groups by making much more of an effort to bridge the gap that had so often separated Mexican immigrants from Mexican Americans. Unlike the G.I. Forum and LULAC, the CSO had no citizenship requirements for membership and actively encouraged noncitizens (and non-Mexicanos) to join.[53] Reflecting this fresh perspective, the CSO also broke new ground in the area of immigration politics in the 1950s and early 1960s. There were several reasons for organization's special interest in these issues. Notably, among the group's founding members were many CIO-affiliated trade unionists who had fought for the right of resident aliens to work in defense industries during the war. For example, Antonio Ríos, Balt Yanez, Arnoldo Torres, and Gilbert Anaya were all active union organizers who had worked on the issue during the war through their various locals and the CIO's Committee to Aid Mexican Workers. Roybal himself had developed an open attitude on the question of the resident Mexican alien population through his work with the California Tuberculosis and Health Association.[54] Significantly, all of these individuals also worked later with the Los Angeles Conference on Immigration and Citizenship, a local organization committed "to provide counsel, assistance, and stimulation to the development of any local projects . . . that might be developed to improve the integration process [of Mexican immigrants]."[55]

Although the CSO actively sought the phasing out of the Bracero Program throughout the 1950s, it also lent assistance to noncitizen residents regardless of their legal status.[56] The fundamental assumption underlying much of the CSO's immigration activities was that resident aliens should become naturalized American citizens, if only to provide themselves with some protection under American law. Indeed, Article II, Section 2 of the organization's by-laws stated: "Residents of the community who are not citizens of the United States shall be encouraged to become citizens and to actively participate in community programs and activities that are for the purpose of improving the general welfare."[57] Beyond this basic instrumental approach, however, the CSO pursued the strategy of persuading Mexican aliens to become citizens, in Roybal's words, "so that they may feel they are a part, and that they do count in the democracy of America."[58]

Significantly, much of this innovative position on immigrants stemmed from the Community Service Organization's expanded conception of just what constituted its community. Reflecting a perspective that other ethnic Mexican activists had developed since the 1920s, the organization advanced the notion that resident Mexican aliens were not merely sojourners in the north but that they had become integral members of the Mexican American community. The CSO's basic assumption was that, because immigrants had made the decision to settle in the United States, they should become American citizens for their own good and for the good of the larger Spanish-speaking community. CSO members believed that many Mexican immigrants had existed for far too long on the margins of American society "uncemented," as one CSO publication put it, "into the strong foundations of American life." The time had come for such persons to be officially incorporated into American society. In the CSO's view the only protection "of home and family," "of justice and a voice in the government," lay in attaining the rights, privileges, and responsibilities of American citizenship.[59]

This attitude was evident early on in the day-to-day operations of the organization, as noncitizen members were encouraged to participate in the CSO's various activities in anticipation of the day they would become Mexican Americans rather than Mexicans who happened to live in the United States. As Roybal explained in 1953, "We are endeavoring to have these *potential citizens* participate actively on our many committees. This, we think, will give them firsthand knowledge of the many civic problems that confront the district and will help them become better Americans."[60]

Such attitudes pointed to the evolution of thinking on the issue of Mexican immigration that became increasingly apparent among other Mexican American activists in southern California during the 1950s. Mexican American concern with Mexicano immigrants reflected a pragmatic, if belated, recognition that such people had sunk deep roots into their communities and, in most cases, fully intended to stay. By this time most Mexican Americans had direct relationships extending into the immigrant community in addition to the more indirect ties and affinities which bound them to the immigrants. Of course, like the majority of Mexican Americans by this time, many CSO members had noncitizen relatives or were themselves the children of immigrant parents.[61] Yet, beyond their expressed concern for the integration of noncitizen Mexicanos into American society "as full-fledged participating member[s] of the American community," CSO members also began to recognize that it was not necessary for noncitizens to abandon their cultural traditions or practices to achieve these goals.[62] The organization's membership requirements and the scope of its activities during the 1950s and early 1960s attest to the comparatively open position the organization adopted with regard to the immigrant question. The fact that so many of the CSO naturalization, citizenship, health, and voter education classes were conducted in Spanish was one more manifestation of its new flexibility with regard to Americanization.

The CSO's legislative lobbying efforts also indicate the extent to which its conception of a more inclusive Mexican American community embraced Mexican immigrants. For example, the CSO joined other Mexican American advocacy groups in fighting a long battle with the California legislature to win old-age pensions for long-term resident aliens. The campaign, which lasted into the early 1960s, advocated the granting of such pensions to aliens who had resided in the United States for more than twenty-five years, regardless of their legal status. When California Governor Edmund G. "Pat" Brown signed Assembly Bill 5 into law in July 1961, the moment marked a hard-won victory for the CSO and other local Mexican American organizations.[63]

As in Texas, external factors had the greatest influence in transforming Mexican American public opinion on the immigration issue after 1950. Passage of the McCarran-Walter Act and increasing, indiscriminate INS sweeps of Mexican American neighborhoods during Operation Wetback not only created confusion and terror but also instigated more forceful community reactions. As a consequence the CSO and other local Mexican American and minority organizations banded together to resist what they gradually came to consider an orchestrated attack on the entire ethnic Mexican community. In the process of defending resident aliens these organizations advanced increasingly sophisticated legal and ethical arguments that also contributed to the further evolution of thought on the issue of their own ethnic identity and affinities.

In the forefront of these new political efforts was an organization founded in 1950 in reaction to passage of the Internal Security Act. Although not specifically a Mexican American organization, this new group, the Los Angeles Committee for the Protection of the Foreign Born (LACPFB), nevertheless worked closely with Mexican American groups, such as the CSO and the Congress of Spanish-Speaking Peoples. In addition, the LACPFB's Eastside branch was especially active in the defense of Mexican immigrants threatened by provisions of the Internal Security and

McCarran-Walter acts, and it included such CSO members as Josephine Yanez and Eliseo Carrillo, Jr.

From its inception the Committee was an outspoken critic of both the Internal Security Act and the McCarran-Walter Act. Considering such legislation discriminatory, repressive, and, indeed, un-American, the LACPFB, led by Los Angeles Jewish community activist Rose Chernin, lobbied for repeal of these laws well into the 1960s. The bulk of its activities during the 1950s, however, was channeled to the defense of noncitizens who were prosecuted under the provisions of the new laws. Under what amounted to ex post facto provisions of both the Internal Security and McCarran-Walter acts, virtually all noncitizens (and many citizens) were subject to summary deportation, regardless of the length of their stay in the United States.[64] The rationale underlying the LACPFB's defense strategy was heard with increasing frequency among numerous ethnic and civil liberties organizations. Perhaps the preeminent argument leveled against the government's policy and actions during the mid-1950s was that such legislation was unconstitutional and inconsistent with American ideals of fair treatment and equality. Indeed, the LACPFB flatly called neighborhood sweeps and raids on factories and fields "militarized terrorist deportation drives." It used similar emotionally charged rhetoric to deride campaigns such as Operation Wetback, describing them as manifestations of "martial law" and "pogroms" that smacked of the odious repatriation campaigns of the Great Depression, the wartime relocation of the Nisei, and even the Holocaust.[65]

LACPFB-sponsored coalitions of trade-unionists, ethnic and civil rights organizations, and such Mexicano-oriented groups as the CSO, the Asociación Nacional México-Americana (a left-leaning Mexican American coalition labor group), and the Comité Defensor del Pueblo Mexicano were also quick to recognize that many of the individuals singled out for persecution happened also to be union and/or community activists. As more and more union organizers were harassed by the INS and local authorities, Mexican American activists argued that the deportation campaigns were, in reality, the thinly veiled actions of a "strike-breaking, union busting force in the fields, shops, and factories."[66] The validity of these charges was born out as many Latino union activists, including Luisa Moreno, Josefina Fierro de Bright, and Frank Dávila, were deported on grounds ranging from technical violations of immigration statutes to their former affiliation with Communist or Communist-front organizations.[67]

Resident Mexican aliens, many of whom had lived in the United States for decades, were virtually powerless against the government's campaigns.

Even when resident aliens attempted to take advantage of the naturalization procedures provided by the McCarran-Walter Act, their backgrounds were researched and they became subject to prosecution. As Rose Chernin described the situation in 1954:

> The only way a non-citizen can avoid the harshest restrictions on his life is to apply for naturalization. The law makes this extremely difficult. Investigations are then made into his activities—social and otherwise. If anything "questionable" from the point of view of the Immigration Service turns up he will be refused, the facts are turned into a weapon and he can become a candidate for deportation.[68]

For long-term resident aliens such circumstances obviously caused immediate and pressing concerns. For years, as Ernesto Galarza had argued, U.S. immigration policy and practices had contributed to the creation of a large class of people who remained in American territory with virtually no legal rights and largely at the whim of the government. Indeed, one reason so few resident alien Mexicans took advantage of the opportunity to become naturalized citizens was that they saw no real benefit to themselves or their families. As José Gastelum, a Mexican immigrant who had resided continuously in the United States for more than forty years, put it in 1963, "I could not see the difference in the treatment of Mexican Americans and the Mexicans who came here from Mexico, so I did not feel it necessary to become a citizen inasmuch as the treatment was the same." "In many instances," he argued, "it was even more acute for the Mexican American than for the non-citizen alien."[69] Gastelum's predicament was one that thousands of Mexicans and their families faced during this period. Having lived in the United States among citizens of their own ancestry for up to four or five decades, many Mexicans now faced expulsion to a country they had never really known. Gastelum's bewilderment was evident when he asked, "Am I an alien? My children and grandchildren have all been born and educated here. I, too, have received all my education here. Which is my native land—Mexico, which I left at the age of ten, or the United States, where I have lived forty-two of my fifty-two years?"[70]

Although the issues most Mexican American activists faced with regard to the immigration question were more indirect than those facing unnaturalized Mexican residents, by the late 1950s they had come to realize the vital stake they had in the constitutional, legal, and moral aspects of the question. Their efforts on behalf of their immigrant neighbors were sincere, and this work served to convince many of them that such advocacy was also necessary for the welfare of Mexican Americans. As Josefina

Yanez, executive secretary of the LACPFB's Eastside branch, explained, "The role of the immigration authorities—their dragnet operations wherein they swoop down upon fields, factories, and entire communities— is so well-known and feared in any Mexican American community that the word 'Los Federales' strikes terror not alone to the non-citizen but to Mexican American citizens of the first, second, and third generations."[71]

Such a realization had significant and lasting political ramifications for Mexican American community leaders. Their increasing awareness of the racist dimensions of immigration policy contributed to the development of a broader sense of community solidarity with resident aliens—especially those who had lived in the United States for years—but it also demonstrated once again how little difference before the law actually existed between citizens and noncitizen members of the extended Mexicano community. Although many activists continued to believe that the presence of Mexican aliens—especially undocumented aliens—helped perpetuate anti-Mexican stereotypes among Anglos, they increasingly held their government, rather than the immigrants, responsible. As a consequence many more Mexican American community leaders began to develop a broader view of the issue, one which was much closer to that previously advanced by such groups as the Congress of Spanish-Speaking Peoples and UCAPAWA than it was to the traditional positions advocated by groups like LULAC and the American G.I. Forum. Indeed, their rhetoric sounded remarkably similar to that of the earlier groups as they defended the right of immigrants to work and live in the United States. For example, in protesting the INS's neighborhood sweeps in 1954, the LACPFB held that "behind the . . . [INS's deportation] figures are human beings: men who have labored under sweltering sun to build this nation's roads and railroads; fruit pickers and packers, laborers in the fields; workers in the nation's economy, who have built industry throughout the Great Southwest."[72]

Such attitudes marked a significant shift in the ideological positions of many Mexican American organizations, and they indicated the degree to which the campaign to achieve civil rights for Americans of Mexican descent had converged or overlapped with the question of the rights of Mexican aliens. This occurred during a period of heightened repression and xenophobia directed specifically at Mexicans, but, ironically enough, the government's campaign against aliens served to encourage greater levels of cooperation between Mexican Americans and Mexican nationals. Even though most Mexican American organizations continued to advocate the abolition of the Bracero Program, greater control of the border, and significant restrictions on future immigration from Mexico, many of those same organizations had begun also to agitate for the rights of those Mexicanos already physically present in the country. They had begun to believe, as the LACPFB did, that "by legislation and long practice, barriers have been set up which, today, as through the years, are designed to make economic, cultural and political outcasts of the Mexican people, whether Mexican nationals, naturalized, or U.S.-born citizens."[73]

For Mexican American organizations ranging from LULAC and the G.I. Forum in Texas to the Congreso, the CSO, and the LACPFB in California, the government's harsh treatment of noncitizens served as a catalyst for the evolution of a new, broader-based civil rights movement. Beyond the purely ideological aspects of their concern with the immigrant question lay the more fundamental belief, shaped by the experience of many of their families and neighbors, that most long-term Mexican residents had earned a legitimate place in American society through their work, contributions, and sacrifices in ways most Americans never had to endure. A Mexican American in San Antonio poignantly expressed such sentiments in 1954 when he asserted in an article in San Antonio's *La Prensa*, "This loyalty has been sealed with their own blood, as it was in Normandie and Korea and wherever else a similar burden was carried; and in peaceful times this loyalty had been work in the foundries and on the railroads, and in the fields of cotton, the vineyards and orange groves of California, as well as the mines of Colorado and Arizona, and in the metropolises of New York and Chicago."[74]

Perhaps the most dramatic and portentous manifestation of this change in attitude occurred in 1959, when the American Committee for the Protection of the Foreign Born presented the United Nations with a petition that described Mexican Americans as an "oppressed national minority." The American Committee, the New York-based parent group of the Los Angeles Committee of the same name, drafted its petition based on what it considered to be the U.S. government's flagrant violations of the UN's Universal Declaration of Human Rights. Although the document is notable for its effrontery alone, it is even more notable as a reflection of the significant change of thought about ethnic identity and immigration evinced by one group of Mexican American activists. In developing their argument the petitioners, who included Los Angeles activists Ralph Acevedo and Eliseo Carrillo, Jr., asserted what they considered the common interests—the basic human rights—of Mexican Americans and Mexican immigrants in the United States. Arguing that "the difficulties faced by the bracero reflect the problems faced by the average Mexican American," the petitioners maintained that Mexican American communities throughout the country were being kept "in a state of permanent insecurity by discrimination, segregation, raids, . . . and repeated deportation drives."[75]

The significance of their position was further underscored in the way they chose to describe the people for whom they claimed to speak. Apparently seeking to make a point about the arbitrary and unjust nature of naturalization and citizenship in American society, the petitioners pointedly referred to the entire 1,101,228 persons the government claimed to have expelled in 1954 under Operation Wetback as Mexican Americans. By refusing to recognize any significant distinction between citizens and aliens (much less the more invidious distinction between citizens and wetbacks), the petitioners advocated what many Americans almost certainly would have considered a radical new basis for ethnic political organization and mobilization. In effect, the committee adopted the view that if the government (and the general public) had never seen fit to distinguish whether an individual of Mexican descent was "a Mexican national, a legally or illegally resident alien of the United States, a naturalized United States citizen," or a native-born American, then Mexican Americans should not make much of the distinction either.[76]

Conclusion

Mexican American organizational responses to the perceived excesses brought about by changes in immigration law during the 1950s indicate the degree to which their political attitudes had evolved since the first large numbers of immigrants from Mexico had crossed into the United States early in the century. Although most mainstream Mexican American groups continued to support some form of strict control of the border, the repressive actions of the U.S. government after 1950 stimulated a serious reconsideration of their position vis-à-vis Mexican immigrants. As always, their immediate concern was with long-term alien residents who had raised American-born families and had otherwise established equities in American society. But at the same time increasing numbers of Mexican American activists began to comprehend how much of their quest for civil rights was tied to the immigrant question. As the American Committee for the Protection of the Foreign Born argued in 1959, a perception was growing among Mexican Americans that the Mexican-descent population—aliens and citizens alike—had been "forced to live lives of second-class citizens or immigrants without rights or status, [and subject to] discrimination, harassment, and great insecurity." In their view, and in the view of a growing number of Mexican American activists, "Their basic human rights [had been] disregarded and violated day in and day out by agents of the United States Immigration and Naturalization Service and its Border Patrol, by the police, [and] by agencies of the United States Departments of Justice, Labor and Agriculture."[77]

This explicit linkage of the rights of Mexican aliens with the civil rights of Mexican Americans occurred at a time when it would have been reasonable to expect widespread Mexican American support for the various immigration reform measures instituted by the government. To the contrary, after their initial support of government immigration enforcement efforts by such organizations as LULAC, the American G.I. Forum, and the NAWU, a growing groundswell of opinion sympathetic to the plight of immigrants began to emerge in these organizations. Though still in nascent form, such sentiments eventually contributed to greater assertions of a positive sense of ethnic identity among many politically active Mexican Americans. This is not to assert that these developments did not continue in the traditional broader context of Mexican Americans' loyalty to the United States, for most Mexican Americans continued to proudly proclaim their Americanness and commitment to American ideals and values. Similarly, most Mexican American advocacy organizations continued to emphasize integration as their stated objective. Yet by the late 1950s integration no longer necessarily meant complete assimilation, for Mexican American activists increasingly began to demand acceptance of their people on their own terms—that is, with the recognition that they were indeed of Mexican descent and proud of it. Perhaps the clearest example of this was the establishment in the late 1950s and early 1960s of organizations like the Mexican American Political Association in California, and the Political Association of Spanish-Speaking Organizations in Texas, which set precedent by simultaneously proclaiming their political activism and strongly asserting their ethnic background. Few activists recognized it at the time, but these developments presaged the emergence of even more militant declarations of ethnic solidarity among Mexican Americans in subsequent years—and also foreshadowed the emergence in the near future of an even more rancorous debate over Mexican immigration to the United States.

6   Sin Fronteras?
The Contemporary Debate

In October 1977 more than two thousand people assembled in San Antonio, Texas, for the First National Chicano/Latino Conference on Immigration and Public Policy. They represented a broad spectrum of Mexican American and other Hispanic interests, ranging from community groups and elected officials to militant ethnic separatist and Marxist organizations.[1] Called in response to President Jimmy Carter's recently announced immigration reform legislation, the conference provided dramatic evidence of the extent to which the immigration controversy had become a major civil rights issue in the 1970s. In three days of meetings the participants passed a series of unanimous resolutions condemning the Carter Plan as discriminatory against both citizens and aliens of Latin descent. With Mexican American organizations leading the way, the delegates specifically criticized the administration's call for the imposition of legal sanctions against habitual employers of illegal aliens and lambasted other aspects of the proposal, including the provisions for extending a limited amnesty to hundreds of thousands of undocumented aliens in the United States.

The unanimous negative response to the Carter Plan by Mexican American community groups, elected officials, and virtually every major national civil rights and political advocacy organization was a dramatic departure from traditional Mexican American positions on the immigration issue. Indeed, as we have seen, ever since the first mass migrations of Mexicans into the United States after the turn of the century, most Mexican American political activists and organizations had consistently demanded many of the same reforms that they were now rejecting. Given this long history of restrictionist sentiment, the overwhelmingly negative Mexican American response to the Carter Plan in 1977 was truly remarkable.

In other ways, however, the united Mexican American opposition to the government's immigration reform proposals was a logical outgrowth of the social ferment that had transformed ethnic politics in the United States in the 1960s and 1970s. After a period of relative quiescence in the early 1960s Mexican immigration reemerged as a national political issue just when politically active Mexican Americans became embroiled in a complex debate over their cultural and ethnic identity. Paralleling developments in the black civil rights and the antiwar movements of the era, Mexican Americans also intensified their demands for equal rights in a series of disparate social protests that became known collectively as the Chicano movement. Mexican American activists—particularly students and youth—built a political campaign characterized by proclamations of cultural pride, ethnic solidarity, and a willingness to employ confrontational political tactics.

Though many Mexican Americans were alienated by the Chicano militants' ideology and rhetoric, the young activists helped to change the political landscape by raising demands for social justice in aggressive new terms and by drawing attention to the nation's second largest minority group. In the process Chicano militants also helped to stimulate a far-reaching debate among Mexican Americans over complex issues concerning their own sense of ethnic identity, the nature of Mexican American (or, as they termed it, Chicano) culture in the United States, and the logic, potential efficacy, and desirability of a strident, ethnically based politics for the Mexican American minority at large.

Coincidentally, the immigration issue reemerged after 1970 at a time when Mexican American and Chicano activists were arguing over the degree to which their ethnicity should be emphasized in Mexican Americans' political and social future in the United States. In this period, as had been true in previous periods when the immigration controversy intensified, many Mexican American advocates initially supported the government's restrictionist reform proposals. As increasing numbers of young Mexican Americans began to reassess the significance of the ethnic heritage for their own sense of identity, however, they began to develop new attitudes about the many hundreds of thousands of Mexican immigrants—and their children—who constituted such a large percentage of the total Mexican-origin population of the United States. By the mid-1970s this broad-based process of reassessment had contributed to the emergence of a remarkable new consensus on the immigration controversy among Mexican American and Chicano political activists. By the late 1970s most major Mexican American and Chicano activists and civil rights organizations had reversed their traditional positions and were actively supporting the civil and human rights of Mexican immigrants in the United States, a stance they maintained well into the 1980s.

A Brief Quiescence: The Early 1960s

By the late 1950s Mexican American organizations had significantly changed their political tactics. Although Mexican American groups had used their ethnic heritage as a primary basis on which to organize, by the end of the decade some activists had concluded that new, more aggressive tactics were warranted. Undoubtedly noting the civil rights successes that African Americans had achieved in the 1950s, some Mexican American political activists argued that Americans of Mexican descent should organize as an interest group based on a new, more aggressive assertion of Mexican ethnic identity. The founding of the Mexican American Political Association (MAPA) in California in 1959 and the Political Association of Spanish-Speaking Organizations in Texas in 1960 provided good examples of this broad shift in political strategy, as Mexican American activists self-consciously concentrated on mobilizing voters as an ethnic bloc (though almost exclusively within the Democratic party). MAPA and similar political groups hoped to empower the Mexican American community by contributing to the election of Mexican American candidates, organizing resistance against such disfranchising policies as gerrymandering and poll taxes, and pressuring the Democratic and Republican parties to include Mexican Americans in mainstream politics.[2] Although such positive political assertions of Mexican ethnicity fell considerably short of the separatist or quasi-nationalistic position that would be adopted within a few years by Chicano militants, the establishment of new Mexican American organizations in the late 1950s and early 1960s marked a significant shift in political strategy and tactics.

Mexican American activists made this sharp turn toward emphasizing ethnic political mobilization, but their activities in the early 1960s concerning the status of Mexican nationals in their communities continued to emphasize education, naturalization and citizenship, and, of course, the abolition of the Bracero Program. Based on the assumption that progress could best be achieved by following established strategies within the American electoral system, Mexican American civil rights advocates continued to stress citizenship training and naturalization as the means by which eventually to expand the Mexican American vote. In California groups such as the CSO and, later, MAPA continued to encourage aliens to attend citizenship and English-language classes and to participate in neighborhood political-organization efforts. In Texas LULAC continued along similar lines and developed an innovative new program, "The Little School of the 400," which strove to provide Mexican preschoolers with a vocabulary of 400 English words. A prototype of subsequent programs like "Project Headstart" and early bilingual-education approaches, the Little School project was designed to help Spanish-speaking preschool students overcome some of the largest language-related obstacles they faced when entering American public schools.[3]

After the tumult over immigration policy during the 1950s, however, the debate waned considerably in the early 1960s. Proponents of the Bracero Program were successful in their efforts to renew the program throughout the 1950s, but by 1960 critics of the program, which now comprised a loose coalition of labor unions, religious organizations, Mexican American groups, and the liberal wing of the Democratic party, began to make headway. The Kennedy administration was open to considering farm-labor reform proposals, and as groups like the National Council of Churches, the Catholic Rural Life Conference, the Catholic Bishops' Committee for the Spanish-Speaking, and Americans for Democratic Action stepped up their criticism, Secretary of Labor Arthur Goldberg publicly announced doubts about the need to continue the Bracero Program. Corporate lobbyists convinced Congress to renew the program twice during Kennedy's tenure as president, but opponents finally succeeded in killing it at the end of 1964, when Congress refused to reauthorize the Mexican farm-labor program.[4]

After the demise of the Bracero Program Mexican immigration virtually disappeared as an issue in national politics. By the mid-1960s the intensifying civil rights movement, urban unrest, and the escalation of the war in Vietnam all served to push the immigration issue out of the political spotlight. Undocumented Mexican immigrants continued to enter the United States during this period, but the INS reported that the rate of apprehensions of deportable aliens recorded between 1960 and 1965 had dropped to one-tenth the rate recorded in the years immediately preceding Operation Wetback.[5]

As in the 1940s, however, the residual effects of years of sustained immigration from Mexico continued to shape the demographic and social development of the permanent ethnic Mexican population of the United States. The native-born Mexican American population continued to grow as a percentage of the total resident Mexican-stock population, but Mexican nationals and their U.S.-born children continued to constitute a very large proportion of the population and thus remained a potent social issue in Mexican American communities. According to U.S. census figures, of the estimated 3,464,999 Spanish-surname persons residing in the Southwest in 1960 nearly 55 percent were natives of native parentage, 15 percent had been born in Mexico, and approximately 30 percent were U.S. natives of mixed parentage (that is, with at least one parent born in Mexico).[6]

By 1970 these percentages had changed very little. Of the 4,532,435 persons of Mexican descent enumerated in the 1970 census, 3,715,408 (nearly 82 percent) were native-born American citizens and 817,027 were resident Mexican nationals. However, of the native-born Mexican American component, 1,579,440 (approximately 35 percent of the total Mexican-descent population and almost 43 percent of the U.S.-born Mexican American cohort) were the children of foreign or mixed parentage.[7] As is evident from this statistical profile, despite the fact that the vast majority of Mexican Americans were native-born Americans, in 1970 immigrants and first-generation Mexican Americans continued to make up a very large percentage of the total Mexican-descent population of the Southwest. This demographic reality continued to exert a powerful influence on both ethnic politics and attitudes about immigration and ethnic identity among Mexican Americans during this volatile period of American history.

The Emergence of the Chicano Movement

The emergence of the Chicano movement in the mid-1960s probably did more than any other series of events to transform Mexican Americans' opinions about the relationship and significance of the immigration issue to their own status in American society. Originating as a series of localized protests erupting in New Mexico, Colorado, Texas, and California early in the decade, by 1968 this militancy had taken on the characteristics of a cohesive social movement. Inspired by the pioneering and widely publicized efforts of César Chávez and the United Farm Workers Union (UFW) in California and by Reies López Tijerina and his irredentist organization in New Mexico, the first stage of this period of accelerating social and political activism helped to lay the foundation for the unprecedented politicization of thousands of Mexican Americans across the country.

By 1966 these initial efforts opened the way for a second phase of Mexican American political activity. At this time young Mexican Americans, particularly high school and college students, began to express increasing dissatisfaction with discrimination, inferior education, and what they perceived as severely limited life opportunities. In many ways these students represented a paradox. Even though their educational and occupational levels continued to lag behind those achieved by other Americans, young Mexican Americans growing up in the late 1950s and early 1960s had significantly outstripped the levels of education and employment their parents had been able to attain. In the context of rising expectations for social reform emanating from the New Frontier and Great Society rhetoric of the Kennedy and Johnson administrations, however, Mexican American students grew increasingly impatient with the pace of social change. As the antiwar and black-power movements intensified in the United States after 1965, young Mexican Americans also began to voice their frustrations and protests. To a certain extent emulating the style and rhetoric of these militant movements, in 1967 and 1968 Mexican American students spontaneously walked out of classes in California, Texas, Colorado, and New Mexico, thus signaling the birth of the Chicano student movement.[8]

One of the most important thrusts of this second stage of increasing political activism—and arguably the development that ultimately had the most impact in transforming Mexican American opinion on the immigration issue—was the adoption and promotion among young Mexican Americans of a new, Chicano identity. Long used as a slang or pejorative in-group reference to lower-class persons of Mexican descent, in the 1960s the term *Chicano* was adopted by young Mexican Americans as an act of defiance and self-assertion and as an attempt to redefine themselves by criteria of their own choosing. Similar to the dynamics involved in the shift from *Negro* to *black* as the preferred self-referent of young African Americans that was taking place at about the same time, young Mexican Americans soon adopted the term *Chicano* as a powerful symbolic code. The term implied pride in the Mexican cultural heritage of the Southwest and symbolized solidarity against what Chicano activists argued was a history of racial oppression and discrimination at the hands of Anglo Americans. Chicanismo—the idea of being Chicano—established strong symbolic ethnic boundaries for young Mexican Americans who explicitly and stridently rejected the notion of inherent Anglo-American superiority. Although adopted and used primarily by young Mexican American high school and university students, by 1970 the student movement had attracted sufficient attention that the term had entered fairly general usage as a descriptor of the Mexican American population at large.[9]

This new assertion of ethnic solidarity was carried one step farther in the concept of Aztlán, an idea first articulated and debated in 1969 at the landmark First National Chicano Youth Liberation Conference in Denver, Colorado. Sponsored by the Crusade for Justice, a Colorado community organization founded by Rodolfo "Corky" Gonzales in 1965, the meeting attracted more than two thousand delegates representing Chicano students, community organizers, and political organizations from across the country. The conference marked the first time a large group of Chicano activists had come together to discuss the goals and strategy of a broad-based national Chicano movement.

In the process of refining their new sense of ethnic identity, the participants at the Denver meeting proclaimed the idea of Aztlán in the conference's famous manifesto, "El Plan Espiritual de Aztlán." The Spiritual Plan of Aztlán drew its inspiration from Aztec myths and from the vivid expressions of Chicano cultural pride explored in the writings of Corky Gonzales and the Chicano poet Alurista. Aztlán referred to the presumed ancestral homeland of the Aztecs and thus, by extension, of the Mexican people. Interpreted as the lost territories that Mexico had surrendered to the United States in 1848 after the Mexican War, to Chicano activists Aztlán represented the symbolic territorial base of the Chicano people.[10] The Plan of Aztlán presented an almost millennial vision of the future, painting an image of a separate Chicano culture and nation that ultimately would be reclaimed by the Chicano descendants of the ancient civilization. Proclaiming, "We are a Bronze People with a Bronze Culture," participants at the First National Chicano Youth Liberation Conference declared, "Before the World, before all of North America, before all our brothers in the Bronze Continent, We are a Nation, We are a Union of free pueblos, we are Aztlán. Por La Raza todo, Fuera de la Raza nada" (For the [Chicano] people everything; for [non-Chicanos] nothing).[11]

The Plan of Aztlán marked an important turning point in young Chicanos' ongoing efforts to refine their conception of a collective Chicano identity and to build a political program based on that identity. In the idea of Aztlán the young activists presented a quasi-nationalist vision of the Chicano people which extolled a pre-Columbian, native ancestry while diminishing or even rejecting their connection with American culture and society. In so doing they also dismissed traditional notions of Americanization and assimilation as nothing more than *gabacho* (a derisive term for Anglo) attempts to maintain hegemony over Chicanos by destroying their culture. Pursuing a logic similar to that followed by black nationalists of the period, the Chicano nationalists at the Denver conference proposed to break Anglo hegemony by demanding community control or local autonomy over schools, elected offices, businesses, and even financial institutions located in areas of high Chicano concentration.[12]

Clearly, much of the ethnic separatism and nationalism expressed in the Plan of Aztlán represented a symbolic act of defiance, rather than a formal declaration of secession from American society. Nevertheless, the conference and its ringing manifesto galvanized the student delegates and stimulated a new level of activism and the formation of numerous new student and community groups throughout the Southwest. In addition, after the

Denver conference Chicano activists Corky Gonzales and south Texas organizer José Angel Gutiérrez attempted to implement their plans for achieving Chicano community control by building an alternative, ethnically based political party in the Southwest, El Partido de La Raza Unida, or La Raza Unida Party (LRUP).[13]

More important, events surrounding the 1969 conference contributed to an intensifying debate among Mexican Americans over the wisdom of pursuing the politics of ethnic militancy. Despite Chicano militants' claim that they represented the true interests of the Mexican-descent people of the United States, their tactics and rhetoric often provoked strong, hostile reactions from more moderate, old-line Mexican American political activists, who tended to view the militants' demands as unrealistic, counterproductive, or even racist.

Perhaps the best known example of this increasingly volatile debate took place in 1969 between José Angel Gutiérrez and Henry B. González, the veteran Mexican American congressman representing San Antonio. Reflecting the views of many others of his generation who had grown up believing that Mexican Americans must work within the system to achieve social justice, Congressman González lambasted Gutiérrez and other Chicano militants. He characterized them as "professional Mexicans" who were attempting "to stir up the people by appeals to emotion [and] prejudice in order to become leader[s] and achieve selfish ends." In González's view the militants' emphasis on Chicano ethnic distinctiveness and their espousal of separatist ideologies represented the "politics of hatred" and "racism in reverse." Articulating the views held by a great many Mexican Americans in that volatile period, González rejected the militants' appeals to ethnic solidarity because he felt that their campaign was based on "a new racism [that] demands an allegiance to race above all else."[14]

For his part, Gutiérrez derided González and Mexican American moderates for denying the importance of their cultural heritage. Gutiérrez accused González of holding "gringo tendencies" and maintained that Mexican Americans who subscribed to the ideology of assimilation were *vendidos* (sellouts) who had abandoned their people and contributed to their oppression. Voicing a view prevalent among other Chicano militants in the late 1960s, Gutiérrez argued that Chicanos should consider the very idea of assimilation offensive, because it implied that Chicano culture was inferior to that of the American mainstream. For Gutiérrez and other militants the key to the liberation of the Chicano people was "social change that will enable La Raza to become masters of their destiny, owners of their resources, both human and natural, and a culturally separate people from the gringo." "We will not try to assimilate into this gringo society," he declared, "nor will we encourage anybody else to do so."[15]

A great many Mexican Americans like González profoundly disagreed with the rhetoric, ideology, and political tactics adopted by Gutiérrez and other militant Chicano activists. Nevertheless, few could deny that the Chicano movement, like the larger civil rights movement itself, was instrumental in raising public and government awareness of the chronic problems facing the Mexican American population. Even if many Mexican Americans refused to accept a Chicano self-identity, much less the ethnic separatism espoused by the militants, the actions of Chicano activists undoubtedly helped to convince at least some government officials that the militants' grievances warranted attention. This trend accelerated after 1971, when a U.S. District Court ruled in the landmark *Cisneros* case that Mexican Americans constituted an identifiable minority group entitled to special federal assistance.[16] By granting official recognition of Mexican Americans as a disadvantaged minority, the court undoubtedly helped to encourage the trend among Mexican American activists to pursue political reform as part of an organized ethnic lobby. Similarly, whether or not one agreed with the ideology and tactics of the militant young Chicanos, it was clear that by challenging the integrationist assumptions of assimilation ideology, Chicano activists in effect had forced Mexican American moderates associated with older civil rights organizations to prove their loyalties and to justify their traditional approaches to achieving social change. Recognizing that the militants had achieved some credibility in Mexican American communities—particularly among the young—many Mexican American mainstream politicians eventually, if reluctantly, acknowledged that the Chicano militants articulated the frustrations of barrio residents who were impatient with the pace of social change. Consequently, some Mexican American moderates began to acknowledge and act upon the militants' demands.[17] As one prominent scholar of this period noted, "The success, albeit limited, of the movement . . . in focusing government attention on Mexican problems softened the initial resistance and pejorative attitudes of the established Mexican [American] community leadership which realized its own interests could be served best by working in the 'movement' framework."[18]

The "Silent Invasion"

One largely unforeseen effect of this internal debate over political ideology, ethnic identity, and the redefinition of the Chicano community was the profound influence it eventually exerted on Mexican Americans' attitudes about the Mexican immigration issue. This development was ironic in that very few Chicano or Mexican American activists had recognized immigration as a significant political issue in the late 1960s. Just when Mexican Americans were becoming embroiled in an escalating debate over such fundamental issues as the appropriate basis for political organization and activism, the sources and salience of ethnic identity in contemporary society, and the very nature of the Mexican American community, however, the immigration issue suddenly reemerged.

After a brief period during which the controversy over Mexican immigration receded, several factors contributed to a renewed movement of immigrants across the international frontier. Among the most important of these were the inability of the Mexican economy to keep pace with population growth and the attraction of the booming American economy of the Vietnam era. Whatever the reason, by the late 1960s a slow but steady increase in the number of undocumented entries was being recorded by the INS. Although the number was still only a fraction of the peak noted during the bracero era, the INS reported that by 1967 apprehensions had again exceeded the one hundred thousand mark. Apprehensions continued to rise steadily over the next decade: the number approached five hundred thousand by 1970, exceeded six hundred eighty thousand in 1974, and neared the one million mark in fiscal 1977.[19]

Americans became aware of the renewal of undocumented immigration when a sharp recession threw Americans out of work in 1970 and 1971, rekindling concern that Mexicans were stealing jobs from American citizens. This impression undoubtedly was reinforced when prominent news publications, including the *New York Times*, the *Washington Post*, the *Los Angeles Times*, and *U.S. News and World Report* began to publish stories describing the illegal alien influx as a human flood or a silent invasion.[20] In a series of particularly inflammatory articles and public statements, INS Commissioner Leonard Chapman described the illegal alien issue in alarming terms, warning of dire long-term consequences to the national interest. In one widely publicized article Chapman termed the illegal alien issue a "national disaster," claiming that illegal aliens were "milking the U.S. taxpayer of $13 billion annually by taking away jobs from legal residents and forcing them into unemployment; by acquiring welfare benefits and public services; by avoiding taxes." "Clearly," Chapman asserted, "the nation can no longer afford these enormous, growing costs."[21]

In response to the growing negative publicity and public outcry surrounding the illegal alien issue, in 1972 and 1973 the INS embarked upon a new effort to control undocumented immigration by instituting a series of neighborhood sweeps in which aliens were apprehended and returned to Mexico. These sweeps were concentrated in predominantly Mexican American neighborhoods in the southwestern states and received extensive news coverage.[22] In addition to these renewed enforcement efforts, both Congress and some state governments began to consider legislation designed to address the latest immigration crisis. At the state level the best-known legislative development unfolded in California in 1970, when State Assemblyman Dixon Arnett of Redwood City introduced a bill that would impose criminal sanctions against employers who knowingly hired an individual "not entitled to lawful residence in the United States."[23] Congress followed a similar approach in its deliberations on immigration reform. In early 1972, after more than a year of hearings and staff research, a House immigration subcommittee synthesized several proposals and drafted a series of recommendations, which were then endorsed by the full Judiciary Committee. This legislation, which quickly became associated with House Judiciary Committee chairman Peter Rodino (Democrat of New Jersey), provided the basis for much of the subsequent congressional debate on immigration policy in the 1970s and 1980s. Such legislative activity also served notice that the illegal immigration question had once again become a prominent national issue.

The centerpiece of the Rodino legislation was similar to the employer sanctions proposed in Arnett's bill in California. Acting on the assumption that the root of the problem of illegal aliens in the United States lay with employers who knowingly hired them for substandard wages, Rodino advocated imposing civil and criminal penalties against anyone who hired such workers. To overcome the obvious difficulties inherent in identifying legal workers Rodino and others advocated the creation of improved Social Security cards, or the development of a new, counterfeit-proof national identification system. Most of the legislation introduced at this time also called for significantly increased appropriations for the INS. Finally, as a gesture to Mexican Americans and other Hispanic groups, some legislation proposed to extend a limited amnesty to aliens who could prove continuous residence in the United States from some arbitrarily set date.[24]

The increasingly negative national press coverage of the so-called illegal alien crisis, the policy debate in Congress, and the intensified and highly publicized enforcement efforts of the INS set the stage for renewal of debate among Mexican American civil rights activists over the Mexican immigration issue. Although, as always, Mexican Americans remained divided on the question, recent political developments contributed to the most far-reaching and broad-based reassessment of the immigration issue in Mexican American history. This process of reassessment had several sources, but the government's reaction and the news media's negative coverage of the immigration question clearly rankled Mexican Americans who remembered the persecution of Mexican nationals (and their families) during the 1930s and 1950s.

Over the long run, however, the discussion over Mexican Americans' ethnic and cultural identity provoked by Chicano movement activists probably influenced Mexican Americans' responses to the immigration issue more than any other factor did. Having attempted to redefine the Chicano community by rejecting the assimilationist model and emphasizing the central importance of Mexican culture, history, and language to contemporary Chicano society, Chicano activists had raised some complex questions as to the boundaries of their community. Few Chicano activists initially made the connection between their efforts to redefine Chicano identity and their need to adopt some position on the immigration issue. At the same time, however, their appropriation of Mexican cultural symbols as integral parts of Chicano culture seemed to open the door to establishing a new level of solidarity with immigrants from Mexico. Consequently, in the context of the significant ethnic awakening symbolized by the emergent Chicano movement, the immigration issue assumed much more complex dimensions and importance in Chicano political discourse.

Initially, few of the early Chicano groups made any connection between their objectives and the immigrant question. The important exception to this was a group known as El Centro de Acción Social Autónoma, Hermandad General de Trabajadores (the Center for Autonomous Social Action, General Brotherhood of Workers, or simply, CASA). Established in 1968 by veteran Mexican American community activists and labor organizers Bert Corona and Soledad "Chole" Alatorre in Los Angeles, CASA was founded as a "voluntary, democratic mutual assistance social welfare organization" to provide needed services to undocumented Mexican workers in the United States. Patterned after the traditional Mexican mutualista, CASA had expanded by 1970 to include autonomous local affiliates in other California cities and in the states of Texas, Colorado, Washington, and Illinois. These locals provided undocumented workers with a variety of direct services, including immigration counseling and notary and legal assistance.[25] Moreover, in 1973 CASA helped to establish the National Coalition for Fair Immigration Laws and Practices, a coalition of a broad range of predominantly Mexican American community and labor groups that played an important role in articulating Mexican American opinion on the immigration controversy throughout the debate in the 1970s.[26]

What most distinguished CASA from other groups was that it was the first Chicano-era organization to explore systematically the significance of the relationship between immigration, Chicano ethnicity, and the status of Mexican Americans in the United States. Basing their political perspective on more than four decades of labor-union organizing and activism in Mexican communities in the Southwest, CASA's founders, particularly Corona and Alatorre, argued that Mexican immigrant laborers historically represented an integral component of the American working class and that, as such, they had legitimate claims to the same rights as other workers in the United States. This assertion represented a significant departure from the views of most other contemporary Mexican American and Chicano organizations, but CASA's organizing slogans, "Somos Un Pueblo Sin Fronteras" (We Are One People without Borders) and "Somos Uno Porque America Es Una" (We Are One Because America Is One), had even more sweeping political connotations. From CASA's point of view the historical and ongoing exploitation of both Mexican American and Mexican immigrant workers in the United States made them virtually indistinguishable. CASA's overriding goal, therefore, was to "unite . . . immigrant workers with the rest of the working class in the United States who 'enjoy' citizenship." CASA's leaders saw "an immediate need to organize and educate the passive individuals who are the victims of these anti-human and anti-legal [*sic*] practices so that they will incorporate physically and consciously to demand the rights and benefits all human beings are entitled to."[27] This statement not only called into question what the organization viewed as more than a century of American exploitation of Spanish speakers but, more significant, also fundamentally challenged Mexican Americans' own responses to the exploitation of Mexican immigrants. Unlike other Mexican American organizations of the period, CASA maintained that Mexican immigrant workers, by virtue of their sacrifices and contributions to American society, had the right to live and work in the United States without harassment from the government or from Mexican Americans.

The political demands that stemmed from these assertions were truly revolutionary, in light of the assimilationist assumptions that had informed nearly two hundred years of American immigration policy and had deeply influenced Mexican American political thought in the twentieth century. CASA asserted that naturalization, and surely Americanization, was largely irrelevant in a society that refused to recognize the full rights of citizenship for its ethnic and racial minorities. CASA's spokespersons argued that immigrant workers had for too long suffered as scapegoats for social and economic dislocations in the United States. CASA members consistently argued that the inferior social, economic, and political position of Mexicans in the United States did not derive from their cultural backwardness and refusal to assimilate into American culture and society but, rather, reflected the inherently exploitative nature of American capitalist development.

CASA's position, as expressed by Corona in a 1971 speech, squarely challenged attempts "to sell to the so-called 'Mexican Americans' the idea that the greatest threat to their well-being is not the capitalist system, not the corporations, not the bad wages, not discrimination, not exploitation . . . [but] our *carnales* [brothers and sisters], who in their poverty come from Mexico to find work." Rejecting what he considered to be a half-century of invidious Anglo-American corporate and governmental propaganda, Corona asserted that Chicanos themselves must reject the false distinctions that traditionally had divided them from other working-class Latin Americans. "Our unity has to include not only Chicanos born here," Corona argued, "but also those who come from Mexico and Central and South America with documents and those who come . . . without."[28] "The[se] workers never cause unemployment," argued another CASA representative, "it's the jobs that are disappearing to other countries and which are being eliminated due to corporate greed." "The aliens contribute much, much more than they remove," he concluded. "They have not only built our country but continue to contribute to it by being taxed superheavily and by consuming, utilizing, and paying for services in this country."[29] Following this logic, CASA maintained that the basic guarantees of American law represented only the bare minimum to which undocumented workers were entitled. CASA's leaders proposed, much as the Congress of Spanish-Speaking Peoples had thirty years earlier, that the undocumented be granted the "right of access to public bodies," a statute of limitations of one year on deportations, eligibility for citizenship after one year's residence, and the right "to be offered employment on equal terms with workers native to the host country."[30]

In many ways CASA's views represented an extreme position on the growing controversy in the early 1970s. However, the government's recent actions in immigration policy and enforcement, the tenor of media coverage on immigration, and Mexican Americans' growing impatience with the pace of social change soon led others to join in a spirited critique of American immigration policy. Moreover, CASA's strong advocacy of working-class solidarity with Mexican immigrants held great appeal for Chicano student activists, who by 1972 had begun to explore Marxian class analyses to help explain the subordination of Mexicans in American society. Utilizing these more sophisticated conceptual frameworks to analyze Chicanos' historical experience, Chicano students and a small but growing number of Mexican American academicians developed a new understanding of the close correspondence between the historical exploitation of Mexican and of Mexican American workers in the American labor market.[31]

Such analyses soon spilled over into Chicanos' evaluation of the immigration debate. On the most basic level young Chicano students, activists, and community organizers began to develop a new perspective on immigration by rejecting the government's contention that undocumented workers represented a threat to the Mexican American working class. As one young activist stated in the militant Los Angeles Chicano newspaper *Regeneración* in 1972: "It is claimed that illegals cause high unemployment of residents; that they oppose the formation of unions; that they drain residents' incomes by adding to welfare costs; that they add to the tax burden by needing special programs." "These are fake claims," he argued. "Illegals . . . do not create unemployment of Chicanos, employers desiring to pay the lowest possible wages do."[32] Over the coming months the combination of INS sweeps, legislative action in Congress, and what Chicano militants perceived as intensifying anti-Mexican rhetoric in the media led other Chicano activists to step up their criticisms of the government's reform efforts, and their increasingly strident rhetoric clearly reflected these trends. In July 1972 LRUP issued a statement in California describing undocumented workers as refugees from hunger and called upon the government to issue a blanket amnesty to those aliens already in the United States. Like CASA, LRUP also demanded that the law be amended so that all aliens would be eligible for American citizenship after three years with no language requirements.[33] In Denver a coalition of Mexican American groups led by the Crusade for Justice went farther by issuing a press statement that decried the Rodino proposal as an attempt to "perpetuate racism" against all Latinos. The coalition charged that if the Rodino bill passed, "all Latinos, Chicanos, [and] Mejicanos will be obligated to produce identity papers, and many applicants for jobs will be denied a chance for employment based solely on the fact that we may 'appear' alien."[34]

Although activists in the Chicano movement led the growing clamor against the government's proposals for immigration reform, some politically moderate and even conservative old-line organizations, such as LULAC and the American G.I. Forum, began to be pulled toward a new position on the question. During the initial Rodino hearings in 1971, even LULAC began to express growing ambivalence on the issue. Before then most LULAC spokesmen seemed to support the government's general approach to the issue. Over the course of the hearings, however, some LULAC leaders seemed to be having second thoughts on the question of undocumented Mexican workers. LULAC's growing ambivalence on the immigration controversy was a new permutation of the group's traditional concern about the impact of immigration on Mexican Americans. During the Rodino hearings some LULAC members criticized proposed legislation by stressing the adverse effects such laws might have on American citizens of Mexican descent. This marked a significant change, because LULAC's representatives had shifted the target of their criticism from undocumented workers themselves to the proposed legislation. Although LULAC at this point still tended to favor the proposals for employer sanctions contained in the Rodino legislation, their testimony indicated a growing concern over the impact this particular reform might have on American citizens of Mexican descent. Consequently, LULAC representatives repeatedly admonished the committee to see to it that the law "did not become a tool of oppression on those people who have a right to live and work here," a concern LULAC would emphasize with increasing frequency in the coming months.[35]

On the other hand, LULAC's rhetoric during the Rodino hearings betrayed a growing sensitivity to the plight of undocumented aliens who entered the country seeking work. Though not nearly as strident on the issue as Chicano militants would soon prove to be, LULAC members nevertheless began to use rhetoric that expressed a new level of empathy with Mexican immigrants in the United States. Albert Armendáriz, Sr., who had been president of the organization when these issues surfaced within LULAC during Operation Wetback, attempted to explain LULAC's changing position to the Rodino committee. He stated that Mexican Americans were "torn between two desires, the desire to be good to our brothers who come from across the border and suffer so much when they are here trying to get ahead, and our desire to have those that are here as citizens advance in our society and become better adjusted to American life with the benefits of American life."[36] Another LULAC leader expressed similar sentiments. Although he made sure to point out that Mexican Americans remained "very much concerned with the problem because our people are . . . in competition with illegal aliens for jobs," he concluded his remarks by flatly asserting that "they are our brothers, we speak the same language . . . we are the same, the same people."[37]

As LULAC was advancing this rather startling departure from traditional mainstream Mexican American opinion on the immigration question, other organizations were beginning to make the same kind of arguments. MAPA also revised its position at this time. Established as an organizational offshoot of the CSO in 1959, MAPA, like LULAC and the G.I. Forum, had been among the strongest critics of the Bracero Program and had lobbied extensively for abolition of the program and for stricter enforcement of laws against undocumented immigration. During the debate over the Arnett bill in the California assembly, however, MAPA executed a reversal in its position on immigration reform that was every bit as remarkable as LULAC's shift.

In testimony before Arnett's subcommittee in late 1971, MAPA's state president, Armando Rodríguez, detailed the logic behind his organization's change in position. Though MAPA had once supported employer sanctions as an effective means of controlling undocumented immigration, he explained, his organization now intended to oppose the Arnett legislation because it would open the door to discrimination against anyone who looked Latino. Although Mexican Americans had made this argument before (most notably during Operation Wetback in 1954), Rodríguez took the criticism a significant step farther. Reminding the committee that MAPA traditionally had "favored employment for legal aliens and [American] citizens as opposed to employment of illegal aliens," MAPA's president went on to insist that the proposed legislation "should not be used by employers to continue harassing Mexican American people seeking employment, be they legals, illegals, citizens or otherwise."[38]

Rodríguez's statement is particularly enlightening because it provides a clear, though in all probability unintentional, indication of the extent to which even Mexican American moderates were beginning to reassess their thinking about the relationship of Mexican immigrants to Americans of Mexican descent. MAPA, LULAC, and similar Mexican American advocacy organizations previously had based much of their civil rights programs on their constituencies' American citizenship and had consistently attempted to emphasize the distinctions separating Mexican Americans from Mexican nationals. Now, MAPA's California state president rhetorically referred to a Mexican American people that included both legal and undocumented aliens from Mexico, along with American citizens of Mexican descent. It must be emphasized that Rodríguez's remarks represented only the views of an activist minority of the Mexican American population (MAPA claimed a membership of twenty-three thousand in 1971), but they did reflect a changing awareness of the civil rights implications of the immigration issue, one that was taking place among a growing number of diverse Mexican American interests.[39] Although it was still common to hear Mexican American citizens voice the opinion that "illegal aliens have no rights, and should be rounded up, and booted back across the border," Mexican American political and civil rights advocates were beginning to see the issue from a new perspective.[40] Clearly, moderate Mexican American advocacy organizations continued to base much of their revised position on their growing concern over the potential that employer sanctions held for creating job discrimination against Americans of Latin descent. Their changing rhetoric suggests, however, that Mexican American advocates were also beginning to recognize a new level of convergence between their civil rights efforts and the issue of the rights of Spanish-speaking immigrants in the United States, a concern Chicano activists were articulating with growing vehemence. Although most Mexican American moderates would not admit that Chicano militants had influenced their thinking on the issue, the changing tenor of debate over the civil rights and social identity of the Chicano people in the past decade had laid the foundations for a fundamental reassessment of the immigration issue. As Armendáriz later recalled, the combined efforts of the militants and mainstream Mexican American civil rights groups had contributed to a growing realization "that our previous position was not a realistic goal in our society. We realized that we needed to include non-citizens—both legal and illegal—in our [civil rights] efforts."[41]

The change in LULAC's and MAPA's positions was significant, but the most dramatic evidence of change was provided by a dispute that developed over the UFW's position on the question. Established in California in 1962 by César Chávez and Dolores Huerta, the UFW undoubtedly had been most instrumental in publicizing the plight of Mexican Americans to a national public. Chávez's farmworkers' movement had begun as a modest struggle merely to gain collective bargaining rights and union recognition for Mexican American and Filipino farmworkers in California. But by skillfully employing nonviolent tactics and utilizing emotionally charged ethnic symbols, such as the union's stylized black Aztec eagle insignia and banners of Mexico's patron saint, the Virgin of Guadalupe, to attract members and garner publicity, Chávez succeeded in capturing the imagination of Mexican Americans across the Southwest. He cultivated the image of a modest, pious man committed to using the powers of civil disobedience on behalf of his downtrodden people. More than any other individual, Chávez gave Mexican Americans a nationally recognized role model and champion. Moreover, by winning the support of priests, nuns, ministers, and a multiethnic horde of idealistic young student volunteers, Chávez imbued his movement with a moral dimension that transcended traditional labor-union politics. His ability to gain mass media attention during the 1960s was also instrumental in eventually garnering the public support of national celebrities, including comedian/musician Steve Allen, writer Peter Matthiessen, labor leader Walter Reuther of the powerful United Autoworkers Union, and such liberal politicians as Robert Kennedy, Eugene McCarthy, and George McGovern.[42]

Chávez was convinced, however, that in order to achieve the UFW's goals, the union's energies needed to be expended exclusively on behalf of American citizens and resident aliens. Consequently, from its inception in 1962 the UFW lobbied for strict control of the Mexican border. Like Ernesto Galarza before him, César Chávez argued that the presence of a large pool of politically powerless noncitizen workers severely hampered efforts to unionize American citizen workers. Moreover, the UFW stressed that American employers had always used undocumented Mexican workers to break strikes by American citizens. Chávez therefore stubbornly argued for the repeal of the Bracero Program and was among the most vocal critics of illegal immigration. The UFW consistently maintained this position in its early years, going so far as to report undocumented Mexican farmworkers to the INS.[43] In 1971 the UFW's leadership quietly supported the Arnett bill, later justifying its position by insisting that the use of undocumented workers was a "massive, well-organized black market in slave labor."[44] A Chicano UFW worker on strike for higher wages summarized his union's position when he told a reporter, "I know these people [that is, undocumented workers] want to work. But we can't let them break our strike, in the end we will benefit and they too will benefit. We are suffering for them, they should suffer a little for us."[45]

By 1973 it was apparent, however, that Chávez's stated position on the immigration issue was seriously out of line with the public views expressed by other Chicano and Mexican American groups. In the spring of that year CASA and the National Coalition for Fair Immigration Laws and Practices led a growing chorus of criticism against the UFW's apparent continued support of the Arnett and Rodino legislation.[46] Such criticism was remarkable in that it simultaneously marked the erosion of support for an individual leader and a political cause that up to this point had enjoyed the overwhelming support of Mexican American and Chicano activists and the crystallization of opinion on the immigration issue.[47]

The UFW's vacillation on the immigration issue renewed conflict among Chicano groups to such a point that the coalition issued an open letter to the union in July 1974. Incensed over an Associated Press story which quoted UFW officials as stating that aliens were "depriving jobs [from] farm workers and posing a threat to all people," the coalition's letter was the clearest statement yet as to the new position of Mexican American and Chicano activists. The coalition insisted that "all workers have the right to seek work in order to support themselves and their families. When we ask for the deportation of all of the workers who have no visas," the letter stated, "we are attacking many good union brothers and sisters that have no visas but would never break a strike." The coalition concluded by pointedly observing: "The [employers'] traditional response has been to deport not only the leaders of strikes but the workers themselves. Thus, when a union calls on the U.S. Immigration [Service] to help them it is calling on a traditional tool of the employers and the United States [government]."[48]

Chávez was made painfully aware of the strength of Mexican American and Chicano advocates' position on the immigration issue when the controversy made newspaper headlines again that autumn. It was reignited when Attorney General William B. Saxbe announced the Justice Department's intention of deporting a million illegal aliens from the country. Saxbe's announcement was particularly inflammatory in light of the increasing Mexican American sensitivity to the INS raids of the previous eighteen months, but when Saxbe claimed the full support of the UFW the issue exploded. Within days a coalition of organizations, including CASA, MAPA, the American G.I. Forum, LULAC, and the Los Angeles-based Chicana organization Comisión Feminil, angrily denounced the government's plan and demanded Saxbe's immediate resignation.[49]

Chávez gamely tried to defend his policies by flatly asserting that "most of the [Chicano] left attacking us has no experience in labor matters. They don't know what a strike is." "They don't know," he continued, "because they're not workers. They don't know because they've never felt the insecurity of being on strike. And they don't know because really they haven't talked to the workers."[50] Aware, however, that he desperately needed to maintain his base of support among urban Mexican Americans— particularly Chicano activists and students—Chávez was compelled to reassess his union's position on the increasingly explosive issue. In a letter to the editor of the *San Francisco Examiner* dated November 22, 1974, Chávez detailed the UFW's latest stand on the question. While reiterating the UFW's long-term objections to the use of undocumented workers as strike breakers, he subtly altered his position by pinning primary responsibility for "the mass recruitment of undocumented workers for the specific purpose of breaking our strikes and jeopardizing the rights of all farm workers" on the Justice Department and the INS. Chávez flatly denied supporting Saxbe's proposal and charged that the government's plan for mass deportation was nothing but "a ploy toward the reinstatement of a bracero program, which would give government sanction once more to the abuse of Mexican farm workers and, in turn, of farm workers who are citizens." Treading a very fine line between his earlier public support of restrictive legislation and his need to mend fences with other Mexican American and Chicano organizations, Chávez further asserted that "the illegal aliens are doubly exploited, first because they are farm workers, and second because they are powerless to defend their own interests. But if there were no illegals being used to break our strikes, we could win those strikes overnight and then be in a position to improve the living and working conditions of all farm workers." Chávez promised that the farmworkers would advocate "amnesty for illegal aliens and support their efforts to obtain legal documents and equal rights, including the right of collective bargaining." Concluding with a clear overture to militant Chicano groups, Chávez pledged his support to the undocumented because "the illegals [are] our brothers and sisters."[51]

The UFW's shifting position on the immigration question provided a good barometer of the extent to which Mexican American thinking on immigration had changed by the mid-1970s. The debate between the UFW and Chicano and Mexican American activists over Mexican immigration was seriously affecting support for Chávez's movement—and for what up to that point had been the most successful and unified political effort in Mexican American history. Clearly, many Mexican Americans continued to believe that political efforts on behalf of immigrants must remain secondary to efforts made on behalf of American citizens. But by 1975 Chicano activists and most major Mexican American advocacy organizations, including the UFW, had come to a new understanding of the relationship between the immigration controversy and the ongoing struggle to achieve equal rights for Americans of Mexican descent. A Mexican American labor union official in Los Angeles captured the spirit of this new position when he insisted that Mexican Americans who continued to support restrictive immigration policies "should realize that they would not be here if their fathers had not been illegal aliens"; an assertion that was certainly true for a large proportion of the Mexican American population.[52] Reflecting this new awareness, these diverse organizations and individuals had reconstructed earlier positions. Even the farmworkers, arguably the group most directly affected by undocumented immigration, expressed solidarity with undocumented workers while excoriating the federal government for proposing many of the same reforms they had once advocated. Although CASA's claim that its view on immigration had gone "from a minority position in the Mexican and Latin communities to the position of the overwhelming majority" was overstated, by 1975 a significant realignment had indeed occurred.[53] Given the ideological gulf that separated such politically moderate organizations as LULAC, MAPA, and the G.I. Forum on one hand and CASA and Chicano student groups on the other, this united front on the immigration controversy was remarkable.

The First Chicano/Latino Conference on Immigration and Public Policy

If anything, the united front of Chicano and Mexican American advocates became more solid after 1975. Facing growing opposition and unable to agree on an approach to immigration reform, Congress and other branches of the federal government commissioned a series of studies on the controversy in an attempt to develop consensus. Taken together, the most publicized of these studies, reports by the General Accounting Office (issued in 1973 and 1976) and by the INS (issued in 1976), accomplished this task by agreeing on the scope of the problem and by making very similar recommendations.[54]

Following the rough policy outlines sketched out in such reports, several members of Congress offered legislation that, though varying in detail, nevertheless embraced the same set of assumptions and policy recommendations. Consequently, separate bills offered by Congressman Rodino, Congressman Joshua Eilberg of Pennsylvania, Senator James Eastland of Mississippi, and Senator Edward Kennedy of Massachusetts advanced four basic recommendations: legal sanctions against employers who knowingly and repeatedly hired illegal aliens; increased INS appropriations and more stringent enforcement of the border; development of some kind of counterfeit-proof workers' identification system; and a limited extension of some type of legal amnesty to workers who had entered the United States before a date to be determined by Congress.[55]

Opponents were able to stymie such legislation until the presidential election of 1976. When Jimmy Carter was narrowly elected (with the overwhelming support of Mexican American voters), many Mexican American political advocates expected the new administration to address the immigration issue from a fresh perspective. Thus, when President Carter announced his immigration reform package in the summer of 1977, Mexican American and Chicano civil rights advocates were shocked to learn that the administration's plan closely resembled Rodino's. Indeed, in arguing that illegal aliens "had breached [the] Nation's immigration laws, displaced many American citizens from jobs, and placed an increased financial burden on many state and local governments," President Carter restated virtually all of the assumptions that had shaped congressional consideration of immigration policy reform since the debate over the Box Bill some forty years earlier.[56]

Virtually every major Mexican American and Chicano organization immediately protested the Carter Plan. In Washington national organizations, including LULAC, the American G.I. Forum, the Mexican American

Women's National Association, the National Council of La Raza, the Mexican American Legal Defense and Education Fund (MALDEF), and a broad range of at least ten other national and local groups established an ad hoc coalition to work against the Carter proposals.[57] The drama of the reaction was underscored when LULAC, completing a process of reevaluation of the issue that had begun in 1971, expressed its unequivocal opposition to the Carter Plan. In an almost complete departure from the organization's founding principles, LULAC's national headquarters issued a statement arguing that it was "unconscionable and objectionable" to subject resident Mexican nationals to the "second-class citizenship" that would be established under Carter's "amnesty" proposal. LULAC's Texas state director, Ruben Bonilla, elaborated on his organization's position, charging that the aliens' impact on American society had been "unduly sensationalized, grossly distorted, and vastly misrepresented." Bonilla expressed LULAC's particular opposition to Carter's proposed development of a national identification system, the reinstitution of some sort of limited foreign-worker program, and the imposition of employer sanctions, arguing that such provisions would create "a dual system of employment [in which] hiring will be based largely on a prospective employee's pigmentation and English-speaking ability."[58] The American G.I. Forum, next to LULAC perhaps the most politically conservative of the organizations in the ad hoc coalition, also derided the Carter Plan, passing a resolution at its national convention that strongly criticized the administration's proposals.[59]

The single most dramatic manifestation of the broad-based agreement on the issue was the landmark First National Chicano/Latino Conference on Immigration and Public Policy, held in San Antonio in October 1977. Organized primarily under the auspices of José Angel Gutiérrez and the Texas LRUP, the conference attracted nearly two thousand participants representing groups and individuals as diverse as LULAC, the American G.I. Forum, MALDEF, the Crusade for Justice, CASA, the Socialist Workers Party, and numerous Latino elected and appointed government officials. In the weeks preceding the conference and during the three-day meeting itself, participants made it clear that the government's proposals would meet with widespread Latino opposition. The conference's "Call for Action" rejected virtually all of the government's stated premises on immigration reform, charging that "the truth of the matter [was] that Latinos are to be made the scapegoat for this administration's ineptness at solving economic problems of inflation, unemployment, wage depression and rising consumer frustration." Voicing their dismay at a president from whom they had expected support, the conference organizers protested that "the very same man our Raza supported for the Presidency now seeks to deport us. The Carter administration is designing a new immigration policy. We are the main target."[60]

The significance of such unprecedented unity among the Mexican American, Chicano, and other Latino organizations and individuals represented at San Antonio was not lost on the participants. Peter Camejo, a Chicano representative of the Socialist Workers Party, observed: "I am speaking. So is LULAC, an organization I have disagreements with. We can disagree. But we can also sit down and talk to each other. Because when they come to deport us, we're all in the same boat."[61] Reflecting just how far Mexican American opinion on the issue had evolved since 1969, LULAC's national leaders now made corresponding claims. LULAC's national director, Edwin Morga, argued that the issue of undocumented workers in the United States represented a fundamental question of human rights. "We should show the world," he asserted, "that we are aware of the continuing political repression, the repression of human rights that is ongoing not only against Blacks, but certainly against Chicanos, against Mexicanos, and other brother Latins."[62]

Acting on this new-found unity, conference delegates passed a series of resolutions demanding full and unconditional amnesty for undocumented workers already in the country and the extension of full constitutional rights to resident aliens. Furthermore, the conference demanded that the government guarantee aliens the right to unionize, to receive unemployment compensation, and to educate their children in the United States.[63] After nearly six years of intense debate, Chicano and Mexican American activists had achieved an unprecedented consensus on the immigration controversy, a consensus that would last well into the debate over the Simpson-Rodino immigration proposals in the 1980s.

Conclusion

In many ways the First National Chicano/Latino Conference on Immigration and Public Policy marked the culmination of nearly a half century of Mexican American debate on Mexican immigration. Though the delegates remained ideologically divided on other issues, the meeting's resolutions demonstrated just how far Mexican American and Chicano activists had come on the complex question of the political, social, and cultural relationships between Mexican Americans and immigrants from Mexico. The conference also demonstrated the degree to which immigration had become a central issue in Mexican American politics.

This state of affairs was the outcome of a complicated historical process in which Chicano and Mexican American activists, in their separate pursuits of equal rights for the Mexican-descent minority in the United States, came to recognize how closely linked their campaigns were to the plight of Mexican immigrants. Forced to confront the recurrent issue of the mass immigration of relatively impoverished Mexican laborers into their communities, Mexican American political activists were also constantly compelled to assess and define their own sense of social and cultural identity vis-à-vis the recent arrivals. In the late 1960s few militant Chicano organizations and activists considered Mexican immigration a pressing concern, but the media's depiction of what it termed the illegal alien crisis and the government's subsequent actions in the immigration arena, combined with their own awakened sense of ethnic identity, soon stimulated a strong response among them. In the context of the ethnic catharsis symbolized by the rise of the Chicano movement, young Chicanos tended to view these reform efforts as yet another attack on the Mexican minority in the United States. By the early 1970s their central concern with exploring the sources of Chicano identity, their attempts to redefine the Chicano community, and a growing recognition that Mexican immigrants were Chicanos in the making led them to adopt a new, empathic stance on the issue. By 1975 most Chicano organizations had come to accept the view, as CASA's San Jose, California, affiliate succinctly put it, that "to learn how to protect the rights of workers without papers is to learn how to protect ourselves."[64]

Mexican American moderates had also come to a new understanding of the immigration dilemma. Indeed, by almost any measure the shift in Mexican American activists' opinion on the immigration issue in the 1970s represented a fundamental realignment on one of the most historically vexing and divisive issues in Mexican American politics. Though initially not nearly as aggressive as their Chicano counterparts, Mexican American moderates responded to what they too had come to perceive as an unwarranted campaign of anti-Mexican hysteria. Once they realized that the proposed immigration policy held potentially grave civil rights implications for American citizens of Mexican descent, organizations spanning the political spectrum began to soften their traditional restrictionist positions. And although few Mexican American advocates would admit it, the rhetoric of Chicano militants on both immigration and ethnic politics contributed to their growing awareness of the close relationships that bound Mexican immigrants to American citizens of Mexican descent.

The unprecedented show of unity on the immigration question should not, however, obscure the paradoxes and disagreements that continued to divide Mexican American and Chicano political activists on the related issues of ethnic identity, ideology, and the direction of Mexican American–Chicano politics. Indeed, when all was said and done, Mexican Americans' changing positions on the immigration controversy in many ways served to magnify what were already very old ideological and philosophical cleavages. Despite their newly sympathetic stand on immigration moderate Mexican American political activists and organizations generally continued to adhere to a vision of America that, while modifying the traditional assimilationist-Americanization perspective so prevalent in Mexican American politics since World War II, still emphasized achieving political and social reform by working within the confines of the existing American political system. For such individuals and organizations, and presumably for a large percentage of the U.S.-born Mexican American population as well, militant, ethnic-based politics held little appeal. Similarly, although Mexican American moderates had substantially altered their thinking on support for the rights of Mexican workers in the United States, few were willing to accept the premise that distinctions between American citizens and Mexican nationals should disappear entirely. As one LULAC member expressed it: "Mexico and its people know, and readily admit, that no one born in the United States is a Mexican, even if his parents were Mexican. . . . We have never been Mexicans nor Mexican Americans . . . much less Chicanos. Wake up, Spanish-speaking Americans—claim your rightful heritage, your real nationality. Tell the world, with the rest of our fellow citizens—I AM AN AMERICAN—don't call me anything else!"[65]

For the more militant wing of the Chicano movement, consideration of ethnic nationalist ideology in conjunction with the immigration issue helped to expose some of the most glaring conflicts and contradictions of leaders who advocated Chicano nationalism without fully and critically examining the sources of their ethnicity, their relationship to Mexicans who had arrived from the other side of the border, or their relationship to other Americans. Although the process of refining and reshaping their cultural identity and political ideology led Chicano activists to reject assimilation and Americanization as sterile strategies that contributed to Chicano oppression, their ultimate inability to provide an alternative vision by precisely defining the parameters of Chicano culture and the ethnocultural boundaries of the community they claimed to represent spoke to an ideological dilemma that is yet to be resolved.

In broader terms the ability of Mexican American and Chicano movement activists and organizations to achieve consensus on the immigration issue while continuing to disagree deeply over issues of culture, ethnic identity, political ideology, and community during the 1960s and 1970s was symptomatic of the fractured nature of the Mexican American experience throughout the twentieth century. These issues all revolved around the fundamental and ultimately inextricable questions of Mexican Americans' and Mexican immigrants' self-perceived place in American society. Was it reasonable to expect that either group could ultimately achieve sociocultural and political assimilation into that society, or was it possible to maintain distinct and viable ethnic cultures in the larger society? Or could some as yet undefined middle path be followed? By the late 1970s internal debate among Mexican Americans and Chicanos over the most basic questions of ethnic and cultural identity, the steadily increasing class, generational, and regional diversity of the population, and fundamental historical disagreements over the best political strategy for the United States' ethnic Mexican minority combined to foil concerted Mexican American–Chicano action. The rapid growth of the Mexican American–Mexican immigrant population of the United States since then, the attendant social dislocations accompanying that growth, and the continuing and increasing pressures inducing emigration from Mexico (and increasingly, from other Latin American "sending nations") are all clear indications that such fundamental questions will continue to be pressing concerns facing Americans of Mexican descent in the years to come.

Epilogue

As the twentieth century comes to a close immigration has reemerged as one of the most divisive controversies in American politics. Resurfacing at a time when the nation is simultaneously experiencing a deep economic recession, increasing political polarization, and a frightening increase in ethnic and racial tensions, many Americans are again venting their frustrations about U.S. immigration policy and about the many cultural issues that immigration has helped to inject into national politics. Although much of the animus toward immigrants is a response to current circumstances, many of the patterns of the most recent wave of anti-immigrant sentiment are eerily reminiscent of earlier periods of American nativism. Indeed, much of the rhetoric about immigrants presently being heard in government and in the media is virtually identical to the anti-immigrant pronouncements that were commonly heard in the 1890s, the 1920s, the 1950s, and again in the 1970s. In a litany that can be found daily in virtually every major newspaper in the country, a new, vocal group of restrictionists argues that immigrants—particularly undocumented immigrants—are stealing jobs from American citizens, undermining wage rates and working conditions, committing crimes, overwhelming the public education and health systems, and abusing welfare and other social programs. Insisting that the current rate of immigration threatens the very fabric of American life, these critics demand that strong action be taken to regain control of the nation's borders by increasing enforcement efforts and by sharply limiting the number of immigrants allowed into the United States in the future.

The debate has become particularly volatile in the Southwest. Although the region has long been a site of intensive contact and conflict among many different cultural groups, the recent recession has helped to raise in-

terethnic and interracial tensions to new, dangerous levels. In a region that
has seen a steady erosion of the quality of public education and other tax-
supported public services, has been particularly hard hit by the economic
dislocations caused by the post–cold war contractions of key industries, and
is still trying to recover from the shock of the conflagration that erupted in
Los Angeles in 1992, the growing apprehension about the growth of non-
white resident immigrant populations comes as no surprise.

As in previous eras, immigrants provide easy targets for people who are
profoundly uneasy about the economic and cultural changes they believe
are transforming their society. Largely as a consequence of this, local politicians have once again raised a hue and cry about the immigrant menace.
Jumping at the chance to gain political capital from an issue that has come
to dominate debate in many states, a growing number of both conservatives and liberals alike have issued grave warnings about the wisdom of
continuing to allow large-scale immigration into the Southwest and the
nation at large. Representing positions across the political spectrum, a
highly visible group of individuals and organizations has mounted campaigns calling for the implementation of new legislative measures designed
to restrict and control the flow of immigrants into the United States. Cities
such as El Paso have already experimented with blockades of the international frontier, and politicians in San Diego are calling for similar action
there. Many other measures have been proposed, ranging from such seemingly benign propositions as the recent move in California to conduct a
census of foreign students in the public school system to more draconian
demands to deny undocumented immigrants access to public education and
medical care. At the more extreme end of the spectrum some regional politicians have revived earlier proposals calling for the development of a
counterfeit-proof national worker identity card and for the construction
along the border of high barbed-wire fences and/or deep trenches permanently manned by armed troops. The most dramatic recent reform proposal is the one supported by several regional politicians, including such
otherwise unlikely allies as conservative California Republican Governor
Pete Wilson and veteran liberal Los Angeles Democratic Congressman Anthony Bielensen, to amend the Constitution so that automatic birthright
citizenship would henceforth be denied to the U.S.-born children of undocumented immigrants. With moderate Democrats like California Senators Diane Feinstein and Barbara Boxer joining such conservatives as Patrick Buchanan and George Will and such influential lobby groups as the
Federation for Immigration Reform in issuing calls for immigration reform, the issue is apparently gaining broad-based support.[1]

Although INS statistics indicate that documented and undocumented immigrants to the United States come from virtually every nation on earth, Spanish-speaking immigrants have borne the brunt of the most recent revival of restrictionism. Long the most publicized of all the so-called illegal aliens in the Southwest, Spanish-speaking immigrants are again receiving most of the negative attention generated by recent campaigns against immigrants.

As a result of this attention Mexican Americans and other Americans of Latin American descent once again find themselves caught in the middle of the immigration controversy. Although a few more politically aware Americans have come to realize that Mexican Americans and other U.S.-born Latinos are themselves deeply divided over the issue, the perception nevertheless persists that Latinos somehow have a natural interest in supporting Latin American immigrants' right to enter, work, and live in the United States. This perception has undoubtedly been reinforced in recent years by the vigorous opposition that Mexican American and other Latino political leaders and lobbies have mounted against efforts to enact restrictive immigration policies. Beginning with the debate over legislation originally proposed by Congressman Peter Rodino in 1971 and 1972, continuing with the controversy over President Jimmy Carter's immigration reform plan in 1977, and resolutely persisting through the long, rancorous debate over various bills that preceded the eventual passage of the Immigration Reform and Control Act in 1986, prominent Mexican American and Latino organizations have been in the forefront of the political forces arrayed against the advocates of immigration restriction. Led by the Congressional Hispanic Caucus and supported by a strong coalition of advocacy organizations, such as LULAC, the American G.I. Forum, MALDEF, and the National Council of La Raza, these oppositional efforts have proved to be remarkably effective. Despite the fact that members of the Hispanic Caucus have never represented more than a tiny fraction of the total membership of Congress, they helped to stymie virtually all efforts to pass restrictive immigration policies at the federal level between 1970 and 1985.[2]

Advocates of immigration control and restriction have become increasingly frustrated by Latino political activists' success in blocking their proposals. Although some proponents of immigration restriction have grudgingly acknowledged that immigration is a particularly sensitive issue for Latino politicians and community groups, others have flatly accused Latino political leaders of being more interested in building the ethnic vote (presumably by allowing the number of their potential constituents to grow) than they are in protecting the national interest. During the intense political wrangling over immigration that occurred in the early 1980s, for example, Wyoming Republican Senator Alan Simpson (a former member of the Select Commission on Immigration and Refugee Policy and the chief sponsor of the Simpson-Mazzoli immigration reform bill in the Senate) used martial terms to characterize the immigration debate, calling it a "battle to regain control of the nation's borders" and "a continuing, running gun battle with tunnel vision, short-term special interests constantly cutting . . . across the long-term national interest." In a thinly veiled reference to Mexican American and other Latino activists, Simpson argued that the debate over immigration could be reduced to a question of whether "U.S. politics [will be] controlled by narrow and wholly selfish special interests [or will be] representative of the broad public will."[3] Former Colorado governor and immigration activist Richard Lamm was even more blunt in his criticism of Latino political leaders. After a revised version of the Simpson-Mazzoli legislation was defeated in 1984 Lamm declared that "Hispanic leaders have remained obdurate, have refused to accept any solution to the problems of massive illegal and legal immigration, and even refused to admit that massive illegal and legal immigration are . . . problems." From Lamm's point of view, "The Simpson-Mazzoli Immigration Reform bill was a start toward getting control over illegal immigration [but] it was killed because a few spokesmen for unrepresentative Hispanic pressure groups and a few members of the Congressional Hispanic Caucus do not want illegal immigration to be controlled."[4]

Although restrictionists like Lamm and Simpson have been particularly harsh in their criticism of their Latino opponents, they have gone to great pains to insist that they are not xenophobes or nativists. They have insisted that they have only the national interest at heart, and they usually try to couch their rhetoric on the issue in only the broadest, most universalistic terms. To cite just one example of this, Senator Simpson has stated at numerous times over the past decade that his only concern is for the future of the American commonwealth. Arguing that "uncontrolled immigration" has become "one of the greatest threats to the future" of the United States because it threatens eventually to undermine "American values, traditions, institutions, and . . . our way of life," Simpson has long tried to convince his Senate colleagues and the American public of the grave threat.[5] As he put it in a speech before the Senate in 1983, "If we in Government or politics are not able to bridle our compassion for the less fortunate people of other lands sufficiently to protect the national interest, then not only will we have failed in our primary duty to the least advantaged in our own nation, but there is a substantial risk that in the long run the American people will be unable or unwilling to respond at all."[6]

If recent public-opinion polls and the tenor of discussions about the immigration issue in the mass media are any indication, a great many Americans apparently have come to agree both with Simpson's conception of the nature of the immigration problem and with the larger questions arising from the changing ethnic composition of the United States.[7] For Simpson, and for a growing proportion of the American public, the issues involved in the immigration controversy are fairly straightforward. Adhering to a view in which the issue of an immigrant's standing in American society and ability to fit into the American way of life should be determined simply by ascertaining the individual's formal status before the law, many apparently believe that devising appropriate immigration policies should be a simple matter. For such individuals the question of who rightly should be considered a fully vested member of the American community is unambiguous: one is either legal or illegal, a citizen or an alien, an American or a foreigner.

If one accepts this starkly bifurcated system of categorization, it follows that coming to basic decisions about who rightfully belongs to, and who must be excluded from, that community should be an easy matter. As I have attempted to demonstrate in this book, however, such a conceptualization of the immigration controversy—and of the politicization of ethnicity in American society that immigration has helped to spawn—is fundamentally flawed in a number of respects. The most glaring flaw in this formulation is, of course, that it ignores the central role that Americans of all walks of life have played, and continue to play, in creating and maintaining the situation that is now ubiquitously portrayed as the crisis of illegal immigration. As we have seen, from the first years of this century to the present, American employers and their allies in government have worked in close partnership to recruit foreign workers and to ensure that the flow of immigrant workers is regulated for the maximum benefit of American businesses and consumers. The long history in this century of the ad hoc implementation of arbitrary immigration laws, the selective enforcement of those laws, and the periodic expulsions of ethnic Mexican workers and their U.S.-born children—in short, the endlessly sliding mechanisms Americans have used to exclude Mexican aliens from becoming vested members of the American community—stands as stark testimony of the extent to which business, government, and the general public have colluded in exploiting and profiting from the fruits of Mexican labor while they simultaneously lamented and decried the cultural transformations of American society caused by those practices. And although virtually all the players in this process would deny it if asked, this alliance of business and government over time helped to erode clear-cut distinctions between juridically bona fide American citizens and members of this society who, in virtually every respect except their formal citizenship status, were as American as anyone else. Thus to rail, as the latest generation of restrictionists does incessantly, that the United States has lost its sovereign right to secure its borders, without also acknowledging that the nation's leaders themselves have consistently abrogated that right, is to engage, at the very least, in selective memory.

It goes without saying that immigrant minorities—particularly the ethnic Mexican minority—have been profoundly affected by Americans' habit of engaging in such selective, sanitized historical memory. Among the most serious effects of this historical amnesia is that it has allowed Americans to continue to deny any knowledge of, or responsibility for, the origins, evolution, and present political and social consequences of more than nine decades of institutionally supported immigration from Mexico. By indulging instead in the demonization of illegal aliens, legislators, journalists, and members of the public at large have chosen the simpler yet infinitely more destructive expedient of creating scapegoats. They thus avoid the responsibility of systematically and critically addressing what has become an immensely complicated set of social, political, cultural, and economic issues affecting millions of people on both sides of the border. Indeed, demonstrating the same kind of self-serving myopia that has characterized Americans' images about Mexican immigrants for generations, most of the individuals and organizations involved in the current controversy over immigration act as though the issue somehow erupted in a vacuum. The result of this social myopia is the perpetuation of one-sided analyses of the immigration phenomenon in which a wide range of social ills, including unemployment, welfare abuses, threats to public health, teen-age pregnancies, and increasing crime rates, drug abuse, and gang activity in the cities, can be blamed, as has occurred so often in the past, on a faceless, dehumanized, horde of Spanish-speaking immigrants. The damage this has done, and is doing, to the nation's large resident immigrant population is obvious. Such negative portrayals have not only increasingly poisoned public opinion about the effects of immigration, they also have clearly contributed to the frightening recent increase in acts of violence committed against immigrants in the United States.

The most insidious long-term result of this persistent shirking of responsibility is that it has helped to obscure the extent to which the uproar over immigration is serving as a surrogate for deeper fears and concerns about the changing nature of society and culture in the United States. I would argue that the current attempt by restrictionists to employ the same loaded, manipulative rhetoric about the immigration issue that nativists used at the turn of the century should be construed as part of a larger political strategy targeted at Mexican American, Latino, and other minority civil rights and community activists who have recently begun to exert a significant influence in American politics.

The current battle over the issue of multiculturalism is particularly illustrative of the ways in which the dispute over immigration has spilled over into other pressing issues in U.S. ethnic and racial politics. Although the term *multiculturalism* has been used by so many people in so many contexts that its meaning has become hopelessly muddled, the concept has nevertheless stimulated one of the fiercest debates in recent American politics. To critics of the concept, multiculturalism represents nothing short of a full frontal assault on "Western civilization, democracy, its representatives and its values."[8] With a growing group of journalists, scholars, politicians, and bureaucrats leading the way, critics who support this general point of view have mounted an increasingly shrill attack on the minority activists whom they accuse of practicing the balkanizing politics of multiculturalism. As historian Arthur Schlesinger, Jr., has put it in a recent series of essays and in his widely publicized polemic, *The Disuniting of America*,

> The recent apotheosis of ethnicity, black, brown, red, yellow, white, has revived the dismal prospect that in happy melting-pot days Americans thought the republic was moving safely beyond—that is, a society fragmented into ethnic groups. The cult of ethnicity exaggerates differences, intensifies resentments and antagonisms, and drives ever deeper the awful wedges between races and nationalities. The end-game is self-pity and self-ghettoization.[9]

According to Schlesinger and others of his ilk the recent "eruption of ethnicity" they so decry "has reversed the movement of American history" by promulgating ethnically based ideologies that "inculcate . . . the illusion that membership in one or another ethnic group is the basic American experience."[10]

In light of the deep hold that assimilationist ideology has exerted on Americans, the fears expressed by such individuals are certainly understandable. A cherished myth since the founding of the republic, the hopeful idea of the melting pot continues to exert a powerful grip on Americans who are worried about the present and uncertain about the future. Indeed, of all the sources of misunderstanding between hard-line proponents of assimilation and members of the ethnic Mexican population, the idea that individuals might choose to reject all or part of this comforting prescription for the eventual social absorption of ethnic minorities is probably the most intractable.

On many other levels, however, the recent criticism leveled at Mexican

American, Latino, and other minority political activists betrays a lack of candor, to say the very least. At the most basic level such analyses diminish, or ignore completely, the extent to which Mexican Americans and other minority activists were in many ways forced by the realities of deeply rooted racism, ethnocentrism, and enforced segregation to struggle for their civil rights by organizing along ethnic or racial lines. In the face of more than a century of a history in which Mexican American activists associated with such organizations as LULAC, the American G.I. Forum, the CSO, and the NAWU had to claw and scratch to see even the most limited progress in their efforts to desegregate public facilities, to gain access to public education and other tax-supported services, to receive equal pay for equal work, and, most recently, to protect the basic human rights of Mexican and other Latino immigrants, it is somewhat disingenuous for critics of the current political scene to expect that these activists should have acted differently in the past or that politically active Mexican Americans should now choose some other basis for pressing their demands. As has been seen repeatedly over the past century, Mexican American and Mexican immigrant activists have consistently organized and struggled to achieve political goals based on whatever room for maneuver they were afforded by the structures of mainstream American politics. To assert otherwise is not only a distortion of history, it is also a lie.

The current attack on ethnic and immigrant rights activists and on the alternative political positions they espouse on immigration and other matters reflects more than a mere distortion of the past. The tragedy of this sustained, withering attack is that it is based on a profound misapprehension or intentional misrepresentation of the kinds of changes and challenges that have slowly emerged in regional ethnic and immigration politics in recent years. Although the individuals who have led the attack against proponents of alternative political and cultural perspectives have doggedly characterized their actions as a last-ditch defense against multicultural barbarians who are bent on destroying everything that is good about American society, their seemingly selfless critique is actually the most egregious distortion of the diverse political and cultural campaigns currently being pursued by ethnic Mexican, Latino, and other activists. To its proponents multiculturalism represents a broad point of view that simply acknowledges, and asks other Americans to acknowledge, that the United States has become an exceedingly polyglot, multiethnic, multicultural society. Proponents also insist that along with this recognition comes a serious reconsideration of the criteria for membership in the American community. Although it is true that many Mexican American and Latino community activists are committed to challenging, and eventually displacing, the long-standing racial ideologies and other modes of cultural domination that have collectively locked ethnic Mexicans into a subordinate position vis-à-vis other Americans, the most progressive of them are also aware of the dangers of replacing one racial, ethnic, or cultural hierarchy with another. On the contrary, the intent of their challenge is not "to rediscover some absolute racial, ethnic, or cultural purity," as one group of scholars engaged in this project put it in another context, but to explore new ways of ensuring the meaningful political inclusion and participation in society of those who historically have been excluded. As the Chicano performance artist Guillermo Gómez-Peña argued, although the advocates of such alternative political and cultural perspectives recognize that "the multicultural process that the U.S. is presently undergoing implies a shift in center, a decentralization of . . . canons and styles," they tend to view these changes not as a trend toward balkanization and chaos but as a positive move in the direction of democratization based on "a multiplication of . . . criteria" by which people may be "validated . . . as full citizens."[11]

Such challenges to the perpetuation of the arbitrary, essentialistic, and exclusionary notions of race, ethnicity, and citizenship that have traditionally characterized interethnic relations in the Southwest have had, and will continue to exert, a profound influence on the ongoing debate over immigration. Given the years of intimate interaction with immigrants from Mexico, it is not at all surprising that significant numbers of Mexican Americans consider immigrants to be functional, contributing members of American society and thus will continue to fight policies that threaten immigrants' rights as human beings and as members of their communities. When considered along with the new forms of ethnic consciousness that gradually evolved out of the civil rights movement after World War II, Mexican Americans' empathy toward Mexican immigrants makes even more sense.

To assert this here, however, is not to imply that Mexican Americans are necessarily moving toward some new consensus on the vexing questions of Mexican and pan-Latino immigration or to diminish the importance of intraethnic differences of opinion on the related question of the appropriateness of pursuing a political strategy predicated on racial, ethnic, or cultural solidarity. On the contrary, if recent public-opinion polls are any indication—and their reliability as a gauge of Latino-American opinion is hotly disputed—Americans of Mexican descent remain about as deeply divided on these issues as other Americans are.[12] One need only consider the apparent gulf in the immigration policy debate between Mexican American legislators and their constituents and the increasing debate among Mexican Americans over such issues as the appropriateness of bilingual education, multicultural curricular reform in education, affirmative action, busing, and, indeed, over their designation as an identifiable minority group in general to recognize that a great many Mexican Americans continue to subscribe to some version of the melting-pot theory in their everyday lives.

Still, as Mexican Americans have discovered throughout their history, the realities of their strong links to Mexican immigrants will continue to compel them to make decisions about who they are, how they want to be perceived by others, and who they want to be as citizens of this society. The choices they make about these walls and mirrors at this crucial historical juncture will not only provide strong indications about the future of ethnic politics in the Southwest but also will determine whether the nation remains a society deeply fractured along lines of race, class, and culture or begins to move in the direction of a truly participatory democracy, one whose members finally acknowledge their society's intricate ethnic heterogeneity—and learn to accept and deal constructively with the political consequences of that ineluctable fact.

Notes

INTRODUCTION

1. The terminology used to describe this population group is steeped in controversy and contention. The term *Hispanic* came into vogue in the 1970s as a descriptor of the total Spanish-heritage population of the United States as conceived of by the U.S. Census Bureau and other agencies of the federal government. Used in this context the term refers to ethnic groups who trace their origins to predominantly Spanish-speaking nations of the Western Hemisphere. The term *Latino,* on the other hand, has been adopted as a self-referent by many Americans of Hispanic descent as a way to denote their sense of a pan-Hispanic solidarity that cuts across national and ethnic lines. For critical discussions of the issues involved in such categorizations, see Leo F. Estrada, José Hernández, and David Alvírez, "Using Census Data to Study the Spanish Heritage Population of the United States," in *Cuantos Somos: A Demographic Study of the Mexican American Population,* ed. Charles H. Teller, Monograph no. 2, Center for Mexican American Studies, University of Texas, Austin (Austin: Center for Mexican American Studies, 1977), 13–60; Martha E. Giménez, "The Political Construction of the Hispanic," in *Estudios Chicanos and the Politics of Community: Selected Proceedings, National Association for Chicano Studies,* ed. Mary Romero et al. (Boulder, Colo.: National Association for Chicano Studies, 1989), 66–85; and Ramón A. Gutiérrez's provocative "Unraveling America's Hispanic Past: Internal Stratification and Class Boundaries," *Aztlán* 17 (Spring 1986):79–102.

2. See Thomas D. Boswell, "The Growth and Proportional Distribution of the Mexican Stock Population in the United States: 1910–1970," *Mississippi Geographer* 7 (Spring 1979):57–76; Frank D. Bean and Marta Tienda, *The Hispanic Population of the United States* (New York: Russell

Sage Foundation, 1987), 36–103; and "Hispanic Population Passes 20 Million, U.S. Says," *New York Times,* October 12, 1989, sec. 1, p. 12.

3. I have been careful to use terminology to describe various subgroups of the Mexican-origin population as they labeled themselves or to otherwise make clear distinctions among the different groups. Thus when I refer to immigrants from Mexico I use the terms *Mexican immigrants, Mexican aliens, Mexican nationals,* or simply *Mexicans.* I have attempted to restrict use of the term *Chicano* to that group of American citizens of Mexican descent who use this term to describe themselves. The term *Mexican American* is more problematic, but again, for the purposes of this study, the term refers specifically to those individuals who label themselves as such. As a matter of convenience, however, I also occasionally use that term to describe all American citizens of Mexican descent, regardless of their political orientation or length of residence in the United States. For reasons that will become clear in the text, I employ *ethnic Mexicans* or *the ethnic Mexican population* when referring to the total Mexican-origin population of the United States, citizen and alien alike.

4. Because of the changing definitions used to enumerate persons of Mexican origin or descent and the presence of large numbers of undocumented Mexicans nationals in the United States, the statistics cited in this study should be considered estimates that suggest population trends rather than absolutely accurate enumerations. For various estimates and discussions of some of the methodological problems associated with enumerating persons of Mexican origin or heritage, see Boswell, "Growth and Proportional Distribution of the Mexican Stock Population," 57–76; Bean and Tienda, *Hispanic Population of the United States;* David E. Lorey, ed., *United States–Mexico Border Statistics Since 1900* (Los Angeles: UCLA Latin American Center Publications, 1990), tables 120–122; Roberto Ham-Chande and John R. Weeks, "A Demographic Perspective of the U.S.–Mexico Border," in *Demographic Dynamics of the U.S.–Mexico Border,* ed. John R. Weeks and Roberto Ham-Chande (El Paso: Texas Western Press, 1992), 1–27; and U.S. Bureau of the Census, *The Hispanic Population in the United States: March 1991,* Current Population Reports, ser. P–20, no. 455 (Washington, D.C.: U.S. Government Printing Office, 1991).

5. See, for example, T. B. Morgan, "The Latinization of America," *Esquire,* May 1983, 47–56; and Joan Didion's penetrating analysis in *Miami* (New York: Simon and Schuster, 1987).

6. Several pioneering scholars recognized that intraethnic relationships between Mexican Americans and Mexican immigrants revealed important insights into the social history of Spanish-speaking people in the United States, but very few attempted systematic analyses of these complex relationships. For some early efforts in this direction, see Emory S. Bogardus,

The Mexican in the United States, University of Southern California Social Science Series, no. 8 (Los Angeles: University of Southern California, 1934); Ernesto Galarza, *Merchants of Labor: The Mexican Bracero Story, An Account of the Managed Migration of Mexican Farmworkers in California, 1942–1960* (Charlotte, N.C.: McNally & Loftin, 1964); Manuel Gamio, *Mexican Immigration to the United States; A Study of Human Migration and Adjustment* (Chicago: University of Chicago Press, 1930), and *The Life Story of the Mexican Immigrant: Autobiographical Documents* (Chicago: University of Chicago Press, 1931); Carey McWilliams, *North from Mexico: The Spanish-Speaking People of the United States* (New York: Lippincott, 1948); and Paul S. Taylor, *Mexican Labor in the United States*, University of California Publications in Economics, vol. 6, nos. 1–5 (Berkeley: University of California Press, 1928–1930), and *An American-Mexican Frontier: Nueces County, Texas* (Chapel Hill: University of North Carolina Press, 1934). More recently, Chicano studies and immigration scholars have made more detailed efforts in this direction, but again, most studies of Mexican American–Mexican immigrant relationships focus on the contemporary situation and are of a preliminary, exploratory nature. For recent examples of this scholarship, see Alejandro Portes and Robert L. Bach, *Latin Journey: Cuban and Mexican Immigrants in the United States* (Berkeley: University of California Press, 1985); Harley Browning and Rodolfo O. de la Garza, eds., *Mexican Immigrants and Mexican Americans: An Evolving Relationship* (Austin: Center for Mexican American Studies Publications, 1986); Douglas Massey et al., *Return to Aztlán: The Social Process of International Migration to the United States from Western Mexico* (Berkeley: University of California Press, 1987); Estevan T. Flores, "Post-Bracero Undocumented Mexican Immigration to the United States and Political Recomposition" (Ph.D. diss., University of Texas, Austin, 1982); Mario T. García, "La Frontera: The Border as Symbol and Reality in Mexican American Thought," *Mexican Studies/Estudios Mexicanos* 1 (Summer 1985):195–225; Juan Gómez-Quiñones, "Notes on the Interpretation of the Relations between the Mexican Community in the United States and Mexico: Historical and Political Contexts of a Dialogue Renewed," in *Mexico–United States Relations: Conflict and Convergence*, ed. Carlos Vásquez and Manuel García y Griego (Los Angeles: Chicano Studies Research Center and Latin American Center Publications, University of California, Los Angeles, 1983), 417–439; and Arturo Santamaría Gómez, *La izquierda norteamericana y los trabajadores indocumentados* (Sinaloa, Mexico: Ediciones de Cultura Popular, Universidad Autónoma de Sinaloa, 1988).

7. Carl Allsup, *The American G.I. Forum: Origins and Evolution*, Monograph no. 6, Center for Mexican American Studies, University of Texas, Austin (Austin: University of Texas Press, 1982), 119.

8. Albert M. Camarillo, *Chicanos in a Changing Society: From Mexican Pueblos to American Barrios in Santa Barbara and Southern California, 1848–1930* (Cambridge, Mass.: Harvard University Press, 1979), 169.

9. The debate is succinctly explicated in the introduction to Nathan Glazer and Daniel Patrick Moynihan, eds., *Ethnicity: Theory and Experience* (Cambridge, Mass.: Harvard University Press, 1975), 1–26; Peter K. Eisinger, "Ethnicity as a Strategic Option: An Emerging View," *Public Administration Review* 38 (January-February 1978):89–93; John Rex and David Mason, eds., *Theories of Race and Ethnic Relations* (Cambridge, England: Cambridge University Press, 1986); George M. Scott, Jr., "A Resynthesis of the Primordial and Circumstantial Approaches to Ethnic Group Solidarity: Towards an Explanatory Model," *Ethnic and Racial Studies* 13 (April 1990):147–171; and Anthony P. Cohen, "Culture as Identity: An Anthropologist's View," *New Literary History* 24 (Winter 1993):195–209.

10. E. K. Francis, "The Nature of the Ethnic Group," *American Journal of Sociology* 52 (March 1947):399. See also Stuart Hall, "Race, Articulation and Societies Structured in Dominance," in *Sociological Theories: Race and Colonialism* (Paris: UNESCO, 1980), 305–345, "New Ethnicities," reprinted in *"Race," Culture, and Difference*, ed. J. Donald and A. Ratansi (London: Sage, 1992), 252–260, "Ethnicity: Identity and Difference," *Radical America* 23 (October-December 1989):9–22, and "Cultural Identity and Diaspora," in *Identity: Community, Culture, Difference*, ed. Jonathan Rutherford (London: Lawrence and Wishart, 1990), 222–237.

11. Indeed, as late as 1990 more than 70 percent of the entire ethnic Mexican population of the United States resided in those two states alone. See U.S. Bureau of the Census, *Hispanic Population in the United States, March 1991*.

ONE. LEGACIES OF CONQUEST

1. For discussions of the so-called All Mexico movement, see John Douglas Pitts Fuller, *The Movement for the Acquisition of All Mexico, 1846–1848* (Baltimore: Johns Hopkins University Press, 1936); Frederick Merk, *Manifest Destiny and Mission in American History* (New York: Vintage Books, 1963), 107–143; and David M. Pletcher, *The Diplomacy of Annexation: Texas, Oregon, and the Mexican War* (Columbia: University of Missouri Press, 1973), 522–526, 551–552, 555–557, 561.

2. Reginald Horsman, *Race and Manifest Destiny: The Origins of American Racial Anglo-Saxonism* (Cambridge, Mass.: Harvard University Press, 1981), 236–237.

3. John L. O'Sullivan, *Democratic Review* 17 (July-August 1845), quoted in Horsman, *Race and Manifest Destiny*, 219.

4. *New York Sun*, November 20, 1847, quoted in Merk, *Manifest Destiny and Mission*, 122. See also Horsman, *Race and Manifest Destiny*, 232–235; and Ronald Takaki, *Iron Cages: Race and Culture in 19th-Century America* (New York: Oxford University Press, 1990), 154–162.

5. *Richmond Whig*, October 9, 1846, quoted in Horsman, *Race and Manifest Destiny*, 239.

6. *Illinois State Register*, December 27, 1844, quoted in Merk, *Manifest Destiny and Mission*, 39.

7. *Congressional Globe*, 29th Cong., 2d sess., February 9, 1847, appendix, 327, and *Congressional Globe*, 30th Cong., 1st sess., January 4, 1848, 98–99, quoted in Horsman, *Race and Manifest Destiny*, 241.

8. *Congressional Globe*, 29th Cong., 2d sess., February 10, 1847, 191, quoted in Horsman, *Race and Manifest Destiny*, 241.

9. See diplomatic correspondence in Hunter Miller, ed., *Treaties and Other International Acts of the United States of America* (Washington, D.C.: U.S. Government Printing Office, 1931); and Pletcher, *Diplomacy of Annexation*, 528–530, 538–540.

10. Nicholas Trist, Department of State, Despatches, Mexico, no. 27, January 25, 1848, quoted in Hunter Miller, *Treaties and Other International Acts*, 306.

11. Algunos documentos sobre el Tratado de Guadalupe, December 30, 1847, quoted in ibid., 300.

12. See the general discussion of the treaty in Hunter Miller, *Treaties and Other International Acts*; and Richard Griswold del Castillo, *The Treaty of Guadalupe Hidalgo: A Legacy of Conflict* (Norman: University of Oklahoma Press, 1990).

13. U.S. Senate, Amendments to Section IX, Treaty of Guadalupe Hidalgo, March 10, 1848, quoted in Hunter Miller, *Treaties and Other International Acts*, 241.

14. Griswold del Castillo, *Treaty of Guadalupe Hidalgo*, 62–72.

15. Horsman, *Race and Manifest Destiny*, 246.

16. Richard Henry Dana, *Two Years Before the Mast* (New York: Airmont Publishing Co., 1966), 136, 137.

17. See Leonard Pitt, *The Decline of the Californios: A Social History of the Spanish-Speaking Californians, 1846–1890* (Berkeley: University of California Press, 1966), 46–68.

18. For the differing estimates of the scope of the demographic transformation of nineteenth-century Texas, see Terry G. Jordan, "A Century and a Half of Ethnic Change in Texas, 1836–1986," *Southwestern Historical Quarterly* 89 (April 1986):386–421, and "Population Origins in Texas, 1850," *Geographical Review* 59 (January 1969):83–103; Oscar J. Martínez, "On the Size of the Chicano Population: New Estimates, 1850–1900," *Aztlán* 6 (Spring 1975):43–67; and Arnoldo de León and Kenneth L.

Stewart, *Tejanos and the Numbers Game: A Socio-Historical Interpretation from the Federal Censuses, 1850–1900* (Albuquerque: University of New Mexico Press, 1989), 15–29.

19. Arnoldo de León, *They Called Them Greasers: Anglo Attitudes toward Mexicans in Texas, 1821–1900* (Austin: University of Texas Press, 1983), 11.

20. Quoted in ibid., 17.

21. For comparative population data for California cities, see Richard Griswold del Castillo, *The Los Angeles Barrio, 1850–1890: A Social History* (Berkeley: University of California Press, 1979), 62–63; and Albert M. Camarillo, *Chicanos in a Changing Society: From Mexican Pueblos to American Barrios in Santa Barbara and Southern California, 1848–1930* (Cambridge, Mass.: Harvard University Press, 1979), 47, 58, 116–117. See also Doris Marion Wright, "The Making of Cosmopolitan California: An Analysis of Immigration, 1848–1870," *California Historical Quarterly* 19 (December 1940):323–343, 20 (March 1941):65–79; and J. S. Holliday, *The World Rushed In: The California Gold Rush Experience* (New York: Simon and Schuster, 1981).

22. Griswold del Castillo, *Los Angeles Barrio,* 150. For discussions of the implications of what Camarillo called the *barrioization* of nineteenth-century California, see Camarillo, *Chicanos in a Changing Society,* 53–78, 142–164; Pedro Castillo, "Mexicans in Los Angeles, 1890–1920" (Ph.D. diss., University of California, Santa Barbara, 1977); Antonio Ríos-Bustamante and Pedro Castillo, *An Illustrated History of Mexican Los Angeles, 1781–1985,* Chicano Research Center Publications, Monograph no. 12 (Los Angeles: Chicano Research Center, University of California, Los Angeles, 1986), 104–109; and Pitt, *Decline of the Californios,* 120–129.

23. Camarillo, *Chicanos in a Changing Society,* 53–54.

24. Draft, Article X, Treaty of Guadalupe Hidalgo, 1848, quoted in Hunter Miller, *Treaties and Other International Acts,* 242.

25. Secretary of State James Buchanan to the Secretary of Foreign Relations of the Mexican Republic, March 18, 1848, quoted in ibid., 256. For concise analyses of the land-grant issue during the treaty negotiations, see also Griswold del Castillo, *Treaty of Guadalupe Hidalgo,* 72–86; and Victor Westphall, *Mercedes Reales: Hispanic Land Grants of the Upper Rio Grande Region* (Albuquerque: University of New Mexico Press, 1983), 67–83.

26. For examples of such practices, see Lorenzo Marquis and Antonio José Ortiz, "A Communal Land Grant," in *Foreigners in Their Native Land: Historical Roots of the Mexican Americans,* ed. David J. Weber (Albuquerque: University of New Mexico Press, 1973), 30–32. For a succinct discussion of the land-grant system under Spain and Mexico, see Westphall, *Mercedes Reales,* 122–145.

27. Of the 750 claims submitted by all parties to the Court of Land

Claims in California, 553 were confirmed. See Warren A. Beck and Ynez D. Haase, *Historical Atlas of California* (Norman: University of Oklahoma Press, 1974).

28. Robert Glass Cleland, *The Cattle on a Thousand Hills* (San Marino, Calif.: Huntington Library Publications, 1951); Camarillo, *Chicanos in a Changing Society*, 35–37; Griswold del Castillo, *Los Angeles Barrio*, 41–51; and Pitt, *Decline of the Californios*, 83–103.

29. See Camarillo, *Chicanos in a Changing Society*, 108–122; Griswold del Castillo, *Los Angeles Barrio*, 150–160; and Pitt, *Decline of the Californios*, 269–276.

30. See Camarillo, *Chicanos in a Changing Society*, 79–81, 83–100, 126–139; Griswold del Castillo, *Los Angeles Barrio*, 51–61; Pitt, *Decline of the Californios*, 195–196, 244–248; and Tomás Almaguer, "Interpreting Chicano History: The 'World-System' Approach to Nineteenth-Century California," *Review* 4 (Winter 1981):459–507.

31. For the evolution of an ethnic division of labor and a dual wage system in California, see Camarillo, *Chicanos in a Changing Society*, 167–168; and Tomás Almaguer, "Class, Race, and Capitalist Development: The Social Transformation of a Southern California County, 1848–1903" (Ph.D. diss., University of California, Berkeley, 1979). For discussions of these issues for the Southwest as a region, see Mario Barrera, *Race and Class in the Southwest: A Theory of Racial Inequality* (Notre Dame, Ind.: University of Notre Dame Press, 1979), 34–57; and Lawrence A. Cardoso, *Mexican Emigration to the United States, 1897–1931* (Tucson: University of Arizona Press, 1980), 18–23.

32. On Tejanos' loss of land in this period, see Weber, *Foreigners in Their Native Land*, 155–156; and Arnoldo de León and Kenneth L. Stewart, "Lost Dreams and Found Fortunes," *Western Historical Quarterly* 14 (July 1983):291–310.

33. David Montejano, *Anglos and Mexicans in the Making of Texas, 1836–1986* (Austin: University of Texas Press, 1987), 51–52.

34. For analysis of these economic trends in different parts of Texas, see Alwyn Barr, "Occupational and Geographic Mobility in San Antonio, 1870–1900," *Southwestern Quarterly* 51 (September 1970):396–403; Barrera, *Race and Class in the Southwest*, 30–33; Arnoldo de León, *The Tejano Community, 1836–1900* (Albuquerque: University of New Mexico Press, 1982), 50–78; and de León and Stewart, "Lost Dreams," 291–310, and *Tejanos and the Numbers Game*, 31–48.

35. De León, *They Called Them Greasers*, 75–76. For the historical debate over the repressive role of the Texas Rangers in South Texas, see Walter Prescott Webb, *The Texas Rangers: A Century of Frontier Defense*, 2d ed. (Austin: University of Texas Press, 1965); and revisionist views in Américo Paredes, *"With a Pistol in His Hand": A Border Ballad and Its Hero* (Austin: University of Texas Press, 1958); and in Julian Samora, Joe

Bernal, and Albert Peña, *Gunpowder Justice: A Reassessment of the Texas Rangers* (Notre Dame, Ind.: University of Notre Dame Press, 1979).

36. For discussions of Mexican Americans' influence in local politics, see Montejano, *Anglos and Mexicans*, 39–41; de León, *Tejano Community*, 23–49; Mario T. García, *Desert Immigrants: The Mexicans of El Paso, 1880–1920* (New Haven, Conn.: Yale University Press, 1981), 6–7, 158–171; and Gilberto Miguel Hinojosa, *A Borderlands Town in Transition: Laredo, Texas, 1755–1870* (College Station: Texas A & M University Press, 1983), 57–58, 71–73, 117–119.

37. See Montejano, *Anglos and Mexicans*, 143–145; Alwyn Barr, *Reconstruction to Reform: Texas Politics, 1876–1906* (Austin: University of Texas Press, 1971), 199–201; Evan Anders, *Boss Rule in South Texas: The Progressive Era* (Austin: University of Texas Press, 1982), 90–94; and Wilbourn E. Benton, *Texas: Its Government and Politics*, 3d ed. (Englewood Cliffs, N.J.: Prentice Hall, 1972), 49–61.

38. For discussions of the impact of the poll tax in Texas, see Benton, *Texas*, 60–61; Barr, *Reconstruction to Reform*, 205–208, 233; Paul S. Taylor, *Mexican Labor in the United States: Dimmitt County, Winter Garden District, South Texas*, University of California Publications in Economics, vol. 6, no. 5 (Berkeley: University of California Press, 1930), 399–410; and O. Douglas Weeks, "The Texas Mexicans and the Politics of South Texas," *American Political Science Review* 24 (August 1930):606–627.

39. Montejano, *Anglos and Mexicans*, 34.

40. Anders, *Boss Rule*, 14. For a discussion of boss politics in El Paso, see García, *Desert Immigrants*, 155–171.

41. Anthony D. S. Smith, *Nationalism in the Twentieth Century* (New York: New York University Press, 1979), 105. For the dynamics of "ethnogenesis" in this context, see also Smith's *The Ethnic Origins of Nations* (Oxford: Basil Blackwell, 1986), and "Nationalism, Ethnic Separatism and the Intelligentsia," in *National Separatism*, ed. Colin H. Williams (Cardiff: University of Wales Press, 1982), 17–42; Andrew W. Orridge, "Separatist and Autonomist Nationalisms: The Structure of Regional Loyalties in the Modern State," in *National Separatism*, 43–74; Cynthia Enloe, *Ethnic Conflict and Political Development* (Boston: Little, Brown and Co., 1973); and Michael Banton, "Analytical and Folk Concepts of Race and Ethnicity," *Ethnic and Racial Studies* 2 (April 1979):127–138. For critical discussions of the questions this raises about "authentic" ethnicity or "culture," see, for example, James Clifford, *The Predicament of Culture: Twentieth-Century Ethnography, Literature, and Art* (Cambridge, Mass.: Harvard University Press, 1988); Stephen Steinberg, *The Ethnic Myth: Race, Ethnicity, and Class in America*, updated and expanded ed. (Boston: Beacon Press, 1989); Eric Hobsbawm and Terrence Ranger, eds., *The Invention of Tradition* (Cambridge, England: Cambridge University Press, 1983);

and Benedict Anderson, *Imagined Communities: Reflections on the Origins and Spread of Nationalism* (London: Verso, 1983).

42. David J. Weber, *The Mexican Frontier, 1821–1846: The American Southwest under Mexico* (Albuquerque: University of New Mexico Press, 1982), 240. See also Ramón A. Gutiérrez, "Unraveling America's Hispanic Past: Internal Stratification and Class Boundaries," *Aztlán* 17 (Spring 1986):79–102.

43. Weber, *Mexican Frontier*, 241.

44. José María Sánchez, "A Trip to Texas in 1828," trans. Carlos E. Castañeda, *Southwestern Historical Quarterly* 29 (April 1926):283, quoted in Weber, *Foreigners in Their Native Land*, 80–81.

45. See Ramón A. Gutiérrez, "Honor Ideology, Marriage Negotiation, and Class-Gender Domination in New Mexico, 1690–1846," *Latin American Perspectives* 12 (Winter 1985):81–104, and *"When Jesus Came, the Corn Mothers Went Away": Marriage, Sexuality, and Power in New Mexico, 1500–1846* (Stanford, Calif.: Stanford University Press, 1991). See also Weber's analysis in *Mexican Frontier*, 207–241.

46. On this phenomenon, see Pitt, *Decline of the Californios*, 277–290; Weber, *Mexican Frontier*, 208–212; Jane Dysart, "Mexican Women in San Antonio, 1830–1860: The Assimilation Process," *Western Historical Quarterly* 7 (October 1976):365–377; and Sandra L. Myres, "Mexican Americans and Westering Anglos: A Feminine Perspective," *New Mexico Historical Review* 57 (October 1982):317–333.

47. Carey McWilliams, *North from Mexico: The Spanish-Speaking People of the United States* (Westport, Conn.: Greenwood Press, 1968), 37. See also Gutiérrez, "Unraveling America's Hispanic Past," 89–98; Kevin Starr, *Americans and the California Dream, 1850–1915* (New York: Oxford University Press, 1973), 46–48, 393–401; and Darlis A. Miller, "Cross-Cultural Marriages in the Southwest: The New Mexico Experience, 1846–1900," *New Mexico Historical Review* 57 (October 1982):335–359.

48. Griswold del Castillo, *Los Angeles Barrio*, 133.

49. For discussions of the complex cultural exchanges and negotiations involved in the process of Mexican American community formation, see Camarillo, *Chicanos in a Changing Society*, 53–78; de León, *Tejano Community*, 87–112; Juan Gómez-Quiñones, *On Culture* (Popular Series, UCLA Chicano Studies Publications, no. 1; Los Angeles: UCLA Chicano Studies Research Center Publications, 1977); and Ernesto Galarza's provocative "Mexicans in the Southwest: A Culture in Process," in *Plural Society in the Southwest*, ed. Edward H. Spicer and Raymond H. Thompson (New York: Weatherhead Foundation, 1972), 261–297.

50. For general overviews of the development of mutualistas in ethnic Mexican communities in the United States, see José Amaro Hernández,

Mutual Aid for Survival: The Case of the Mexican Americans (Malabar, Fla.: Robert Krieger Publishers, 1983); and Carlos G. Vélez-Ibáñez, *Bonds of Mutual Trust: The Cultural Systems of Rotating Credit Associations among Urban Mexicans and Chicanos* (New Brunswick, N.J.: Rutgers University Press, 1983).

51. Robert J. Rosenbaum, *Mexicano Resistance in the Southwest: "The Sacred Right of Self-Preservation"* (Austin: University of Texas Press, 1981). For examples of "social banditry" among Mexican Americans, see Pitt, *Decline of the Californios,* 69–82, 148–180; and Pedro Castillo and Albert M. Camarillo, eds., *Furia y Muerte: Los Bandidos Chicanos,* Aztlán Publications, Monograph no. 4 (Chicano Research Center, University of California, Los Angeles, 1973).

52. For examples of the usage of such terminology in the nineteenth-century Spanish-language press, see the following articles and/or numbers of *El Clamor Público*: untitled editorial, July 24, 1855; "Los mexicanos en la Alta California," August 7, 1855; "Muerte a los españoles," August 28, 1855; "Hospitalidad californiana," September 18, 1855; "El periodismo en California," February 23, 1856; and "Reclamaciones al gobierno mexicano," April 12, 1856; and "Revenge Took Possession of Me" (interview with Tiburcio Vásquez), in Weber, *Foreigners in Their Native Land,* 226–228. For the evolution of such terminology in other areas of the Southwest, refer to Gutiérrez, "Unraveling America's Hispanic Past."

53. Griswold del Castillo, *Los Angeles Barrio,* 133–134.

54. De León, *Tejano Community,* xiv–xv, 78–79. For similar assessments of the evolution of Mexican American ethnic identity in nineteenth-century Texas, see also Hinojosa, *Borderlands Town in Transition;* Dellos U. Buckner, "Study of the Lower Rio Grande Valley as a Culture Area" (M.A. thesis, University of Texas, Austin, 1929); and Jovita González, "Social Life in Cameron, Starr, and Zapata Counties" (M.A. thesis, University of Texas, Austin, 1930).

TWO. ECONOMIC DEVELOPMENT AND IMMIGRATION

1. George I. Sánchez, *Forgotten People: A Study of New Mexicans* (Albuquerque: University of New Mexico Press, 1940). Indeed, as late as 1903 one scholar observed in an essay on the evolution of American society that "while the acquisition of Florida, Texas, New Mexico and California brought in a Spanish element, most . . . presently disappeared into Mexico and Cuba." See F. H. Giddings, "The American People," *The International Quarterly* 7 (June 1903):285, quoted in Julius Drachsler, *Democracy and Assimilation* (New York: Macmillan, 1920), 47.

2. Slason Thompson, comp., *Railway Statistics of the United States of America, 1921* (Chicago: Bureau of Railway News and Statistics, 1921), 142.

3. Lawrence A. Cardoso, *Mexican Emigration to the United States, 1897–1931* (Tucson: University of Arizona, 1980), 19.

4. O. W. Israelson, "Irrigation and Drainage," in *California and the Southwest*, ed. Clifford M. Zierer (New York: John Wiley & Sons, 1956), 143–144; and Donald Worster, *Rivers of Empire: Water, Aridity & the Growth of the American West* (New York: Pantheon Books, 1985), 214.

5. Walton Bean, *California: An Interpretive History* (New York: McGraw-Hill, 1968), 227–237; Mansel G. Blackford, *The Politics of Business in California, 1890–1920* (Columbus: Ohio State University Press, 1977), 3–5; Cletus E. Daniel, *Bitter Harvest: A History of California Farmworkers, 1870–1941* (Ithaca, N.Y.: Cornell University Press, 1981), 33–34; Carey McWilliams, *North from Mexico: The Spanish-Speaking People of the United States* (Westport, Conn.: Greenwood Press, 1968), 174–188, and *Factories in the Fields: The Story of Migratory Farm Labor in California* (Boston: Little, Brown and Co., 1939), 59–65; Mark Reisler, *By the Sweat of Their Brow: Mexican Immigrant Labor in the United States, 1900–1940* (Westport, Conn.: Greenwood Press, 1976), 4–8; and Worster, *Rivers of Empire*, 205.

6. Reisler, *By the Sweat of Their Brow*, 78–79; and McWilliams, *Factories in the Fields*, 81–102.

7. Walter Prescott Webb, ed., *Handbook of Texas*, vol. 1 (Austin: Texas State Historical Society, 1952), 421; Edwin L. Caldwell, "Highlights of the Development of Manufacturing in Texas," *Southwestern Historical Quarterly* 68 (April 1965):409; and Mario T. García, *Desert Immigrants: The Mexicans of El Paso, 1880–1920* (New Haven, Conn.: Yale University Press, 1981), 15–27.

8. Ronald Takaki, *Strangers from a Different Shore: A History of Asian Americans* (New York: Penguin, 1990), 99–131; and Alexander Saxton, *The Indispensable Enemy: Labor and the Anti-Chinese Movement in California* (Berkeley: University of California Press, 1971).

9. See Takaki, *Strangers from a Different Shore*, 45–53; Roger Daniels, *The Politics of Prejudice: The Anti-Japanese Movement in California and the Struggle for Japanese Exclusion* (Berkeley: University of California Press, 1960); and Daniel, *Bitter Harvest*, 73–76.

10. Cardoso, *Mexican Emigration*, 1–2.

11. Reisler, *By the Sweat of Their Brow*, 8–12, 57–59, 100–103; and García, *Desert Immigrants*, 51–61.

12. James D. Cockcroft, *Outlaws in the Promised Land: Mexican Immigrant Workers and America's Future* (New York: Grove Press, 1986), 49. See also Oscar J. Martínez, "On the Size of the Chicano Population: New Estimates, 1850–1900," *Aztlán* 6 (Spring 1975):43–67.

13. See José Hernández Alvarez, "A Demographic Profile of the Mexican Immigration to the United States, 1910–1950," *Journal of Inter-American Studies* 8 (July 1966):471–496; and Thomas D. Boswell, "The

Growth and Proportional Distribution of the Mexican Stock Population in the United States: 1910–1970," *Mississippi Geographer* 7 (Spring 1979): 57–76.

14. For discussions of the growing Mexican presence in a wide variety of occupations, see Jeremiah W. Jenks and W. Jett Lauck, *The Immigrant Problem: A Study of American Immigration Conditions and Needs* (New York: Funk and Wagnalls, 1917), 227–228; Edwin F. Bamford, "The Mexican Casual Problem in the Southwest," *Journal of Applied Sociology* (8) (1923–1924):364–371; Roden Fuller, "Occupations of the Mexican-Born Population of Texas, New Mexico, and Arizona, 1900–1920," *American Statistical Association Journal* 23 (March 1928):64–67; Albert M. Camarillo, *Chicanos in a Changing Society: From Mexican Pueblos to American Barrios in Santa Barbara and Southern California, 1848–1930* (Cambridge, Mass.: Harvard University Press, 1979), 137–139, 142–164; Cardoso, *Mexican Emigration*, 18–27; McWilliams, *North from Mexico*, 169–172, 181–186; Reisler, *By the Sweat of Their Brow*, 5–7, 82, 97; García, *Desert Immigrants*, 9–32; and Zaragosa Vargas, "Armies in the Fields and the Factories: The Mexican Working Classes in the Midwest in the 1920s," *Mexican Studies/Estudios Mexicanos* 7 (Winter 1991):47–72.

15. Victor S. Clark, *Mexican Labor in the United States*, U.S. Bureau of Labor Statistics Bulletin no. 78; Washington, D.C., 1908, 464–522.

16. U.S. Immigration Commission, *Reports of the Immigration Commission, Immigrants in Industries* (Washington, D.C.: U.S. Government Printing Office, 1911), pt. 25 (3), 31, quoted in Reisler, *By the Sweat of Their Brow*, 13.

17. Statement of Harry Chandler, in U.S. Congress, House of Representatives, Committee on Immigration and Naturalization, *Immigration from Countries of the Western Hemisphere: Hearings*, 71st Cong., 2d sess., 1930, 60.

18. Congressman Edward T. Taylor, in U.S. Congress, House of Representatives, Committee on Immigration and Naturalization, *Seasonal Agricultural Workers from Mexico: Hearings*, 69th Cong., 1st sess., 1926, 262. For more detailed discussions of the development of such a rationale among southwestern employers, see Daniel, *Bitter Harvest*, esp. 24–28; and Lloyd Fisher, *The Harvest Labor Market in California* (Cambridge, Mass.: Harvard University Press, 1953).

19. Ralph H. Taylor, "Brief in Opposition to Application of Any Quota to Mexico," in House Committee on Immigration, *Immigration from Countries of the Western Hemisphere: Hearings*, 1930, 228.

20. George P. Clements to the Men's Lemon Club (typescript), October 2, 1929, Box 62, George P. Clements Collection, Department of Special Collections, University Research Library, University of California, Los Angeles (hereafter cited as Clements Collection). See also the similar testimony of A. C. Hardison in U.S. Congress, House of Representatives,

Committee on Immigration and Naturalization, *Immigration from Countries of the Western Hemisphere: Hearings*, 70th Cong., 1st session, 1928, 252.

21. Clements to Men's Lemon Club. Ralph Taylor of the California Agricultural Legislative Committee advanced a very similar argument. See his comments in House Committee on Immigration, *Immigration from Countries of the Western Hemisphere: Hearings*, 1930, 237–238.

22. Ralph Taylor in House Committee on Immigration, *Immigration from Countries of the Western Hemisphere: Hearings*, 1930, 265.

23. Testimony of S. Parker Frisselle, in House Committee on Immigration, *Seasonal Agricultural Laborers from Mexico: Hearings*, 6, quoted in Reisler, *By the Sweat of Their Brow*, 178. For further discussions of Mexicans' purported homing instinct, see McWilliams, *Factories in the Fields*, 148–150; Mark Reisler, "Always the Laborer, Never the Citizen: Anglo Perceptions of the Mexican Immigrant during the 1920s," *Pacific Historical Review* 45 (1976):231–254; and Douglas Monroy, "Like the Swallows at the Old Mission: Mexicans and the Racial Politics of Growth in Los Angeles in the Interwar Period," *Western Historical Quarterly* 14 (October 1983):435–458.

24. Testimony of Olger B. Burtness, in House Committee on Immigration, *Immigration from Countries of the Western Hemisphere: Hearings*, 1928, 546.

25. Ibid., 321. For expressions of similar views on the use of Mexican labor, see, for example, statement of Fred H. Bixby, National Cattlemen's Association, in ibid., 160; J. H. Powell, Navasota Cooperage Company, to U.S. Representative John L. Box, January 29, 1926, Box 2, Folder 3, O. Douglas Weeks Papers, LULAC Archives, Benson Latin American Library, University of Texas, Austin (hereafter cited as Weeks Papers); El Paso Conference of the Central Chamber of Commerce and Agriculture, memorandum, November 18, 19, 1927, Box 62, Clements Collection; and Charles C. Teague (President, California Fruit Growers' Exchange), "A Statement on Mexican Immigration," *Saturday Evening Post* March 10, 1928, 169–170.

26. Testimony of Alfred P. Thom, General Counsel, Association of Railroad Executives and National Railroad Association, in House Committee on Immigration, *Immigration from Countries of the Western Hemisphere: Hearings*, 1928, 390.

27. Ibid., 406.

28. "Immigration: History of U.S. Policy," in *Harvard Encyclopedia of American Ethnic Groups*, ed. Stephan Thernstrom (Cambridge, Mass.: Harvard University Press, 1980), 491–492. See also John Higham, *Strangers in the Land: Patterns of American Nativism 1860–1925* (New York: Atheneum, 1963); David H. Bennett, *The Party of Fear: From Nativist Movements to the New Right in American History* (Chapel Hill:

University of North Carolina Press, 1988), 159–237; Thomas J. Archdeacon, *Becoming American: An Ethnic History* (New York: Free Press, 1983), 143–172; and Roger Daniels, *Coming to America: A History of Immigration and Ethnicity in American Life* (New York: HarperCollins, 1990), 265–284.

29. See Otey M. Scruggs, "The First Mexican Farm Labor Program," *Arizona and the West* 2 (Winter 1960):319–326; and Manuel García y Griego, "The Importation of Mexican Contract Laborers to the United States, 1942–1964: Antecedents, Operation and Legacy," in *The Border That Joins: Mexican Migrants and U.S. Responsibility*, ed. Peter G. Brown and Henry Shue (Totowa, N.J.: Rowman and Littlefield, 1983).

30. See, for example, U.S. Congress, U.S. Immigration Commission, *Report of the United States Immigration Commission*, Part 25 (Washington, D.C.: U.S. Government Printing Office, 1911), 448–450.

31. *Congressional Record*, 68th Cong., 1st sess., 1923–1924, 65, pt. 6:6129.

32. Reisler, *By the Sweat of Their Brow*, 153. Similar expressions of racial animosity toward Mexican immigrants were communicated to restrictionist Congressman John C. Box of Texas. See, for example, the following documents in Box 2, Folder 8, Weeks Papers: J. E. Farnsworth, Vice-President, Southwestern Bell, Dallas, Texas, to Box, April 22, 1927; O. M. Goethe, President, Immigration Study Commission, Sacramento, California, to Box, February 4, 1928; and California State Commission on Immigration and Housing to Box, February 24, 1926.

33. House Committee on Immigration, *Immigration from Countries of the Western Hemisphere: Hearings*, 1930, 4.

34. Statement of U.S. Representative John C. Box, in ibid., 221.

35. Statement of U.S. Representative John C. Box, *Congressional Record*, 70th Cong., 1st sess., 1928, 69, pt. 3:2817–2818. For an earlier expressions of Box's views, see House Committee on Immigration, *Seasonal Agricultural Laborers from Mexico: Hearings*, 323–345.

36. *Bob Shuler's Magazine*, January 1928, as quoted in Reisler, *By the Sweat of Their Brow*, 161. For similar articulations of the "racial aspects" of the Mexican immigration debate in the 1920s, see also Roy L. Garis, "Are Aliens Lowering American Standards?—The Necessity of Excluding Inferior Stocks," *Current History* 24 (August 1926):666–677; C. M. Goethe, "Other Aspects of the Problem," *Current History* 28 (August 1928):766–768; S. J. Holmes, "Perils of the Mexican Invasion," *North American Review* 227 (May 1929):615–623; Kenneth L. Roberts, "Mexicans or Ruin," *Saturday Evening Post*, February 18, 1928, 14–15, 142, 145–146, 149–150, 154 and "The Docile Mexican," *Saturday Evening Post*, March 10, 1928, 39, 41, 165–166; and C. M. Goethe, "Peons Need Not Apply," *World's Work* 59 (November 1930):47–48.

37. See Roy L. Garis, "Report on Mexican Immigration" submitted to

House Committee on Immigration and Naturalization, in House Committee on Immigration, *Immigration from Countries of the Western Hemisphere: Hearings*, 1930, 436.

38. Fourth Report of the Committee on Selected Immigration of the American Eugenics Society, Inc., 1928, John Randolph Haynes Collection, "Immigration and Emigration—United States," Box 78, University Research Library, University of California, Los Angeles. See also statement by James H. Patten, Chairman, National Legislative Committee, Immigration Restriction League, in House Committee on Immigration, *Immigration from Countries of the Western Hemisphere: Hearings*, 1930, 392–402.

39. Garis, "Mexican Immigration," 435.

40. O. W. Killan, South Texas Chamber of Commerce, quoted in Roy L. Garis, "The Mexicanization of American Business," *Saturday Evening Post*, February 8, 1930, 46. See also Roberts, "Docile Mexican," 41; and statement of Edgar Wallace, American Federation of Labor, in House Immigration Committee, *Seasonal Agricultural Workers from Mexico: Hearings*, 295–299.

41. "The Mexican Conquest," *Saturday Evening Post*, June 22, 1929, 26. For a similar analysis of the impact of Mexican immigrants on American labor, see Glenn E. Hoover, "Our Mexican Immigrants," *Foreign Affairs* 8 (October 1929):99–107; and the statement of William C. Hushing, Legislative Representative, American Federation of Labor, in House Committee on Immigration, *Immigration from Countries of the Western Hemisphere: Hearings*, 1930, 361–368.

42. Reisler, *By the Sweat of Their Brow*, 143.

43. Camarillo, *Chicanos in a Changing Society*, 200. For estimates of Los Angeles' ethnic Mexican population between annexation and 1890, see Richard Griswold del Castillo, *The Los Angeles Barrio, 1850–1890: A Social History* (Berkeley: University of California Press, 1979), 40; and Ricardo Romo, *East Los Angeles: History of a Barrio* (Austin: University of Texas Press, 1983), 29, 61–62, 80.

44. See Ricardo Romo, "The Urbanization of Southwestern Chicanos in the Early Twentieth Century," in *New Directions in Chicano Scholarship*, ed. Ricardo Romo and Raymund Paredes (La Jolla: Chicano Studies Monograph Series, Chicano Studies Program, University of California, San Diego, 1978), 185, 192–193. See also Arnoldo de León and Kenneth L. Stewart's demographic estimates in *Tejanos and the Numbers Game: A Socio-Historical Interpretation from the Federal Censuses, 1850–1900* (Albuquerque: University of New Mexico Press, 1989), 15–29.

45. See Reisler, *By the Sweat of Their Brow*, 268–270.

46. M. Colette Standart, "The Sonoran Migration to California, 1848–1856: A Study in Prejudice," *Southern California Quarterly* 57 (Fall 1976):342. The conflict between the Californios and recent immigrants

from Mexico in the nineteenth century is noted by several observers. See, for example, J. M. Guinn, "The Sonoran Migration," *Annual Publication, Historical Society of Southern California* 7 (1909–1911):32; Richard A. Peterson, "Anti-Mexican Nativism in California, 1848–1853: A Study of Cultural Conflict," *Southern California Quarterly* 62 (Winter 1980):309–328; and David J. Weber, *The Mexican Frontier, 1821–1846: The American Southwest under Mexico* (Albuquerque: University of New Mexico Press, 1982), 188–190, 239.

47. For discussions of these tensions, see Fane Downs, "The History of Mexicans in Texas, 1820–1845" (Ph.D. diss., Texas Tech University, 1970), 44–49; and W. H. Timmons, "The El Paso Area in the Mexican Period, 1821–1848," *Southwestern Historical Quarterly* 84 (July 1980):1–28.

48. For succinct analyses of the ambiguities involved in Mexican-Tejano intraethnic relations in this volatile period, see J. Fred Rippy, "Border Troubles Along the Rio Grande, 1848–1860," *Southwestern Historical Quarterly* 23 (October 1919):91–111; Andrés A. Tijerina, "Tejanos and Texas: The Native Mexicans of Texas, 1820–1850" (Ph.D. diss., University of Texas, Austin, 1977), esp. 259–260, 318–328; and Homer L. Kerr, "Migration into Texas, 1860–1880," *Southwestern Historical Quarterly* 70 (October 1966):184–216.

49. For discussions of the significance of regional differences in greater Mexican society see, for example, Ida Altman and James Lockhart, eds., *Provinces of Early Mexico: Variants of Spanish American Regional Evolution* (Los Angeles: UCLA Latin American Research Center Publications, 1976); Miguel León-Portilla, "The Norteño Variety of Mexican Culture: An Ethnohistorical Approach," in *Plural Society in the Southwest*, ed. Edward H. Spicer and Raymond H. Thompson (New York: Weatherhead Foundation, 1972), 77–114; William B. Taylor, "Between Global Process and Local Knowledge: An Inquiry into Early Latin American Social History, 1500–1900," in *Reliving the Past: The Worlds of Social History*, ed. Olivier Zunz (Chapel Hill: University of North Carolina Press, 1985), 115–190; and Eric Van Young, ed. *Mexico's Regions: Comparative History and Development* (La Jolla: Center for U.S.–Mexican Studies, University of California, San Diego, 1992).

50. Camarillo, *Chicanos in a Changing Society*, 188.

51. Clark, "Mexican Labor in the United States," 513.

52. Although repetitive, ethnocentric, and at times overly impressionistic, Emory S. Bogardus's research on Mexicans and Mexican Americans in the early twentieth century provides useful insights. See, for example, his major work, *The Mexican in the United States*, University of Southern California Social Science Series, no. 8 (Los Angeles: University of Southern California, 1934), as well as his "The Mexican Immigrant," *Journal of Applied Sociology* 11 (1927):470–488, "Mexican Immigration and Segregation," *American Journal of Sociology* 36 (July 1930):74–80, and "At-

titudes and the Mexican Immigrant," in *Social Attitudes*, ed. Kimball Young (New York: Henry Holt and Co., 1931), 291–327.

53. Manuel Gamio, *Mexican Immigration to the United States: A Study of Human Migration and Adjustment* (New York: Dover Publications, 1971), and *The Life Story of the Mexican Immigrant: Autobiographical Documents* (New York: Dover Publications, 1971).

54. Gamio, *Mexican Immigration to the United States*, 129.

55. Ibid., 130.

56. Gamio, *Life Story of the Mexican Immigrant*, 268–269.

57. Ibid., 272.

58. Ibid., 273.

59. Ibid., 46.

60. Ibid., 139.

61. Ibid., 172.

62. Ibid., 65.

63. Paul S. Taylor, *Mexican Labor in the United States: Dimmitt County, Winter Garden District, South Texas*, University of California Publications in Economics, vol. 6, no. 5 (Berkeley: University of California Press, 1930), 452.

64. Paul S. Taylor, *Mexican Labor in the United States: Valley of the South Platte, Colorado*, University of California Publications in Economics, vol. 6, no. 2 (Berkeley: University of California Press, 1929), 213.

65. Ibid., 214.

66. Ibid.

67. Paul S. Taylor, *Mexican Labor in the United States: Dimmitt County*, 413. For Taylor's reports of similar expressions of such sentiments by both immigrants and natives of Mexican descent, see, in particular, ibid., 409, 454, and his *Mexican Labor in the United States: Imperial Valley*, University of California Publications in Economics, vol. 6, no. 1 (Berkeley: University of California Press, 1928), 90, and *Mexican Labor in the United States: Chicago and the Calumet Region*, University of California Publications in Economics, vol. 7, no. 2 (Berkeley: University of California Press, 1932), 110–115; and *An American-Mexican Frontier: Nueces County, Texas* (Chapel Hill: University of North Carolina Press, 1934), 241–249 and passim. Jovita González made almost identical observations about social relations in South Texas in her "Social Life in Cameron, Starr, and Zapata Counties" (M.A. thesis, University of Texas, Austin, 1930), 110.

68. Terrence L. Hansen, "Corridos in Southern California," *Western Folklore* 18 (July 1959):202–232; 18 (October 1959):295–315.

THREE. THE SHIFTING POLITICS OF ETHNICITY
IN THE INTERWAR PERIOD

1. *Imperial Valley Farmer*, September 12, 1929.

2. *Brawley News*, March 15, 1935. Articles along a similar vein can be found in the *Brawley News*, March 13 and April 14, 1935.

3. Repatriation campaigns elsewhere in the United States during this era are discussed in Neil Betten and Raymond A. Mohl, "From Discrimination to Repatriation: Mexican Life during the Great Depression," *Pacific Historical Review* 42 (August 1973):370–388; D. H. Dinwoodie, "Deportation: The Immigration Service and the Chicano Labor Movement in the 1930s," *New Mexico Historical Review* 52 (July 1977):193–206; and George C. Kiser and David Silverman, "Mexican Repatriation during the Great Depression," *Journal of Mexican American History* 3 (1973):139–164.

4. Abraham Hoffman, *Unwanted Mexican Americans in the Great Depression, Repatriation Pressures, 1929–1939* (Tucson: University of Arizona Press, 1974), 120. See also Abraham Hoffman, "Stimulus to Repatriation: The 1931 Federal Deportation Drive and the Los Angeles Mexican Community," *Pacific Historical Review* 42 (May 1973):203–219; Mark Reisler, *By the Sweat of Their Brow: Mexican Immigrant Labor in the United States, 1900–1940* (Westport, Conn.: Greenwood Press, 1976), 232; and George J. Sánchez, "Becoming Mexican American: Ethnicity and Acculturation in Chicano Los Angeles, 1900–1943" (Ph.D. diss., Stanford University, 1989), 294–334.

5. To state that these individuals returned to Mexico at this time is somewhat inaccurate, given the fact that many of the U.S.-born children of Mexican immigrants had never even seen Mexico. For discussions of the difficulties in establishing accurate data for the number of Mexican-descent repatriates during the depression, see Hoffman, *Unwanted Mexican Americans*, 100–104, 126; Manuel García y Griego, "The Importation of Mexican Contract Laborers to the United States, 1942–1964: Antecedents, Operation and Legacy," in *The Border That Joins: Mexican Migrants and U.S. Responsibility*, ed. Peter G. Brown and Henry Shue (Totowa, N.J.: Rowman and Littlefield, 1983), 52–53; Lawrence A. Cardoso, *Mexican Emigration to the United States, 1897–1931* (Tucson: University of Arizona Press, 1980), 144–152; and Arthur F. Corwin and Lawrence A. Cardoso, "Vamos al Norte: Causes of Mass Mexican Migration to the United States," in *Immigrants and Immigrants: Perspectives on Mexican Labor Migration to the United States*, ed. Arthur F. Corwin (Westport, Conn.: Greenwood Press, 1978), 53.

6. For discussions of the Mexican government's role in the various repatriation campaigns of the period, see Francisco E. Balderrama, *In Defense of La Raza: The Los Angeles Mexican Consulate and the Mexican Com-*

munity, 1929–1936 (Tucson: University of Arizona Press, 1982); and Juan Gómez-Quiñones, "Piedras contra la luna, México en Aztlán y Aztlán en México: Chicano-Mexican Relations in the Mexican Consulates, 1900–1920," in *Contemporary Mexico: Papers of the IV International Congress of Mexican History* (Mexico City: El Colegio de México and UCLA Latin American Studies Center, 1975), 494–527.

7. Leo Grebler, *Mexican Immigration to the United States: The Record and Its Implications*. Mexican American Study Project Advance Report 2 (Los Angeles: Division of Research, Graduate School of Business Administration, University of California, Los Angeles, 1966), 25.

8. For this, and for similar examples of corridos of the depression era, see Nellie Foster, "The Corrido: A Mexican Culture Trait Persisting in Southern California" (M.A. thesis, University of Southern California, 1939).

9. James L. Slayden, "Some Observations on the Mexican Immigrant," *Annals of the American Academy of Political and Social Science* 93 (January 1921):125.

10. Edward D. Garza, *LULAC: The League of United Latin American Citizens* (San Francisco: R and E Research Associates, 1972), 4; Mario T. García, *Mexican Americans: Leadership, Ideology, and Identity, 1930–1960* (New Haven, Conn.: Yale University Press, 1989), 29–30. For an insightful recent analysis of the formation of these organizations, see Cynthia E. Orozco, "The Origins of the League of United Latin American Citizens (LULAC) and the Mexican American Civil Rights Movement in Texas with an Analysis of Women's Political Participation in a Gendered Context, 1910–1929" (Ph.D. diss., University of California, Los Angeles, 1993).

11. O. Douglas Weeks, "The League of United Latin American Citizens: A Texas Mexican Civic Organization," *Southwestern Political and Social Science Quarterly* 10 (December 1928):257–278.

12. Preamble, "Constitución y Leyes de la Orden Hijos de América," 1927, Box 1, Folder 3, O. Douglas Weeks Papers, LULAC Archives, Benson Latin American Library, University of Texas, Austin (hereafter cited as Weeks Papers).

13. See Weeks's "League of United Latin American Citizens," and "The Texas Mexican and the Politics of South Texas," *American Political Science Review* 24 (August 1930):606–627.

14. See *El Paladín*, May 17, 1929; and "Fueron numerosos los delegados que asistieron a la convención verificada en Corpus Christi, Texas," *La Prensa*, May 19, 1929.

15. Weeks, "League of United Latin American Citizens."

16. LULAC Constitution, Box 1, Folder 7, Weeks Papers.

17. August Meier, *Negro Thought in America, 1880–1915: Racial Ideologies in the Age of Booker T. Washington* (Ann Arbor: University of Michigan Press, 1963), 192. Although there is little evidence that DuBois's

ideas directly influenced LULAC's leadership, the similarities between LULAC's evolving political ideas and those of the NAACP during this period are striking.

18. Mario T. García, *Mexican Americans*, 33.

19. For descriptions of LULAC's general political and legal efforts during this period, see Mario T. García, *Mexican Americans*, 40–41, 46–53; and Richard A. García, *Rise of the Mexican American Middle Class: San Antonio, 1929–1941* (College Station: Texas A & M University Press, 1991), 282–299. For discussions of LULAC's efforts in the struggle to desegregate public schools, see Guadalupe San Miguel's "The Struggle against Separate and Unequal Schools: Middle Class Mexican Americans and the Desegregation Campaign in Texas, 1929–1957," *History of Education Quarterly* 23 (Fall 1983):343–359, and *"Let All of Them Take Heed": Mexican Americans and the Campaign for Educational Equality in Texas, 1910–1981* (Austin: University of Texas Press, 1987), 74–82; Gilbert G. González, *Chicano Education in the Era of Segregation* (Philadelphia: Balch Institute Press, Associated University Presses, 1990), 28–29, 155–156; and Guadalupe Salinas, "Mexican Americans and the Desegregation of Schools in the Southwest," *Houston Law Review* 8 (1971):929–951.

20. "The Mexico Texan," *LULAC News*, July 1937. Bonilla-Wilmot Collection, Box 1, Folder 2, LULAC Archives, Benson Library.

21. The first version of "The Mexico-Texan" was written by the distinguished Mexican American folklorist Américo Paredes in 1934, when he was a high-school senior in south Texas. For a more extensive analysis of the poem and the political circumstances that stimulated Paredes to write it, see Ramón Saldívar, *Chicano Narrative: The Dialectics of Difference* (Madison: University of Wisconsin Press, 1990), 10–25.

22. See LULAC Constitution, esp. Article II, No. 7, and LULAC Code, Box 1, Folder 7, Weeks Papers.

23. "History of LULAC" (1977), Box 1, Folder 1, LULAC Archives, Benson Latin American Library, University of Texas, Austin. For a more detailed analysis of the Harlingen meeting, see Orozco, "Origins of . . . LULAC," 222–261.

24. See, for example, Benjamin Márquez's "The Politics of Race and Assimilation: The League of United Latin American Citizens, 1929–1940," *Western Political Quarterly* 42 (June 1989):355–375, "The Politics of Race and Class: The League of United Latin American Citizens in the Post–World War II Period," *Social Science Quarterly* 68 (March 1987):84–101, and *LULAC: The Evolution of a Mexican American Political Organization* (Austin: University of Texas Press, 1993).

25. In an informal survey of local LULAC councils conducted in late 1929, O. Douglas Weeks reported that although many LULAC members were small ethnic entrepreneurs (such as barbers, druggists, butchers, or

store owner/operators) or white-collar professionals (such as teachers, newspaper reporters, or attorneys) most LULAC members were either skilled or semi-skilled workers or small farm or ranch owner/operators. Weeks's notes are in Box 1, Folder 10, Weeks Papers.

26. Alonso S. Perales to Ben Garza, June 22, 1928, Box 1, Folder 1, Andrés de Luna Papers, LULAC Archives, Benson Latin American Library, University of Texas, Austin.

27. Mario T. García, *Mexican Americans*, 28. For a similar interpretation of LULAC's early ideology and activities, see also Richard A. García, *Rise of the Mexican American Middle Class*, 253–299.

28. M. C. Gonzales, "The Aim of LULAC," *LULAC News*, March 1932, 3.

29. Ibid.

30. Ibid.

31. "And LULAC Was Born . . . ," *LULAC News*, February, 1949.

32. Ibid.

33. Alonso S. Perales, "The Unification of Mexican Americans, Part III," *La Prensa*, September 6, 1929.

34. Alonso S. Perales, "The Unification of Mexican Americans, Part VI," *La Prensa*, September 9, 1929.

35. Ibid.

36. Perales, "The Unification of Mexican Americans, Part III," *La Prensa*, September 6, 1929.

37. Testimony of Alonso S. Perales, in U.S. Congress, House of Representatives, Committee on Immigration and Naturalization, *Immigration from Countries of the Western Hemisphere: Hearings*, 71st Cong., 2d sess., 1930, 182.

38. Andrés Hernández, "In Relation to Our Civil Liberties," *LULAC News*, August 1938, 12.

39. "Are Texas-Mexicans 'Americans'?" *LULAC News*, April 30, 1932, 7.

40. Mario T. García, *Mexican Americans*, 15.

41. Richard A. García, *Rise of the Mexican American Middle Class*, 4.

42. Ibid., 116.

43. Ibid., 301. For a more judicious explication of a similar argument, see Roberto R. Treviño, "*Prensa y Patria*: The Spanish-Language Press and the Biculturation of the Tejano Middle Class, 1920–1940," *Western Historical Quarterly* 22 (November 1991):451–472.

44. Special survey of the Mexican colony at Hick's Camp, California, conducted by the California Division of Immigration and Housing (typescript, January, 1940), Box 27, Folder marked "Mexicans—Housing," Carey McWilliams Collection, Department of Special Collections, University Research Library, University of California, Los Angeles (hereafter cited as McWilliams Collection).

45. Ibid.

46. Ibid.

47. Ibid.

48. Julia Kirk Blackwelder, *Women of the Depression: Caste and Culture in San Antonio, 1929–1939* (College Station: Texas A & M University Press, 1984), 112.

49. Selden C. Menefee, *Migratory Workers of South Texas* (Washington, D.C.: Works Progress Administration, 1941), 41.

50. California, Governor C. C. Young's Mexican Fact-Finding Committee, *Mexicans in California* (San Francisco: State of California, 1930), 178.

51. Ibid.

52. Ibid., 183. Similar mortality rates were reported in ethnic Mexican communities in other parts of the state. In Santa Barbara, for example, Camarillo notes that the infant mortality rate among Mexicans was five times that of the general population. See Albert M. Camarillo, *Chicanos in a Changing Society: From Mexican Pueblos to American Barrios in Santa Barbara and Southern California, 1848–1930* (Cambridge, Mass.: Harvard University Press, 1979), 160.

53. California, Commission on Immigration and Housing, *Annual Report* (Sacramento: State of California, 1927), 18.

54. California, Mexican Fact-Finding Committee, *Mexicans in California*, 185.

55. Edyth Tate Thompson, Chief, Bureau of Tuberculosis, Division of Communicable Diseases, California Department of Public Health, to John Anson Ford, Los Angeles County Board of Supervisors, July 7, 1936, Box 65, Folder B, John Anson Ford Collection, Huntington Library and Art Museum, San Marino, California (hereafter cited as Ford Collection). See also U.S. Department of Labor, "Labor and Social Conditions of Mexicans in California," *Monthly Labor Review* 32 (January 1932):81–89; and Edward C. McDonagh, "Status Levels of Mexicans," *Sociology and Social Research* 33 (July 1949):449–459.

56. Lizabeth Cohen, *Making a New Deal: Industrial Workers in Chicago, 1919–1939* (Cambridge, England: Cambridge University Press, 1990), 356.

57. For the estimated generational composition of the Mexican-origin population for the period 1930 to 1960, see Thomas D. Boswell, "The Growth and Proportional Distribution of the Mexican Population in the United States: 1910–1970" *Mississippi Geographer* 7 (Spring 1979):57–76; J. Allan Beegle, Harold F. Goldsmith, and Charles P. Loomis, "Demographic Characteristics of the United States–Mexican Border," *Rural Sociology* 25 (March 1960):107–162; and Leo Grebler, Joan W. Moore, and Ralph C. Guzmán, *The Mexican-American People: The Nation's Second Largest Minority* (New York: Free Press, 1970), 30.

58. Like many of the Census Bureau's categories, mother tongue data must be used as an approximation of social trends rather than as incontrovertible evidence. However, sociolinguist Joshua Fishman notes that the Census Bureau defined the category as "the principal language spoken in the home of [a] person in his earliest childhood. This definition [has been] frequently interpreted as referring to the language spoken by the person himself." See Joshua Fishman, *Language Loyalty in the United States* (The Hague: Mouton & Co., 1966), 39.

59. Fishman, *Language Loyalty*, 36, 38. See also Grebler, Moore, and Guzmán, *Mexican American People*, 423–432; and Rosaura Sánchez, *Chicano Discourse: Socio-Historical Perspectives* (Rowley, Mass.: Newbury House, 1983).

60. Indeed, according to the 1930 census an estimated 55 percent of the foreign-born ethnic Mexican population over the age of 10 did not speak any English. See McDonagh, "Status Levels of Mexicans," 455.

61. This argument has been raised for some ethnic groups in contemporary American society. For an explication of some of the theoretical issues suggested by this, see Dale C. Nelson, "Ethnicity and Socioeconomic Status as Sources of Participation: The Case for Ethnic Political Culture," *American Political Science Review* 73 (December 1979):1024–1038.

62. For a discussion of such strategies, see Manuel Peña's insightful *The Texas-Mexican Conjunto: History of a Working-Class Music* (Austin: University of Texas Press, 1985). For broader theoretical treatments, see Richard Oestreicher, "Urban Working-Class Political Behavior and Theories of American Electoral Politics, 1870–1940," *Journal of American History* 74 (March 1988):1257–1286; Douglas E. Foley, "Does the Working Class Have a Culture in the Anthropological Sense?" *Cultural Anthropology* 4 (May 1989):137–162; and Rick Fantasia, *Cultures of Solidarity: Consciousness, Action, and Contemporary American Workers* (Berkeley: University of California Press, 1988).

63. I am grateful to Professor Emilio Zamora for generously sharing with me his then unpublished work on mutualistas. For his insightful analysis, see Emilio Zamora, *The World of the Mexican Worker in Texas* (College Station: Texas A & M University Press, 1993).

64. See Julie Leininger Pycior, "La Raza Organizes: Mexican American Life in San Antonio, 1915–1930 as Reflected in Mutualista Activities" (Ph.D. diss., University of Notre Dame, 1979). For discussions of the ways in which mutualista activities often intersected with political debates, see also Hernández, *Mutual Aid for Survival*, 97–98; Paul S. Taylor, *Mexican Labor in the United States: Imperial Valley*, University of California Publications in Economics, vol. 6, no. 1 (Berkeley: University of California Press, 1928), 64, *Mexican Immigration to the United States: Valley of the South Platte, Colorado*, University of California Publications in Economics, vol. 6, no. 2 (Berkeley: University of California Press, 1929), 185, and

An American-Mexican Frontier: Nueces County, Texas (Chapel Hill: University of North Carolina Press, 1934), 174; and Zamora, *World of the Mexican Worker in Texas,* 86–109.

65. James Officer, "Sodalities and Systemic Linkage: The Joining Habits of Urban Mexican-Americans" (Ph.D. diss., University of Arizona, 1964), 55. See also Kaye Lynn Briegel, "The Alianza Hispano Americana, 1894–1965: A Mexican Fraternal Insurance Society" (Ph.D. diss., University of Southern California, 1974); and Thomas J. Sheridan, *Los Tucsonenses: The Mexican Community in Tucson, 1854–1941* (Tucson: University of Arizona Press, 1986), 108–116.

66. Hernández, *Mutual Aid for Survival,* 33.

67. José Limón, "El Primer Congreso Mexicanista de 1911: A Precursor to Contemporary Chicanismo," *Aztlán* 5 (Spring-Fall 1974):85–117. See also Hernández, *Mutual Aid for Survival,* 61–77.

68. Pycior, "La Raza Organizes," 42–50.

69. See, for example, Taylor, *American-Mexican Frontier,* 173–175; Camarillo, *Chicanos in a Changing Society,* 151–154; Mario T. García, *Desert Immigrants: The Mexicans of El Paso, 1880–1920* (New Haven, Conn.: Yale University Press, 1981), 223; Richard Griswold del Castillo, *The Los Angeles Barrio, 1850–1890: A Social History* (Berkeley: University of California Press, 1979), 138; and Ricardo Romo, *East Los Angeles: History of a Barrio* (Austin: University of Texas Press, 1983), 149.

70. Pycior, "La Raza Organizes," 46.

71. Taylor, *American-Mexican Frontier,* 174. See also Romo, *East Los Angeles,* 148–155; Briegel, "Alianza Hispano Americana," 78; and Arnoldo de León, *The Tejano Community, 1836–1900* (Albuquerque: University of New Mexico Press, 1982), 195–196.

72. Pycior, "La Raza Organizes," 34.

73. Manuel Gamio, *Mexican Immigration to the United States: A Study of Human Migration and Adjustment* (New York: Dover Publications, 1971), 136.

74. Ralph C. Guzmán, "The Political Socialization of the Mexican American People" (Ph.D. diss., University of California, Los Angeles, 1970), 197.

75. Mario Barrera, "The Historical Evolution of Chicano Ethnic Goals: A Bibliographic Essay," *Sage Race Relations Abstracts* 10 (February 1985):1, 8. For similar interpretations, see Rodolfo Alvarez, "The Psycho-Historical and Socioeconomic Development of the Chicano Community in the United States," *Social Science Quarterly* 53 (March 1973):920–942.

76. Grebler, Moore, and Guzmán, *Mexican American People,* 381, emphasis in original.

77. See, for example, Juan Gómez-Quiñones, "The First Steps: Chicano Labor Conflict and Organizing, 1900–1920," *Aztlán* 3 (Spring 1972):13–50; Luis Leobardo Arroyo, "Notes on Past, Present, and Future Directions of Chicano Labor Studies," *Aztlán* 6 (Summer 1975):137–150;

and Tomás Almaguer and Albert Camarillo, "Urban Chicano Workers in Historical Perspective: A Review of the Literature," in *The State of Chicano Research on Family, Labor, and Migration: Proceedings of the First Stanford Symposium on Chicano Research and Public Policy,* ed. Armando Valdez, Albert Camarillo, and Tomás Almaguer (Stanford, Calif.: Stanford Center for Chicano Research, 1983), 3–32. For a more general interpretive overview, see Juan Gómez-Quiñones, *Development of the Mexican Working Class North of the Rio Bravo: Work and Culture among Laborers and Artisans, 1600–1900* (Los Angeles: Chicano Studies Research Center Publications, University of California, Los Angeles, 1982). For discussions of the development and influence of socialist and anarchist thought in the transborder Mexican labor movement, see James D. Cockcroft, *Intellectual Precursors of the Mexican Revolution, 1900–1913* (Austin: University of Texas Press, 1968); Juan Gómez-Quiñones, *Sembradores, Ricardo Flores Magón y El Partido Liberal Mexicano: A Eulogy and Critique,* rev. ed. (Los Angeles: Chicano Studies Center Publications, University of California, Los Angeles, 1977); John M. Hart, *Anarchism and the Mexican Working Class, 1860–1931* (Austin: University of Texas Press, 1978); and W. Dirk Raat, *Revoltosos: Mexico's Rebels in the United States, 1903–1923* (College Station: Texas A & M University Press, 1981).

78. See Stuart M. Jamieson, *Labor Unionism in American Agriculture,* U.S. Department of Labor, Bureau of Labor Statistics, Bulletin no. 836 (Washington, D.C.: U.S. Government Printing Office, 1945), 34–42.

79. For the background to ethnic Mexican workers' labor activities in the Arizona copper mines, see James R. Kluger, *The Clifton-Morenci Strike: Labor Difficulty in Arizona* (Tucson: University of Arizona Press, 1970); Philip Taft, "The Bisbee Deportation," *Labor History* 13 (Winter 1972):3–40; Byrkit James Ward, "Life and Labor in Arizona, 1901–1921: With Particular Reference to the Deportations of 1917" (Ph.D. diss., Claremont Graduate School, 1972); and Michael E. Parrish, *Mexican Workers, Progressives and Copper: The Failure of Industrial Democracy in Arizona during the Wilson Years* (San Diego: Chicano Research Publications, University of California, San Diego, 1979). The mutualistas' role in the Arizona Mexican labor movement is discussed in Hernández, *Mutual Aid for Survival,* 35–44; James D. McBride, "La Liga Protectora Latina: An Arizona Mexican-American Benevolent Society," *Journal of the West,* 14 (October 1975):82–90; and Sheridan, *Los Tucsonenses,* 172–180.

80. Emilio Zamora, "Chicano Socialist Labor Activity in Texas, 1900–1920," *Aztlán* 6 (Summer 1975):224.

81. Union of United Workers of Imperial Valley, Inc. to Imperial Valley Growers Association, April 18, 1928, quoted in Taylor, *Mexican Labor in the United States: The Imperial Valley,* 47.

82. President, Mutualista Benito Juárez, to Mexican Vice-consul, Calexico, Mexico, quoted in ibid., 52.

83. For a detailed overview of strike activity among ethnic Mexican

workers during the depression, see Jamieson, *Labor Unionism in American Agriculture*. For California, see Cletus E. Daniel, *Bitter Harvest: A History of California Farmworkers, 1870–1941* (Ithaca, N.Y.: Cornell University Press, 1981), 141–257; and Linda C. Majka and Theo J. Majka, *Farm Workers, Agribusiness, and the State* (Philadelphia: Temple University Press, 1982). For Texas, see Victor B. Nelson-Cisneros, "La clase trabajadora en Tejas, 1920–1940," *Aztlán* 6 (Summer 1975):239–266; and Victor B. Nelson-Cisneros, "UCAPAWA Organizing Activities in Texas, 1935–50," *Aztlán* 9 (Spring-Fall 1978):71–85.

84. Daniel, *Bitter Harvest*, 105.

85. Jamieson, *Labor Unionism in American Agriculture*, 75.

86. In 1938 Paul S. Taylor estimated that at least 29 percent of agricultural workers in California resided in urban communities. See State of California, Division of Immigration and Housing, *Report for the First Half of 1939* (mimeo copy), John Randolph Haynes Collection, Box 16, Department of Special Collections, URL, University of California, Los Angeles. On the general proliferation of these informal communication networks among Mexican American and Mexican immigrant workers, see Jamieson, *Labor Unionism in American Agriculture*, 15, 31–42, 80; and Devra Anne Weber, "The Struggle for Stability and Control in the Cotton Fields of California: Class Relations in Agriculture, 1919–1942" (Ph.D. diss., University of California, Los Angeles, 1986).

87. For discussions of the initial organization of the various Mexican societies into an umbrella group prior to the fall of 1927, see articles on the Confederación de Sociedades Mexicanas in *La Opinión*, May 31, June 2, and October 24, 1927. CUOM's initial activities are analyzed in *La Opinión*, November 5, 6, and 9, 1927. The background to CUOM's development and its relationship to CROM is discussed in California, Mexican Fact-Finding Committee, *Mexicans in California*, 123–144; William E. Walling, *The Mexican Question: Mexico and American-Mexican Relations under Calles and Obregón* (New York: Robins Press, 1927), 81–144; and Devra Anne Weber, "The Organizing of Mexicano Agricultural Workers: Imperial Valley and Los Angeles, 1928–1934, An Oral History Approach," *Aztlán* 3 (Fall 1972):307–347.

88. CUOM Constitution, as cited in California, Mexican Fact-Finding Committee, *Mexicans in California*, 125–126. See also *La Opinión*, November 5 and 9, 1927.

89. California, Mexican Fact-Finding Committee, *Mexicans in California*, 124, 127. The evolution of CUOM's position on immigration is followed in *La Opinión*, January 25, January 31, and February 26, 1928. For expressions in *La Opinión* of growing sentiment among at least some local Mexicans that immigration should be restricted, see, for example, "La Nueva Repatriación," February 2, 1927; "Ayuda a Los Sin Trabajo," February 25, 1927; "Deportados," March 4, 1927; "Sin Trabajo," March 17,

1927; and "California No Es Tierra de Promisión para Los Trabajadores Mexicanos" May 29, 1927; and similar articles on May 30, June 14, June 29, July 20, August 13, and September 12, 1927, and January 7, 1928. I would also like to acknowledge and thank George Sánchez for sharing with me copies of correspondence during this period between representatives of CUOM and the Mexican Consulate in Los Angeles. For a more general analysis of the many issues involved in the Mexican immigration debate of this period, see Mario T. García, "La Frontera: The Border as Symbol and Reality in Mexican American Thought," *Mexican Studies/Estudios Mexicanos* 1 (Summer 1985):195–225.

90. Quoted in California, Mexican Fact-Finding Committee, *Mexicans in California*, 125–126. See also Ampelio González, Confederación de Sociedades Mexicanas, "Memorandum Number 244," January 3, 1931, and response from Mexican Consulate, Los Angeles, ca. February 1931, in author's files, courtesy George Sánchez. Although some scholars may view such rhetoric as a simple extension of the kind of logic used by the editors of *La Opinión* and *La Prensa* urging *mexicanos de afuera* to remain true to Mexico by steadfastly refusing to become Americanized, CUOM's position differed significantly in that the organization seemed to recognize that many Mexicans, for better or worse, had decided to remain permanently in the United States. CUOM apparently chose to accept this fact and thus encouraged its members to retain—and train their children in—the essence of their culture even if they chose to remain in the United States. For good discussions of the positions of the small number of Mexican exiles who stridently advocated the *Mexico de afuera* position, see Mario T. García, "La Frontera"; Arturo Rosales, "Shifting Self-Perceptions and Ethnic Consciousness in Houston, 1908–1946," *Aztlán* 16 (1985):71–91; and Richard A. García's analysis in *Rise of the Mexican American Middle Class*, 221–252.

91. See, for example, Daniel, *Bitter Harvest*; Weber, "Struggle for Stability," and "Organizing of Mexicano Agricultural Workers"; Charles B. Spaulding, "The Mexican Strike at El Monte, California," *Sociology and Social Research* 18 (July-August 1934):571–580; Ronald W. López, "The El Monte Berry Strike of 1933," *Aztlán* 1 (Fall 1970):101–114; and Abraham Hoffman, "The El Monte Berry Pickers Strike, 1933: International Involvement in a Local Labor Dispute," *Journal of the West* 12 (1973):71–84.

92. Jamieson, *Labor Unionism in American Agriculture*, 19–20; Menefee, *Migratory Workers*; and Raúl A. Ramos, "La Huelga de los Nueceros de San Antonio, Texas, Febrero 1938" (senior thesis, Princeton University, 1989).

93. Paul Taylor and Clark Kerr made this clear in their report on the massive 1933 California cotton strike to the La Follette Committee when they noted, "The excitement of the parades, the fiery talks, the cheering,

appealed to the Mexicans particularly, and race discrimination, poor housing, and low pay, especially the latter, were rallying cries which appealed to
a class of workers with adequate personal experience to vivify the charges
hurled by Communist leaders and rendered exposition of the theories of
Marx superfluous." U.S. Congress, Senate, Committee on Education and
Labor, *Violations of the Rights of Free Speech and Assembly and Interference with Rights of Labor: Hearings,* 74th Cong., 2d sess., pt. 53:19957.

94. Weber, "Struggle for Stability," 123–176.

95. Cannery and Agricultural Workers Industrial Union, *Trabajador
Agrícolo* (newsletter), December 20, 1933, Box 1, Folder 10, Paul S. Taylor
Papers, Bancroft Library, University of California, Berkeley..

96. See Jamieson, *Labor Unionism in American Agriculture,* 81–103.
Jamieson noted similar dynamics at work among ethnic Mexican workers
in Colorado during the sugar-beet strike of 1929, asserting that "many local representatives in the [beet-workers' association] were strongly nationalistic in sentiment, for the status and prestige of a community leader
among Mexicans rested upon his upholding, at least vocally, their rights as
a national minority. Some representatives favored the formation of a separate union, exclusively Mexican and unaffiliated with other organizations. Others sought to obtain a charter from the State federation [of the
AFL] for an all-Mexican or Spanish-speaking organization whose members
would be allowed to work in other unionized industries." Ibid., 238.

97. Weber, "Struggle for Stability," 111, 123, 166.

98. Jamieson, *Labor Unionism in American Agriculture,* 261.

99. Although a detailed analysis of Tenayuca's life and career has yet to
be published, her background and influence on Mexican American labor
politics is discussed in Roberto R. Calderón and Emilio Zamora, "Manuela
Solis Sager and Emma B. Tenayuca: A Tribute," in *Between Borders: Es-
says on Mexicana/Chicana History,* ed. Adelaida R. del Castillo (Encino,
Calif.: Floricanto Press, 1990), 269–280; "La Pasionaria de Texas," *Time,*
February 28, 1938, 17; Blackwelder, *Women of the Depression,* 141–151;
Don E. Carleton, *Red Scare! Right Wing Hysteria, Fifties Fanaticism, and
Their Legacy in Texas* (Austin: Texas Monthly Press, 1985), 28–38; and
Matt S. Meier, *Mexican American Biographies: A Historical Dictionary,
1836–1987* (New York: Greenwood Press, 1988), 218.

100. Emma Tenayuca and Homer Brooks, "The Mexican Question in
the Southwest," *The Communist,* March 1939, 267.

101. Ibid., 266.

102. Ibid.

103. Ibid., 264, emphasis in the original.

104. For discussions of UCAPAWA's significance, see Vicki L. Ruiz,
*Cannery Women, Cannery Lives: Mexican Women, Unionization, and
the California Food Processing Industry, 1930–1950* (Albuquerque: University of New Mexico Press, 1987); Nelson-Cisneros, "UCAPAWA Or-

ganizing Activities"; and Nelson-Cisneros, "UCAPAWA in California: The Farm Worker Period," *Aztlán* 7 (Fall 1976):453–478.

105. See Dinwoodie, "Deportation," 193–206.

106. The background to El Congreso is discussed in Albert M. Camarillo's *Chicanos in California: A History of Mexican Americans in California* (San Francisco: Boyd and Fraser Publishing Co., 1984), 58–64, and "The Development of a Pan-Hispanic Civil Rights Movement: The 1939 Congress of Spanish-Speaking People" (paper presented at the annual meeting of the Organization of American Historians, Los Angeles, 1986). I am grateful to Professor Camarillo for graciously sharing with me his extensive file of unpublished documents and oral-history transcripts on the congress's activities. For a different reading of the activities and significance of the congress, see Mario T. García, *Mexican Americans,* 145–174.

107. "Call to the First Congress of the Mexican and Spanish American Peoples of the United States—Signers of the Call," Box 31, McWilliams Collection. See also *La Opinión,* December 4, 1938, and February 26, March 5, March 19, April 19, and April 26, 1939.

108. Camarillo, *Chicanos in California,* 61; *La Opinión,* April 26, 28, and 29, 1939; *People's World,* April 28 and 30, 1939. The congress's objectives were also laid out in a letter from the organization's secretary to Los Angeles County Supervisor John Anson Ford. See Josefina Fierro de Bright to Ford, September 1, 1939, Box 65, Folder B, Ford Collection.

109. "Call to the First Congress," McWilliams Collection.

110. "Statement and Resolution of the English-Speaking Panel," in Draft Program of the National Congress of Spanish-Speaking Peoples, Digest of Proceedings, Box 14, Folder 9, Ernesto Galarza Papers, Department of Special Collections, Stanford University Libraries, Stanford, California (hereafter cited as Digest of Proceedings).

111. Ibid., 7.

112. "Call to the First Congress," McWilliams Collection.

113. Luisa Moreno, "Caravans of Sorrow," address delivered at the panel on Deportation and the Right of Asylum of the Fourth Annual Conference of the American Committee for the Protection of the Foreign Born, Washington, D.C., March 3, 1940, Box 1, Folder 1, McWilliams Collection.

114. "Resolution on Illiteracy," Digest of Proceedings, 10, emphasis added.

115. "Resolution on Discrimination and Civil Rights," Digest of Proceedings, 11, emphasis added.

116. Digest of Proceedings, 12.

FOUR. THE CONTRADICTIONS OF ETHNIC POLITICS

1. Mario T. García, *Mexican Americans: Leadership, Ideology, and Identity, 1930–1960* (New Haven, Conn.: Yale University Press, 1989), 2. For other examples of this general interpretive line, see Mario T. García, "Americans All: The Mexican American Generation and the Politics of Wartime Los Angeles, 1941–1945," in *The Mexican American Experience: An Interdisciplinary Anthology*, ed. Rodolfo O. de la Garza et al. (Austin: University of Texas Press, 1985), 201–212; Raúl Morín, *Among the Valiant: Mexican Americans in WWII and Korea* (Alhambra, Calif.: Borden Publishing Co., 1966); Rodolfo Alvarez, "The Psycho-Historical and Socioeconomic Development of the Chicano Community in the United States," *Social Science Quarterly* 53 (March 1973):920–942, and "The Unique Psycho-Historical Experience of the Mexican American People," *Social Science Quarterly* 52 (June 1971):15–29; John R. Chávez, *The Lost Land: The Chicano Image of the Southwest* (Albuquerque: University of New Mexico Press, 1984), 106, 113, 116; and most recently, Richard A. García, *Rise of the Mexican American Middle Class: San Antonio, 1929–1941* (College Station: Texas A & M University Press, 1991).

2. Indeed, at the time of Pearl Harbor some Los Angeles officials were still discussing plans to reduce the county's welfare roles by offering voluntary repatriation and one hundred dollars cash to resident Mexican nationals who chose to return to Mexico, a situation that would change very quickly once manpower demands began to rise. It is interesting to note, however, that the mindset of California government officials on the eve of the World War II was that there were still too many Mexicans living in the state. These contingency plans are discussed in "Memorandum Regarding Repatriation of Mexican Citizens in California," December 26, 1941, and in correspondence between Los Angeles County Supervisor John Anson Ford and California Governor Culbert Olsen and Mexican Consul-General Rodolfo Salazar between November 1941 and January 1942, Box 65, Folder B, John Anson Ford Collection, Huntington Library and Art Museum, San Marino, California (hereafter cited as Ford Collection)..

3. Manuel Gamio, *Mexican Immigration to the United States: A Study of Human Migration and Adjustment* (New York: Dover Publications, 1971), 93–94.

4. Cited in Carey McWilliams, *North from Mexico: The Spanish-Speaking People of the United States* (New York: Greenwood Press, 1968), 225–226.

5. Emory S. Bogardus, "Attitudes and the Mexican Immigrant," in *Social Attitudes*, ed. Kimball Young (New York: Henry Holt and Co., 1931), 318.

6. Emory S. Bogardus, "Current Problems of Mexican Immigrants," *Sociology and Social Research* 25 (November 1940):171. See also Emory

S. Bogardus, "Second Generation Mexicans," *Sociology and Social Research* 13 (January 1929):276–283.

7. Ernesto Galarza, "Life in the United States for Mexican People: Out of the Experience of a Mexican," in *National Conference of Social Work, Proceedings of 1929* (Chicago: University of Chicago Press, 1930), 402. For similar analyses, see Paul S. Taylor, *Mexican Labor in the United States: Chicago and the Calumet Region*, University of California Publications in Economics, vol. 7, no. 2 (Berkeley: University of California Press, 1932), 193–195; and Carey McWilliams, "The Mexican Problem," *Common Ground* 8 (Spring 1948), 3–17.

8. For discussions of the limitations of the 1940 Census in accurately estimating the native-born Mexican American population, see Thomas D. Boswell, "The Growth and Proportional Distribution of the Mexican Stock Population in the United States: 1910–1970," *Mississippi Geographer* 7 (Spring 1979):57–58; and José Hernández, Leo Estrada, and David Alvírez, "Census Data and the Problem of Conceptually Defining the Mexican American Population," *Social Science Quarterly* 53 (March 1973):671–687.

9. U.S. Bureau of the Census, *Sixteenth Census of the United States, 1940: Population, Nativity, and Parentage of the White Population. Country of Origin of the Foreign Stock* (Washington, D.C., 1943), 9.

10. U.S. Bureau of the Census, *Sixteenth Census of the United States, 1940: Population, Nativity, and Parentage of the White Population. Mother Tongue* (Washington, D.C., 1943), 20, 22.

11. Ibid., 42.

12. Ibid., 50.

13. Bureau of the Census, *Sixteenth Census, Country of Origin of the Foreign Stock*, 5.

14. Ruth D. Tuck, *Not with the Fist* (New York: Harcourt, Brace and Co., 1946), 207. The 1940 Census reported that of the 34,900 Mexican aliens enumerated in Los Angeles in 1940, only 3,980 were naturalized, 1,800 had taken out "first papers," and 28,160 had not applied for American citizenship. See Bureau of the Census, *Sixteenth Census, Country of Origin of the Foreign Stock*, 83. Carey McWilliams, Ernesto Galarza, and War Manpower Commission member Guy T. Nunn all ventured similar analyses of Mexicans' reluctance to become American citizens. See, for example, the testimony of Carey McWilliams and Guy T. Nunn to Special Committee of the Los Angeles Grand Jury, October 8, 1942, Box 27, Carey McWilliams Collection, Department of Special Collections, University Research Library, University of California, Los Angeles. Mexican immigrants interviewed thirty years later expressed similar reluctance to become American citizens. See survey of the Mexican colonia in Oxnard, California, in Ventura County Neighborhood Youth Corps, "Colonia Family Living Study," Summer, Fall 1971, Box 16, Folder 5, Ernesto Galarza Papers,

Department of Special Collections, Stanford University, Stanford, California (hereafter cited as Galarza Papers).

15. For discussions of the evolution of the pachuco subculture and the context of the Sleepy Lagoon and Zoot-Suit incidents, see Beatrice Griffith's "The Pachuco Patois," *Common Ground* 7 (Summer 1947):77–84, and *American Me* (Boston: Houghton Mifflin Co., 1948), esp. 42–90; George Carpenter Barker, *Pachuco: An American-Spanish Argot and Its Social Function in Tucson, Arizona* (Tucson: University of Arizona Press, 1950); and Arturo Madrid-Barela's incisive "In Search of the Authentic Pachuco, An Interpretive Essay," *Aztlán* 4 (Spring 1973):31–57. The implications of these developments for the ethnic Mexican population at large are sensitively treated in Joan W. Moore's *Homeboys: Gangs, Drugs, and Prison in the Barrios of Los Angeles* (Philadelphia: Temple University Press, 1978); and James Diego Vigil, *Barrio Gangs: Streetlife and Identity in Southern California* (Austin: University of Texas Press, 1988). For an example of a contemporary analysis of the emergence of the pachuco phenomenon, see the editorial, "Glorificacíon del 'Pachuquismo,'" in *La Opinión*, November 11, 1943.

16. For general discussions of the Sleepy Lagoon incident and the Zoot-Suit Riots, see Lloyd H. Fisher, "The Problem of Violence: Observations on Race Conflict in Los Angeles" (Los Angeles: American Council on Race Relations, 1946); McWilliams, *North from Mexico*, 228–233; Rodolfo Acuña, *Occupied America: A History of Chicanos*, 2d ed. (New York: Harper & Row, 1981), 324–326; Gerald D. Nash, *The American West Transformed: The Impact of the Second World War* (Bloomington: Indiana University Press, 1985), 110–121; Robin F. Scott, "The Mexican American in the Los Angeles Area, 1920–1950: From Acquiescence to Activity" (Ph.D. diss., University of Southern California, 1971), 222–227, and 234–247; and Mauricio Mazón, *The Zoot-Suit Riots: The Psychology of Symbolic Annihilation* (Austin: University of Texas Press, 1984), 20–30.

17. See, for example, "Youth Gangs Leading Cause of Delinquency," *Los Angeles Times*, June 2, 1943; "Zoot-Suiters Learn," *Los Angeles Herald Express*, June 8, 1943; "Zoot Girls Stab Woman; State Probes Rioting—Grand Jury to Act in Zoot-Suit War," *Los Angeles Herald Express*, June 10, 1943; "Zoot Cyclists Snatch Purses," *Los Angeles Times*, June 16, 1943; and "Youthful Gang Secrets Exposed—Young Hoodlums Smoke 'Reefers,' Tattoo Girls and Plot Robberies," *Los Angeles Times*, July 16, 1944. For examples of national coverage of the Zoot-Suit phenomenon, see "California: Zoot-Suit War," *Time*, June 21, 1943, 18–19; "The Zoot-Suit Riots," *New Republic*, June 21, 1943, 818–820; and "Zoot-Suit Riots," *Life*, June 21, 1943, 30–31.

18. Lt. Ed Duran Ayres, "Statistics" (typescript), Box 65, Folder B, Ford Collection.

19. See Griffith, *American Me*, 3–41; McWilliams, *North from Mex-*

ico, 235–239; and Scott, "Mexican American in the Los Angeles Area," 216–222.

20. California, Legislature, Joint Fact-Finding Committee on Un-American Activities, *Report of the Joint Fact-Finding Committee on Un-American Activities in California* (Sacramento, 1945), 209 (hereafter cited as Tenney Committee Report).

21. Testimony of C. B. Horrall, Chief, Los Angeles Police Department, to Tenney Committee, ibid., 160, 173.

22. See Tenney Committee Report, 173, 208–210.

23. Sleepy Lagoon Defense Committee, *The Sleepy Lagoon Case* (Los Angeles: Sleepy Lagoon Defense Committee, 1944). See also Nash, *The American West Transformed*, 113–114; Carlos Larralde, *Mexican American Movements and Leaders* (Los Alamitos, Calif.: Hwong Publishing Co., 1976), 172–174, Mazón, *The Zoot-Suit Riots*, 24; and Tenney Committee Report, 210.

24. Sleepy Lagoon Defense Committee, *The Sleepy Lagoon Case*, (n.p.), ca. 1944.

25. Ibid.

26. Ibid.

27. Ibid.

28. Ibid.

29. Citizens' Committee for Latin American Youth, roster, 1943, Box 62, Folder IV, Ford Collection; and Los Angeles County Committee for Interracial Progress, "Report of Interracial Committees in Los Angeles County," April 17, 1944, Box 4, Folder 9, Manuel Ruiz Papers, Department of Special Collections, Stanford University Libraries, Stanford, California (hereafter cited as Ruiz Papers).

30. Coordinating Council on Latin American Youth, "Petition," November 24, 1942, Box 62, Folder 4, Ford Collection.

31. Manuel Ruiz to *Los Angeles Times* and *Los Angeles Examiner*, August 6, 1942, Box 1, Folder 6, Ruiz Papers.

32. Coordinating Council on Latin American Youth, Petition to Los Angeles City Council, November 11, 1942, Box 4, Folder 11, Ruiz Papers. Manuel Ruiz elaborated on this position later in the war, asserting flatly that "the Mexican is integrating rapidly. He has not organized as a pressure group or put on porcupine defensive armour. The sons of Mexico generally do not possess the consciousness of being a minority, for where he comes from there were nothing but Mexicans. The proximity of our sister republic keeps him from accepting or succumbing to the feelings of class consciousness, as suffered by some other minorities, who feel isolated by reason of the fact that historically they have always constituted a special group." See "The Racial Problem Is Being Solved," typescript of radio address broadcast June 24, 1945, Box 1, Folder 6, Ruiz Papers. Later, during the Chicano movement of the 1960s, Ruiz maintained this position despite

the fact that so many younger Mexican Americans clearly wanted to make more of the cultural differences that divided them from other Americans. Writing in 1963 to Eduardo Quevedo, former president of the Congress of Spanish-Speaking Peoples, Ruiz complained, "If you recall, I originally lost interest when some political actions groups, without political experience, began to seek recognition upon the predicate that our Spanish-speaking Americans had a distinct interest from the rest of the community and began to single themselves out as special [interest] groups. These groups finally succeeded in putting the stamp of 'minority groups' upon themselves and so it is today." Manuel Ruiz to Eduardo Quevedo, June 1963, Box 1, Folder 5, Ruiz Papers.

33. Coordinating Council, "Petition to Los Angeles City Council," November 11, 1942, Ruiz Papers. See also "Report and Recommendations of the Citizens' Advisory Committee on Youth in Wartime," June 12, 1943, Box 4, Folder 1, Ruiz Papers.

34. Testimony of Carey McWilliams, Chief, California Division of Immigration and Housing, to the Special Committee of the Los Angeles County Grand Jury, October 8, 1942, Box 65, Folder B, Ford Collection.

35. These issues, which dominated Mexican Americans' civil rights agenda throughout the war years, were articulated by a great number of political activists in this period. See, for example, George I. Sánchez, President-General, League of United Latin American Citizens, to Nelson A. Rockefeller, Coordinator of Inter-American Affairs, December 31, 1941, Box 42, Correspondence file "R," George I. Sánchez Papers, Benson Latin American Library, University of Texas, Austin (hereafter cited as Sánchez Papers); and Manuel C. Gonzales to Sánchez, August 10, 1942, in author's files.

36. Sánchez to Rockefeller, December 31, 1941, Box 42, Correspondence file "R," Sánchez Papers.

37. Sánchez to Rockefeller, February 7, 1942, Box 42, Correspondence file "R," Sánchez Papers.

38. Sánchez to Roger Baldwin, American Civil Liberties Union, September 15, 1942, Box 67, Sánchez Papers. Like Manuel Ruiz in California, Sánchez also objected to the continued common use of the term *Mexican* to describe American citizens of Mexican descent. Such usage, he argued, provided the very "basis for biased public opinion which is later expressed by individuals in business, the Army, etc." See Sánchez to Baldwin, September 21, 1942, Box 67, Sánchez Papers.

39. Hector E. Valdez, Hector Benítez, José Garza, J. G. Robles, Manuel Cirilo, and Johnny Leal to J. T. Canales, May 22, 1943, Box 67, Sánchez Papers.

40. J. T. Canales to George I. Sánchez, May 22, 1943, Box 67, Sánchez Papers. Almost identical arguments were raised by Mexican Americans across Texas throughout the war. Leocadio Durán of Rosenberg, Texas,

wrote to Texas Governor Coke Stevenson that "since the United States of America and the Government of Mexico are . . . united in the war against a common enemy who threatens to take away from us the right to be free and sovereign," widespread discrimination against Mexicans in Texas must come "from a number of bad citizens . . . bent on destroying those efforts on the part of your governments and bringing to naught the sacrifice of our soldiers now giving their very lives so that Democracy might live." See Durán to Stevenson, October 16, 1943, Box 67, Sánchez Papers. Similar sentiments are evident in a number of other sources. See, for example, Sánchez to Roger Baldwin, American Civil Liberties Union, January 4, September 15, and September 21, 1942, Box 67, Sánchez Papers; Santiago Vargas, José Iram Hernández, and Alejos Lara to Sánchez, February 1, 1942, Box 42, Correspondence File "R," Sánchez Papers; and similar testimonies in Alonso S. Perales, *Are We Good Neighbors?* (New York: Arno Press, 1974).

41. Although the actual extent of the labor shortage claimed by agricultural interests was open to debate, U.S. Department of Agriculture statistics that reported a decline in the American hired farm labor force from 3,421,000 on October 1, 1944, to 2,494,000 one year later seemed to support at least some of these claims. See U.S. Department of Agriculture, Bureau of Agricultural Economics, *Farm Labor* (Washington, D.C., October 12, 1945), 1, quoted in Otey Scruggs, *Braceros, "Wetbacks," and the Farm Labor Problem: Mexican Agricultural Labor in the United States, 1942–1954* (New York: Garland Publishing, 1988), 339. For lobbyists' arguments during this period, see, for example, U.S. Congress, House of Representatives, Committee on Agriculture, *Farm Labor and Production: Hearings,* 77th Cong., 2d sess., September 23, September 25, September 28, and October 2, 1942; the statement and testimony of Charles C. Teague, President of the California Fruit Growers' Exchange, in U.S. Congress, Senate, Committee on Appropriations, *Farm Labor Program, 1943: Hearings,* 78th Cong., 1st sess., March 1943, 151–169; Richard B. Craig, *The Bracero Program: Interest Groups and Foreign Policy* (Austin: University of Texas Press, 1971), 24–28, 36–39; and Wayne D. Rasmussen, *A History of the Emergency Farm Labor Supply Program, 1943–1947,* Agricultural Monograph no. 13, U.S. Department of Agriculture, Bureau of Economics (Washington, D.C.: U.S. Government Printing Office, 1951), 1–15.

42. For the evolution of various versions of the Bracero Program, see Otey Scruggs, *Braceros, "Wetbacks," and the Farm Labor Problem;* Craig, *Bracero Program;* Ernesto Galarza, *Merchants of Labor: The Mexican Bracero Story, An Account of the Managed Migration of Mexican Farmworkers in California, 1942–1960* (Charlotte, N.C.: McNally & Loftin, 1964); and Manuel García y Griego, "The Importation of Mexican Contract Laborers to the United States, 1942–1964: Antecedents, Operation,

and Legacy," in *The Border That Joins: Mexican Migrants and U.S. Responsibility*, ed. Peter G. Brown and Henry Shue (Totowa, N.J.: Rowman and Littlefield, 1983), 49–98. The texts of both the executive bilateral agreements signed by the United States and Mexico and of a typical agreement between the U.S. government and American employers can be found in U.S. Congress, House of Representatives, Committee on Appropriations, *Farm Labor Program, 1943: Hearings*, 78th Cong., 1st sess., 1943, 49–53.

43. See Rasmussen, *Emergency Farm Labor Supply Program*, 199, 226. Although the overwhelming majority of agricultural and railroad workers employed in the Southwest were Mexicans, workers were also recruited under the terms of the program from Canada, the Bahamas, Barbados, and Jamaica.

44. For brief discussions of the lack of publicity surrounding the bracero negotiations, see Scruggs, *Braceros, "Wetbacks," and the Farm Labor Problem*, 150–199; and Cletus E. Daniel, *Chicano Workers and the Politics of Fairness: The FEPC in the Southwest, 1941–1945* (Austin: University of Texas Press, 1991), 40–41.

45. See Scruggs, *Braceros, "Wetbacks," and the Farm Labor Problem*, 157–159.

46. Letter from Davis McIntire, Regional Leader, Bureau of Agricultural Economics, to J. H. Province, Acting Head, Division of Farm Population and Rural Welfare, U.S. Department of Agriculture, April 13, 1942, quoted in ibid., 159.

47. Theodore A. Chacón to George I. Sánchez, July 12, 1941, Box 68, "Correspondence File—LULAC, 1941–43," Sánchez Papers. Sánchez apparently agreed with his counterpart in California. Although he expressed "hope that we can make our opposition felt in a discreet and diplomatic manner . . . we want . . . our Mexican friends to know that our objections are a result of our sincere desire to see that they are not exploited and then mistreated." "We would be for letting down such bars," Sánchez asserted, "if we were not convinced that such a move is against the base interest of both the American and the Mexican people." Sánchez to Chacón, July 31, 1941, Box 68, "Correspondence File—LULAC, 1941–43," Sánchez Papers.

48. *The Mexican Voice*, Winter 1941, 2. See also Mexican American Movement, Constitution, "Cardinal Aims of the Movement," Box 15, Folder 5, Galarza Papers; and Félix Gutiérrez, "Mexican-American Youth and Their Media: *The Mexican Voice*, 1938–1945," unpublished paper presented at the 77th annual meeting of the Organization of American Historians, Los Angeles, April 1984.

49. Paul Coronel, "The Pachuco Problem," *The Mexican Voice*, ca. Summer 1943, 3.

50. *The Mexican Voice*, Winter 1941, 2.

51. *The Mexican Voice*, September, 1938, 5, emphasis in original.

52. *The Mexican Voice*, February 1940, 6.

53. *The Mexican Voice*, October-November 1938, 7.

54. For discussions of the historical role played by Mexican consulates in the United States, see Francisco Balderrama, *In Defense of La Raza: The Los Angeles Mexican Consulate and the Mexican Community, 1929 to 1936* (Tucson: University of Arizona Press, 1982); Juan Gómez-Quiñones, "Piedras contra la luna, México en Aztlán y Aztlán en México: Chicano-Mexican Relations in the Mexican Consulates, 1900–1920," in *Contemporary Mexico: Papers of the IV International Congress of Mexican History* (Mexico City: El Colegio de México and UCLA Latin American Studies Center, 1975), 494–527; and José Amaro Hernández, *Mutual Aid for Survival: The Case of the Mexican Americans* (Malabar, Fla.: Robert Krieger Publishers, 1983).

55. Pauline R. Kibbe, *Latin Americans in Texas* (Albuquerque, University of New Mexico Press, 1946), 172.

56. Texas farmers' bid to recruit braceros is detailed in Johnny M. McCain, "Texas and the Mexican Labor Question, 1942–1947," *Southwestern Historical Quarterly* 85 (July 1981):48; Rasmussen, *Emergency Farm Labor Supply Program*, 200; and Otey Scruggs's series of articles, "The United States, Mexico, and the Wetbacks," *Pacific Historical Review* 30 (May 1961):149–164, "Texas, Good Neighbor?" *Southwestern Social Science Quarterly* 43 (September 1962):118–125, and "Texas and the Bracero Program, 1942–1947," *Pacific Historical Review* 32 (August 1963):251–264.

57. Testimony of Edward A. O'Neal, President, American Farm Bureau Federation, in Senate Committee on Appropriations, *Farm Labor Program, 1943: Hearings*, 70–71.

58. See Hensley C. Woodbridge, "Mexico and U.S. Racism: How Mexicans View Our Treatment of Minorities," *Commonweal*, June 22, 1945, 235.

59. For the official Mexican response to developments in Texas, see "No Mexicans Allowed," *Inter-American* 11 (September 1943), 8–9; Kibbe, *Latin Americans in Texas*, 172; and Craig, *Bracero Program*, 50–51.

60. McCain, "Texas and the Mexican Labor Question," 53–56; and Scruggs, "Texas and the Bracero Program," 254–256. See also the official correspondence between Padilla and Stevenson in "The Good Neighbor Policy and Mexicans in Texas," in *The Mexican American and the Law*, ed. Carlos Cortés (New York: Arno Press, 1974).

61. Kibbe, *Latin Americans in Texas*, 121.

62. Ibid.

63. For general discussions of the gradual gains Mexican Americans in Texas made during the war decade, see Vernon M. Briggs, Jr., Walter Fogel, and Fred H. Schmidt, *The Chicano Worker* (Austin: University of Texas Press, 1977); Mario Barrera, *Race and Class in the Southwest: A Theory*

of Racial Inequality (Notre Dame, Ind.: University of Notre Dame Press, 1979); Manuel Peña, *The Texas-Mexican Conjunto: History of a Working-Class Music* (Austin: University of Texas Press, 1985), 113–133; Guadalupe San Miguel, Jr., *"Let All of Them Take Heed": Mexican Americans and the Campaign for Educational Equality in Texas, 1910–1981* (Austin: University of Texas Press, 1987), 91–112; David Montejano, *Anglos and Mexicans in the Making of Texas, 1836–1986* (Austin: University of Texas Press, 1987), 262–287; and Mario T. García, *Mexican Americans*, 114–116.

64. The terminology used to describe unsanctioned entrants into the United States has always been politically charged and thus fraught with controversy. As the debate over officially sanctioned and unsanctioned immigrants intensified again in the 1940s and 1950s, manipulation of terminology became part of the political struggle over U.S. immigration and labor policies. Those who opposed large-scale undocumented entry of Mexican immigrants into the country tended to use derogatory terms, such as *wetbacks* (or simply *wets*), *fence jumpers, illegal aliens,* or, in Spanish, *mojados* (*wet ones*), to describe unsanctioned entrants. This usage is problematic because it tends to ignore or mystify the role that U.S. business interests and the federal government played throughout this period to recruit Mexican laborers and, perhaps more important, ignores the fact that Americans in both the private and public sectors routinely broke existing U.S. immigration, labor, and civil statutes concerning Mexican immigrants when it suited them or the interests they represented. Consequently, I prefer to use the more neutral terms *undocumented* or *unsanctioned* immigrants or workers when I am referring to Mexican nationals who entered the United States outside officially established and sanctioned procedures.

65. As with all such statistics, because many undocumented aliens were apprehended more than once in a year and many were never apprehended, INS tallies of apprehensions should be considered rough approximations of the magnitude of the flow of unsanctioned entries into the United States. For discussions of the different estimates of undocumented Mexican entrants at this time, see Galarza, *Merchants of Labor,* 58–59; Julian Samora, *Los Mojados: The Wetback Story* (Notre Dame, Ind.: University of Notre Dame Press, 1971), 43–46; and David M. Reimers, *Still the Golden Door: The Third World Comes to America* (New York: Columbia University Press, 1985), 39–52. In its 1951 report, President Harry S. Truman's Commission on Migratory Labor noted that the Bracero Program also seemed to have contributed to an unprecedented population buildup in northern Mexico as people used northern Mexican cities as staging grounds from which to enter the United States. Between 1940 and 1950, for example, the population of the Mexican border town of Mexicali grew by 240 percent; of Tijuana, by 259 percent; of Ciudad Juárez, by 149 percent; and of Matamoros, by 179 percent. See President's Commission on

Migratory Labor, *Migratory Labor in American Agriculture* (Washington, D.C.: U.S. Government Printing Office, 1951), 72.

66. The debate within LULAC is discussed in M. C. Gonzales to George I. Sánchez, August 20, 1943, Box 67, Sánchez Papers. The quotation is from George J. Garza, "Editorial," *LULAC News*, March 1947, 5, 17.

67. José R. Moreno, "The Price We Must Pay for Equality," *LULAC News* (date obscured, but article dated October 25, 1946). The issue was debated in the pages of the *LULAC News* and in LULAC's official functions for the next decade, although several LULAC national conventions chose not to take action on the proposed change of the organization's name. See George J. Garza's "Our Classification—What Is It?" *LULAC News*, June 1947, 7, and "Editorial," *LULAC News*, July 1947, 3; and Albert Armendáriz, "Hello from Your National President," *LULAC News*, May 1954, 3.

68. See the open letter from Raoul A. Cortez, President General, LULAC, to all LULAC Councils, October 28, 1948, Box 67, "Minority Correspondence, 1950–51," Sánchez Papers; and Jacob I. Rodríguez to John J. Herrera, July 1, 1952, Box 67, "Minority Correspondence, 1950–51," Sánchez Papers. See also the summary statement on the issue in the resolution adopted by the LULAC National Convention, June 26, 1966, GEN HU2/MC, WHCF, Box 24, Lyndon Baines Johnson Presidential Papers, Lyndon Baines Johnson Presidential Library, Austin, Texas; "Editorial," *LULAC News*, October 1947, 5; and "State Convention Features," *LULAC News*, October 1947, 11.

69. "Night Classes for Aliens Being Planned," *LULAC News*, November 1946, 17; Ike Martínez, "LULAC-ism in Action," *LULAC News* January 1949, 23, 25; untitled article in *LULAC News*, February 1954, 50; and LULAC, "LULAC Education Fund" (brochure, n.d.), Jake Rodríguez Collection, Box 2, Folder 1, LULAC Archives, Benson Latin American Library, University of Texas, Austin.

70. Sánchez to Ernesto Galarza, October 12, 1948, Box 1, Folder 3, Galarza Papers.

71. Sánchez to Galarza, January 19, 1949, Box 67, Sánchez Papers.

72. Sánchez to Ernest Schwarz, Executive Secretary, Committee on Latin American Affairs, CIO, January 19, 1949, "Immigration," Box 1, Galarza Papers. See also Sánchez's comments in "Peons in West Lowering Culture," *New York Times*, March 27, 1951.

73. Gladwyn Hill, "Peons in West Lowering Culture," *New York Times*, March 27, 1951.

74. These included various versions of the following works, which are in the Sánchez Papers: George I. Sánchez and Lyle Saunders, ed. "Wetbacks: A Preliminary Report to the Advisory Committee; Study of Spanish-Speaking People" (mimeo, University of Texas, Austin, 1949); Lyle Saunders, "The Social History of Spanish-Speaking People in the Southwestern United States since 1846" (paper delivered at the 4th Regional

Conference, Southwest Council on the Education of Spanish-Speaking People, January 23–25, 1950); and Lyle Saunders, "Sociological Study of the Wetbacks in the Lower Rio Grande Valley" (paper presented at the 5th Annual Conference, Southwest Council on the Education of Spanish-Speaking People, Pepperdine College, Los Angeles, California, 1951). The final version of this extended research project, written by Lyle Saunders and Olin Leonard, was published as "The Wetback in the Lower Rio Grande Valley of Texas," Inter-American Education Occasional Papers, 7, University of Texas, Austin, 1951.

75. Lyle Saunders, "The Wetback Problem in the Lower Rio Grande Valley" (typescript), Box 36, Sánchez Papers.

76. For a brilliant explication of this argument, see Manuel Peña's analysis of the evolution of the distinctive "Texas-Mexican" musical style, *conjunto*, and other forms of what he argues were symbolic forms of cultural resistance in *Texas-Mexican Conjunto*.

77. The details of Mexican Americans' activities in CIO unions during the 1940s and 1950s are still largely unknown, but for good overview discussions, see Douglas Monroy, "Mexicanos in Los Angeles, 1930–1941: An Ethnic Group in Relation to Class Forces" (Ph.D. diss., University of California, Los Angeles, 1978), 115–128 and passim; and Luis Leobardo Arroyo, "Chicano Participation in Organized Labor: The C.I.O. in Los Angeles, 1938–1950, An Extended Research Note," *Aztlán* 6 (Summer 1975):290–299.

78. Monroy, "Mexicanos in Los Angeles," 138–139; and Arroyo, "Chicano Participation in Organized Labor," 290–299. For Bert Corona's reminiscences about the CIO's Committee to Aid Mexican Workers, see Mario T. García, "Working for the Union," *Mexican Studies/Estudios Mexicanos* 9 (Summer 1993), 254–257.

79. U.S. Office of Production Management, press release, January 10, 1942, Box 65, Folder B, Ford Collection. The background of this development is discussed in Nash, *The American West Transformed*, 121–123; and Daniel, *Chicano Workers and the Politics of Fairness*.

80. Minutes, Los Angeles Committee for Latin American Youth, January 18 and February 15, 1943, Box 4, Folder 6, Ruiz Papers.

81. Los Angeles Coordinating Council on Latin American Youth to David Carrasco, California State Commissioner of Labor, April 15, 1942, Box 3, Folder 2, Ruiz Papers. The committee referred to President Roosevelt's Executive Order 8802, "Re: Official Policy on Full Participation in the Defense Program by All Persons, Regardless of Race, Creed, Color, or National Origin," June 25, 1941.

82. Los Angeles Coordinating Council on Latin American Youth, petition to the mayor of Los Angeles, November 11, 1942, Box 62, Folder IV, Ford Collection. See also Manuel J. Avila, "Constructive Approach to the Youth Problem," *Los Angeles Daily Journal*, March 15, 1943.

83. Minutes, Los Angeles Citizens' Committee for Latin American Youth, July 12, 1942, p. 2, Box 4, Folder 6, Ruiz Papers.

84. Testimony of Eduardo Quevedo, Los Angeles Coordinating Council on Latin American Youth, to U.S. Congress, Senate, Committee on Education and Labor, *Hearings on the Fair Employment Practices Act*, March 12–14, 1945, quoted in Perales, *Are We Good Neighbors?* 110–111.

FIVE. ETHNIC POLITICS, IMMIGRATION POLICY, AND THE COLD WAR

1. The founding of the G.I. Forum is recounted in "The Three Rivers Incident," *New Republic*, May 2, 1949, 7; Stanford P. Dyer and Merrell A. Knighten, "Discrimination after Death: Lyndon Johnson and Felix Longoria," *Southern Studies* 17 (Winter 1978):411–426; and Carl Allsup, *The American G.I. Forum: Origins and Evolution*, Monograph no. 6, Center for Mexican American Studies (Austin: University of Texas Press, 1982).

2. American G.I. Forum of Texas and Texas State Federation of Labor, "What Price Wetbacks?" in *Mexican Migration to the United States*, ed. Carlos Cortés (New York: Arno Press, 1976), 2. See also Juan Ramón García, *Operation Wetback: The Mass Deportation of Mexican Undocumented Laborers in 1954* (Westport, Conn.: Greenwood Press, 1980), 210.

3. "What Price Wetbacks?" 5, 38.

4. Ibid., 54–55. See also American Council of Spanish Speaking People, *Civil Liberties Newsletter*, November 15, 1951, Box 14, Folder 1, Ernesto Galarza Papers, Department of Special Collections, Stanford University Libraries, Stanford, California (hereafter cited as Galarza Papers); and Cristobal P. Aldrete, State Chairman, American G.I. Forum of Texas, to Representative Clifford Hope, Chairman, House Agriculture Committee, February 10, 1954, in U.S. Congress, House of Representatives, Committee on Agriculture, *Mexican Farm Labor: Hearings*, 83d Cong., 2d sess., 1954, 188.

5. Allsup, *American G.I. Forum*, 119.

6. Ibid., 106.

7. *Texas Observer*, August 16, 1957, 4.

8. *Texas Observer*, June 28, 1957, 8.

9. Indeed, Galarza's basic position on the immigrant question already seemed to be well formed by the late 1920s. See his early analysis of the issue, "Life in the United States for Mexican People: Out of the Experience of a Mexican," in *National Council of Social Work, Proceedings of 1929* (Chicago: University of Chicago Press, 1930), 399–404.

10. *Associated Farmer*, March 3, 1943, 2.

11. National Farm Workers Union, "Statement on the Importation of Agricultural Workers from Mexico," June 4, 1948, Box 67, George I. Sán-

chez Papers, Benson Latin American Library, University of Texas, Austin (hereafter cited as Sánchez Papers).

12. See, for example, testimony of H. L. Mitchell, NAWU, to House Agriculture Committee, June 18, 1947, U.S. Congress, House of Representatives, Committee on Agriculture, *Permanent Farm Labor Program: Hearings*, 80th Cong., 1st sess., 1947, 84–85; Ernesto Galarza, speech to Albuquerque Conference on the Status of Spanish-Speaking People, January 25, 1950, Box 67, Sánchez Papers; and Galarza to California State Federation of Labor, June 14, 1950, Box 14, Folder 7, Galarza Papers.

13. George I. Sánchez to Ernesto Galarza, October 12, 1948, Box 67, Sánchez Papers.

14. Ernesto Galarza, "Big Farm Strike: A Report on the Labor Dispute at DiGiorgio's," *Commonweal*, June 4, 1948, 179–180.

15. Ernesto Galarza, *Merchants of Labor: The Mexican Bracero Story, An Account of the Managed Migration of Mexican Farmworkers in California, 1942–1960* (Charlotte, N.C.: McNally & Loftin, 1964), 238.

16. House Committee on Agriculture, *Mexican Farm Labor: Hearings*, 159–160.

17. Galarza, "Big Farm Strike," 182. See also Ernesto Galarza, Herman Gallegos, and Julian Samora, *Mexican Americans in the Southwest* (Santa Barbara, Calif.: McNally & Loftin, 1969), ix.

18. Margaret Clark, *Health in the Mexican American Culture: A Community Study* (Berkeley: University of California Press, 1959), 79–80.

19. Lyle Saunders and Olen Leonard, "Tentative Report" (a draft version of "The Wetback in the Lower Rio Grande Valley of Texas"), 52, Box 38, Sánchez Papers.

20. National Farm Labor Union, "Summer Brings the Mexicans—Statement of the National Farm Labor Union," *Commonweal*, July 2, 1948, 275–278.

21. U.S. Congress, House of Representatives, Committee on Agriculture, *Mexican Farm Labor Program: Hearings*, 84th Cong., 1st sess., 1955, 186–188.

22. Ernesto Galarza, "The Burning Light" (transcript, oral history interview), Galarza Papers, 17.

23. House Committee on Agriculture, *Mexican Farm Labor Program: Hearings*, 176.

24. Ibid., 177.

25. For the politics surrounding the passage of the Immigration and Nationality Act of 1952, see Marius A. Dimmitt, "The Enactment of the McCarran-Walter Act of 1952" (Ph.D. diss., University of Kansas, 1970); and Robert A. Divine, *American Immigration Policy, 1924–1952* (New Haven, Conn.: Yale University Press, 1957), 164–191. For the civil rights aspects of this, and similar, legislation, see Milton R. Konvitz, *Civil Rights*

in Immigration (Ithaca, N.Y.: Cornell University Press, 1953); Elizabeth Hull, *Without Justice for All: The Constitutional Rights of Aliens* (Westport, Conn.: Greenwood Press, 1985); William Preston, Jr., *Aliens and Dissenters: Federal Suppression of Radicals, 1903–1933* (Cambridge, Mass.: Harvard University Press, 1963), 1–10, 273–276; and Steven R. Shapiro, "Ideological Exclusions: Closing the Border to Political Dissidents," *Harvard Law Review* 100 (February 1987):930–945.

26. Of the more than 450,000 resident Mexican nationals enumerated in 1950, only about 26 percent had become naturalized citizens, an increase of less than 2 percent over the naturalization rate reported for Mexicans in 1940. For analysis of demographic trends in the United States' ethnic Mexican population between 1950 and 1960, see J. Allan Beegle, Harold F. Goldsmith, and Charles P. Loomis, "Demographic Characteristics of the United States–Mexico Border," *Rural Sociology* 25 (March 1960):107–162. For estimates of rates of naturalization and the ratio of the U.S.-born to the Mexican-born cohorts of the total resident ethnic population at this time, see U.S. Bureau of the Census, *Census of Population, 1950: Special Reports—Nativity and Parentage* Vol. 4, P–E No. 3A (Washington, D.C., 1954), 71, 75, and 130.

27. See statement of H. L. Mitchell in U.S. Congress, House of Representatives, Committee on Agriculture, *Extension of the Mexican Farm Labor Program: Hearings*, 83d Cong., 1st sess., 1953, 93. For the tenor of the popular discussion over the issue of "communist infiltration" from Mexico, see, for example: "Reds Slip into U.S., Congress Warned," *New York Times*, February 10, 1954, 23; statement of Dave Beck of the Teamsters Union, *New York Times*, February 15, 1954, 39; statements by Senators Herbert Lehman of New York and Hubert Humphrey of Minnesota, *New York Times*, March 3, 1954; and statement of INS officials warning of a "mass invasion . . . of foreign agents," *New York Times*, March 8, 1954, 6. See also George I. Sánchez to Ernesto Galarza, October 12, 1948, Box 1, Folder 3, Galarza Papers; and statement of Ernesto Galarza, *New York Times*, March 3, 1954, 18.

28. The differences in the "LULAC Code" can be seen by comparing *LULAC News*, July 1945, 36, with *LULAC News*, July 1953, back cover. I have been unable to locate any documentary evidence explaining this change, and none of the LULAC members I interviewed seemed to recall the reasons behind it.

29. "Aims and Purposes," *LULAC News*, February 1954. Interestingly, in a development that reminds one of Orwell's *Animal Farm*, LULAC reamended its constitution in the 1960s, during the "ethnic resurgence" of the Chicano movement era. Under Article III, "Aims and Purposes," LULAC members once again were asked to pledge "to foster the learning and fluent use of the English language that we may thereby equip ourselves and our families for the fullest enjoyment of our rights and privi-

leges and the efficient discharge of our duties and responsibilities to our country *but at the same time, exerting equal effort to foster the fluent mastery of the Spanish language which is part of our cultural heritage and a means of extending the cultural horizons of our nation. . . .* " See Article III, Section 2, "Aims and Purposes," LULAC Constitution (as amended, 1969), Box 1, Folder 1, LULAC Archives, Benson Latin American Library, University of Texas, Austin (emphasis added).

30. The most thorough treatment of Operation Wetback remains Juan Ramón García, *Operation Wetback*.

31. "Resolution No. 9," 24th Annual LULAC National Convention, Santa Fe, New Mexico, June 12–14, 1953, *LULAC News*, August 1953, 35.

32. *LULAC News*, May 1954, 3.

33. Editorial, *LULAC News*, August 1954, 1–2.

34. *LULAC News*, August 1954, 1–2. See also "Wetback Roundup Needs Support of LULAC," *LULAC News*, July 1954, 4.

35. Albert Armendáriz, "Hello from Your National President," *LULAC News*, May 1954, 3.

36. Ibid.

37. See Resolution No. 3, 25th Annual LULAC National Convention, Austin, Texas, June 11–13, 1954, *LULAC News*, July 1954, 12–13.

38. See, for example, resolution and discussion on the McCarran-Walter Act, LULAC National Convention, El Paso, Texas, June 22–24, 1956, *LULAC News*, July 1956, 9; and Resolution No. 19, 29th Annual LULAC Convention, Laredo, Texas, *LULAC News*, June 29, 1958, 8. A similar process of reassessment was occurring within the American G.I. Forum as well. Indeed, as early as 1949 the American G.I. Forum was voicing concern that INS practices toward Mexican nationals were violating the rights of U.S. citizens of Mexican descent. "Such practices are detrimental and injurious to . . . American citizens of Latin and Mexican [descent]," a Forum resolution argued. "Therefore be it resolved," the resolution concluded, "that the American G.I. Forum of Texas go on record . . . expressing . . . its dissatisfaction with the inhuman treatment given to some of our people, particularly to those of Spanish or Mexican descent and respectfully ask the Immigration Service to exercise a little more kindness and to be more respectful of the rights of others and to modify their methods of questioning people of Spanish or Mexican origin and that if members of the Immigration Service be required to demand evidences of Citizenship, that they also demand such evidences from people of all other nationalities as well." Resolution adopted by the annual convention of the American G.I. Forum of Texas, Corpus Christi, Texas, September 24–25, 1949, File on "Minorities—American G.I. Forum, 1949–51," Sánchez Papers. See also Juan Ramón García, *Operation Wetback*, 196.

39. Indeed, it is particularly revealing that although Galarza spent much of his life fighting against the Bracero Program and trying to stop

undocumented immigration, he often referred to himself as "the original wetback" and actively assisted braceros (and sometimes even wetbacks) in the United States while fighting to abolish the system under which such workers entered the country. Such assistance included pursuing with various government agencies braceros' grievances over hours, wages, and working conditions, and providing food, temporary shelter, and medical assistance to braceros and undocumented workers. See Ernesto Galarza, *Farmworkers and Agribusiness in California, 1947–1977* (Notre Dame, Ind.: University of Notre Dame Press, 1977), 111–112, 211.

40. Ernesto Galarza, "Mexicans in the Southwest: A Culture in Process," in *Plural Society in the Southwest*, ed. Edward H. Spicer and Raymond H. Thompson (New York: Weatherhead Foundation, 1972), 272, 274.

41. Testimony of Ernesto Galarza to House Committee on Agriculture, *Mexican Farm Labor Program: Hearings*, 172. This situation was repeated on numerous occasions over the life of the Bracero Program. For example, on the same day that INS Commissioner Joseph Swing crowed about his agency's successes in "stemming the wetback flow" in the Southwest, President Eisenhower requested an additional $350 million to cover costs of recruiting more braceros from Mexico. According to the *New York Times* report, "The funds are necessary, the White House spokesman said, because the intensified drive against wetback labor has increased the demand for legally recruited field workers." See *New York Times*, July 3, 1954, 11.

42. Author interview with Antonio Ríos, State Director, Community Service Organization, Los Angeles, California, December 12, 1984. For the establishment of the CSO, see Memorandum, Art Miley to Supervisor John Anson Ford, September 16, 1948, Box 65, Folder B, Ford Collection; Beatrice Griffith, "Viva Roybal—Viva America," *Common Ground* 10 (Autumn 1949):61–70; "Acute Problems of Los Angeles' Mexican American Residents Told," *Los Angeles Daily News*, December 26, 1950, 3; and J. Craig Jenkins, *The Politics of Insurgency: The Farm Worker Movement in the 1960s* (New York: Columbia University Press, 1985), 131–133.

Saul Alinsky's organizing techniques, which have been adopted by many Hispanic and other ethnic advocacy organizations, are described in Robert Bailey, Jr., *Radicals in Urban Politics: The Alinsky Approach* (Chicago: University of Chicago Press, 1972); and in Alinsky's own works, *Reveille for Radicals* (New York: Vintage Books, 1969), and *Rules for Radicals: A Pragmatic Primer for Realistic Radicals* (New York: Vintage Books, 1971).

43. "Mexican American Affairs," American Council on Race Relations—Programs Under Way (n.d.), 2, Box 65, Folder B, Ford Collection.

44. Interview with Ríos, December 12, 1984.

45. Griffith, "Viva Roybal"; Fred W. Ross, "Mexican Americans on the March," *Catholic Charities Review* 44 (June 1960):13–16; Martin Hall,

"Roybal's Candidacy and What It Means," *Frontier* 5 (June 1954):5–7; and Minutes, National Community Service Organization, Executive Board Meetings, July 17, 1955, Fresno, California, Box 9, Edward R. Roybal Papers, Department of Special Collections, University Research Library, University of California, Los Angeles (hereafter cited as Roybal Papers, UCLA).

46. Ross, "Mexican Americans on the March"; and Community Service Organization, "Highlights of the Past Twenty Years" (mimeo, n.d., in author's files, courtesy Antonio Ríos).

47. Griffith, "Viva Roybal."

48. Los Angeles Municipal Official Election Returns, Primary Nominating Election, Bulletin No. 7, April 3, 1945, and Official Election Returns, Los Angeles Municipal Election, May 31, 1949, Box 37, Fletcher C. Bowron Collection, Huntington Library and Art Museum, San Marino, California (hereafter cited as Bowron Collection).

49. Los Angeles Municipal Official Election Returns, Primary Nominating Election, Bulletin No. 7, Box 37, Bowron Collection; and "Community Service Organization Doing Much to Clean Up City's Slum Areas," *Los Angeles Daily News*, December 25, 1950.

50. Community Service Organization, "Help Us Build This Bridge" (ca. 1955?), Box 14, Folder 8, Galarza Papers.

51. See the following documents in Box 9, Roybal Papers, UCLA: Community Service Organization, "Los Angeles Community Service Organization Presents a Proven Formula" (pamphlet, n.d.); Edward R. Roybal to David Orozco, August 16, 1955; J. J. Rodríguez to Housing Authority of the City of Los Angeles, November 22, 1955; and Community Service Organization Fourth Annual Convention, *Chapter Reports*, March 23–24, 1957. See also Community Service Organization, "Democracy is Not a Fake" (mimeo, 1965), 6, Box 14, Folder 8, Galarza Papers, and Community Service Organization, "Highlights of the Past Twenty Years."

52. Ross, "Mexican Americans on the March."

53. Community Service Organization, By-Laws (n.d.), Box 9, Roybal Papers, UCLA. By mid-decade the CSO estimated that 85 percent of its members were of Mexican ancestry and that 25 percent of its members were noncitizens. Community Service Organization, "Application for Funds to the United Steelworkers of America" (n.d.), Box 8, Roybal Papers, UCLA.

54. Interview with Ríos, December 12, 1984; Monroy, "Mexicanos in Los Angeles," 115–139; and Arroyo, "Chicano Participation in Organized Labor," 299.

55. Memorandum, Los Angeles Conference on Immigration and Citizenship (n.d.), Box 17, Roybal Papers, UCLA.

56. See Joseph B. Kelley and Walter Collett, "The Deportation of Mexican Aliens and Its Impact on Family Life," *Catholic Charities Review* 37

(October 1954):161–171; and Ross, "Mexican Americans on the March," 13–16.

57. Community Service Organization, By-Laws (ca. 1967), Box 14, Folder 7, Galarza Papers.

58. Edward R. Roybal to Samuel Otto, Vice President, Pacific Coast Division, International Ladies Garment Workers Union, April 4, 1953, Box 9, Roybal Papers, UCLA.

59. Community Service Organization, "Help Us Build This Bridge."

60. Roybal to Otto, April 4, 1953, Box 9, Roybal Papers, UCLA (emphasis added).

61. Antonio Ríos, current president and founding member of the CSO, pointed out that much of the organization's leadership and membership had parents or other close relatives who had emigrated from Mexico. Interview with Ríos, December 12, 1984. See also Monroy, "Mexicanos in Los Angeles," 132.

62. Community Service Organization, "Los Angeles Community Service Organization Presents a Proven Formula."

63. The CSO joined a number of California Mexican American advocacy organizations, including the Los Angeles Committee for Latin American Youth and the newly established Mexican American Political Association (MAPA), in supporting the pension measure. The pension campaign is discussed in the following documents in Box 8, Roybal Papers, UCLA: Community Service Organization, "CSO Stirs Up Sleeping Giant" (flyer, n.d.); CSO, Fourth Annual Convention, *Chapter Reports*, March 23–24, 1957; and California Committee for Fair Practices, "The Civil Rights Record of the 1961 Session of the California State Legislature" (mimeo, ca. 1961); Community Service Organization, "Democracy is Not a Fake," 7; and Eliseo Carrillo, Jr., "A Yoke on the Mexican People," in Los Angeles Committee for the Protection of the Foreign Born, *Journal for 1960* (Los Angeles: The Committee, 1961), 25.

64. For a thorough critique of the legal and civil liberties implications of these statutes during this period, see Will Maslow, "Recasting Our Deportation Law: Proposals for Reform," *Columbia Law Review* 56 (March 1956):309–366.

65. See Patricia Morgan, *Shame of a Nation: A Documented Story of Police-State Terror against Mexican Americans in the U.S.A.* (Los Angeles: Los Angeles Committee for the Protection of the Foreign Born, 1954), 7–8. Congressman Walter was not amused by such attacks on his pet legislation, arguing that opposition to the INA was a "truly devilish scheme" to wreak havoc on the Good Neighbor Policy. From his perspective, attacks on the INA could only give "aid and comfort" to the Communists in their plans for the conquest of Latin America. See Walter's comments in the *New York Times*, March 3, 1955, 4, and November 21, 1956, 8. Consequently, the House Un-American Activities Committee quickly called

hearings to investigate the membership and activities of the American Committee for the Protection of the Foreign-Born. According to a *New York Times* story, "The Committee's point, apparently, is to show again that many of those persons or groups favoring modification of the present immigration laws have been touched by communism." See *New York Times*, November 14, 1956, 19. For Congressional harassment of the ACPFB, see: *New York Times*, December 2, 1955, 12; November 15, 1956, 24; December 7, 1956, 2; December 8, 1956, 12; December 10, 1956, 55; and December 19, 1956, 79.

66. Morgan, *Shame of a Nation*.

67. Interview with Bert Corona, January 16, 1984, Sun Valley, California. See also Morgan, *Shame of a Nation*, 38–47; Arroyo, "Chicano Participation in Organized Labor," 287–290; Mario T. García, "Mexican American Labor and the Left: the Asociación Nacional México-Americana, 1949–1954," in *The Chicano Struggle: Analyses of Past and Present Efforts*, ed. John A. García et al. (Binghamton, N.Y.: Bilingual Press for the National Association for Chicano Studies, 1984), 80–81; Mario T. García, *Mexican Americans: Leadership, Ideology, and Identity, 1930–1960* (New Haven, Conn.: Yale University Press, 1989), 199–227; and Vicki L. Ruiz, *Cannery Women, Cannery Lives: Mexican Women, Unionization, and the California Food Processing Industry, 1930–1950* (Albuquerque: University of New Mexico Press, 1987), 116–117.

68. Rose Chernin, "How the McCarran-Walter Act Affects the Mexican People," Los Angeles Committee for the Protection of the Foreign Born, in *Journal for 1957* (Los Angeles: The Committee, 1958), 7–8.

69. Ethel Bertolini, "Joe Gastelum Asks a Question," in Los Angeles Committee for the Protection of the Foreign Born, *13th Annual Conference Journal* (Los Angeles: The Committee, 1962), 43. Bertolini herself was harassed by immigration officials seeking to deport her until the courts upheld her right to remain in the United States. See "Finally an American," *Los Angeles Times*, August 9, 1985.

70. Bertolini, "Joe Gastelum Asks a Question."

71. Quoted in Morgan, *Shame of a Nation*, 38.

72. Ibid., 37.

73. Ibid., 12.

74. Manuel Pacheco Moreno, "La Cultura Mexicana en Norteamerica," *La Prensa*, December 29, 1954.

75. American Committee for the Protection of the Foreign Born, "Our Badge of Infamy," in *The Mexican American and the Law*, ed. Carlos Cortés (New York: Arno Press, 1974), v.

76. Ibid., 32–34.

77. Ibid., 45.

SIX. SIN FRONTERAS? THE CONTEMPORARY DEBATE

1. As mentioned previously, the term *Hispanic* has become popular—especially in agencies of the federal government—as a descriptor of the total Spanish-heritage population of the United States. For discussions of the recent evolution of such nomenclature, see David E. Hayes-Bautista and Jorge Chapa, "Latino Terminology: Conceptual Basis for Standardized Terminology," *American Journal of Public Health* 77 (January 1987):69–72; and Martha E. Giménez, "The Political Construction of the Hispanic," in *Estudios Chicanos and the Politics of Community,* ed. Mary Romero and Cordelia Candelaria (Boulder, Colo.: National Association for Chicano Studies, 1989), 66–85.

2. See Wilson Craig, "The Mexican American Political Association of California" (M.A. thesis, Sonoma State University, 1970); Miguel David Tirado, "Mexican American Community Political Organization: The Key to Chicano Political Power," *Aztlán* 1 (Spring 1970):53–78; Ralph C. Guzmán, *The Political Socialization of the Mexican American People* (New York: Arno Press, 1976), 143–147; Mario Barrera, *Beyond Aztlán: Ethnic Autonomy in Comparative Perspective* (New York: Praeger, 1988), 21–31; and Juan Gómez-Quiñones, *Chicano Politics: Reality and Promise, 1940–1990* (Albuquerque: University of New Mexico Press, 1990), 67–68, 92–93.

3. "LULAC Naturalization Manual" (ca. 1970), Box 1, Folder 1, LULAC Archives, Benson Latin American Library, University of Texas, Austin (hereafter cited as LULAC Archives); LULAC Preschool Recruitment Committee, "Report for the Seminar on Education," 39th Annual LULAC Convention, San Antonio, Texas, June 28–30, 1968, Box 2, Folder 1, Jake Rodríguez Papers, LULAC Archives (hereafter cited as Rodríguez Papers).

4. For succinct discussions of the demise of the Bracero Program, see Ellis Hawley, "The Politics of the Mexican Labor Issue, 1950–1965," *Agricultural History* 40 (July 1966):157–176; and Manuel García y Griego, "The Importation of Mexican Contract Laborers to the United States, 1942–1964: Antecedents, Operation, and Legacy," in *The Border That Joins: Mexican Migrants and U.S. Responsibility,* ed. Peter G. Brown and Henry Shue (Totowa, N.J.: Rowman and Littlefield, 1983), 49–98.

5. For INS estimates of apprehensions of "deportable Mexican aliens," refer to U.S. Department of Justice, Immigration and Naturalization Service, *Annual Report, 1954* (Washington, D.C., 1955), and tables 24 and 24a for each annual report published between 1965 and 1971; and Immigration and Naturalization Service (INS), "Deportable Aliens Located, Aliens Deported, and Aliens Required to Depart—Years Ended June 30, 1892–1976, July-September 1976, and Years Ended September 30, 1977–1978," cited in U.S. Congress, Library of Congress, Congressional Re-

search Service, *Selected Readings on U.S. Immigration Law and Policy* (Washington, D.C.: Congressional Research Service, 1980), 16.

6. For discussions of the demographics of the Mexican-descent population of the Southwest in 1960, see Leo Grebler, Joan W. Moore, and Ralph C. Guzmán, *The Mexican American People: The Nation's Second Largest Minority* (New York: Free Press, 1970), 30; and Richard L. Nostrand, "The Hispanic-American Borderland: Delimitation of an American Culture Region," *Annals of the Association of American Geographers* 60 (December 1970):640.

7. See U.S. Bureau of the Census, *Census of Population, 1970: Subject Reports*, Final Report PC (2)–1C, *Persons of Spanish Origin* (Washington, D.C., 1973), 32; and *Census of Population, 1970: Subject Reports*, Final Report PC (2)–1A, *National Origin and Language* (Washington, D.C., 1973), 70.

8. The best discussions of the evolution of the Chicano student movement are Gerald Paul Rosen, "The Development of the Chicano Movement in Los Angeles, from 1967 to 1969," *Aztlán* 4 (Spring 1973):155–184; Juan Gómez-Quiñones, *Mexican Students por La Raza: The Chicano Student Movement in Southern California, 1967–1977* (Santa Barbara, Calif.: Editorial La Causa, 1978); Carlos Muñoz, Jr., and Mario Barrera, "La Raza Unida Party and the Chicano Student Movement in California," *Social Science Journal* 19 (April 1982):101–120; Barrera, *Beyond Aztlán*; Carlos Muñoz, Jr., *Youth, Identity, Power: The Chicano Movement* (London: Verso, 1989); and most recently, Gómez-Quiñones, *Chicano Politics*.

9. For differing interpretations on the origins and significance of the term *Chicano*, see Tino Villanueva, "Sobre el término 'chicano'," *Cuadernos Hispano-Americanos* (June 1978):387–410; and José Limón, "The Folk Performance of 'Chicano' and the Cultural Limits of Political Ideology," in *And Other Neighborly Names: Social Process and Cultural Image in Texas Folklore*, ed. Richard Bauman and Roger D. Abrahams (Austin: University of Texas Press, 1981), 197–225. Evidence that awareness of the Chicano movement was growing in the media and in government is scattered, but trends in this direction were clearly evident by 1969. See, for example, "Mexican Americans and 'La Raza'," *Christian Century*, March 1969, 325–328; Patrick H. McNamara, "Rumbles along the Rio," *Commonweal* 14 (March 1969):730–732; and "Chicanos Stirring with New Ethnic Pride," *New York Times*, September 20, 1970. For a discussion of the evolution and use of different self-referents in the Mexican-descent population of the Southwest, see Ramón A. Gutiérrez, "Unraveling America's Hispanic Past: Internal Stratification and Class Boundaries," *Aztlán* 17 (Spring 1986):79–102.

10. The background to the 1969 Chicano Youth Liberation Conference is assessed in Barrera, *Beyond Aztlán*, chap. 4. For an interpretation of the historical evolution of the concept of Aztlán, see John R. Chávez, *The Lost*

Land: The Chicano Image of the Southwest (Albuquerque: University of New Mexico Press, 1984); and Rudolfo A. Anaya and Francisco Lomelí, eds., *Aztlán: Essays on the Chicano Homeland* (Albuquerque: El Norte Publications, 1989).

11. First National Chicano Youth Liberation Conference, "El Plan Espiritual de Aztlán," in *Aztlán: An Anthology of Mexican American Literature,* ed. Luis Valdez and Stan Steiner (New York: Alfred A. Knopf, 1972), 403–404; and Barrera, *Beyond Aztlán,* 37.

12. For elaboration of the concept of community control, as used by Chicano activists of this period, see Rodolfo "Corky" Gonzales, "Chicano Nationalism: The Key to Unity for La Raza," in *A Documentary History of the Mexican Americans,* ed. Wayne Moquin (New York: Bantam Books, 1972), 488–493; and John C. Hammerback, Richard J. Jensen, and José Angel Gutiérrez, *A War of Words: Chicano Protest in the 1960s and 1970s* (Westport, Conn.: Greenwood Press, 1985), 53–100. Compare the similarities in black militants' rhetoric on this point in Raymond L. Hall, *Black Separatism in the United States* (Hanover, N.H.: University Press of New England, 1978).

13. See Gómez-Quiñones, *Chicano Politics,* 128–138; and Ignacio M. García, *United We Win: The Rise and Fall of La Raza Unida Party* (Tucson: Mexican American Studies and Research Center, University of Arizona, 1989).

14. Henry B. González to Jake Rodríguez, June 5, 1967, Box 11, Folder 4, Rodríguez Papers. See also González's remarks in the *Congressional Record,* 91st Cong., 1st sess., 1969, 115, pt. 6:8590, and 1969, 115, pt. 7:9058. For a succinct overview of González's critique of Chicano militants, see "The Rhetorical Counter-Attack of Mexican American Political Leaders," in Hammerback, Jensen, and Gutiérrez, *War of Words,* 101–120. See also Ruben Salazar's insightful analysis "Chicanos vs. Traditionalists," *Los Angeles Times,* March 6, 1970.

15. José Angel Gutiérrez, quoted in the *Congressional Record,* 91st Cong., 1st sess., 1969, 115, pt. 7:9059.

16. Cabinet Committee on Opportunity for the Spanish Speaking, "Judge Identifies Mexican Americans in School Suit" (news release, June 1970), Box 14, Folder 5, Ernesto Galarza Papers, Department of Special Collections, Stanford University Libraries, Stanford, California. On the far-reaching significance of *Cisneros v. Corpus Christi Independent School District,* see Guadalupe San Miguel, Jr., *"Let All of Them Take Heed": Mexican Americans and the Campaign for Educational Equality in Texas, 1910–1981* (Austin: University of Texas Press, 1987), 177–181.

17. Edward R. Roybal, the veteran moderate Mexican American politician, by then a congressman representing East Los Angeles, acknowledged the influence Chicano militants exerted on Mexican American politics of the period when he complained in a House subcommittee hearing

that "[Chicano] students are asking questions. The militants in our community are on our backs almost every moment of the day. And the question that is being asked of me . . . and other elected officials is, 'Is it necessary for us to riot? Is it necessary for us to burn a town before the Government looks at our problems objectively? What are we to do if our community is not recognized?'" See U.S. Congress, House of Representatives, Committee on Government Operations, *Establishing a Cabinet Committee on Opportunities for Spanish-Speaking People: Hearings*, 91st Cong., 1st sess., 1969, 18.

18. Gómez-Quiñones, *Mexican Students*, 14.

19. INS, "Deportable Aliens." See also U.S. Congress, Library of Congress, Congressional Research Service, "U.S. Immigration Law and Policy: 1952–1979" (Washington, D.C.: Congressional Research Service, 1979), 34.

20. All of these publications provided extensive coverage of the evolving immigration controversy during the 1970s, but *U.S. News and World Report* paid special attention to the issue. For examples of the tenor of the *USN&WR* reportage during this period, see "Why Wetbacks Are So Hard to Control," October 18, 1971, 50; "Surge of Illegal Immigrants Across American Borders," January 17, 1972, 32–34; "'Invasion' of Illegal Aliens and the Problems They Create," July 23, 1973, 32–35; "How Millions of Illegal Aliens Sneak into the U.S.," July 22, 1974, 27–30; and "Rising Flood of Illegal Aliens," February 3, 1975, 27–30.

21. Leonard F. Chapman, "Illegal Aliens: Time to Call a Halt!" *Reader's Digest*, October 1976, 189. See also Chapman's statements to the *New York Times*, October 22, 1974; and his "Illegal Aliens—A Growing Population," *Immigration and Naturalization Reporter* 24 (Fall 1975):15–18.

22. See, for example, the following articles in the *Los Angeles Times*: "600 More Aliens Rounded Up in Continuing L.A.-Area Raids," May 30, 1973; "U.S. Roundup of Suspected Aliens Hit in Suit," June 23, 1973; "Roundup of Illegal Aliens Stirs Angry Charges," June 27, 1973; "Suit Asks Curb on Questioning of Suspected Aliens," June 21, 1974.

23. See Kitty Calavita, *California's 'Employer Sanctions': The Case of the Disappearing Law*, Research Report Series, 39 (La Jolla: Center for U.S.–Mexican Studies, University of California, San Diego, 1982).

24. The development of the Rodino and similar legislation is summarized in Donald C. Hohl and Michael G. Wenk, "Current U.S. Immigration Legislation: Analysis and Comment," *International Migration Review* 5 (Fall 1971):339–356; Austin T. Fragomen, "Legislative and Judicial Developments," *International Migration Review* 6 (Fall 1972):296–302; Donald C. Hohl and Michael G. Wenk, "The Illegal Alien and the Western Hemisphere Immigration Dilemma," *International Migration Review* 7 (Fall 1973):323–332; Donald C. Hohl, "United States Immigration Legislation: Prospects in the 94th Congress," *International Migration Review*

9 (Spring 1975):59–62; and U.S. Congress, House of Representatives, Committee on the Judiciary, *Amending the Immigration and Nationality Act, and for Other Purposes: House Report 94–506*, 94th Cong., 1st sess., 1975.

25. Author's interview with Bert Corona; Centro de Acción Social Autónoma (CASA), "Articles of Incorporation, Article II" (1969), Box 7, Folder 14, Centro de Acción Social Autónoma Collection, Department of Special Collections, Stanford University Libraries, Stanford, California (hereafter cited as CASA Collection); CASA, "What is CASA?" (ca. 1974, mimeo), Box 31, Folder 13, CASA Collection; and CASA, "History of CASA" (ca. 1978, typescript draft), Box 4, Folder 4, CASA Collection. For an interpretation of CASA's role in immigration politics and the Chicano movement in southern California, see David G. Gutiérrez, *CASA in the Chicano Movement: Ideology and Organizational Politics in the Chicano Community, 1968–1978*, Working Papers Series, no. 5, Stanford Center for Chicano Research, Stanford University, 1984; and Arturo Santamaría Gómez's insightful study *La izquierda norteamericana y los trabajadores indocumentados* (Sinaloa, Mexico: Ediciones de Cultura Popular, Universidad Autónoma de Sinaloa, 1988).

26. National Coalition for Fair Immigration Laws and Practices, "A Call to Action" (December 1973), Box 32, Folder 11, CASA Collection.

27. CASA, "What is CASA?"

28. Bert Corona, *Bert Corona Speaks!* (New York: Pathfinder Press, 1972), 13–14.

29. Letter from Steve Hollopeter, Vice President, CASA, to Editor, *Los Angeles Times*, November 8, 1972.

30. CASA, "What is CASA?"

31. Employing variants of the internal colonial model in attempts to analyze the historical position of minorities in American society, Chicano scholars of this period built on the early work of sociologists Robert Blauner and Joan W. Moore to develop new, class-based interpretations of the Chicano experience. For examples of early Chicano scholarship in this vein, see Tomás Almaguer, "Toward the Study of Chicano Colonialism," *Aztlán* 2 (Spring 1971):137–142; and Mario Barrera, Carlos Muñoz, Jr., and Charles Ornelas, "The Barrio as an Internal Colony," in *People and Politics in Urban Society*, ed. Harlan Hahn, Urban Affairs Annual Reviews, vol. 6 (Los Angeles: Sage Publications, 1972), 465–498. For an insightful recent review and critique of the evolution of the internal colonial model in Chicano studies, see Tomás Almaguer, "Ideological Distortions in Recent Chicano Historiography: The Internal Colonial Model and Chicano Historical Interpretation," *Aztlán* 18 (Spring 1987):7–28.

32. Steve Teixeira, "Dixon-Arnett Bill," *Regeneración*, ca. 1972.

33. "La Raza Platform Prohibits Support of Non-Chicano," *Los Angeles Times*, July 4, 1972.

34. "Rodino Immigration Proposal Protested," *Denver Post*, October 4, 1974.

35. Albert Armendáriz, Sr., testimony before U.S. Congress, House of Representatives, Committee on the Judiciary, Subcommittee No. 1, *Illegal Aliens: Hearings*, Part 2 (El Paso, Texas, July 10, 1971), Serial No. 13, 92d Cong., 1st sess., 596.

36. Ibid., 592.

37. Statement of Manny Villareal, Past District Director, LULAC, in ibid., 596–597, 600. For an expression of similar sentiments, see also *LULAC News*, November-December 1973, 9.

38. *La Voz de MAPA* (February 1972), Box 8, Folder 17, Manuel Ruiz Papers, Department of Special Collections, Stanford University Libraries, Stanford, California. See also "The Vicious Circle of the Illegal Alien Hiring Ban," *Los Angeles Times*, January 23, 1973.

39. See "Latin Political Unit Elects President in Stormy Session," *Los Angeles Times*, August 2, 1971.

40. See published letter to the editor, *Los Angeles Times*, July 1, 1973. For the range of opinion on the issue expressed by members of the public, see the letters to the editor, *Los Angeles Times*, November 8, 1974.

41. Author's telephone interview with Albert Armendáriz, Sr., September 18, 1989.

42. For the evolution of the UFW, see Peter Matthiessen, *Sal Si Puedes: César Chávez and the New American Revolution* (New York: Random House, 1969); Jacques Levy, *César Chávez: An Autobiography of La Causa* (New York: W. W. Norton, 1975); Ronald B. Taylor, *Chávez and the Farm Workers: A Study in the Acquisition and Use of Power* (Boston: Beacon Press, 1975); and J. Craig Jenkins, *The Politics of Insurgency: The Farm Worker Movement in the 1960s* (New York: Columbia University Press, 1985).

43. For the UFW's position on braceros and undocumented workers see Taylor, *Chávez and the Farm Workers*, 218–219, 287–289; Jenkins, *Politics of Insurgency*, 108–109, 144–146; and the statement of Len Avila, Colorado Labor Council, United Farm Worker Organizing Committee, in House Judiciary Subcommittee No. 1, *Illegal Aliens: Hearings* (Denver, Colorado, June 24–25, 1971), 403–416. The UFW's official newspaper, *El Malcriado*, published many articles during the 1970s decrying the use of "illegal alien labor." For some representative stories, see, for example, "Hiring Illegals Challenged," December 1, 1972, 11; "Growers Use Illegals for Scabs," July 27, 1973, 4; "Illegal Aliens—Million Dollar Import Business," August 24, 1973; "New Proposal for 'Bracero' Slave Labor," December 14, 1973, 3; "Chávez Assails Use of 'Illegals' in Mendota Rally," and "The 'Illegals' and the Growers," July 31, 1974, 3, 10.

44. "UFW Campaign against Illegal Aliens—Farm Workers Ask for Citizens' Drive against Illegal Workers," *Acción!*, July 1974. See also Calavita, "California's 'Employer Sanctions'," 29–30.

45. See "UFW Border Patrol," *El Malcriado*, November 18, 1974, 5.

46. By the end of 1973 the National Coalition claimed the support of a broad range of Mexican-American and Chicano groups and individuals, including chapters of LULAC, the American G.I. Forum, labor unions, and numerous Hispanic government officials.

47. The growing divisions between Chávez and other Chicano activists are summarized in "Chicanos Divided by Sympathy for Aliens, Fear for Own Jobs," *Los Angeles Times*, March 25, 1972; "Chávez Union Does Turnabout, Opposes Alien Worker Bill," *Los Angeles Times*, March 27, 1973; and "Why Citizen Chicanos Fear Fresh Turmoil," *Los Angeles Times*, February 23, 1975.

48. National Coalition for Fair Immigration Laws and Practices and CASA, "Open Letter to Our Brothers and Sisters of the United Farm Workers of America, AFL–CIO" (July 20, 1974), Box 32, Folder 11, CASA Collection.

49. "Saxbe Calls Illegal Aliens a U.S. Crisis," *Los Angeles Times*, October 31, 1974; "Chicanos Criticize Saxbe on Alien Deportation Proposal," *Los Angeles Times*, November 8, 1974; "Chicano Activists Ask Ford to Seek Saxbe's Resignation," *Los Angeles Times*, November 18, 1974.

50. See "UFW Leader Talks with *El Malcriado*," *El Malcriado*, October 18, 1974, 11.

51. Chávez to *San Francisco Examiner*, November 22, 1974. See also his similar statement in *El Malcriado*, September 9, 1974, 10. Chávez and the UFW maintained this new position throughout the rest of the decade and into the 1980s, as shown in the union's forceful opposition to President Jimmy Carter's immigration reform proposals in 1977. For the union's revised position, see "UFW Denounces Carter Program on Illegal Aliens," *Los Angeles Times*, August 28, 1977; and United Farm Workers of America, AFL-CIO, Third Constitutional Convention, "Resolution 73" (August 1977), Box 32, Folder 11, CASA Collection.

52. Trinidad Flores, President, Los Angeles Mexican American Labor Council, to Antonio Rodríguez, CASA (ca. 1975), Box 31, Folder 6, CASA Collection.

53. National Coalition for Fair Immigration Laws and Practices, "Stop Inhuman Rodino Bill" (1975), Box 32, Folder 11, CASA Collection. The American G.I. Forum's position during this period provides further evidence that even Mexican American moderates were changing their views on the immigration issue. As late as March 1974 the forum was supporting legislation such as Rodino's bill because the use of braceros and undocu-

mented workers "pits Mexicanos from south of the border and Chicanos del norte against each other in . . . the farm labor market . . . [and because] it hampers César Chávez's farmworkers union in their organizing efforts." See *The Forumeer*, March 1974, 3. By May of the following year, however, *The Forumeer* reported that the forum was actively advising undocumented workers about their legal rights in the United States. By October of 1975 the forum's position had changed sufficiently for the organization's national chairman, Tony Morales, to publicly demand the ouster of INS Commissioner Leonard Chapman. "Maybe we should give amnesty to illegal aliens and let them vote," argued Morales. "Then maybe we could remove people like Mr. Chapman from our government." See *The Forumeer*, May 1975, 3; and "Morales Asks Ouster of U.S. 'Migra' Boss," *The Forumeer*, October 1975, 1–2.

54. See U.S. General Accounting Office, Office of the Comptroller General, *More Needs to Be Done to Reduce the Number and Adverse Impact of Illegal Aliens in the United States* (Washington, D.C.: U.S. General Accounting Office, 1973); *Report to Congress: Immigration—Need to Reassess U.S. Policy* (Washington, D.C.: U.S. General Accounting Office, 1976); U.S. Department of Justice, Immigration and Naturalization Service, *Fraudulent Entrants Study: A Study of Malefide Applicants for Admission at Selected Airports and Southwest Land Border Ports* (Washington, D.C.: U.S. Government Printing Office, 1976); and U. S. Department of Justice, Immigration and Naturalization Service, *Preliminary Report: Domestic Council Committee on Illegal Aliens* (Washington, D.C., U.S. Government Printing Office, 1976).

55. For a brief explanation of the various legislative proposals being considered on Capitol Hill during this period, see *Illegal Aliens: Issue Brief Number IB74137* (Washington, D.C.: Congressional Research Service, 1978).

56. See President Jimmy Carter, "Communication to Congress," *Congressional Record*, 95th Cong., 1st sess., 1977, 123, pt. 21; "Carter Asks Congress to Let Illegal Aliens Stay," *Los Angeles Times*, August 5, 1977; and "President Seeks Legalized Status for Many Aliens," *New York Times*, August 5, 1977.

57. Hispanic Ad Hoc Coalition on Immigration, "Response by Hispanics to Changes in Immigration Law Proposed by President Jimmy Carter" (Washington, D.C., February 15, 1978, mimeo), in author's personal files. Members of the ad hoc coalition included the American G.I. Forum, LULAC, the Mexican American Legal Defense and Education Fund (MALDEF), the Mexican American Women's National Association, the National Coalition of Hispanic Mental Health and Human Services Organizations, the National Congress of Hispanic American Citizens, the National Council of La Raza, National IMAGE, and La Raza National Lawyers Association. Local endorsers included the Bishop's Committee for the

Spanish Speaking (East Chicago, Indiana), Centro Cultural Aztlán (San Antonio, Texas), Centro de Inmigración (Georgetown University Law Center, Washington, D.C.), the Hispanic Advisory Committee, Immigration and Naturalization Service (Washington, D.C.), and the National Association of Farm Worker Organizations (Washington, D.C.). See also Mexican American Legal Defense and Education Fund, "Statement of Position Regarding the Administration's Undocumented Alien Legislative Proposal" (Washington, D.C., September 26, 1977), in author's personal files. A summary of MALDEF's statement can be found in Congressional Research Service, *Selected Readings*, 133–134. For the broad-based nature of the Hispanic response to the Carter Plan, see Congressman Roybal's and the Congressional Hispanic Caucus's criticism in "Carter Asks Congress," *Los Angeles Times*, August 5, 1977, and "President Seeks Legalized Status," *New York Times*, August 5, 1977; "Southland Group Assails Plan for Aliens," *Los Angeles Times*, August 5, 1977; Art Hernández, "The Peril Peering In on Us—A Hungry Human," *Los Angeles Times*, August 22, 1977; and "Latins Ready Lobby Effort," *Los Angeles Times*, October 16, 1977.

58. LULAC, Office of the Texas State Director, "Analysis of the Immigration Proposals—A Civil Rights Dilemma" (September 12, 1978), Box 3, Folder 3, LULAC Archives. See also "Alien Plan Criticized by LULAC," *San Antonio Express*, August 6, 1977.

59. See "G.I. Forum Knocks Alien Plan," *El Paso Times*, August 15, 1977; "Resolutions Seek Equality for Aliens, Advancement for Women," *The Forumeer*, September 1, 1977, 1; and "The American G.I. Forum Continues to Fight for Human Rights," *The Forumeer*, September 1, 1977, 4. This constituted a complete reversal of the Forum's position presented in the Rodino hearings just six years earlier. Compare the Forum's testimony in House Judiciary Subcommittee No. 1, *Illegal Aliens: Hearings*, Part 1 (Los Angeles, California, June 21, 1971), 254–255.

60. National Chicano/Latino Conference on Immigration and Public Policy, "A Call for Action" (ca. August 1977), Box 34, Folder 2, CASA Collection. The conference organizers' political perspective is further elaborated in Estevan Flores and the Research Task Force, Conference on Immigration and Public Policy, "A Call to Action: An Analysis of Our Struggles and Alternatives to Carter's Immigration Program," Box 34, Folder 2, CASA Collection.

61. Pedro Camejo, "Human Rights for Immigrants," *The Militant*, December 9, 1977.

62. "Latino Leadership Rips Carter Deportation Plan," *The Militant*, November 18, 1977.

63. See, "Chicanos Will Fight Carter's Alien Plan," *Los Angeles Times*, October 31, 1977; and "Hispanics Rap Amnesty Plan," *San Antonio Press*, October 31, 1977. For contemporary Chicano assessments of the San An-

tonio Conference, see Richard A. García, "The Chicano Movement and the Mexican American Community, 1972–1978: An Interpretive Essay," *Socialist Review* 40–41 (July-October 1978):117–136; and Tomás Almaguer, "Chicano Politics in the Present Period: Comment on García," *Socialist Review* 40–41 (July-October, 1978):137–142.

64. CASA—San José, "Editorial," *El Inmigrante Militante*, August 24, 1974. Or, as a UFW supporter put it in a letter to the union in 1974, "There is no such thing as an illegal worker. These so-called 'illegal aliens' are your brothers and sisters. . . . If you allow the brothers and sisters to be divided, I'm afraid your struggle will be in vain, the movement will be ripped apart." See Thomas J. Morgan to editor, *El Malcriado*, October 18, 1974, 9.

65. Jake Rodríguez, "Exploring and Analyzing 'Mexican' Misnomers and Misconceptions" (1971, typescript), and Rodríguez, draft typescript correspondence addressed to Associated Press (n.d.), Rodríguez Papers.

EPILOGUE

1. For discussion of such recent proposals, see, for example, Peter Brimelow, "Time to Rethink Immigration?" *National Review*, June 22, 1992; "Sacramento Struggles in the Immigration-Issue Thicket" *Los Angeles Times*, May 17, 1993, B6; "Immigration Policy Failures Invite Overhaul," *Los Angeles Times*, July 11, 1993, A1; Patrick J. Buchanan, "GOP Is Caught Napping on Immigration," *Los Angeles Times*, July 11, 1993, M5; "U.S. Blockade Halts El Paso Migrant Flow," *San Diego Union*, September 27, 1993, A1; and "'El Paso Blockade' Here?: Yes and No," *San Diego Union*, September 30, 1993, A1. For an extended discussion of proposals to change the basis of American citizenship, see Peter H. Schuck and Rogers M. Smith, *Citizenship Without Consent: Illegal Aliens in the American Polity* (New Haven, Conn.: Yale University Press, 1985); and Peter H. Schuck, "Membership in the Liberal Polity: The Devaluation of American Citizenship," in *Immigration and the Politics of Citizenship in Europe and North America*, ed. William Rogers Brubaker (Lanham, Md.: University Press of America, 1989), 51–66.

2. For discussion of the activities of the Congressional Hispanic Caucus and other Latino organizations in the recent immigration debate, see Aristide R. Zolberg, "Reforming the Back Door: The Immigration Reform and Control Act of 1986 in Historical Perspective," in *Immigration Reconsidered: History, Sociology, and Politics*, ed. Virginia Yans-McLaughlin (New York: Oxford University Press, 1990), 315–339; Christine Marie Sierra, *Latinos and the "New Immigration": Responses from the Mexican American Community*, Renato Rosaldo Lecture Series Monograph 3 (Tucson: Mexican American Studies and Research Center, University of Arizona, 1987), 33–61; and Christine Marie Sierra, "Mexican Americans and

Immigration Reform: Consensus and Fragmentation" (paper presented at the annual meeting of the Western Political Science Association, Salt Lake City, Utah, March 1989).

3. See address delivered on the floor of the U.S. Senate by Simpson on April 28, 1983, quoted in the *Congressional Record*, 98th Cong., 1st sess., 1983, 129, pt. 56:S–5531.

4. Richard D. Lamm and Gary Imhoff, *The Immigration Time Bomb: The Fragmenting of America* (New York: Truman Talley Books, E. P. Dutton, 1985), 230, 233.

5. See the *Congressional Record*, 98th Cong., 1st sess., 1983, 129, pt. 56:S–5531.

6. See ibid., 1983, 129, pt. 16:S–1345.

7. For a detailed recent study of these attitudes in California, see Jack Citrin, Beth Reingold, and Donald P. Green, "American Identity and the Politics of Ethnic Change," *Journal of Politics* 52 (November 1990):1124–1154. For the changing opinions on the immigration issue at the national level, see "Democrat About-Face on Immigration," *San Diego Union*, July 27, 1993, B6; "Is America Still a Melting Pot?" *Newsweek*, August 9, 1993, 16–26; "Majority in State Are Fed Up with Illegal Immigration," *Los Angeles Times*, September 19, 1993, A1; and the references cited in note 1 above.

8. For an incisive critique of the conservative assault on the idea of multiculturalism, see Joan Wallach Scott, "The Campaign against Political Correctness: What's Really at Stake," *Radical History Review* 54 (Fall 1992):59–79.

9. Arthur M. Schlesinger, Jr., "The American Creed: From Dilemma to Decomposition," *New Perspectives Quarterly* 8 (Summer 1991):24.

10. Ibid., 21. For similar critiques of the so-called new politics of ethnicity, see Arthur M. Schlesinger, Jr., *The Disuniting of America* (New York: W. W. Norton, 1992); Thomas Sowell, "Promoting Alienation," *Forbes*, November 25, 1991, 112; and Robert Hughs, *The Culture of Complaint: The Fraying of America* (New York: Oxford University Press, 1993). For an extended recent analysis that applies such a point of view to the specific case of Mexican Americans, see Peter Skerry, *Mexican Americans: The Ambivalent Minority* (New York: Free Press, 1993).

11. See Guillermo Gómez-Peña, "The Multicultural Paradigm: An Open Letter to the Arts Community," *High Performance*, 12 (Fall 1989):18–27.

12. For discussion of recent Mexican American public opinion on these issues, see, for example, Rodolfo O. de la Garza, *Chicano Political Elite Perceptions of the Undocumented Worker: An Empirical Analysis*, Working Papers in U.S.–Mexican Studies, no. 31 (La Jolla: Center for U.S.–Mexican Studies, University of California, San Diego, 1981); Gallup Opinion Index Reports, *Immigration 151*, November 1983, and *Immigration 232–*

233, January-February 1985; Lawrence W. Miller, Jerry L. Polinard, and Robert D. Wrinkle, "Attitudes toward Undocumented Workers: The Mexican American Perspective," *Social Science Quarterly* 65 (June 1984):482–494; Jerry L. Polinard, Robert D. Wrinkle, and Rodolfo O. de la Garza, "Attitudes of Mexican Americans toward Irregular Mexican Immigration," *International Migration Review* 18 (Fall 1984):782–799; and "Survey of Attitudes and Opinions Regarding Immigration in Southern California," in *The Fourth Wave: California's Newest Immigrants*, ed. Thomas Muller and Thomas J. Espenshade (Washington, D.C.: Urban Institute Press, 1985), 199–206. For a discussion of the vicissitudes of polling U.S. Latinos, see Rodolfo O. de la Garza, ed., *Ignored Voices: Public Opinion Polls and the Latino Community* (Austin: Center for Mexican American Studies Publications, University of Texas Press, 1987).

Bibliography

ARCHIVAL AND MANUSCRIPT COLLECTIONS

Bonilla-Wilmot Collection. League of United Latin American Citizens (LULAC) Archives. Benson Latin American Library, University of Texas, Austin.

Fletcher C. Bowron Collection. Huntington Library and Art Museum, San Marino, California.

Centro de Acción Social Autónoma Collection. Department of Special Collections, Stanford University Libraries, Stanford, California.

George P. Clements Collection. Department of Special Collections, University Research Library, University of California, Los Angeles.

Andrés de Luna Papers. LULAC Archives. Benson Latin American Library, University of Texas, Austin.

John Anson Ford Collection. Huntington Library and Art Museum, San Marino, California.

Ernesto Galarza Papers. Department of Special Collections, Stanford University Libraries, Stanford, California.

John Randolph Haynes Collection. University Research Library, University of California, Los Angeles.

Lyndon Baines Johnson Presidential Papers. Lyndon Baines Johnson Presidential Library, Austin, Texas.

League of United Latin American Citizens (LULAC) Archives. Benson Latin American Library, University of Texas, Austin.

Carey McWilliams Collection. Department of Special Collections, University Research Library, University of California, Los Angeles.

Eduardo Quevedo Papers. Department of Special Collections, Stanford University Libraries, Stanford, California.

Jake Rodríguez Papers. LULAC Archives. Benson Latin American Library, University of Texas, Austin.

Edward R. Roybal Papers. Department of Special Collections, California State University, Los Angeles.

Edward R. Roybal Papers. Department of Special Collections, University Research Library, University of California, Los Angeles.

Manuel Ruiz Papers. Department of Special Collections, Stanford University Libraries, Stanford, California.

George I. Sánchez Papers, Benson Latin American Library, University of Texas, Austin.

Paul S. Taylor Papers. Bancroft Library, University of California, Berkeley.

O. Douglas Weeks Papers. LULAC Archives. Benson Latin American Library, University of Texas, Austin.

PUBLISHED PRIMARY SOURCES

Books and Journal Articles

American Committee for the Protection of the Foreign Born. "Our Badge of Infamy: A Petition to the United Nations on the Treatment of the Mexican Immigrant." N.p., 1959. Reprinted in *The Mexican American and the Law*, edited by Carlos Cortés. New York: Arno Press, 1974.

American G.I. Forum of Texas and Texas State Federation of Labor. *What Price Wetbacks?* Austin: G.I. Forum of Texas, 1954. Reprinted in *Mexican Migration to the United States*, edited by Carlos Cortés. New York: Arno Press, 1976.

Corona, Bert. *Bert Corona Speaks!* New York: Pathfinder Press, 1972.

First National Chicano Youth Liberation Conference. "El Plan Espiritual de Aztlán." In *Aztlán: An Anthology of Mexican American Literature*, edited by Luis Valdez and Stan Steiner, 402–406. New York: Alfred A. Knopf, 1972.

González, Henry B. "The Hate Issue Speech." In *Introduction to Chicano Studies*, edited by Livie Isauro Durán and H. Russell Bernard, 561–67. 2d ed. New York: Macmillan Publishing Co., 1982.

Los Angeles Committee for the Protection of the Foreign Born. *Journal for 1957*. Los Angeles: The Committee, 1958.

———. *Journal for 1960*. Los Angeles: The Committee, 1961.

———. *13th Annual Conference Journal*. Los Angeles: The Committee, 1962.

Morgan, Patricia. *Shame of a Nation: A Documented Story of Police-State Terror against Mexican Americans in the U.S.A.* Los Angeles: Los Angeles Committee for the Protection of the Foreign Born, 1954.

Sleepy Lagoon Defense Committee. *The Sleepy Lagoon Case*. Los Angeles: The Committee, 1944.

Government Documents and Publications

California. Commission on Immigration and Housing. *Annual Report.* Sacramento: State of California, 1927.

California. Governor C. C. Young's Mexican Fact-Finding Committee. *Mexicans in California.* San Francisco: State of California, 1930.

California. Legislature. Joint Fact-Finding Committee on Un-American Activities. *Report of the Joint Fact-Finding Committee on Un-American Activities in California.* Sacramento, 1945.

Clark, Victor S. *Mexican Labor in the United States.* U.S. Bureau of Labor Statistics Bulletin no. 78. Washington, D.C., 1908.

Congressional Record. Washington, D.C., 1929, 1969, 1977, 1983.

Jamieson, Stuart. *Labor Unionism in American Agriculture.* U.S. Department of Labor, Bureau of Labor Statistics Bulletin no. 836. Washington, D.C.: U.S. Government Printing Office, 1945.

Menefee, Selden C. *Mexican Migratory Workers of South Texas.* Washington, D.C.: Works Progress Administration, 1941.

President's Commission on Migratory Labor. *Migratory Labor in American Agriculture.* Washington, D.C.: U.S. Government Printing Office, 1951.

Rasmussen, Wayne D. *A History of the Emergency Farm Labor Supply Program, 1943–1947.* Agricultural Monograph No. 13. U.S. Department of Agriculture, Bureau of Economics. Washington, D.C.: U.S. Government Printing Office, 1951.

U.S. Bureau of the Census. *Census of Population, 1950: Special Reports— Nativity and Parentage.* Vol. 4, P–E No. 3A. Washington, D.C.: U.S. Government Printing Office, 1954.

————. *Census of Population, 1970: Subject Reports.* Final Report PC (2)– 1A, National Origin and Language. Washington, D.C.: U.S. Government Printing Office, 1973.

————. *Census of Population, 1970: Subject Reports.* Final Report PC (2)– 1C, Persons of Spanish Origin. Washington, D.C.: U.S. Government Printing Office, 1973.

————. *The Hispanic Population in the United States: March 1991.* Current Population Reports, ser. P–20, no. 455. Washington, D.C.: U.S. Government Printing Office, 1991.

————. *Historical Statistics of the United States, Colonial Times to 1970,* Part 1. Washington, D.C.: U.S. Government Printing Office, 1975.

————. *1980 Census of Population: Persons of Spanish Origin by State, 1980: Supplementary Report.* Washington, D.C.: U.S. Government Printing Office, August 1982.

————. *Sixteenth Census of the United States, 1940: Population, Nativity, and Parentage of the White Population. Country of Origin of the*

Foreign Stock. Washington, D.C.: U.S. Government Printing Office, 1943.

———. *Sixteenth Census of the United States, 1940: Population, Nativity, and Parentage of the White Population. Mother Tongue.* Washington, D.C.: U.S. Government Printing Office, 1943.

U.S. Congress. House of Representatives. Committee on Agriculture. *Extension of the Mexican Farm Labor Program: Hearings.* 83d Cong., 1st sess., 1953.

———. *Farm Labor: Hearings.* 82d Cong., 1st sess., 1951.

———. *Farm Labor and Production: Hearings.* 77th Cong., 2d sess., 1942.

———. *Farm Labor Program, 1943: Hearings.* 78th Cong., 1st sess., 1943.

———. *Mexican Farm Labor: Hearings.* 83d Cong., 2d sess., 1954.

———. *Mexican Farm Labor Program: Hearings.* 84th Cong., 1st sess., 1955.

———. *Permanent Farm Labor Program: Hearings.* 80th Cong., 1st sess., 1947.

U.S. Congress. House of Representatives. Committee on Appropriations. *Farm Labor Program, 1943: Hearings.* 78th Cong., 1st sess., 1943.

U.S. Congress. House of Representatives. Committee on Government Operations. *Establishing a Cabinet Committee on Opportunities for Spanish-Speaking People: Hearings.* 91st Cong., 1st sess., 1969.

U.S. Congress. House of Representatives. Committee on Immigration and Naturalization. *Immigration from Countries of the Western Hemisphere: Hearings.* 70th Cong., 1st sess., 1928.

———. *Immigration from Countries of the Western Hemisphere: Hearings.* 71st Cong., 2d sess., 1930.

———. *Immigration from Countries of the Western Hemisphere: House Report No. 898.* 71st Cong., 1st sess., 1930.

———. *Seasonal Agricultural Workers from Mexico: Hearings.* 69th Cong., 1st sess., 1926.

U.S. Congress. House of Representatives. Committee on the Judiciary. *Amending the Immigration and Nationality Act, and for Other Purposes: House Report 94–506.* 94th Cong., 1st sess., 1975.

———. Subcommittee No. 1. *Illegal Aliens: Hearings.* Serial No. 13, 92d Cong., 1st sess., 1971.

U.S. Congress. Immigration Commission. *Report of the United States Immigration Commission.* Washington, D.C.: U.S. Government Printing Office, 1911.

U.S. Congress. Library of Congress. Congressional Research Service. *Comparative Analysis of H.R. 1663 and H.R. 9531/S. 2252.* Washington, D.C.: Congressional Research Service, 1977.

———. *Illegal Aliens: Issue Brief Number IB74137.* Washington, D.C.: Congressional Research Service, 1978.

———. *Selected Readings on U.S. Immigration Law and Policy.* Washington, D.C.: Congressional Research Service, 1980.

———. *U.S. Immigration Law and Policy: 1952–1979.* Washington, D.C.: Congressional Research Service, 1979.

U.S. Congress. Senate. Committee on Appropriations. *Farm Labor Program, 1943: Hearings.* 78th Cong., 1st sess., 1943.

U.S. Congress. Senate. Committee on Education and Labor. *Violations of Free Speech and Assembly and Interference with Rights of Labor: Hearings.* 74th Cong., 2d sess., 1939.

U.S. Department of Justice. Immigration and Naturalization Service. *Annual Reports.* Washington, D.C., 1955–1978.

———. *Fraudulent Entrants Study: A Study of Malefide Applicants for Admission at Selected Airports and Southwest Land Border Ports.* Washington, D.C.: U.S. Government Printing Office, 1976.

———. *Preliminary Report: Domestic Council Committee on Illegal Aliens.* Washington, D.C., U.S. Government Printing Office, 1976.

U.S. Department of Labor. Bureau of Labor Statistics. "Labor and Social Conditions of Mexicans in California." *Monthly Labor Review* 32 (January 1932):81–89.

U.S. General Accounting Office. Office of the Comptroller General. *More Needs to Be Done to Reduce the Number and Adverse Impact of Illegal Aliens in the United States.* Washington, D.C.: U.S. General Accounting Office, 1973.

———. Report to Congress: *Immigration—Need to Reassess U.S. Policy.* Washington, D.C.: U.S. General Accounting Office, 1976.

U.S. Select Committee on Immigration and Refugee Policy. *U.S. Immigration Policy and the National Interest: The Final Report and Recommendations.* Washington, D.C.: U.S. Government Printing Office, 1981.

Newspapers and Magazines

Acción! (United Farmworkers Union)
Associated Farmer (California)
Brawley News (Brawley, California)
Christian Science Monitor
El Clamor Público (Los Angeles)
Congressional Quarterly Weekly Report (Washington, D.C.)
Denver Post
El Paso Times
The Forumeer (American G.I. Forum)

Imperial Valley Farmer (Imperial Valley, California)
El Inmigrante Militante (San Jose, California)
Life
Los Angeles Daily Journal
Los Angeles Daily News
Los Angeles Herald Express
Los Angeles Times
LULAC News
El Malcriado (Delano, California)
The Mexican Voice (Los Angeles)
The Militant
New Republic
Newsweek
New York Times
La Opinión (Los Angeles)
El Paladín (Corpus Christi, Texas)
People's World
La Prensa (San Antonio, Texas)
Reader's Digest
Regeneración (Los Angeles)
San Antonio Express
San Antonio Press
San Antonio Times
San Diego Union
San Francisco Chronicle
San Francisco Examiner
Sin Fronteras (Los Angeles)
Texas Observer
Time
U.S. News and World Report
La Voz de MAPA (California)

SECONDARY SOURCES

Books

Acuña, Rodolfo. *Occupied America: A History of Chicanos,* 2d ed. New York: Harper & Row, 1981.
Alinsky, Saul. *Reveille for Radicals.* New York: Vintage Books, 1969.
————. *Rules for Radicals: A Pragmatic Primer for Realistic Radicals.* New York: Vintage Books, 1971.
Allsup, Carl. *The American G.I. Forum: Origins and Evolution.* Center for Mexican American Studies, University of Texas, Austin, Monograph no. 6. Austin: University of Texas Press, 1982.

Altman, Ida, and James Lockhart, eds. *Provinces of Early Mexico: Variants of Spanish American Regional Evolution.* Los Angeles: UCLA Latin American Center Publications, 1976.

Anaya, Rudolfo A., and Francisco Lomelí, eds. *Aztlán: Essays on the Chicano Homeland.* Albuquerque, N.Mex.: El Norte Publications, 1989.

Anders, Evan. *Boss Rule in South Texas: The Progressive Era.* 1979. Reprint. Austin: University of Texas Press, 1982.

Anderson, Benedict. *Imagined Communities: Reflections on the Origins and Spread of Nationalism.* London: Verso, 1983.

Archdeacon, Thomas J. *Becoming American: An Ethnic History.* New York: Free Press, 1983.

Bailey, Robert, Jr. *Radicals in Urban Politics: The Alinsky Approach.* Chicago: University of Chicago Press, 1972.

Balderrama, Francisco E. *In Defense of La Raza: The Los Angeles Mexican Consulate and the Mexican Community, 1929 to 1936.* Tucson: University of Arizona Press, 1982.

Barker, George Carpenter. *Pachuco: An American-Spanish Argot and Its Social Function in Tucson, Arizona.* Tucson: University of Arizona Press, 1950.

Barr, Alwyn. *Reconstruction to Reform: Texas Politics, 1876–1906.* Austin: University of Texas Press, 1971.

Barrera, Mario. *Beyond Aztlán: Ethnic Autonomy in Comparative Perspective.* New York: Praeger, 1988.

———. *Race and Class in the Southwest: A Theory of Racial Inequality.* Notre Dame, Ind.: University of Notre Dame Press, 1979.

Bean, Frank D., and Marta Tienda. *The Hispanic Population of the United States.* New York: Russell Sage Foundation, 1987.

Bean, Walton. *California: An Interpretive History.* New York: McGraw-Hill, 1968.

Beck, Warren A., and Ynez D. Haase. *Historical Atlas of California.* Norman: University of Oklahoma Press, 1974.

Becker, Stephen D. *Marshall Field III: A Biography.* New York: Simon and Schuster, 1965.

Bennett, David H. *The Party of Fear: From Nativist Movements to the New Right in American History.* Chapel Hill: University of North Carolina Press, 1988.

Benton, Wilbourn E. *Texas: Its Government and Politics,* 3d ed. Englewood Cliffs, N.J.: Prentice Hall, 1972.

Blackford, Mansel G. *The Politics of Business in California, 1890–1920.* Columbus: Ohio State University Press, 1977.

Blackwelder, Julia Kirk. *Women of the Depression: Caste and Culture in San Antonio, 1929–1939.* College Station: Texas A & M University Press, 1984.

Bogardus, Emory S. *The Mexican in the United States.* University of

Southern California Social Science Series, no. 8. Los Angeles: University of Southern California, 1934.

Bonacich, Edna, and John Modell. *The Economic Basis of Ethnic Solidarity: Small Business in the Japanese-American Community.* Berkeley: University of California Press, 1980.

Briggs, Vernon M., Jr., Walter Fogel, and Fred H. Schmidt. *The Chicano Worker.* Austin: University of Texas Press, 1977.

Browning, Harley, and Rodolfo O. de la Garza, eds. *Mexican Immigrants and Mexican Americans: An Evolving Relationship.* Austin: Center for Mexican American Studies, University of Texas at Austin, 1986.

Calavita, Kitty. *California's 'Employer Sanctions': The Case of the Disappearing Law.* Research Report Series, 39. La Jolla: Center for U.S.–Mexican Studies, University of California, San Diego, 1982.

Camarillo, Albert M. *Chicanos in California: A History of Mexican Americans in California.* San Francisco: Boyd and Fraser Publishing Co., 1984.

———. *Chicanos in a Changing Society: From Mexican Pueblos to American Barrios in Santa Barbara and Southern California, 1848–1930.* Cambridge, Mass.: Harvard University Press, 1979.

Cardoso, Lawrence A. *Mexican Emigration to the United States, 1897–1931.* Tucson: University of Arizona Press, 1980.

Carleton, Don E. *Red Scare! Right Wing Hysteria, Fifties Fanaticism, and Their Legacy in Texas.* Austin: Texas Monthly Press, 1985.

Castillo, Pedro, and Albert M. Camarillo, eds. *Furia y Muerte: Los Bandidos Chicanos.* Aztlán Publications, Monograph no. 4. Chicano Studies Center, University of California, Los Angeles, 1973.

Chávez, John R. *The Lost Land: The Chicano Image of the Southwest.* Albuquerque: University of New Mexico Press, 1984.

Clark, Margaret. *Health in the Mexican American Culture: A Community Study.* Berkeley: University of California Press, 1959.

Cleland, Robert Glass. *The Cattle on a Thousand Hills.* San Marino, Calif.: Huntington Library Publications, 1951.

Clifford, James. *The Predicament of Culture: Twentieth-Century Ethnography, Literature, and Art.* Cambridge, Mass.: Harvard University Press, 1988.

Cockcroft, James D. *Intellectual Precursors of the Mexican Revolution, 1900–1913.* Austin: University of Texas Press, 1968.

———. *Outlaws in the Promised Land: Mexican Immigrant Workers and America's Future.* New York: Grove Press, 1986.

Cohen, Lizabeth. *Making a New Deal: Industrial Workers in Chicago, 1919–1939.* Cambridge, England: Cambridge University Press, 1990.

Congressional Quarterly Service. *Congress and the Nation, 1945–1964: A Review of Government and Politics in the Postwar Years.* Washington, D.C.: Congressional Quarterly Publishing, 1965.

Craig, Richard B. *The Bracero Program: Interest Groups and Foreign Policy*. Austin: University of Texas Press, 1971.

Dana, Richard Henry. *Two Years Before The Mast*. Boston, 1840. Reprint. New York: Airmont Publishing Co., 1966.

Daniel, Cletus E. *Bitter Harvest: A History of California Farmworkers, 1870–1941*. Ithaca, N.Y.: Cornell University Press, 1981.

———. *Chicano Workers and the Politics of Fairness: The FEPC in the Southwest, 1941–1945*. Austin: University of Texas Press, 1991.

Daniels, Roger. *Coming to America: A History of Immigration and Ethnicity in American Life*. New York: HarperCollins, 1990.

———. *The Politics of Prejudice: The Anti-Japanese Movement in California and the Struggle for Japanese Exclusion*. Berkeley: University of California Press, 1960.

de la Garza, Rodolfo O., ed. *Ignored Voices: Public Opinion Polls and the Latino Community*. Austin: Center for Mexican American Studies Publications, University of Texas Press, 1987.

de León, Arnoldo. *The Tejano Community, 1836–1900*. Albuquerque: University of New Mexico Press, 1982.

———. *They Called Them Greasers: Anglo Attitudes toward Mexicans in Texas, 1821–1900*. Austin: University of Texas Press, 1983.

———, and Kenneth L. Stewart. *Tejanos and the Numbers Game: A Socio-Historical Interpretation from the Federal Censuses, 1850–1900*. Albuquerque: University of New Mexico Press, 1989.

de Witt, Howard. *Violence in the Fields: California Filipino Farm Labor Unionization during the Great Depression*. Saratoga, Calif.: Century Twenty-One Publishing, 1980.

Didion, Joan. *Miami*. New York: Simon and Schuster, 1987.

Divine, Robert A. *American Immigration Policy, 1924–1952*. New Haven, Conn.: Yale University Press, 1957.

Drachsler, Julius. *Democracy and Assimilation*. New York: Macmillan, 1920.

Enloe, Cynthia. *Ethnic Conflict and Political Development*. Boston: Little, Brown and Co., 1973.

Fantasia, Rick. *Cultures of Solidarity: Consciousness, Action, and Contemporary American Workers*. Berkeley: University of California Press, 1988.

Fehrenbach, T. R. *Fire and Blood: A History of Mexico*. New York: Macmillan Publishing Co., 1973.

Fisher, Lloyd. *The Harvest Labor Market in California*. Cambridge, Mass.: Harvard University Press, 1953.

Fishman, Joshua. *Language Loyalty in the United States*. The Hague: Mouton & Co., 1966.

Francis, E. K. *Interethnic Relations: An Essay in Sociological Theory*. New York: Elsevier, 1976.

Fuller, John Douglas Pitts. *The Movement for the Acquisition of All Mexico, 1846–1848*. Baltimore: Johns Hopkins University Press, 1936.

Galarza, Ernesto. *Farmworkers and Agribusiness in California, 1947–1977*. Notre Dame, Ind.: University of Notre Dame Press, 1977.

————. *Merchants of Labor: The Mexican Bracero Story, An Account of the Managed Migration of Mexican Farmworkers in California, 1942–1960*. Charlotte, N.C.: McNally & Loftin, 1964.

————, Herman Gallegos, and Julian Samora. *Mexican Americans in the Southwest*. Santa Barbara, Calif.: McNally & Loftin, 1969.

Gamio, Manuel. *The Life Story of the Mexican Immigrant: Autobiographical Documents*. Chicago: University of Chicago Press, 1931. Reprint. New York: Dover Publications, 1971.

————. *Mexican Immigration to the United States: A Study of Human Migration and Adjustment*. Chicago: University of Chicago Press, 1930. Reprint. New York: Dover Publications, 1971.

García, F. Chris, and Rodolfo O. de la Garza. *The Chicano Political Experience: Three Perspectives*. North Scituate, Mass.: Duxbury Press, 1977.

García, Ignacio M. *United We Win: The Rise and Fall of La Raza Unida Party*. Tucson: Mexican American Studies and Research Center, University of Arizona, 1989.

García, Juan Ramón. *Operation Wetback: The Mass Deportation of Mexican Undocumented Workers in 1954*. Westport, Conn.: Greenwood Press, 1980.

García, Mario T. *Desert Immigrants: The Mexicans of El Paso, 1880–1920*. New Haven, Conn.: Yale University Press, 1981.

————. *Mexican Americans: Leadership, Ideology, and Identity, 1930–1960*. New Haven, Conn.: Yale University Press, 1989.

García, Richard A. *Rise of the Mexican American Middle Class: San Antonio, 1929–1941*. College Station: Texas A & M University Press, 1991.

Gardner, Richard. *Grito*. New York: Bobbs-Merrill, 1970.

Garza, Edward D. *LULAC: The League of United Latin American Citizens*. San Francisco: R and E Research Associates, 1972.

Glazer, Nathan, and Daniel Patrick Moynihan, eds. *Ethnicity: Theory and Experience*. Cambridge, Mass.: Harvard University Press, 1975.

Gómez-Quiñones, Juan. *Chicano Politics: Reality and Promise, 1940–1990*. Albuquerque: University of New Mexico Press, 1990.

————. *Development of the Mexican Working Class North of the Rio Bravo: Work and Culture among Laborers and Artisans, 1600–1900*. Los Angeles: Chicano Studies Research Center Publications, University of California, Los Angeles, 1982.

————. *Mexican Students por La Raza: The Chicano Student Movement in Southern California, 1967–1977*. Santa Barbara, Calif.: Editorial La Causa, 1978.

————. *Sembradores, Ricardo Flores Magón y El Partido Liberal Mexicano: A Eulogy and Critique*. rev. ed. Los Angeles: Chicano Studies Center Publications, University of California, Los Angeles, 1977.

González, Gilbert G. *Chicano Education in the Era of Segregation*. Philadelphia: Balch Institute Press, Associated University Presses, 1990.

Gordon, Milton M. *Human Nature, Class, and Ethnicity*. New York: Oxford University Press, 1978.

Grebler, Leo, Joan W. Moore, and Ralph C. Guzmán. *The Mexican-American People: The Nation's Second Largest Minority*. New York: Free Press, 1970.

Griffith, Beatrice. *American Me*. Boston: Houghton Mifflin Co., 1948.

Griswold del Castillo, Richard. *The Los Angeles Barrio, 1850–1890: A Social History*. Berkeley: University of California Press, 1979.

————. *The Treaty of Guadalupe Hidalgo: A Legacy of Conflict*. Norman: University of Oklahoma Press, 1990.

Gutiérrez, Ramón A. *"When Jesus Came, the Corn Mothers Went Away": Marriage, Sexuality, and Power in New Mexico, 1500–1846*. Stanford, Calif.: Stanford University Press, 1991.

Guzmán, Ralph C. *The Political Socialization of the Mexican American People*. New York: Arno Press, 1976.

Hall, Raymond L. *Black Separatism in the United States*. Hanover, N.H.: University Press of New England, 1978.

Hammerback, John C., Richard J. Jensen, and José Angel Gutiérrez. *A War of Words: Chicano Protest in the 1960s and 1970s*. Westport, Conn.: Greenwood Press, 1985.

Hart, John M. *Anarchism and the Mexican Working Class, 1860–1931*. Austin: University of Texas Press, 1978.

Hays, Samuel P. *American Political History as Political Analysis*. Knoxville: University of Tennessee Press, 1980.

Heizer, Robert F., and Alan F. Almquist. *The Other Californians: Prejudice and Discrimination under Spain, Mexico, and the United States*. Berkeley: University of California Press, 1971.

Hernández, José Amaro. *Mutual Aid for Survival: The Case of the Mexican Americans*. Malabar, Fla.: Robert Krieger Publishers, 1983.

Higham, John. *Strangers in the Land: Patterns of American Nativism 1860–1925*. New Brunswick, N.J.: Rutgers University Press, 1955. Reprint. New York: Atheneum, 1963.

Hinojosa, Gilberto Miguel. *A Borderlands Town in Transition: Laredo, Texas, 1755–1870*. College Station: Texas A & M University Press, 1983.

Hobsbawm, Eric, and Terrence Ranger, eds. *The Invention of Tradition*. Cambridge, England: Cambridge University Press, 1983.

Hoffman, Abraham. *Unwanted Mexican Americans in the Great Depression: Repatriation Pressures, 1929–1939*. Tucson: University of Arizona Press, 1974.

Holliday, J. S. *The World Rushed In: The California Gold Rush Experience.* New York: Simon and Schuster, 1981.

Horsman, Reginald. *Race and Manifest Destiny: The Origins of American Racial Anglo-Saxonism.* Cambridge, Mass.: Harvard University Press, 1981.

Hughs, Robert. *The Culture of Complaint: The Fraying of America.* New York: Oxford University Press, 1993.

Hull, Elizabeth. *Without Justice for All: The Constitutional Rights of Aliens.* Westport, Conn.: Greenwood Press, 1985.

Hutchinson, E. P. *Immigrants and their Children.* New York: John Wiley & Sons, 1956.

Jankowski, Martin Sánchez. *City Bound: Urban Life and Political Attitudes among Chicano Youth.* Albuquerque: University of New Mexico Press, 1986.

Jelenik, Lawrence. *Harvest Empire: A History of California Agriculture.* San Francisco: Boyd and Fraser Publishing Co., 1979.

Jenkins, J. Craig. *The Politics of Insurgency: The Farm Worker Movement in the 1960s.* New York: Columbia University Press, 1985.

Jenks, Jeremiah W., and W. Jett Lauck. *The Immigrant Problem: A Study of American Immigration Conditions and Needs.* New York: Funk and Wagnalls, 1917.

Johnson, David R., John A. Booth, and Richard J. Harris, eds. *The Politics of San Antonio: Community, Progress, and Power.* Lincoln: University of Nebraska Press, 1983.

Kibbe, Pauline R. *Latin Americans in Texas.* Albuquerque: University of New Mexico Press, 1946.

Kluger, James R. *The Clifton-Morenci Strike: Labor Difficulty in Arizona.* Tucson: University of Arizona Press, 1970.

Konvitz, Milton R. *Civil Rights in Immigration.* Ithaca, N.Y.: Cornell University Press, 1953.

Lamm, Richard D., and Gary Imhoff. *The Immigration Time Bomb: The Fragmenting of America.* New York: Truman Talley Books, E. P. Dutton, 1985.

Larralde, Carlos. *Mexican American Movements and Leaders.* Los Alamitos, Calif.: Hwong Publishing Co., 1976.

Levy, Jacques. *César Chávez: An Autobiography of La Causa.* New York: W. W. Norton, 1975.

Light, Ivan H. *Ethnic Enterprise in America: Business and Welfare Among Chinese, Japanese, and Blacks.* Berkeley: University of California Press, 1980.

Lorey, David E., ed. *United States–Mexico Border Statistics Since 1900.* Los Angeles: UCLA Latin American Center Publications, 1990.

McWilliams, Carey. *Factories in the Fields: The Story of Migratory Farm Labor in California.* Boston: Little, Brown and Co., 1939.

————. *North from Mexico: The Spanish-Speaking People of the United States.* New York: Lippincott, 1948. Reprint. Westport, Conn.: Greenwood Press, 1968.

Majka, Linda C., and Theo J. Majka. *Farm Workers, Agribusiness, and the State.* Philadelphia: Temple University Press, 1982.

Marín, Christine. *A Spokesman of the Mexican American Movement: Rodolfo "Corky" González and the Fight for Chicano Liberation, 1966–1972.* San Francisco: R and E Research Associates, 1977.

Márquez, Benjamin. *LULAC: The Evolution of a Mexican American Political Organization.* Austin: University of Texas Press, 1993.

Massey, Douglas, Rafael Alarcón, Jorge Durand, and Humberto González. *Return to Aztlán: The Social Process of International Migration to the United States from Western Mexico.* Berkeley: University of California Press, 1987.

Matthiessen, Peter. *Sal Si Puedes: César Chávez and the New American Revolution.* New York: Random House, 1969.

Mazón, Mauricio. *The Zoot-Suit Riots: The Psychology of Symbolic Annihilation.* Austin: University of Texas Press, 1984.

Meier, August. *Negro Thought in America, 1880–1915: Racial Ideologies in the Age of Booker T. Washington.* Ann Arbor: University of Michigan Press, 1963.

Meier, Matt S. *Mexican American Biographies: A Historical Dictionary, 1836–1987.* Westport, CT.: Greenwood Press, 1988.

Meinig, Donald W. *Southwest: Three Peoples in Geographical Change, 1600–1970.* New York: Oxford University Press, 1971.

Merk, Frederick. *Manifest Destiny and Mission in American History.* New York: Vintage Books, 1963.

Miller, Hunter, ed. *Treaties and Other International Acts of the United States of America.* Washington, D.C.: U.S. Government Printing Office, 1931.

Montejano, David. *Anglos and Mexicans in the Making of Texas, 1836–1986.* Austin: University of Texas Press, 1987.

Moore, Joan W. *Homeboys: Gangs, Drugs, and Prison in the Barrios of Los Angeles.* Philadelphia: Temple University Press, 1978.

————, with Alfredo Cuéllar. *Mexican Americans.* Englewood Cliffs, N.J.: Prentice Hall, 1970.

Morín, Raúl. *Among the Valiant: Mexican Americans in WWII and Korea.* Alhambra, Calif.: Borden Publishing Co., 1966.

Muñoz, Carlos, Jr. *Youth, Identity, Power: The Chicano Movement.* London: Verso, 1989.

Nabakov, Peter. *Tijerina and the Courthouse Raid.* Albuquerque: University of New Mexico Press, 1969.

Nash, Gerald D. *The American West Transformed: The Impact of the Second World War.* Bloomington: Indiana University Press, 1985.

Olson, James Stuart. *The Ethnic Dimension in American History*. New York: St. Martin's Press, 1979.

Ortiz, Roxanne Dunbar. *Roots of Resistance: Land Tenure in New Mexico, 1680–1980*. Los Angeles: Chicano Studies Research Center Publications, University of California, Los Angeles, 1980.

Paredes, Américo. *"With a Pistol in His Hand": A Border Ballad and Its Hero*. Austin: University of Texas Press, 1958.

Parrish, Michael E. *Mexican Workers, Progressives and Copper: The Failure of Industrial Democracy in Arizona during the Wilson Years*. San Diego: Chicano Research Publications, University of California, San Diego, 1979.

Paz, Octavio. *The Labyrinth of Solitude: Life and Thought in Mexico*. New York: Grove Press, 1961.

Peña, Manuel. *The Texas-Mexican Conjunto: History of a Working-Class Music*. Austin: University of Texas Press, 1985.

Perales, Alonso S. *Are We Good Neighbors?* San Antonio, Tex.: Artes Gráficas, 1948. Reprint. New York: Arno Press, 1974.

Pitt, Leonard. *The Decline of the Californios: A Social History of the Spanish-Speaking Californians, 1846–1890*. Berkeley: University of California Press, 1966.

Pletcher, David M. *The Diplomacy of Annexation: Texas, Oregon, and the Mexican War*. Columbia: University of Missouri Press, 1973.

Portes, Alejandro, and Robert L. Bach. *Latin Journey: Cuban and Mexican Immigrants in the United States*. Berkeley: University of California Press, 1985.

Preston, William, Jr. *Aliens and Dissenters: Federal Suppression of Radicals, 1903–1933*. Cambridge, Mass.: Harvard University Press, 1963.

Raat, W. Dirk. *Revoltosos: Mexico's Rebels in the United States, 1903–1923*. College Station: Texas A & M University Press, 1981.

Reed, S. G. *A History of the Texas Railroads and of Transportation Conditions under Spain and Mexico and the Republic and the State*. Houston, Tex.: St. Clair Publishing Co., 1941.

Reimers, David M. *Still the Golden Door: The Third World Comes to America*. New York: Columbia University Press, 1985.

Reisler, Mark. *By the Sweat of Their Brow: Mexican Immigrant Labor in the United States, 1900–1940*. Westport, Conn.: Greenwood Press, 1976.

Rex, John, and David Mason, eds. *Theories of Race and Ethnic Relations*. Cambridge, England: Cambridge University Press, 1986.

Riding, Alan. *Distant Neighbors: A Portrait of the Mexicans*. New York: Alfred K. Knopf, 1984.

Ríos-Bustamante, Antonio, and Pedro Castillo. *An Illustrated History of Mexican Los Angeles, 1781–1985*. Chicano Studies Research Center

Publications, Monograph no. 12. Los Angeles: Chicano Research Center, University of California, Los Angeles, 1986.

Romo, Ricardo. *East Los Angeles: History of a Barrio.* Austin: University of Texas Press, 1983.

Rosenbaum, Robert J. *Mexicano Resistance in the Southwest: "The Sacred Right of Self-Preservation."* Austin: University of Texas Press, 1981.

Ruiz, Vicki L. *Cannery Women, Cannery Lives: Mexican Women, Unionization, and the California Food Processing Industry, 1930–1950.* Albuquerque: University of New Mexico Press, 1987.

Saldívar, Ramón. *Chicano Narrative: The Dialectics of Difference.* Madison: University of Wisconsin Press, 1990.

Samora, Julian. *Los Mojados: The Wetback Story.* Notre Dame, Ind.: University of Notre Dame Press, 1971.

————, Joe Bernal, and Albert Peña. *Gunpowder Justice: A Reassessment of the Texas Rangers.* Notre Dame, Ind.: University of Notre Dame Press, 1979.

Sánchez, George I. *Forgotten People: A Study of New Mexicans.* Albuquerque: University of New Mexico Press, 1940.

Sánchez, Rosaura. *Chicano Discourse: Socio-Historical Perspectives.* Rowley, Mass.: Newbury House, 1983.

San Miguel, Guadalupe, Jr. *"Let All of Them Take Heed": Mexican Americans and the Campaign for Educational Equality in Texas, 1910–1981.* Austin: University of Texas Press, 1987.

Santamaría Gómez, Arturo. *La izquierda norteamericana y los trabajadores indocumentados.* Sinaloa, Mexico: Ediciones de Cultura Popular, Universidad Autónoma de Sinaloa, 1988.

Saxton, Alexander. *The Indispensable Enemy: Labor and the Anti–Chinese Movement in California.* Berkeley: University of California Press, 1971.

Schlesinger, Arthur M., Jr. *The Disuniting of America.* New York: W. W. Norton, 1992.

Schuck, Peter H., and Rogers M. Smith. *Citizenship Without Consent: Illegal Aliens in the American Polity.* New Haven, Conn.: Yale University Press, 1985.

Scruggs, Otey M. *Braceros, "Wetbacks," and the Farm Labor Problem: Mexican Agricultural Labor in the United States, 1942–1954.* New York: Garland Publishing, 1988.

Sheridan, Thomas J. *Los Tucsonenses: The Mexican Community in Tucson, 1854–1941.* Tucson: University of Arizona Press, 1986.

Shockley, John Staples. *Chicano Revolt in a Texas Town.* Notre Dame, Ind.: University of Notre Dame Press, 1974.

Skerry, Peter. *Mexican Americans: The Ambivalent Minority.* New York: Free Press, 1993.

Smith, Anthony D. S. *The Ethnic Origins of Nations*. Oxford: Basil Blackwell, 1986.

———. *Nationalism in the Twentieth Century*. New York: New York University Press, 1979.

Starr, Kevin. *Americans and the California Dream, 1850–1915*. New York: Oxford University Press, 1973.

Steinberg, Stephen. *The Ethnic Myth: Race, Ethnicity, and Class in America*. Updated and expanded ed. Boston: Beacon Press, 1989.

Stoddard, Ellwyn. *Mexican Americans*. New York: Random House, 1973.

Takaki, Ronald. *Iron Cages: Race and Culture in 19th-Century America*. New York: Alfred A. Knopf, 1979. Reprint. New York: Oxford University Press, 1990.

———. *Strangers from a Different Shore: A History of Asian Americans*. New York: Penguin, 1990.

Taylor, Paul S. *An American-Mexican Frontier: Nueces County, Texas*. Chapel Hill: University of North Carolina Press, 1934.

———. *Mexican Labor in the United States: Chicago and the Calumet Region*. University of California Publications in Economics, vol. 7, no. 2. Berkeley: University of California Press, 1932.

———. *Mexican Labor in the United States: Dimmitt County, Winter Garden District, South Texas*. University of California Publications in Economics, vol. 6, no. 5. Berkeley: University of California Press, 1930.

———. *Mexican Labor in the United States: Imperial Valley*. University of California Publications in Economics, vol. 6, no. 1. Berkeley: University of California Press, 1928.

———. *Mexican Labor in the United States: Valley of the South Platte, Colorado*. University of California Publications in Economics, vol. 6, no. 2. Berkeley: University of California Press, 1929.

Taylor, Ronald B. *Chávez and the Farm Workers*. Boston: Beacon Press, 1975.

Thernstrom, Stephan, ed. *Harvard Encyclopedia of American Ethnic Groups*. Cambridge, Mass.: Harvard University Press, 1980.

Thompson, Slason, comp. *Railway Statistics of the United States of America, 1921*. Chicago: Bureau of Railway News and Statistics, 1921.

Tuck, Ruth D. *Not with the Fist*. New York: Harcourt Brace and Co., 1946.

Van Young, Eric, ed. *Mexico's Regions: Comparative History and Development*. La Jolla: Center for U.S.–Mexican Studies, University of California, San Diego, 1992.

Vélez-Ibáñez, Carlos G. *Bonds of Mutual Trust: The Cultural Systems of Rotating Credit Associations among Urban Mexicans and Chicanos*. New Brunswick, N.J.: Rutgers University Press, 1983.

Vigil, James Diego. *Barrio Gangs: Streetlife and Identity in Southern California*. Austin: University of Texas Press, 1988.

Walling, William E. *The Mexican Question: Mexico and American-*

Mexican Relations under Calles and Obregón. New York: Robins Press, 1927.

Webb, Walter Prescott. *Handbook of Texas,* vols. 1–2. Austin: Texas State Historical Society, 1952.

———. *The Texas Rangers: A Century of Frontier Defense.* 2d ed. Austin: University of Texas Press, 1965.

Weber, David J. *The Mexican Frontier, 1821–1846: The American Southwest under Mexico.* Albuquerque: University of New Mexico Press, 1982.

———, ed. *Foreigners in Their Native Land: Historical Roots of the Mexican Americans.* Albuquerque: University of New Mexico Press, 1973.

Westphall, Victor. *Mercedes Reales: Hispanic Land Grants of the Upper Rio Grande Region.* Albuquerque: University of New Mexico Press, 1983.

Worster, Donald. *Rivers of Empire: Water, Aridity & the Growth of the American West.* New York: Pantheon Books, 1985.

Zamora, Emilio. *The World of the Mexican Worker in Texas.* College Station: Texas A & M University Press, 1993.

Zunz, Olivier. *The Changing Face of Inequality: Urbanization, Industrial Development, and Immigration in Detroit, 1880–1920.* Chicago: University of Chicago Press, 1982.

Articles, Chapters, and Pamphlets

Almaguer, Tomás. "Chicano Politics in the Present Period: Comment on García." *Socialist Review* 40–41 (July-October 1978):137–142.

———. "Ideological Distortions in Recent Chicano Historiography: The Internal Colonial Model and Chicano Historical Interpretation." *Aztlán* 18 (Spring 1987):7–28.

———. "Interpreting Chicano History: The 'World System' Approach to Nineteenth Century California." *Review: A Journal of the Fernand Braudel Center for the Study of Economies, Historical Systems, and Civilizations* 4 (Winter 1981):459–507.

———. "Toward the Study of Chicano Colonialism." *Aztlán* 2 (Spring 1971):137–142.

———, and Albert Camarillo. "Urban Chicano Workers in Historical Perspective: A Review of the Literature." In *The State of Chicano Research on Family, Labor, and Migration: Proceedings of the First Stanford Symposium on Chicano Research and Public Policy,* edited by Armando Valdez, Albert Camarillo, and Tomás Almaguer, 3–32. Stanford, Calif.: Stanford Center for Chicano Research, 1983.

Alvarez, Rodolfo. "The Psycho-Historical and Socioeconomic Development of the Chicano Community in the United States." *Social Science Quarterly* 53 (March 1973):920–942.

——. "The Unique Psycho-Historical Experience of the Mexican American People." *Social Science Quarterly* 52 (June 1971):15–29.

Arroyo, Luis Leobardo. "Chicano Participation in Organized Labor: The C.I.O. in Los Angeles, 1938–1950; An Extended Research Note." *Aztlán* 6 (Summer 1975):277–304.

——. "Notes on Past, Present, and Future Directions of Chicano Labor Studies." *Aztlán* 6 (Summer 1975):137–150.

Bamford, Edwin F. "The Mexican Casual Problem in the Southwest." *Journal of Applied Sociology* 8 (1923–1924):364–371.

Banton, Michael. "Analytical and Folk Concepts of Race and Ethnicity." *Ethnic and Racial Studies* 2 (April 1979):127–138.

Barr, Alwyn. "Occupational and Geographic Mobility in San Antonio, 1870–1900." *Southwestern Quarterly* 51 (September 1970):396–403.

Barrera, Mario. "The Historical Evolution of Chicano Ethnic Goals: A Bibliographic Essay." *Sage Race Relations Abstracts* 10 (February 1985):1–48.

——, Carlos Muñoz, Jr., and Charles Ornelas. "The Barrio as an Internal Colony." In *People and Politics in Urban Society*, edited by Harlan Hahn, 465–498. Urban Affairs Annual Reviews, vol. 6. Los Angeles: Sage Publications, 1972.

Bean, Frank D., Elizabeth H. Stephen, and Wolfgang Opitz. "The Mexican Origin Population in the United States: A Demographic Overview." In *The Mexican American Experience: An Interdisciplinary Anthology*, edited by Rodolfo O. de la Garza et al., 57–75. Austin: University of Texas Press, 1985.

Beegle, J. Allan, Harold F. Goldsmith, and Charles P. Loomis. "Demographic Characteristics of the United States–Mexican Border." *Rural Sociology* 25 (March 1960):107–162.

Betten, Neil, and Raymond A. Mohl. "From Discrimination to Repatriation: Mexican Life during the Great Depression." *Pacific Historical Review* 42 (August 1973):370–388.

Blauner, Robert. "Internal Colonialism and Ghetto Revolt." *Social Problems* 16 (Spring 1969):393–408.

Bogardus, Emory S. "Attitudes and the Mexican Immigrant." In *Social Attitudes*, edited by Kimball Young, 291–327. New York: Henry Holt and Co., 1931.

——. "Current Problems of Mexican Immigrants." *Sociology and Social Research* 25 (November 1940):166–174.

——. "The Mexican Immigrant." *Journal of Applied Sociology* 11 (1927):470–488.

——. "Mexican Immigration and Segregation." *American Journal of Sociology* 36 (July 1930):74–80.

——. "Second Generation Mexicans." *Sociology and Social Research* 13 (January 1929):276–283.

Boswell, Thomas D. "The Growth and Proportional Distribution of the Mexican Stock Population in the United States: 1910–1970." *Mississippi Geographer* 7 (Spring 1979):57–76.

Brimelow, Peter. "Time to Rethink Immigration?" *National Review*, June 22, 1992, 30–46.

Calderón, Roberto R., and Emilio Zamora. "Manuela Solis Sager and Emma B. Tenayuca: A Tribute." In *Between Borders: Essays on Mexicana/Chicana History*, edited by Adelaida R. del Castillo, 269–280. Encino, Calif.: Floricanto Press, 1990.

Caldwell, Edwin L. "Highlights of the Development of Manufacturing in Texas." *Southwestern Historical Quarterly* 68 (April 1965):405–431.

Cárdenas, Gilberto, Rodolfo O. de la Garza, and Niles Hansen. "Mexican Immigrants and the Chicano Ethnic Enterprise: Reconceptualizing an Old Problem." In *Mexican Immigrants and Mexican Americans: An Evolving Relationship*, edited by Harley L. Browning and Rodolfo O. de la Garza, 157–174. Austin: Center for Mexican American Studies Publications, University of Texas, Austin, 1984.

Chacón, Ramón. "The 1933 San Joaquin Valley Cotton Strike: Strikebreaking Activities in California Agriculture." In *Work, Family, Sex Roles, and Language*, edited by Mario Barrera, Albert Camarillo, and Francisco Hernández, 33–70. Berkeley: Tonatiuh-Quinto Sol, 1980.

Chapman, Leonard F. "Controversy Over Proposed Amnesty for Illegal Aliens: Pro and Con." *Congressional Digest* 56 (October 1977):234–241.

———. "Illegal Aliens—A Growing Population." *Immigration and Naturalization Reporter* 24 (Fall 1975):15–18.

———. "Illegal Aliens: Time to Call a Halt." *Reader's Digest*, October 1976, 188–192.

Citrin, Jack, Beth Reingold, and Donald P. Green. "American Identity and the Politics of Ethnic Change." *Journal of Politics* 52 (November 1990):1124–1154.

Cohen, Anthony P. "Culture as Identity: An Anthropologist's View." *New Literary History* 24 (Winter 1993):195–209.

Corwin, Arthur F., and Lawrence A. Cardoso. "Vamos al Norte: Causes of Mass Mexican Migration to the United States." In *Immigrants and Immigrants: Perspectives on Mexican Labor Migration to the United States*, edited by Arthur F. Corwin, 38–66. Westport, Conn.: Greenwood Press, 1978.

Cuéllar, Alfredo. "Perspective on Politics." In *Mexican Americans*, by Joan Moore, with Alfredo Cuéllar, 137–156. Englewood Cliffs, N.J.: Prentice Hall, 1970.

de la Garza, Rodolfo O. "American as Tamale Pie: Mexican-American Political Mobilization and the Loyalty Question." In *Mexican Americans in Comparative Perspective*, edited by Walker Conner, 227–242. Washington, D.C.: Urban Institute Press, 1985.

———. "Attitudes of Mexican Americans toward Irregular Mexican Immigration." *International Migration Review* 18 (Fall 1984):782–799.

———. *Chicano Elite Perceptions of the Undocumented Worker: An Empirical Analysis*. Working Papers in U.S.–Mexican Studies, no. 31. La Jolla: Center for U.S.–Mexican Studies, University of California, San Diego, 1981.

———. "Chicano-Mexican Relations: A Framework for Research." *Social Science Quarterly* 63 (1982):115–130.

———. "Chicanos and Mexican Foreign Policy: The Future of Chicano-Mexican Relations." *Western Political Quarterly* 33 (1980):571–582.

De León, Arnoldo, and Kenneth L. Stewart. "Lost Dreams and Found Fortunes: Mexicans and Anglo Immigrants in South Texas, 1850–1910." *Western Historical Quarterly* 14 (July 1983):291–310.

Dinwoodie, D. H. "Deportation: The Immigration Service and the Chicano Labor Movement in the 1930s." *New Mexico Historical Review* 52 (July 1977):193–206.

Dyer, Stanford P., and Merrell A. Knighten. "Discrimination after Death: Lyndon Johnson and Felix Longoria." *Southern Studies* 17 (Winter 1978):411–426.

Dysart, Jane. "Mexican Women in San Antonio, 1830–1860: The Assimilation Process." *Western Historical Quarterly* 7 (October 1976):365–377.

Eisinger, Peter K. "Ethnicity as a Strategic Option: An Emerging View." *Public Administration Review* 38 (January-February 1978):89–93.

Estrada, Leo F., José Hernández, and David Alvírez. "Using Census Data to Study the Spanish Heritage Population of the United States." In *Cuantos Somos: A Demographic Study of the Mexican American Population*, edited by Charles H. Teller et al., 13–59. Center for Mexican American Studies, University of Texas, Austin, Monograph no. 2. Austin: Center for Mexican American Studies, 1977.

Fernández, Celestino. "Newspaper Coverage of Undocumented Mexican Immigration during the 1970s: A Qualitative Analysis of Pictures and Headings." In *History, Culture, and Society: Chicano Studies in the 1980s*, edited by Mario T. García et al., 177–198. Ypsilanti, Mich.: Bilingual Press/Editorial Bilingüe, 1983.

Fisher, Lloyd H. *The Problem of Violence: Observations on Race Conflict in Los Angeles*. Los Angeles: American Council on Race Relations, 1946.

Foley, Douglas E. "Does the Working Class Have a Culture in the Anthropological Sense?" *Cultural Anthropology* 4 (May 1989):137–162.

Fragomen, Austin T. "Legislative and Judicial Developments." *International Migration Review* 6 (Fall 1972):296–302.

Francis, E. K. "The Nature of the Ethnic Group." *American Journal of Sociology* 52 (March 1947):393–400.

Fuller, Roden. "Occupations of the Mexican-Born Population of Texas, New Mexico, and Arizona, 1900–1920." *American Statistical Association Journal* 23 (March 1928):64–67.

Galarza, Ernesto. "Big Farm Strike: A Report on the Labor Dispute at DiGiorgio's." *Commonweal*, June 4, 1948, 179–180.

————. "Life in the United States for Mexican People: Out of the Experience of a Mexican." In *National Council of Social Work, Proceedings of 1929*, 399–404. Chicago: University of Chicago Press, 1930.

————. "Mexicans in the Southwest: A Culture in Process." In *Plural Society in the Southwest*, edited by Edward H. Spicer and Raymond H. Thompson, 261–297. New York: Weatherhead Foundation, 1972.

Gallup Opinion Index Reports. *Immigration* 51, November 1983.

————. *Immigration* 232–233, January-February 1985.

García, John A. "Political Integration of Mexican Immigrants: Explorations into the Naturalization Process." *International Migration Review* 15 (Winter 1981):608–625.

García, Mario T. "Americanization and the Mexican Immigrant, 1880–1930." *Journal of Ethnic Studies* 6 (Summer 1978):19–34.

————. "Americans All: The Mexican American Generation and the Politics of Wartime Los Angeles, 1941–1945." In *The Mexican American Experience: An Interdisciplinary Anthology*, edited by Rodolfo O. de la Garza et al., 201–212. Austin: University of Texas Press, 1985.

————. "La Frontera: The Border as Symbol and Reality in Mexican American Thought." *Mexican Studies/Estudios Mexicanos* 1 (Summer 1985):195–225.

————. "Mexican American Labor and the Left: The Asociación Nacional México-Americana, 1949–1954." In *The Chicano Struggle: Analyses of Past and Present Efforts*, edited by John A. García, Theresa Córdova, and Juan R. García, 65–86. Binghamton, N.Y.: Bilingual Press for the National Association for Chicano Studies, 1984.

————. "Working for the Union." *Mexican Studies/Estudios Mexicanos* 9 (Summer 1993):241–258.

García, Richard A. "The Chicano Movement and the Mexican American Community, 1972–1978: An Interpretive Essay." *Socialist Review* 40–41 (July-October 1978):117–136.

————. "Class, Consciousness, and Ideology—The Mexican Community of San Antonio, Texas: 1930–1940." *Aztlán* 9 (Fall 1978):23–70.

García y Griego, Manuel. "The Importation of Mexican Contract Laborers to the United States, 1942–1964: Antecedents, Operation, and Legacy." In *The Border That Joins: Mexican Migrants and U.S. Responsibility*, edited by Peter G. Brown and Henry Shue, 49–98. Totowa, N.J.: Rowman and Littlefield, 1983.

Garis, Roy L. "Are Aliens Lowering American Standards?—The Necessity of Excluding Inferior Stocks." *Current History* 24 (August 1926):666–677.

———. "The Mexicanization of American Business." *Saturday Evening Post*, February 8, 1930, 46, 51, 178, 181, 182.

Giménez, Martha E., "The Political Construction of the Hispanic." In *Estudios Chicanos and the Politics of Community: Selected Proceedings, National Association for Chicano Studies*, edited by Mary Romero and Cordelia Candelaria, 66–85. Boulder, Colo.: National Association for Chicano Studies, 1989.

Gleason, Philip. "Identifying Identity: A Semantic History." *Journal of American History* 69 (March 1983):910–931.

Goethe, C. M. "Other Aspects of the Problem." *Current History* 28 (August 1928):766–768.

———. "Peons Need Not Apply." *World's Work* 59 (November 1930):47–48.

Gómez-Peña, Guillermo. "The Multicultural Paradigm: An Open Letter to the Arts Community." *High Performance* 12 (Fall 1989):18–27.

Gómez-Quiñones, Juan. "Critique on the National Question, Self-Determination, and Nationalism." *Latin American Perspectives* 9 (Spring 1982):62–83.

———. "The First Steps: Chicano Labor Conflict and Organizing, 1900–1920." *Aztlán* 3 (Spring 1972):13–50.

———. "Notes on the Interpretation of the Relations between the Mexican Community in the United States and Mexico: Historical and Political Contexts of a Dialogue Renewed." In *Mexico–United States Relations: Conflict and Convergence*, edited by Carlos Vásquez and Manuel García y Griego, 417–439. Los Angeles: Chicano Studies Center and the Latin American Research Center Publications, University of California, Los Angeles, 1983.

———. *On Culture*. Popular Series, UCLA Chicano Studies Publications, no. 1. Los Angeles: UCLA Chicano Studies Research Center Publications, 1977.

———. "Piedras contra la luna, México en Aztlán y Aztlán en México: Chicano-Mexican Relations in the Mexican Consulates, 1900–1920." In *Contemporary Mexico: Papers of the IV International Congress of Mexican History*, 494–527. Mexico City: El Colegio de México and UCLA Latin American Studies Center, 1975.

———. "Toward a Perspective on Chicano History." *Aztlán* 2 (Fall 1971):1–49.

Gonzales, Rodolfo "Corky." "Chicano Nationalism: The Key to Unity for La Raza." In *A Documentary History of the Mexican Americans*, edited by Wayne Moquin, 488–493. New York: Bantam Books, 1972.

Graham, Otis L., Jr. *Illegal Immigration and the New Reform Movement.*

Federation for American Immigration Reform, Immigration Paper 2. Washington, D.C.: FAIR, 1980.

———. "Illegal Immigration and the New Restrictionism." *Center Magazine*, May-June 1979, 54–64.

Grebler, Leo. *Mexican Immigration to the United States: The Record and Its Implications*. Mexican American Study Project Advance Report 2. Los Angeles: Division of Research, Graduate School of Business Administration, University of California, Los Angeles, 1966.

Griffith, Beatrice. "The Pachuco Patois." *Common Ground* 7 (Summer 1947):77–84.

———. "Viva Roybal—Viva America." *Common Ground* 10 (Autumn 1949):61–70.

Guinn, J. M. "The Sonoran Migration." *Annual Publication, Historical Society of Southern California* 7 (1909–1911):31–36.

Gutiérrez, David G. *CASA in the Chicano Movement: Ideology and Organizational Politics in the Chicano Community, 1968–1978*. Working Papers Series, no. 5. Stanford Center for Chicano Research, Stanford University, 1984.

———. "An Ethnic Consensus? Mexican American Political Activism since the Great Depression." *Reviews in American History* 19 (Summer 1991):289–295.

Gutiérrez, Ramón A. "Honor Ideology, Marriage Negotiation, and Class-Gender Domination in New Mexico, 1690–1846." *Latin American Perspectives* 12 (Winter 1985):81–104.

———. "Unraveling America's Hispanic Past: Internal Stratification and Class Boundaries." *Aztlán* 17 (Spring 1986):79–102.

Hall, Martin. "Roybal's Candidacy and What It Means." *Frontier* 5 (June 1954):5–7.

Hall, Stuart. "Cultural Identity and Diaspora." In *Identity: Community, Culture, Difference*, edited by Johnathan Rutherford, 222–237. London: Lawrence and Wishart, 1990.

———. "Ethnicity: Identity and Difference." *Radical America* 23 (October-December 1989):9–22.

———. "New Ethnicities." *Black Film, British Cinema*. London, 1988. Reprinted in *"Race," Culture, and Difference*, edited by J. Donald and A. Ratansi, 252–260. London: Sage, 1992.

———. "Race, Articulation and Societies Structured in Dominance." In *Sociological Theories: Race and Colonialism*, 305–345. Paris: UNESCO, 1980.

Ham-Chande, Roberto, and John R. Weeks. "A Demographic Perspective of the U.S.–Mexico Border." In *Demographic Dynamics of the U.S.–Mexico Border*, edited by John R. Weeks and Roberto Ham-Chande, 1–27. El Paso: Texas Western Press, 1992.

Hansen, Terrence L. "Corridos in Southern California." *Western Folklore* 18 (July 1959):202–232; 18 (October 1959):295–315.

Hawley, Ellis. "The Politics of the Mexican Labor Issue, 1950–1965." *Agricultural History* 40 (July 1966):157–176.

Hayes-Bautista, David E., and Jorge Chapa. "Latino Terminology: Conceptual Basis for Standardized Terminology." *American Journal of Public Health* 77 (January 1987):61–68.

Hernández, José, Leo Estrada, and David Alvírez. "Census Data and the Problem of Conceptually Defining the Mexican American Population." *Social Science Quarterly* 53 (March 1973):671–687.

Hernández Alvarez, José. "A Demographic Profile of the Mexican Immigration to the United States, 1910–1950." *Journal of Inter-American Studies* 8 (July 1966):471–496.

Hoffman, Abraham. "The El Monte Berry Pickers Strike, 1933: International Involvement in a Local Labor Dispute." *Journal of the West* 12 (January 1973):71–84.

———. "The Federal Bureaucracy Meets a Superior Spokesman for Alien Deportation." *Journal of the West* 14 (October 1975):91–106.

———. "Stimulus to Repatriation: The 1931 Federal Deportation Drive and the Los Angeles Mexican Community." *Pacific Historical Review* 42 (May 1973):203–219.

Hohl, Donald C. "United States Immigration Legislation: Prospects in the 94th Congress." *International Migration Review* 9 (Spring 1975):59–62.

———. "The Illegal Alien and the Western Hemisphere Immigration Dilemma." *International Migration Review* 7 (Fall 1973):323–332.

———, and Michael G. Wenk. "Current U.S. Immigration Legislation: Analysis and Comment." *International Migration Review* 5 (Fall 1971):339–356.

Holmes, S. J. "Perils of the Mexican Invasion." *North American Review* 227 (May 1929):615–623.

Hoover, Glenn E. "Our Mexican Immigrants." *Foreign Affairs* 8 (October 1929):99–107.

Israelson, O. W. "Irrigation and Drainage." In *California and the Southwest*, edited by Clifford M. Zierer, 135–159. New York: John Wiley & Sons, 1956.

Jordan, Terry G. "A Century and a Half of Ethnic Change in Texas, 1836–1986." *Southwestern Historical Quarterly* 89 (April 1986):386–421.

———. "Population Origins in Texas, 1850." *Geographical Review* 59 (January 1969):83–103.

Kelley, Joseph B., and Walter Collett. "The Deportation of Mexican Aliens and Its Impact on Family Life." *Catholic Charities Review* 37 (October 1954):161–171.

Kerr, Homer L. "Migration into Texas, 1860–1880." *Southwestern Historical Quarterly* 70 (October 1966):184–216.

Kirstein, Peter N. "American Railroads and the Bracero Program, 1943–1946." *Journal of Mexican American History* 5 (1975):57–90.

Kiser, George C. "Mexican Labor Before World War II." *Journal of Mexican American History* 2 (Spring 1972):122–142.

————, and David Silverman. "Mexican Repatriation during the Great Depression." *Journal of Mexican American History* 3 (1973):139–164.

León-Portilla, Miguel. "The Norteño Variety of Mexican Culture: An Ethnohistorical Approach." In *Plural Society in the Southwest*, edited by Edward H. Spicer and Raymond H. Thompson, 77–114. New York: Weatherhead Foundation, 1972.

Limón, José. "The Folk Performance of 'Chicano' and the Cultural Limits of Political Ideology." In *And Other Neighborly Names: Social Process and Cultural Image in Texas Folklore*, edited by Richard Bauman and Roger D. Abrahams, 197–225. Austin: University of Texas Press, 1981.

————. "El Primer Congreso Mexicanista de 1911: A Precursor to Contemporary Chicanismo." *Aztlán* 5 (Spring-Fall 1974):85–117.

López, Ronald W. "The El Monte Berry Strike of 1933." *Aztlán* 1 (Spring 1970):101–114.

McBride, James D. "La Liga Protectora Latina: An Arizona Mexican-American Benevolent Society." *Journal of the West* 14 (October 1975): 82–90.

McCain, Johnny M. "Texas and the Mexican Labor Question, 1942–1947." *Southwestern Historical Quarterly* 85 (July 1981):45–64.

McDonagh, Edward C. "Status Levels of Mexicans." *Sociology and Social Research* 33 (July 1949):449–459.

McNamara, Patrick H. "Rumbles along the Rio." *Commonweal*, March 1969, 730–732.

McWilliams, Carey. "The Mexican Problem." *Common Ground* 8 (Spring 1948):3–17.

Madrid-Barela, Arturo. "In Search of the Authentic Pachuco, An Interpretive Essay." *Aztlán* 4 (Spring 1973):31–57.

Manuel, Hershel T. "The Mexican Population of Texas." *Southwestern Political and Social Science Quarterly* 15 (June 1934):29–51.

Márquez, Benjamin. "The Politics of Race and Assimilation: The League of United Latin American Citizens, 1929–1940." *Western Political Quarterly* 42 (June 1989):355–375.

————. "The Politics of Race and Class: The League of United Latin American Citizens in the Post–World War II Period." *Social Science Quarterly* 68 (March 1987):84–101.

Martínez, Oscar J. "On the Size of the Chicano Population: New Estimates, 1850–1900." *Aztlán* 6 (Spring 1975):43–67.

Maslow, Will. "Recasting Our Deportation Law: Proposals for Reform." *Columbia Law Review* 56 (March 1956):309–366.

"Mexican Americans and 'La Raza'." *Christian Century*, March 1969, 325–328.

"The Mexican Conquest." *Saturday Evening Post*, June 22, 1929, 26.

Miller, Darlis A. "Cross-Cultural Marriages in the Southwest: The New Mexico Experience, 1846–1900." *New Mexico Historical Review* 57 (October 1982):335–359.

Miller, Lawrence W., Jerry L. Polinard, and Robert D. Wrinkle. "Attitudes toward Undocumented Workers: The Mexican American Perspective." *Social Science Quarterly* 65 (June 1984):482–494.

Miller, Michael V., and Avelardo Valdez. "Immigration and Perceptions of Economic Deprivation among Working-Class Mexican American Men." In *The Mexican American Experience: An Interdisciplinary Anthology*, edited by Rodolfo O. de la Garza et al., 153–162. Austin: University of Texas Press, 1985.

Monroy, Douglas. "Like the Swallows at the Old Mission: Mexicans and the Racial Politics of Growth in Los Angeles in the Interwar Period." *Western Historical Quarterly* 14 (October 1983):435–458.

Montejano, David. "Frustrated Apartheid: Race, Repression and Capitalist Agriculture in South Texas." In *The World System of Capitalism: Past and Present*, edited by Walter L. Goldfrank, 131–168. Beverly Hills, Calif.: Sage Publications, 1979.

Moore, Joan W. "American Minorities and 'New Nation' Perspectives." *Pacific Sociological Review* 19 (October 1976):447–467.

———. "Colonialism: The Case of the Mexican Americans." *Social Problems* 17 (Spring 1970):463–471.

Mora, Magdalena. "The Tolteca Strike: Mexican Women and the Struggle for Union Representation." In *Mexican Immigrant Workers in the United States*, edited by Antonio Ríos-Bustamante, 111–117. Los Angeles: Chicano Research Center Publications, University of California, Los Angeles, 1981.

Morgan, T. B. "The Latinization of America." *Esquire*, May 1983, 47–56.

Muñoz, Carlos, Jr. "Toward a Chicano Perspective of Political Analysis." *Aztlán* 1 (Fall 1970):15–26.

———, and Mario Barrera. "La Raza Unida Party and the Chicano Student Movement in California." *Social Science Journal* 19 (April 1982):101–120.

Myres, Sandra L. "Mexican Americans and Westering Anglos: A Feminine Perspective." *New Mexico Historical Review* 57 (October 1982):317–333.

National Farm Labor Union. "Summer Brings the Mexicans—Statement of the National Farm Labor Union." *Commonweal*, July 2, 1948, 275–278.

Nelson, Dale C. "Ethnicity and Socioeconomic Status as Sources of Participation: The Case for Ethnic Political Culture." *American Political Science Review* 73 (December 1979):1024–1038.

Nelson-Cisneros, Victor B. "La clase trabajadora en Tejas, 1920–1940."
Aztlán 6 (Summer 1975):239–266.

———. "UCAPAWA in California: The Farm Worker Period." *Aztlán* 7
(Fall 1976):453–478.

———. "UCAPAWA Organizing Activities in Texas, 1935–50." *Aztlán* 9
(Spring-Fall 1978):71–85.

"No Mexicans Allowed." *Inter-American* 11 (September 1943):8–9.

Nostrand, Richard L. "The Hispanic-American Borderland: Delimitation
of an American Culture Region." *Annals of the Association of American Geographers* 60 (December 1970):638–661.

Oestreicher, Richard. "Urban Working-Class Political Behavior and Theories of American Electoral Politics, 1870–1940." *Journal of American
History* 74 (March 1988):1257–1286.

Orridge, Andrew W. "Separatist and Autonomist Nationalisms: The
Structure of Regional Loyalties in the Modern State." In *National Sep-
aratism*, edited by Colin H. Williams, 43–74. Cardiff: University of
Wales Press, 1982.

Peñalosa, Fernando. "Recent Changes among Chicanos." *Sociology and
Social Research* 55 (October 1970):47–52.

———. "Toward an Operational Definition of the Mexican American."
Aztlán 1 (Spring 1970):1–12.

Peterson, Richard A. "Anti-Mexican Nativism in California, 1848–1853:
A Study of Cultural Conflict." *Southern California Quarterly* 62 (Winter 1980):309–328.

Polinard, Jerry L., Robert D. Wrinkle, and Rodolfo O. de la Garza. "Attitudes of Mexican Americans toward Irregular Mexican Immigration."
International Migration Review 18 (Fall 1984):782–799.

Reisler, Mark. "Always the Laborer, Never the Citizen: Anglo Perceptions
of the Mexican Immigrant during the 1920s." *Pacific Historical Review*
45 (May 1976):231–254.

———. "Mexican Unionization in California Agriculture, 1927–1936."
Labor History 14 (Fall 1973):562–579.

Ríos-Bustamante, Antonio. *Mexicans in the United States and the National Question: Current Polemics and Organizational Positions.* Santa
Barbara, Calif.: Editorial La Causa, 1978.

Rippy, J. Fred. "Border Troubles Along the Rio Grande, 1848–1860."
Southwestern Historical Quarterly 23 (October 1919):91–111.

Roberts, Kenneth L. "The Docile Mexican." *Saturday Evening Post*, March
10, 1928, 39–41, 165–166.

———. "Mexicans or Ruin." *Saturday Evening Post*, February 18, 1928,
14–15, 142, 145–146, 149–150, 154.

Romo, Ricardo. "The Urbanization of Southwestern Chicanos in the Early Twentieth Century." In *New Directions in Chicano Scholarship*, edited by Ricardo Romo and Raymund Paredes, 183–207. La Jolla: Chicano Studies Monograph Series, Chicano Studies Program, University of California, San Diego, 1978.

Rosales, Arturo. "Shifting Self-Perceptions and Ethnic Consciousness in Houston, 1908–1946." *Aztlán* 16 (1985):71–91.

Rosen, Gerald Paul. "The Development of the Chicano Movement in Los Angeles, from 1967 to 1969." *Aztlán* 4 (Spring 1973):155–184.

Ross, Fred W. "Mexican Americans on the March." *Catholic Charities Review* 44 (June 1960):13–16.

Salamone, Frank A., and Charles H. Swanson. "Identity and Ethnicity: Ethnic Groups and Interactions in a Multi-Ethnic Society." *Ethnic Groups* 2 (1979):167–183.

Salinas, Guadalupe. "Mexican Americans and the Desegregation of Schools in the Southwest." *Houston Law Review* 8 (1971):929–951.

San Miguel, Guadalupe. "The Struggle against Separate and Unequal Schools: Middle Class Mexican Americans and the Desegregation Campaign in Texas, 1929–1957." *History of Education Quarterly* 23 (Fall 1983):343–359.

Saunders, Lyle, and Olin Leonard. *The Wetback in the Lower Rio Grande Valley of Texas*. Inter-American Education Occasional Papers, 7. Austin: University of Texas, 1951.

Schlesinger, Arthur M., Jr. "The American Creed: From Dilemma to Decomposition." *New Perspectives Quarterly* 8 (Summer 1991):20–25.

Schuck, Peter H. "Membership in the Liberal Polity: The Devaluation of American Citizenship." In *Immigration and the Politics of Citizenship in Europe and North America*, edited by William Rogers Brubaker, 51–65. Lanham, Md.: University Press of America, 1989.

Scott, George M., Jr. "A Resynthesis of the Primordial and Circumstantial Approaches to Ethnic Group Solidarity: Towards an Explanatory Model." *Ethnic and Racial Studies* 13 (April 1990):147–171.

Scott, Joan Wallach. "The Campaign against Political Correctness: What's Really at Stake." *Radical History Review* 54 (Fall 1992):59–79.

Scruggs, Otey M. "The Evolution of the Mexican Farm Labor Agreement of 1942." *Agricultural History* 34 (July 1960):140–149.

———. "The First Mexican Farm Labor Program." *Arizona and the West* 2 (Winter 1960):319–326.

———. "Texas and the Bracero Program, 1942–1947." *Pacific Historical Review* 32 (August 1963):251–264.

———. "Texas, Good Neighbor?" *Southwestern Social Science Quarterly* 43 (September 1962):118–125.

———. "The United States, Mexico, and the Wetbacks, 1942–1947." *Pacific Historical Review* 30 (May 1961):149–164.

Segade, Gustavo. "Identification and Power: An Essay on the Politics of

Culture and the Culture of Politics in Chicano Thought." *Aztlán* 9 (Spring-Fall 1978):85–100.

Shapiro, Steven R. "Ideological Exclusions: Closing the Border to Political Dissidents." *Harvard Law Review* 100 (February 1987):930–945.

Sierra, Christine Marie. *Latinos and the "New Immigration": Responses from the Mexican American Community.* Renato Rosaldo Lecture Series Monograph 3. Tucson: Mexican American Studies and Research Center, University of Arizona, 1987.

Slayden, James L. "Some Observations on the Mexican Immigrant." *Annals of the American Academy of Political and Social Science* 93 (January 1921):121–126.

Smith, A. D. "Nationalism, Ethnic Separatism, and the Intelligentsia." In *National Separatism,* edited by Colin H. Williams, 17–41. Cardiff: University of Wales Press, 1982.

Sowell, Thomas. "Promoting Alienation." *Forbes,* November 25, 1991, 112.

Spaulding, Charles B. "The Mexican Strike at El Monte, California." *Sociology and Social Research* 18 (July-August 1934):571–580.

Standart, M. Colette. "The Sonoran Migration to California, 1848–1856: A Study in Prejudice." *Southern California Quarterly* 57 (Fall 1976):333–358.

"Survey of Attitudes and Opinions Regarding Immigration in Southern California." In *The Fourth Wave: California's Newest Immigrants,* edited by Thomas Muller and Thomas J. Espenshade, 199–206. Washington, D.C.: Urban Institute Press, 1985.

Swadesh, Frances L. "The Alianza Movement of New Mexico: The Interplay of Social Change and Public Commentary." In *Minorities and Politics,* edited by Henry J. Tobias and Charles E. Woodhouse, 53–84. Albuquerque: University of New Mexico Press, 1969.

Taft, Philip. "The Bisbee Deportation." *Labor History* 13 (Winter 1972):3–40.

Taylor, Paul S. "Mexicans North of the Rio Grande." *Survey Graphic,* May 1, 1931, 135–140, 197, 200–202, 205.

Taylor, William B. "Between Global Process and Local Knowledge: An Inquiry into Early Latin American Social History, 1500–1900." In *Reliving the Past: The Worlds of Social History,* edited by Olivier Zunz, 115–190. Chapel Hill: University of North Carolina Press, 1985.

Tenayuca, Emma, and Homer Brooks. "The Mexican Question in the Southwest." *The Communist* (March 1939), 257–268.

Timmons, W. H. "The El Paso Area in the Mexican Period, 1821–1848." *Southwestern Historical Quarterly* 84 (July 1980):1–28.

Tirado, Miguel David. "Mexican American Community Political Organization: The Key to Chicano Political Power." *Aztlán* 1 (Spring 1970): 53–78.

Treviño, Roberto R. "*Prensa y Patria:* The Spanish-Language Press and the Biculturation of the Tejano Middle Class, 1920–1940." *Western Historical Quarterly* 22 (November 1991):451–472.

Vargas, Zaragosa. "Armies in the Fields and the Factories: The Mexican Working Classes in the Midwest in the 1920s." *Mexican Studies/Estudios Mexicanos* 7 (Winter 1991):47–72.

Villanueva, Tino. "Sobre el término 'chicano'." *Cuadernos Hispano-Americanos* (June 1978):387–410.

Walker, Helen W. "Mexican Immigrants and American Citizenship." *Sociology and Social Research* 13 (May 1929):465–471.

Weber, Devra Anne. "The Organizing of Mexicano Agricultural Workers: Imperial Valley and Los Angeles, 1928–1934, An Oral History Approach." *Aztlán* 3 (Fall 1972):307–347.

Weeks, O. Douglas. "The League of United Latin American Citizens: A Texas Mexican Civic Organization." *Southwestern Political and Social Science Quarterly* 10 (December 1928):257–278.

———. "The Texas Mexican and the Politics of South Texas." *American Political Science Review* 24 (August 1930):606–627.

Woodbridge, Hensley C. "Mexico and U.S. Racism: How Mexicans View Our Treatment of Minorities." *Commonweal*, June 22, 1945, 234–236.

Wright, Doris Marion. "The Making of Cosmopolitan California: An Analysis of Immigration, 1848–1870." *California Historical Quarterly* 19 (December 1940):323–343; 20 (March 1941):65–79.

Zamora, Emilio. "Chicano Socialist Labor Activity in Texas, 1900–1920." *Aztlán* 6 (Summer 1975):221–238.

Zolberg, Aristide R. "Reforming the Back Door: The Immigration Reform and Control Act of 1986 in Historical Perspective." In *Immigration Reconsidered: History, Sociology, and Politics*, edited by Virginia Yans-McLaughlin, 315–339. New York: Oxford University Press, 1990.

Unpublished Sources

Almaguer, Tomás. "Class, Race, and Capitalist Development: The Social Transformation of a Southern California County, 1848–1903." Ph.D. diss., University of California, Berkeley, 1979.

Briegel, Kaye Lynn. "The Alianza Hispano Americana, 1894–1965: A Mexican Fraternal Insurance Society." Ph.D. diss., University of Southern California, 1974.

Buckner, Dellos U. "Study of the Lower Rio Grande Valley as a Culture Area." M.A. thesis, University of Texas, Austin, 1929.

Camarillo, Albert M. "The Development of a Pan-Hispanic Civil Rights Movement: The 1939 Congress of Spanish-Speaking People." Paper presented at the annual meeting of the Organization of American Historians, Los Angeles, 1986.

Castillo, Pedro. "Mexicans in Los Angeles, 1890–1920." Ph.D. diss., University of California, Santa Barbara, 1977.

Craig, Wilson. "The Mexican American Political Association of California." M.A. thesis, Sonoma State College, 1970.

Dimmitt, Marius A. "The Enactment of the McCarran-Walter Act of 1952." Ph.D. diss., University of Kansas, 1970.

Downs, Fane. "The History of Mexicans in Texas, 1820–1845." Ph.D. diss., Texas Tech University, 1970.

Flores, Estevan T. "Post-Bracero Undocumented Mexican Immigration to the United States and Political Recomposition." Ph.D. diss., University of Texas, Austin, 1982.

Foster, Nellie. "The Corrido: A Mexican Culture Trait Persisting in Southern California." M.A. thesis, University of Southern California, 1939.

García, Richard A. "The Making of the Mexican American Mind, San Antonio, Texas, 1929–1941: A Social and Intellectual History of an Ethnic Community." Ph.D. diss., University of California, Irvine, 1980.

González, Jovita. "Social Life in Cameron, Starr, and Zapata Counties." M.A. thesis, University of Texas, Austin, 1930.

Gutiérrez, David G. "Ethnicity, Ideology, and Political Development: Mexican Immigration as a Political Issue in the Chicano Community, 1910–1977." Ph.D. diss., Stanford University, 1987.

Gutiérrez, Félix. "Mexican-American Youth and Their Media: *The Mexican Voice*, 1938–1945." Paper presented at the 77th annual meeting of the Organization of American Historians, Los Angeles, April 1984.

Gutiérrez, José Angel. "Toward a Theory of Community Organization in a Mexican American Community in South Texas." Ph.D. diss., University of Texas, Austin, 1977.

Guzmán, Ralph C. "The Political Socialization of the Mexican American People." Ph.D. diss., University of California, Los Angeles, 1970.

Kiser, George C. "The Bracero Program: A Case Study of Its Development, Termination, and Political Aftermath." Ph.D. diss., University of Massachusetts, 1974.

Monroy, Douglas. "Mexicanos in Los Angeles 1930–1941: An Ethnic Group in Relation to Class Forces." Ph.D. diss., University of California, Los Angeles, 1978.

Montejano, David. "A Journey through South Texas, 1910–1930: The Making of a Segregated Society." Ph.D. diss., Yale University, 1982.

Officer, James. "Sodalities and Systemic Linkage: The Joining Habits of Urban Mexican-Americans." Ph.D. diss., University of Arizona, 1964.

Orozco, Cynthia E. "The Origins of the League of United Latin American Citizens (LULAC) and the Mexican American Civil Rights Movement in Texas with an Analysis of Women's Political Participation in a Gendered Context, 1910–1929." Ph.D. diss., University of California, Los Angeles, 1993.

Pycior, Julie Leininger. "La Raza Organizes: Mexican American Life in San Antonio, 1915–1930 as Reflected in Mutualista Activities." Ph.D. diss., University of Notre Dame, 1979.

Ramos, Raúl A. "La Huelga de los Nueceros de San Antonio, Texas, Febrero 1938." Senior thesis, Princeton University, 1989.

Ruiz, Vicki L. "UCAPAWA, Chicanas, and the California Food Processing Industry, 1937–1950." Ph.D. diss., Stanford University, 1982.

Sánchez, George J. "Becoming Mexican American: Ethnicity and Acculturation in Chicano Los Angeles, 1900–1943." Ph.D. diss., Stanford University, 1989.

Scott, Robin F. "The Mexican American in the Los Angeles Area, 1920–1950: From Acquiescence to Activity." Ph.D. diss., University of Southern California, 1971.

Sierra, Christine Marie. "Mexican Americans and Immigration Reform: Consensus and Fragmentation." Paper presented at the annual meeting of the Western Political Science Association, Salt Lake City, Utah, March 1989.

Tijerina, Andrés A. "Tejanos and Texas: The Native Mexicans of Texas, 1820–1850." Ph.D. diss., University of Texas, Austin, 1977.

Tirado, Miguel David. "The Mexican Minority's Participation in Voluntary Political Associations." Ph.D. diss., Claremont Graduate School, 1970.

Ward, Byrkit James. "Life and Labor in Arizona, 1901–1921: With Particular Reference to the Deportations of 1917." Ph.D. diss., Claremont Graduate School, 1972.

Weber, Devra Anne. "The Struggle for Stability and Control in the Cotton Fields of California: Class Relations in Agriculture, 1919–1942." Ph.D. diss., University of California, Los Angeles, 1986.

Index

Compositor: Terry Robinson & Co., Inc.
Text: 10/13 Aldus
Display: Aldus
Printer: Sheridan Books, Inc.
Binder: Sheridan Books, Inc.